autobiography
of a blue-eyed devil

my life and times in a racist
imperialist society

inga muscio

Autobiography of a Blue-Eyed Devil
My Life and Times in a Racist, Imperialist Society

Published by
Seal Press
An Imprint of Avalon Publishing Group, Incorporated
1400 65th Street, Suite 250
Emeryville, CA 94608

Library of Congress Cataloging-in-Publication Data
Muscio, Inga.
Autobiography of a blue-eyed devil : my life and times in a racist, imperialist society / by Inga Muscio.— 1st ed.
p. cm.
Includes bibliographical references.
ISBN 1-58005-119-7
1. Muscio, Inga. 2. Feminists—United States—Biography. 3. Racism—United States. 4. United States—Race relations. I. Title.
HQ1413.M87A3 2005
305.8'00973—dc22
2005006573

9 8 7 6 5 4 3 2 1

Cover painting: Devil © Eli Halpin
Cover design by Kathleen Szawiola
Interior design by Jacob Goolkasian
Printed in Canada by Transcontinental
Distributed by Publishers Group West

This book is lovingly dedicated to
the soldiers and families of
South Central Los Angeles,
for showing me what war, autogenocide, loyalty, and honor are.
I thank you.
This book is also lovingly dedicated to
the people of Venezuela and
the Bolívarian Revolution,
for showing me what freedom and democracy look like.
Muchas gracias,
con todo mi corazón.

Contents

Conceptions of a Pale-Skinned Savage

$\mathfrak{C}$onsider this redaction of world history, the sort of thing to be found in any grade school textbook:

> Sixteenth-century South Asia had little that was in
> demand in the rest of the world. So its most important
> export was force. Bolstered by superior firepower,
> the conquerors that burst forth from the Indian
> subcontinent were more than able to shoulder the

Brown Man's Burden of bringing the pale savages in
the far northwest to their rightful dharma. Owing to
this, the succeeding five centuries granted the works
of esoteric regional authors like Shakespeareji and
Chaucerji an otherwise-unobtainable immortality
through their transliteration into that most universal
of scripts, Devanagari. Similarly, Dickensji received
rare admittance to the otherwise exclusive canons
of world literature with his powerfully narrated con-
demnations of the occasional abuses committed by a
handful of overzealous "Hindoo" administrators upon
the yeomanry of the English countryside.

Of course, this is not to be found in any textbook. South
Asia had a great deal that was in demand in the rest of the
world, and by and large had little interest in exporting force. So
I have begun with a fiction, a lie, my own deliberately twisted
misrepresentation. What's worse, I have begun with a plagia-
rism as well, a misrepresentation of a story I pilfered from
somebody else. This is the story I stole: "Europe had little that
was in demand in the rest of the world. Our most important
export was force."[1] And unlike my own narration, this one is not
a fiction, a lie, nor a misrepresentation. It is a fact.

Facts, though, only go so far. They are the components
from which truths are manufactured, but they do not come with
instructions for assembly. Consider, for example, this fact: I am
white. Fair enough, but what to make of this? One possible con-
figuration is that I possess a relatively small amount of melanin

per square inch of skin, from which one may conclude that my ancestors made their livelihoods in locales where sunburn was a lesser issue than was the body's hunger for vitamin D. Personally, I am comfortable labeling this constellation of facts a truth. One might also conclude from this that being so cursed with melanin insufficiency, I am not a member of those other chromas arrayed along the spectrum we compulsively employ to paint humanity: black, yellow, red, and sometimes brown. Again, fair enough.

But what other meanings can one draw from my whiteness? That I am lactose tolerant, perhaps? Not so fast. One finds lactose tolerance and intolerance spread across all hues of the human spectrum. Indeed, one could speak of the two races of humanity—the lactose tolerant and the lactase insufficient—and I could join with my fellow ice cream eaters (regardless of the shade of their dermis) to celebrate our well-deserved mastery over the hordes of frozen-dairy-treat-hating savages (pale-skinned ones included). Could one, then, at least conclude that my blood cells are not prone to sickle and so deprive my body of oxygen? In my particular instance, a fair guess, but a hypothetical blood-cell-sickling-anemic race would include representatives of at least three chromatic distinctions: people from spots scattered across the European subcontinent, a sizable contingent from the lowlands of Southeast Asia, and people from only certain parts of Africa below the Sahara.[2]

The color of one's skin, then, tells us only one thing for certain: the color of one's skin. So how could it even be imagined that one might be able to deduce from whiteness such notions as this: To be white is to be hardworking and ingenious, for it is to have come from a clime harsh enough to demand diligent effort if one was to thrive, but not so harsh as to render diligence futile. Yet we have all heard this story so many times and in so many ways, this Tale of the European Miracle, that we know it by heart. Here's another one: To be white is to be a barbarian, a savage incapable of governing oneself or others, for it is to have come from a clime that overfills one with spirit and deprives one of the leisure to develop intelligence or skill. The ancient Athenians, no slouches themselves in the exportation of force, came up with that one. And in retrospect, I am not convinced that it is the Athenians who are further from the mark. If white could tell me anything more than the color of my skin, of course.

Here I feel compelled to make a further confession. I have inflicted upon you yet another fiction. No spectrum is composed of just primary colors, and to the discerning eye I am not merely white. I am pale, but with a distinctly olive tinge. And for those whose eyes discern, this is no small thing. One such pair of eyes was upon me during a long-ago trip through ol' Virginny. After some while, the markedly pink-ish body behind those eyes approached me with an inquiry, "Where are you from?" Naïvely, I answered with the city of my origin, Los Angeles. "No," the questioner interjected, "where are your parents from?" An odd question that, and I answered with the rust belt city of their birth. Frustration was clearly mounting, and my questioner demanded, "I mean, where is your family from?!" He wanted a simple answer, and my family had none to offer. So I described the procession

Foreword: Conceptions of a Pale-Skinned Savage

of ancestors across the undulating steppes of central Asia to Crimea, the hope-filled strides of others due south across the frostbitten fields of the Russian empire, the involuntary eastward flight of yet others from the violated glories of El Andalus (just at the moment Columbus set out from the same point, albeit in the opposite direction) and across the farther Mediterranean shore. All the while, I was certain I could hear the most spectacular of terminological gymnastics straining my interrogator's imagination: two-humped-camel-jockey-oriental-dune-coon-rag-headed-spic-kike-russki trash. But I need not have feared; he was far too parsimonious for that. "I got it," he burst out, in a matter-of-fact tone tinged with relief but not the slightest hint of malice. "You're lessthanwhite."

Lessthanwhite. The very term gives the game away, doesn't it? If white constitutes the absence of color, doesn't an additional tint or tinge constitute . . . well . . . something additional? A plus, if you will? Would it not therefore be technically correct to refer to me as "morethanwhite"?[3] Sure. But of course the world is entirely different than that. The human spectrum is hierarchically ranked, with white having exported itself to the top (no absence of anything there!) quite forcibly indeed. To have even the slightest something extra is to be adulterated, fallen, a miscegenated "less than." Off-white, ethnic white, "probationary white"[4] as one friend puts it—suffered to pass provided we've the good sense to keep our mouths shut. The creeping cryptic legions of the unwhite, clawing at civilization's door like a horde of B-movie zombies, driven by a hunger to grind your children into piroshki filling or bake their heads

into *besbarmak* served atop a bed of couscous. This final judgment, rendered against me unbidden in some Virginia barroom,
put me in mind of my great-grandparents' experience: Despite
being no less pale than I, they were colloquially (and denigrat-
ingly) referred to as "black" in the "old country."

New world, same old shit. America is particularly rich
with ingenious just-so stories of why police flashlights are fed
to errant motorists predicated upon the shade of their skins,
and why we must tithe a piece of our ever-shrinking paychecks
to baptize distant lessthanwhites in depleted uranium. Such
are the straws that broke this camel jockey's back, so love it or
not, leave it I have ("go north, young man") . . . only to discover
one final fact. There is no escape. At the moment I crossed the
border, the alchemical mysteries of statistical censusing trans-
muted me—abracadabra presto change-o—from white to West
Asian, a new and improved geographical brand name stamped
by bureaucratic fiat into the hides of anyone with ancestors
spread from Istanbul to Ürümqi. And I must be thankful for
such small transmutations, here in this professedly unracist
corner of the world where a surfeit of melanin can relegate the
most gifted and credentialed newcomer to a bright future of
piloting taxis, sanitizing hotel rooms, or assembling corrugated
cardboard boxes.

Others, however, are made of tougher (and less portable)
stuff than I—when seized by the instinct to fight or fly, they fight.
Inga Muscio, for instance. She is a fighter, and every word in this
book is a fighting word. I began this modest rant with a fanciful
vision, a world in which His Imperial Majesty the Maharaja's

expeditionary forces come pouring across the English Channel, cannons a-blazin', charged with a missionary zeal to civilize the pasty brutes. But Inga's world is more outrageous still. It is a place where the drunken binge of a legendary ancestor commands the enslavement of entire peoples, in perpetuity. A place in which to be kidnapped and repeatedly raped is to be a voracious Jezebel. A place in which storybooks tell children charming tales of slow-motion genocide. A place in which the color of one's skin tells not just the color of one's skin, but also how, where, and for how long one may live. And, for all its outrageousness, it is the place wherein we all must live. How fortunate, then, that Inga lives here too, and cannot help but stand against what she witnesses, with more than ample outrage of her own.

From the frozen waste of the Canucki Southeast,
Annexia, Year 5 of the Arbusto Era

Steven E. Flusty, PhD
York University
Department of Geography

Preface

$\mathcal{I}$n my first book, *Cunt: A Declaration of Independence,* there is a chapter called "Acrimony of Cunts," where I discuss some of the intimate ways women learn to distrust one another in a patriarchal society. This was a very difficult chapter for me to briefly articulate because so much of this distrust is based on the complex influences of white supremacist racism. I worked hard to keep this much larger reality from running away with me and not letting me finish *Cunt.*

It was a big struggle, and I ended up striking a deal. I promised the Deeply Complex Reality of White Supremacist Racism that if it would please stand aside and allow me to do a good job of saying what I was saying in *Cunt,* I would allow it to fully possess me for my next book.

Which is, um, this one.

Hi.

"White supremacist racism" is the term I have chosen to describe much of what I discuss in this book. Dr. Frances Cress Welsing, author of the absolutely requisite reading *The Isis Papers,* hooked me up with a brilliant and all-encompassing definition for this term:

> As a Black behavioral scientist and practicing general and child psychiatrist, my current functional definition of racism (white supremacy) is as follows: the local and global power system structured and maintained by persons who classify themselves as white, whether consciously or subconsciously determined; this system consists of patterns of perception, logic, symbol formation, thought, speech, action and emotional response, as conducted in all areas of people activity (economics, education, entertainment, labor, law, politics, religion, sex and war). The ultimate purpose of the system is to prevent white genetic annihilation on Earth—a planet in which the overwhelming

majority of people are classified as non-white (black, brown, red and yellow) by white-skinned people. All of the non-white people are genetically dominant (in terms of skin coloration) compared to the genetically recessive white-skinned people.[1]

This definition helped me to understand the huge disconnect I see between indoctrinated, unconscious white and white-identified people here in the United States of Amerikkka and the rest of the population on the planet.

When I started touring around and doing *Cunt* readings, I grew increasingly aware of something very striking. When white people mentioned "Acrimony of Cunts," they focused on the general catty nature women often entertain when dealing with one another. When indigenous people and people of color mentioned this same chapter, they focused on the larger point of racial complexities and unaccountability among white women. I encountered but a slim population of white folks who talked about these larger points in "Acrimony of Cunts."

It got kinda surreal after a while—traveling all over the country, and the same thing happening whether I was in Flagstaff, New York City, Los Angeles, Chicago, Minneapolis, Tampa, or Seattle. It became clear that many people mysteriously fogged out all the parts of my book they did not wish to see—as if they'd read the book they wanted to read and not the book I wrote.

Sometimes people ask me why I have "shifted" from the topic of feminism to the topics of racism and imperialism.

There have been no shiftings.

When I was in my early twenties, I tended bar at a tavern.

One night, a Nisqually grandfather came in with two of his grandsons. They were all fairly drunk. They laughed about something funny while the grandfather ordered a pitcher of beer. As I handed it over, foamy down the sides, the grandfather's eyes seared into me. He wrapped his hand firmly over mine and his spirit moshed with perfection into my heart, my bloodstream, the pulse of my life. He completely sobered, as if the effects of alcohol were accessories he could don and discard at will.

He simply was not drunk anymore.

This moment in time froze, still as a pretty meadow landscape, with all the same chaos that you can't see from far away.

He said, "Child, you feel too much."

No one blinked.

There was a big joke underneath the deadly seriousness.

I half-smiled and whispered, "I know."

I mean, what *do* you say when someone reaches into your soul like greased lightning while you are handing them a plastic pitcher of beer?

We stared at each other.

I felt the alcohol inside him, as a force utilized to negotiate a not-told/not-listened-to history that decimated his people and later pillaged their graves. I felt his history, his life, in my body. It staggered me for a breath and then his eyes steadied me. Hand over mine, he filled my heart with his stories.

Then the grandsons broke into it all and said, "He's drunk, don't listen to him."

We looked at each other again for the briefest moment. We were both completely present as a pristine babbling mountain brook as he released my hand. The deadly seriousness slipped away and the big joke rose up. This is when he laughed, loud and raucous. Elegantly slipped back into drunkenness, kicked up his heels, and wheeled around to play pool with his grandsons.

"Child, you feel too much," he said, as he passed his stories into my body so that I could feel them.

It was a telling of the telling.

The big joke underneath the whole interaction.

Geddit?

In the environment we are born into, there are many ways we learn to categorize each other, our selves, and our lived realities. This book, however, simply comes to you from the heart of a person who feels too much.

Part 1 **Roots**

It would be a serious mistake to conclude that the current behavior of the United States represents something temporary that will change when George Bush Jr. leaves the presidency. Never in its history has the United States taken a backward step in its drive towards universal domination and never has it corrected its behavior, going from bad to worse from the point of view of the rights of the rest of humanity.

—Miguel D'Escoto,
former Nicaraguan foreign minister

Introduction to Part 1

Since I was a child, I've experienced history as a study in disconnectedness. I was blessed with parents who had actual history books in the house, so I was never reliant on the pap that's passed off as history in schools.

Still, it took me a long time to understand that U.S. history, alone, is at least eighteen mall-size libraries crammed tight with books, films, music, zines, art, and microfiche up the ass. In my country, though, history is presented as one big book, and everyone is expected to read this book, memorize the facts, know them, love them, and *move the fuck on*. Similar to some of the reactions I saw to "Acrimony of Cunts," this take on U.S. history fogs out everything that people living under the constructed perspective of learned white supremacist racism do not wish to see.

In the genuine, authentic, normal history of the U.S., indigenous people are not slaughtered, raped, and forcibly displaced. They're just "removed." Slavery was a few bad apples in the back-ass South, and that has all been cleared up. Ditto the internment of Japanese Americans during World War II, and every other atrocity that has somehow managed to seep into the U.S.'s mainstream collective consciousness.

Meanwhile, all white men are heroes and brave and noble and so are some white women and no on Nat Turner, but yes on Harriet Tubman.

So yeah.

One starts to wonder why *exactly* it just so happens that almost every U.S. street, building, and landmark that isn't named after Rosa Parks, Pocahontas, César Chávez, or Martin Luther King Jr. is named after a white person.

Is it some kind of bizarre coincidence that superficially portrayed good and noble white people are almost exclusively the gods and heroes of U.S. history?

What *kind* of culture names its federal police headquarters after a virulently racist, homophobic, closeted cross-dresser who was responsible for the deaths and/or ruined lives of thousands of men and women who dared to dream of a better world?

Why's it considered perfectly natural for elite white alpha-dog-eat-dog concepts such as "survival of the fittest" and manifest destiny to so *seamlessly* serve as the basis of— and justification for—our economic, spiritual, political, and emotional life?

Without a willingness to question history, folks tend not to address any of these highly interesting queries, and there's plenty more where they came from, believe you me. Dig deep into *any* moment of U.S. history, and any learned sense of truth, justice, humanity, freedom, and democracy will be confounded, if not irreparably sundered.

For instance, early on a December morning in 1969, twenty-one-year-old Black Panther leader Fred Hampton was murdered at the behest of J. Edgar Hoover's FBI while he slept in bed.

White mainstream society portrays black resistance groups such as the Black Panthers as "militants." In truth, "militants" are merely those who are unwilling to compromise with oppression. Many demographics in Amerikkka are punished when they step out of line, but white society reserves a special vitriol for black people who dare to resist white supremacy.

And so, Chicago police busted into Fred Hampton's home and fired anywhere between eighty-two and two hundred submachine gun and shotgun rounds. As part of the covert FBI operation COINTELPRO (counterintelligence program), an informant had provided a floor plan, including a sketch of exactly where Mr. Hampton slept. The FBI then handed this information over to the Chicago police, who evidently felt the need to fill the walls with lead.

The Civil Rights Movement is packed with incidents such as this one.

Filled to the gills in a mall-size library.

In existence from 1956 to 1971,[†] this FBI program commands quite a bit of space in the history of the Civil Rights Movement. COINTELPRO agents and operatives executed a known (as opposed to actual) 295 covert actions against black resistance groups alone. This program was fully enacted against indigenous, Chicano, Puerto Rican, and war resistance groups, and everybody else COINTELPRO-thinkers could think to hassle.

Fred Hampton is one of many, many people who lost their lives, freedom, and/or sanity during this specific time period. Maybe you didn't know this, but now you do.

And whether you knew this before or you just found out, how does that sit with your heart? The knowledge that the name of the man responsible for Mr. Hampton's death graces the federal police headquarters? What does this say about our country? What does

---

[†] It's inaccurate to assert that COINTELPRO ended. Though it may be called other things at this point, similarly disruptive, infiltrative, and illegal tactics are enacted against resistance-minded organizations and individuals to this day. If anything, COINTELPRO provided a blueprint for PATRIOT Acts I and II.

this say about you and me, for allowing the man responsible for Mr. Hampton's murder to be honored in our nation's capital?

Knowing about the lived and stolen life of Fred Hampton presents *many further questions* about the death, incarceration, co-optation, and exile of enough individuals to populate a large, thriving city.

Addressing ignorance tends to have this effect. It raises more questions, not only about history but about the present and future as well. That's the thing with learning history. There's not much sense of accomplishment involved. Answers lead only to more questions.

Learning history is an ongoing and somewhat demanding relationship, requiring unconditional love and dedication. In a society that honors everything temporary and disposable—from diapers to sexual partners—the kind of commitment that history demands is not all that attractive. For me, learning about history involves reeducating myself, finding the time to read books, magazines, comics, and graphic novels, listening to music, watching films and documentaries, talking to my elders, and researching stuff on the internet.

This commitment to history also means ditching most all of my face time with the teevee.

In this country, we are ignorant about an awful, awful lot of history—largely, but by no means solely, because of the exorbitant amount of time spent in front of teevee sets.

While I gaily concede that some folks have the luxury of elders who offer living renditions of history, and some have enough money and/or community resources to be educated within a completely different paradigm than the one presently lording it over the U.S. public education system, and some go to a college or university where history is very much alive and well, and some read a lot, all in all, what people of the U.S. learn from the public education system is lightly veiled white male supremacist racist propaganda.

It's just *called* history.

This history we learn in school is a brand. Since it is first introduced to us when we are five years old, we develop a kind of brand loyalty to this history, but, as any conscientious consumer knows, brand loyalty does not necessarily signify a high-quality product.

As a school subject, history is "ALL THIS STUFF FROM THE PAST that we overcame, and look at us now, see how smart and evolved we are." In fact, other than invoking a sense of evolution, where we perpetually marvel at how back-ass people once were, history serves little purpose.

It means remembering dates of wars and names of "discoverers," knowing that slavery and the Nazis were "wrong," and being happy that (white) people would never, ever stoop that low again.

Whew!

Glad that chapter's over!

Hope I do well on the test!

The cultural practice of categorizing (and by proxy, ghettoizing and trivializing) the autobiography of Assata Shakur and the writing of Mary Crow Dog as "African American" and

"Native American" literature, respectively, rather than presenting them as the U.S. history texts that they actually are, would
not be conceptualized by, much less acceptable to, a population
on the up-and-up with its history.

If you do not know exactly who Assata Shakur and Mary Crow
Dog are, it is safe to assume you are not on the up-and-up with
your U.S. history.

Without a vital connection to the actual lived history of *everyone* in this country, children who are indigenous, mixed race,
poor, gender variant, queer, and/or of color will continue to be
burdened by (among many other things) completely extraneous
self-esteem issues that they must face off with as young adults,
which, in turn, often render them vulnerable to the forces of
silence and control that rule our society. If you and your family
are only reflected through stereotypes and innocuous "role
models" who have received the stamp of approval from a dominant white supremacist racist culture, then no matter how wonderful life may or may not be, you are *forced to create* a positive
racial identity.

   Meanwhile, white children not only learn that it is fine and
dandy to accept ridiculous racial stereotypes, but also remain
oblivious to how surrealistically "normal" all this whiteness is
designed to appear. White children never have to bother ourselves with creating a positive racial identity. As long as we do

not resist the legacy of white supremacist racism, we inherit a positive racial identity.

The other day, I saw a white man standing on the street protesting the invasion of Iraq and Afghanistan. His sign said, "I want my country back." This is not funny, but I laughed anyway, thinking, "This man wants his country back, huh?" I wondered how it would be perceived if a tribe of Tlingit indians were to stand on the corner—not necessarily protesting any foreign U.S. invasion—with a sign like that. In what has been called the United States of America for the past two hundred plus years, there are lots of indian tribes and nations who would very much like the four-thousand-plus-year-old ancient land of their sacred ancestors back as well.

It is through our ignorance that we can create and condone protest signs of this nature. Is this *really* what democracy looks like? How can white people want "our" country back when we are collectively unwilling to recognize and acknowledge the history of "our" country?

Almost every day lately, I've read political essays that are kinda like the protest sign that man was holding. These articles are written by white or white-identified people who want our democracy back, our right to free speech, our government, our media, our schools, our libraries, our jobs, our freedom.

Don't these folks care about all the people in this country who haven't had jobs, libraries, or schools very often at all? Those who are never free to speak unless they are saying things white society wishes to hear, those who are never represented by the government, those who have no voice in the media, no freedom or democracy or other such luxurious things?

Only if we are living in the white world, created by and for whites and white-identified "allies" of color, do we believe that the wonderful luxuries of a true, representational democracy have but recently absconded.

Then, and only then, do tremors of shock and outrage unsettle our consciousness.

For people of color and indigenous people living in the Americas "our democracy" has, on the whole, never ever ever ever ever ever ever ever ever ever ever ever ever existed.

The biggest difference I am able to presently discern between the old democracy and the present one is that the **Arbusto**† administration has engendered a reality where the United States of Amerikkka is now in a constant, overt state of being undeniably and glaringly itself.

We're out and proud, livin' loud, waving forty-five-foot flags from car dealerships from sea to shining sea, and killin' us passels of sand nigger terrorists on their turf, which keeps them the fuck offa ours.

For people living in countries where the U.S. decides "our democracy" is needed, it has not only never existed, but our imposition of "democracy" generally creates a vacuum, sucking everything alive and beautiful—old trees who are the earth's sentinels, the innocence of children, sustainable organic farms, loving family-centered communities who argue, debate, and

---

† Yo, look it up in the glossary.

deal with each other, and all who call the rainforest home—into its insatiable sweatshop, torture chamber, clear-cut maw.

This did not start when an Arbusto became a president, and it will not end just because an Arbusto is no longer a president.[†]

U.S. citizens who are not *personally familiar* with how the nature of present—and deeply rooted—U.S. policies affect life for folks in (for instance) Vietnam, El Salvador, Bosnia, Iraq, or Somalia tend to ignore how our daily choices wreak continued havoc on populations all over the globe.

Many—if not all—of the gravest social, environmental, and economic problems in the world can be traced to the indoctrination of the U.S. population. It is through our painstakingly learned complacency that our government and corporations continue to create debilitating situations throughout the world, to the benefit of the elite white **Lucky Sperm Club** and the dictators the CIA coup d'etats into power. The impacts are felt far and wide. Entire nations and communities are enslaved in the service of producing goods for us.

The "us" who "outlawed slavery" over 140 years ago.

Us, who are descended from slaves, masters, autonomous indigenous nations, refugees, and immigrants seeking, if not a

---

† Though, it must be noted, Arbustos really have enjoyed pulling strings in the background since pilgrims alit on these shores.

better life, subsistence in a brutal world—we heedlessly patronize businesses that *could not exist* without slavery.

Wal-Mart.

Starbucks.

Target.

Home Depot.

Banana Republic.

And, oh yes, on.

Every day of our lives, we literally *pay* to keep this system in place. Economies that do not perpetuate slavery are considered "alternative," "guerrilla," or "communist," if they are considered at all.

Why the fuck, then, pray tell, do we continue to allow history to pat "us" on the back about the Emancipation Proclamation?

At its very, very, very best, U.S. history is an unimaginative and superficial saga, with a beginning, middle, and end, as told by the victors of history's present telling.

What would this country be like if the victors of history's present telling were people who placed Marcus Garvey in the position presently reserved for John D. Rockefeller? How would our ideas be different if the victors exalted Billy Tipton as "the King," mindlessly named federal government buildings after Black Elk and main thoroughfares for Yuri Kochiyama? How would our world be different if Magdalen Hsu-Li were in charge of AOL, Annie Sprinkle headed Time, and Cheryl Dunye ran Warner? How about if Amma's beliefs about love and survival dwarfed those of Sigmund Freud and Charles Darwin?

How would our world be different?

These things are difficult to imagine because:

a.) We don't.

b.) We are taught that entrenched white supremacist racist ideology is such a perfectly normal occurrence that to imagine such things is (you pick:) silly, absurd, idealistic, utopian, a conspiracy theory, unrealistic, unpatriotic, un-American, un-Godly, and/or just plain evil.

I imagine all the time how U.S. culture could be different, and it's rather fun.

I mean, jeez, this is the United States of America, right? The big melting pot? Why embrace the tendency to draw the line on a white national heritage and culture? It gets really boring after a while. United States celebrations and national rites of passage have no depth or meaning. The Fourth of July? Memorial Day? Valentine's Day? Come on, do these holidays hold any true meaning for you in your deepest heart of hearts? Why can't we have a U.S. Constitution Day, with a twenty-four-hour, live call-in talk show where, by referendum, we address new ways to improve the rules for everyone's quality of life? Or how about merging Christmas and Arbor Day so folks don't have tree carcasses in their homes, and then on their front curbs, once a year?

Compared with, say, Día de los Muertos in Mexico, our hol-

idays suck. We never get down in the graveyard with marigolds
and sugared skeletons and portraits of all the dead people we
love, and laugh and dance and sing and visit with our past.

We do lame-ass shit like set off explosives and buy teddy
bears that are hugging red satin hearts emblazoned with mass-
produced, silk-screened endearments that say, "Forget the Rest,
You're the Best!"

Here we are, in a country filled with people from millions
of historical experiences, not to mention every nation on the
planet, and the best we can come up with is stuffing turkeys
with stale bread and thanking indians for feeding the pilgrims
who committed acts of genocide against them?

Is this *really* the best we can come up with?

And you know, if the true actions and choices of white
men such as John Brown were celebrated on the same scale as
the false actions and choices of white men such as Abraham
Lincoln, people would be far more inclined to associate their
humanity with actions and choices involving honesty and justice for all, because truth cuts deep into hearts.

And lies do not.

In a perfect world, *Lies My Teacher Told Me,* by the eminent
historian James W. Loewen, would be the first book you read
directly after finishing this one.

Well, actually, in a *perfect* world, you'd already have read it.

When I was fifteen years old, I developed a theory that
my fascination with history was sabotaged by the very civic

propagandists who were allegedly teaching it to me.[†] *Lies My Teacher Told Me* represents a formal acknowledgment that this tenth grade analysis was indeed correct. For this alone, I am greatly indebted to Mr. Loewen.

But my gratitude goes deeper than that.

I thank him for validating all the times I sat in history classes, bored off my ass.

I thank him for validating my frustration that my captivation with the subject of history was quelled with platitudes about some war in 1812, with completely unremarkable personalities like Betsy Ross, and with minutiae like whose elite white male alpha dog signature took up the most space on the Declaration of Independence.

I thank him for validating that time I busted my ass writing a paper for which my primary resource was lyrics to songs from a vegan, system-smashing punk rock band from England called Crass. I was proud of this paper. I remember it as one of my last stabs at making any effort, whatsoever, in high school. The teacher's comment was something along the lines of "Punk

---

[†] I need to qualify my negative feelings about the public education system. I know so many teachers who truly care and bust their asses to provide quality education. I am thankful to all the educators and librarians who work so hard to teach children in a criminally underfunded, negative milieu. I still love Mrs. Lingle and Mrs. House—my second and third grade teachers, respectively. From fourth grade to the holysacred end of high school, however, my experience with public education was so completely demoralizing, the thought of college didn't enter my mind until I was twenty-two and heard about the Evergreen State College: no tests, no grades, I could design my own classes, and I qualified for cheap-ass in-state tuition.

rock music is not a reputable citation for this class." I don't remember her exact words, but I do remember my exact grade. I got a big fuck-you of a D-.

That was in the 1980s, when punk served me in a similar way that rap and hiphop serve many (young) people today. So you can maybe imagine the flash of recognition I had when Loewen described an uncannily similar scenario:

> Standard history textbooks and courses discriminate against students who have been educated by rap songs or by Van Sertima. Imagine an eleventh-grade classroom in American history in early fall. The text is *Life and Liberty;* students are reading chapter two, "Exploration and Colonization." What happens when an African American girl shoots up her hand to challenge the statement "Not until 1497–1499 did the Portuguese explorer Vasco da Gama sail around Africa"? From rap songs the girl has learned that Afro-Phoenicians beat Da Gama by more than 2,000 years. Does the teacher take time to research the question and find that the student is right, the textbook wrong? More likely, s/he puts down the student's knowledge: "Rap songs aren't appropriate in a *history* class!" Or s/he humors the child: "Yes, but that was long ago and didn't lead to anything. Vasco da Gama's discovery is the important one." These responses allow the class to move "forward" to the next topic. They also contain some truth: the Afro-Phoenician circumnavigation

didn't lead to any new trade routes or national alliances, because the Afro-Phoenicians were already trading with India through the Red Sea and the Persian Gulf.[1]

In Chicago's O'Hare International Airport, I once struck up conversation with a woman from Italy. At one point she said, "I love America because there is no history here." The breath left my body like I'd been sucker punched. "Of course there's history here," I said. "There's *positively scads* of history here." She smiled the "Stupid American" smile of someone who strolls through piazzas that reverberate with the hoofbeat memories of Roman emperors' horses, and quietly replied, "No. No. There is no history here."

As with all other countries on the planet, the history of this land predates Jesus Christ. It didn't, however, pertain to white folks until Columbus bamboozled Queen Isabella into funding a voyage for him—a mere five hundred plus years ago.

Acknowledging this land's true history would involve paying respect to all the people who were here before Columbus, and see, that just wouldn't make sense. For that to make sense, Amerikkkans would have to be willing to openly acknowledge our foredaddies' role in a very messy (and continuing) genocide, not to mention the perpetuation of an extremely uninteresting, propagandistic mutation of American history, where white people are the stars, role models, and heroes. Loewen continues:

Textbooks don't name Vasco da Gama because something came from his "discovery," however. They name him because he was white. Two pages later, *Life and Liberty* tells us that Hernando De Soto "discovered [the] Mississippi River." (Of course, it had been discovered and named Mississippi by ancestors of the Indians who were soon to chase De Soto down it.) Textbooks portray De Soto in armor, not showing that by the time he reached the river, his men and women had lost almost all their clothing in a fire set by Indians in Alabama and were wearing replacements woven from reeds. De Soto's "discovery" had no larger significance and led to no trade or white settlement. His was merely the first *white* face to gaze upon the Mississippi. That's why ten of the twelve American history textbooks [that Loewen analyzed for his book] include him. From Erik the Red to Peary at the North Pole to the first man on the moon, we celebrate most discoverers because they were first and because they were white, not because of events that flowed or did not flow from their accomplishments. . . . In this way students learn that black [or Chicano, Asian, or indigenous] feats are not considered important while white ones are.[2]

My Italian buddy in the airport obviously didn't learn about United States history while hanging out with Yaqui people. Either that, or she too believes history is based solely on the deeds of whites.

If I flow along this train of thought for a while, it starts to seem like there really are no such things as mountains called "Rainier," "McKinley," or "Everest," or states like "New Hampshire," "Washington," or "Colorado." "Old Faithful," "the Everglades," and "the Great Salt Lake" also start to look like arbitrary names chosen by the victors of history's present telling.

History is not an easy thing to learn because no matter how much you find out, you still never know much more than jack shit. There is not an historian breathing air on this planet who will not corroborate this fact. Any thorough retelling of the bebop jazz era, for instance, would span the globe and discuss gender, white supremacist racism, wars, slavery, social ignorance, sexuality, and the repercussions of violent white hate groups emerging within the mainstream culture—to offer a minute sprinkling of topics.

History is a gorgeous, fascinating, endless fractal.

Basic questions lead to deeply intimate realities. For instance:
Where did your family come from?
Why are they where they are?
Were there global weather changes that led your family to

migrate here thousands and thousands of years ago? If so, how did those changes come about? Is your family on the land they originally migrated to or have they been displaced countless times? If the latter applies, how does the history of controlled movement manifest in your life today, and how do members of your family and community deal with this?

Or perhaps you can trace the reasons why your family is in this country back to slavery, a long-past or quite recent war, unbearable economic conditions, and/or a colonial occupation. If so, how much do you know about slavery? Which war brought your parents or grandparents together, or, for that matter, tore them apart? Why were the economic conditions so extreme? In what manner, and to what effect, did colonialists occupy your family's country of origin?

The year Hitler started bombing London, my maternal grandmother had a fling with an Irish UK soldier. She went on to marry a nice man and have four kids with him, but my mother was the result of this wartime assignation.

This means: No WWII = no Mom = no Inga.

Soon after she was born, baby Mom was whisked out to the English countryside, for absolutely no children were allowed in London during this time. So my mom set her pink baby ass on the planet and went to live with strangers.

I think this would suck and result in serious-ass abandonment issues, and so I think about ALL the London children who grew up with these potential abandonment issues and wonder how that affects their millions of children and grand-children. I wonder how that affects my siblings, myself, my nephews, and niece.

WWII lives on in billions of ways, and that's one of them.

Here's another: When I was a kid, my mom would only serve potatoes on holidays, and then only if we kids bugged her. She hated the sight and smell of potatoes because that's what was for breakfast, lunch, and dinner during the war. Consequently, the four of us mostly enjoyed french fries and baked spuds when we were at a relative's or a restaurant.

Because of WWII, it wasn't until I was well into my thirties—that is, roughly sixty years after Hitler started bombing London—that I stopped (unthinkingly) thinking of potatoes as some kind of special treat.

I mean, how intimate is that?

Dear Adolf,
*   I love potatoes in a really weird way because of your actions and choices.*
Peace out,
Inga

History spans out into teevee, ads, and movies, plays into the naming of cars, towns, streets, and buildings. Sitcom plots, dreams, songs, plays, dances, languages, and paintings are all influenced by history.

It is everywhere, you cannot avoid it, but in this culture, we do.

Oh, we do.

The history we've come to recognize is an institution of intellectual, economic, political, and spiritual apartheid that pretty much everyone in this country buys into until they realize the glaring back-ass stupidity of it and start teaching themselves the real, live-action history of everyone in this land, which, despite slavery, genocide, enforced displacement, legalized lynching, poverty, police brutality, death rows, corporate greed, and racial profiling, is still a beautiful, fascinating, and complex nation, absolutely rife with possibility.

This is a country where a college team named itself the "Fighting Whites" to protest the culture's willingness to accept team names such as the "Washington Redskins" or the "Atlanta Braves." In this place, a preacher momentarily swept the mainstream media's environmental consciousness by asking, "What Would Jesus Drive?" Here, a group of teenagers named the "Brown Barrettes" (in hilarious honor of the 1960s civil rights group the Brown Berets, whom you would know all about if history were actually taught in our schools) took part in a citizen-led "weapons inspection" at a weapon research facility in Livermore, "California."

Even our celebrities—a demographic I generally can't manage to muster much respect for—nonetheless delight me from time to time. In response to the outpouring of protest to the brutal occupation of Iraq, Renée Zellweger was quoted as saying, "I am *so* getting arrested this year."[†]

People crack me the fuck up.

We are irreverent, imaginative, hilarious, and whimsical.

I am consistently thrilled and honored to be a part of this country—to witness the antics, celebrations, resistances, foibles, and art of my people.

Oh my god, I am so in love with y'all.

Yet, I know people all over the world wonder why we let our government do the things they do. It is truly surreal that we will raise millions of dollars for places pillaged by famine or natural disaster, while our taxes pay for corporations and military theaters to disease, enslave, and environmentally pillage entire foreign and domestic demographics. The sick irony of our nation giving "aid" to victims of the 2004 tsunami disaster while we brutally occupy Iraq and Afghanistan is probably not lost on many people in the world.

I think the reason we are so willing to help people out is because we know in our hearts what our government does, but this frightens us terribly, so we dig deep in our pockets to help hurt people far, far away.

Like when *The Oprah Winfrey Show* went to bat for Amina Lawal, a Nigerian woman who was sentenced to death by stoning for the "crime" of having a child out of wedlock. Millions of

---

† She did not get arrested, however, and if Zellweger were black or indigenous, she might very well experience the possibility of getting arrested as much less of a novelty. Still, I laughed when she said that.

people in the U.S. signed petitions on Oprah.com, demanding that the Nigerian government stop this madness.

I am completely down with this action. I signed Oprah's petition and hope it impacts the life of every woman living under a brutal and unquestioningly misogynistic regime.

Meanwhile, the *very week* this show aired, the Florida government—one-fiftieth of a no less brutal and unquestioningly misogynistic regime—snuffed Aileen Wuornos, a woman who killed men known for torturing and raping prostitutes. The newspapers reported she killed "six businessmen," instead of "six sadistic rapists."

Not a peep was heard from the millions of *Oprah* watchers who were outraged by Nigeria's policies. Being pissed at faraway men in Nigeria is within our collective comfort zone, while being outraged at the U.S. and "Florida" governments is not.

Helping Ms. Lawal doesn't just help Ms. Lawal.

It reinforces the pipe dream that we live in a humane, loving, egalitarian society, where democratic representation has, in the past, fairly governed over all of us, like a cool dad who lets us use the car.

Richard M. Nixon once referred to U.S. citizens as "the children."

Of course, he was evincing his sociopathic megalomania—rather than his kickass mass-fathering skills—when he said this, but it is also quite true.

Unlike older kids in the family, such as Africa and India, we have, in the past, been sheltered from many of the massive abuses the white "fathers" enact. (Which is not to say that they don't also enact massive abuses here, but we generally choose not to know about them, much less express widespread outrage over them and thereby demand a new constitution.)

From a global point of view, U.S. citizens are often perceived to be ignorant, insular, and pathologically self-absorbed. Of late, these qualities have taken on a much deadlier tone, as our government brazenly commits crimes against humanity for all the world to see. We have also, conversely, been viewed as warmhearted, spontaneous, generous souls, always ripe for a rollicking good, weird-ass time. We are very much the youngest, most spoiled kid in the world family. As such, as a population, we have been coddled by the rest of the world, oftentimes to the extreme disadvantage of older, poorer nations.

We—*as diametrically opposed to our government*—have enjoyed being generally well loved for a while. With Arbusto claiming the presidency again in 2004, however, the world has lost all patience with us.

Some time after that latest Arbusto fraud-election, I spent a few hours on the website sorryeverybody.com. People from all over the country posted photos of themselves, their children, or, mysteriously, their pets, holding signs of apology to the rest of the world for allowing Arbusto to remain in power.

Some of the sentiments—expressing infantile forms of unaccountability like "Hey! Don't bomb Smith County! We voted for Kerry!"—deeply annoyed me. Many of the images made me laugh at how dear and loving my people are, and others moved me to tears. Even the ones that bugged me still rang with two key things people in this country have not collectively embraced in my lifetime:

1.) Humility.

2.) The knowledge that there is a whole, wide world that is unfairly and detrimentally affected by our government.

It was also very interesting to see how many gracious people in other countries posted answering images and messages that basically said, "Well, we forgive you, but you all really need to learn the time-tested art of taking your asses to the streets and not going home until you get what you want."

I will never understand the curious practice of asking for "permission" to hold protests and marches on the very streets that we have paid for with our tax dollars, and then dispersing when told to do so. People in the U.S. could learn many things from people in Mexico, Venezuela, and Bolivia if we were able to admit that we are not, in fact, the smartest people on earth.

This is a time of great possibilities. People in this country are at a point where we can, literally, eat a slice of humble pie, grow, and learn what U.S. history really and truly is. This is incredibly important because if we do not, regardless of our gender, religion, sexuality, ethnicity, or race, we will continue to be informed by a white male imperialist and supremacist ideology that debilitates us all, globally, locally, intimately, indivisibly.

And nobody wants that anymore.

Columbus and the New World Order

Myth: The Americas did not exist before a courageous man named Christopher Columbus discovered them. Before he and other like-minded white men alit upon these shores, nothing of worth was happening here, and no one of worth lived here.

In 1492 Christopher Columbus sailed the ocean blue. He had three boats: the *Niña*, the *Pinta*, and the *Santa María*. I was consistently reminded of this growing up in Santa Maria, "California," because the town logo is that boat.

In school, I learned that Columbus discovered the

Americas like maybe it was a quarter under his pillow that the tooth fairy left.

When I grew up, I found out that to "discover" actually involves being THE FIRST to start a five-hundred-year campaign of spiritually and physically raping and killing all the people whom you can't squeeze into your perception of civilization.

The historian Howard Zinn unveils some cognitive permutations from Columbus's journal about the Arawak people of the Bahama Islands, which resonate rather sonorously with this latter-year definition.

Ahem:

> They . . . brought us parrots and balls of cotton
> and spears and many other things, which they
> exchanged for the glass beads and hawks' bells. They
> willingly traded everything they owned. . . . They
> were well-built, with good bodies and handsome fea-
> tures. . . . They do not bear arms, and do not know
> them, for I showed them a sword, they took it by the
> edge and cut themselves out of ignorance. They have
> no iron. Their spears are made of cane. . . . They
> would make fine servants. . . . With fifty men we
> could subjugate them all and make them do what-
> ever we want.[1]

I am reminded of the scene in *Willy Wonka and the Chocolate Factory* when Augustus Gloop first lays eyes on Mr. Wonka's living candy garden with the waterfall-churned chocolate river. As a result of his completely self-absorbed gluttony, our ungainly Mr. Gloop falls into the otherwise serenely flowing chocolate and gets sucked up a tube.

My sister, Liz, tells me that my face "gets all ugly" when I am bitter, but my heart will probably always contain a modicum of bitterness that Columbus—and the self-absorbed gluttony he represents—didn't share a comparable fate.

I accept the fact that my face "getting all ugly" is part of the legacy I inherited as a citizen of the United States of Amerikkka.

Columbus's men worked the Arawak people to death, and in the meantime subjected them to horrors I am quite certain they never imagined in their most grotesque nightmares. People were forced to carry the beastly Spaniards around on their backs, children were beheaded for sport, and bodies were casually sliced to test the sharpness of beloved Spanish swords.

Eduardo Galeano—the Uruguayan writer who is single-handedly responsible for reawakening a fascination with history in my post-traumatic-stressed, publicly educated mind—describes one of many wanton atrocities casually performed by Columbus and his men:

The shadow of the sails spreads across the sea. Gulf-weed and jellyfish, moved by the waves, drift over the surface toward the coast.

From the quarterdeck of one of the caravels, Columbus contemplates the white beaches where he has again planted the cross and the gallows. This is his second voyage. How long it will last he doesn't know; but his heart tells him that all will come out well, and why wouldn't the admiral believe it? Doesn't he have the habit of measuring the ship's speed with his hand against his chest, counting the heartbeats?

Belowdecks in another caravel, in the captain's cabin, a young girl shows her teeth. Miquele de Cuneo reaches for her breasts, and she scratches and kicks him and screams. Miquele received her a while ago. She is a gift from Columbus.

He lashes her with a rope. He beats her hard on the head and stomach and legs. Her screams become moans, the moans become wails. Finally all that can be heard are the comings and goings of sea gulls and the creak of rocked timbers. From time to time waves send a spray through the porthole.

Miquele hurls himself upon the bleeding body and thrusts, gasps, wrestles. The air smells of tar, of saltpeter, of sweat. Then the girl, who seems to have fainted or died, suddenly fastens her nails in Miquele's back, knots herself around his legs, and rolls him over in a fierce embrace.

After some time, when Miquele comes to, he doesn't know where he is or what has happened.

Livid, he detaches himself from her and knocks her
away with his fist.

He staggers up on deck. Mouth open, he takes
a deep breath of sea breeze. In a loud voice, as if
announcing an eternal truth, he says, "These Indian
women are all whores."[2]

Columbus *never set foot* in the continental United States,
yet we are the only "New World" nation in the Americas that
celebrates his deeds.

There are many more indigenous and mixed-race people
in the southern Americas, and like indigenous folks in the U.S.,
they don't feel much of a call to honor those responsible for the
decimation of their children and ancestors.

Also, memories of colonization, slavery, genocide, and
imperialism dance in our DNA strands, whether one is aware of
it or not.

The past is very much alive in the present.

If you've ever sat next to a representative of white male imperialism on an airplane, you have probably had the opportunity
to notice that he or she will command the armrest and generate
vast amounts of passive-aggressive low-level hostility if you in
any way question his or her right to it. Only in the event that
you are a more dominant and powerful representative of white
male imperialism will he or she willingly (and kiss-assingly)
concede the armrest to you.

Over five hundred years ago, Columbus symbolically begat mundane pathologies of this stripe in what is now known as Haiti.

It was white male supremacist imperialist racism then, and so it is now as we witness the U.S. and French governments[†] respond with shady coups, puppet dictators, and indirect military involvement whenever the present-day Haitian people so much as *glance* in the direction of their armrests.

In this context, "armrests" might represent schools, a medical university, food, and other such things that sustain and improve the quality of life. Recently, the Haitian government was doing a lot more than "glancing" at the armrest. The government under Aristide was *resting its arm in the space perceived by the white man to belong to him,* pulling people out of the cycle of U.S.- and French-owned factory slavery.

Hence the coup d'etat against the extremely democratically elected President Aristide on February 29, 2004.

Hence, also, the U.S. government shutdown of the sole aforementioned medical university for use as a base of operations for the U.S. Marines.

[†] Who famously "hate" one another in regard to new imperial conquests, such as the "War" on Terrorism, but can still manage to work together quite swimmingly on the more time-honored and vested interest of subjugating the people of Haiti.

Columbus and the New World Order

It appears that a maddening lack of consciousness based on a consciously manipulated version of history serves as the foundation for honoring Christopher Columbus in my country.

In *Lies My Teacher Told Me,* I came across this 1989 Arbusto I quote: "Christopher Columbus not only opened the door to a New World, but also set an example for us all by showing what monumental feats can be accomplished through perseverance and faith."[3]

It certainly does require an enormous amount of perseverance and faith to live with the monumental feat of enacting mass murder for over five hundred years, but let's, shall we, be, er, *different* from the Arbustos of this world. Let's eviscerate any sense of "accomplishment" from this—quite ongoing—bloodbath. Folks of the Arbusto strain are very fond of phrases like "opened the door to a New World." They sound so much more valiant, patriotic, and kindhearted than "massacring, raping, and enslaving everyone who resists being dominated by us."

I am filled with shame.

And shame is a shitty feeling.

I can understand why so many people opt to drown this true-life emotional response inside man-made constructs like "patriotism," which can't even "exist" without borders that are graphically designed in Hammond World Atlas Corporation's survival-of-the-fittest, xenophobic, punk-ass cartography rooms, located in Union, "New Jersey," USA. Why does

Hammond give an entire page of its "world" atlases to countries in Europe, to Australia, and to individual states in the USA, while cramming entire regions of Africa, Asia, South America, and India onto a few pages? These are carefully considered choices residing under the jurisdiction of white supremacist racism.

In this country, many people file many such choices into a cerebral folder labeled *Just the Way It Is*. We believe in experientially retarded concepts such as *Good vs. Evil* and *Absolute Truth*. Laws are crafted, states 'n' nations are created, and maps are cartographed into existence based on the reality of white supremacist imperialist racism. An *ideology* informs the entire structure of the planet we live on. Not knowing this is a choice.

> Believing otherwise is a choice.
> Living in vitriolic denial is a choice.
> Honoring Columbus gives credence to choices such as these.
> Or perhaps:
> Choices such as these give credence to honoring Columbus.
> I am not sure which.

It's not *difficult* to make other choices about Columbus, but (thanks to such fundamental sources of information as, say, world atlases, encyclopedias, and history textbooks) the knowledge *informing* these choices is not passed along with a clap on the shoulder and a high school diploma—in the event one has lived a life that affords one the opportunity to be handed a high school diploma.

In order to make other choices, you have to *want to know*.

You have to *first note* that, for instance, Palestine is excluded from world atlases published in the United States, *and then you hafta wonder why*. And once you do note and wonder why about this, a whole world of pain, suffering, genocide, poverty, child imprisonment, and wholesale oppression will open its heart to you. If you really start wondering about this, then you will see the same horror enacted not just in places far away, but in your community as well.

And this shit hurts.

No one is saying that making other choices about Columbus and everything he represents does not open one up to a world of hurt.

No one is saying that.

This world is filled with hurt. If you choose to embrace your own humanity and be present in this world, there is no way to protect yourself from being hurt.

So forget that.

I am hurt pretty much every day, but I am a happy, functioning person, with love and laughter in my life. I think I have actually learned to be happier by consciously acknowledging my blessings in the midst of the heartbreak of my environment.

When my sister, Liz, called the other day to tell me that her boy, Evan, looked up from a picture he was drawing and sighed and said, "I miss Inga," my heart just exploded with joy.

I carried that joy around with me for weeks, while forty public schools closed in Detroit due to lack of funding.

Thousands of beautiful Iraqi people are being killed, injured, and psychologically maimed for life by thousands of beautiful U.S. troops, who are also being killed, injured, and psychologically maimed for life.

I carry joy in much the same way that I imagine a soldier carries her gun.

It has the power to save my life in detrimental circumstances.

One doesn't need to be an emotionally distant scholar who pores over obscure volumes in the bowels of an esteemed research library in order to acquire a non-Marvel Comics perspective of Christopher Columbus.

If you noted the page number of the passage I quoted at the beginning of this chapter, you saw that I didn't have to venture more than a couple paragraphs into Howard Zinn's 634-page opus to make the, uh, discovery that Columbus was a wholesale piece of shit.

It's no big secret.

When we pull our heads out of our asses just the eentsiest bit, this is almost guaranteed to be the first thing we find out.

Most historians take care not to cast the "present morality" on Columbus and his ilk. I guess if you're an historian who wants to be "taken seriously," you have to refrain from projecting the present onto the past. I, on the other hand, am quite sure I would have despised Columbus five hundred years ago, every bit as much as I despise his progeny today. Consequently, I suffer no misgivings about passing value judgments on the sadistic, prune-hearted asshole. Furthermore, I don't need to time-travel, to hearken yon to yesteryear and drum up images of big wooden boats charging across whitecapped seas, to imagine what things were like in the 1490s.

It's repeated quite frequently in daily life:

My parking spot.

My phone conversation in the line at the post office.

My kids. My job.

My house, my car, my dog.

My armrest, my handhold, my seat on the bus.

My neighborhood Starbucks.

My right of way.

My turn.

Mine mine mine me me me.

Just yesterday afternoon I had a conversation that vividly recalled how incredibly widespread this modern version of Columbus's pathological self-absorption is.

My next-door neighbor expends a painfully surreal amount of energy policing the easements on either side of him, walking up and down both sides of his home at least three times a week to ascertain whether his neighbors' possessions—

even so much as the handle of a wayward paintbrush—are *touching* his property.[†]

After witnessing this phenomenon a number of times, I asked my landlord about it. He threw his hands up to the heavens and proclaimed, "Yeah, christ, it's like he's Balboa or something."

Columbus, Balboa, whatever.

On a grander scale, Columbus's ideology is also very much alive, well, and still brutalizing, enslaving, and killing indigenous people and people of color the world over. Nowadays, the New World no longer means kings and queens and gold and discoveries. The International Monetary Fund, World Bank, and World Trade Organization are the royalty of today, backing CEOs instead of explorers. What was colonization in the past is globalization today. The new New World trades in Dole bananas, Folgers coffee, and Hershey's chocolate. Georgia-Pacific's deforestation rids Central America of land-hogging mahogany, which will then be transformed into executive desks and boardroom conference tables, so that the banana, coffee, and cocoa plantations will have more space. The new New World's palaces are Hiltons and Marriotts lording it over entire stretches of coastline, with police who allow only tourists and on-duty employee-slaves to view "their" beaches.

[†] Meanwhile, the bamboo he has planted—in his white male Orientalist Fantasy of Feng Shui Democracy, which also compels him to fly Tibetan flags on his front porch—will someday uproot the foundations of every house on the block.

Nowadays the soldiers in the pay of the New World Order wear suits and ties and private corporation military uniforms. Some patrol the world's streets in limousines or tanks; others use machetes, chainsaws, guns, cattle prods, and abandoned sports arenas when carrying out their nefarious actions.

Many of these contemporary enforcers of white imperialism learn everything they know about death, coercion, and torture—about the New World and its Order—in Fort Benning, "Georgia," at the Western Hemisphere Institute for Security Cooperation.

Opened in 1946, the recently renamed School of the Americas teaches Central and South American soldiers how to seize and control entire populations who resist their lives, land, and children being co-opted in the service of white imperialism.

In what I am only able to perceive as revisionist wishful thinking—not unlike that of a wealthy older man who dumps his wife of forty years and marries a young trophy wife in the dim hope that she will make him feel "young" again—the "new" Western Hemisphere Institute for Security Cooperation was "established" in January 2001, a mere month after the School of the Americas "closed" on December 15, 2000. After searching the web for twenty minutes, I managed to find a government-associated site about the SOA. The banner at the top of this site proclaimed: "The U.S. Army School of the Americas officially closed its doors at 1200 Noon on December 15, 2000, after a long tradition of service to the United States of America. This site is available only for historical purposes."[4]

Uh-huh. Right.

Lately, I am usually reading or rereading one of Arundhati Roy's books. She is one of the people who keep me sane in these times.

Right now, I'm involved with *War Talk,* where Ms. Roy writes that sixty thousand people have been trained to serve the New World Order at the School of the Americas in Fort Benning, "Georgia."

This factoid inspired some math in my mind.

If each of this much-reviled institution's "graduates" has tortured, raped, or killed "only" five people, that adds up to a minimum of three hundred thousand psychologically maimed or altogether stolen lives. If each of these people has at least ten friends, coworkers, or relatives who grieved at the fate of their dearly loved one, tack another three million victims onto the walls of the School of the Americas in Fort Benning, "Georgia."

Who do you think funds this place?

Who pays the "teachers" and the janitors and the grounds-keepers at the School of the Americas in Fort Benning, "Georgia"?

Who buys the food that nourishes the bodies that learn how to properly attach live electric currents to someone's mother's, nephew's, grandchild's genitals?

We do, we do, that poison arrow through our hearts.

As I write this passage, some elderly white nuns are sitting in prison cells for peacefully protesting the curriculum of torture this school teaches. You see, it is against the law to barricade oneself behind the doors that the New World's Order steadfastly opens.

You do not have to be an indigenous person or person of color to witness this completely arbitrary and unjust reality firsthand.

But, my god, it helps.

I close my eyes, spin the globe.

My finger lands on: Ecuador.

In Ecuador, more than 70 percent of the fifty thousand people employed by the rose plantation industry are women. Corporations that operate in poor countries to provide products for wealthy ones simply *adore* employing women. Like men, women are willing to work long hours in order to feed their families and children. Unlike men, however, when people who nourish others at their breasts mention the prospect of human rights and unions, they can count on being completely disregarded— even laughed at—by most governments.

Some of the health hazards that arise from being around the pesticides, insecticides, fumigants, and fungicides that keep roses red, vibrant, and youthful looking include: nausea, fatigue, miscarriages, blurred vision, hair loss, aching kidneys, loss of appetite, respiratory problems, conjunctivitis, and rashes.

What is important for a plantation rose's survival is not

taken into consideration for the people who tend, cut, wrap, and box them up for shipping to the U.S., where they will symbolize people's undying Valentine love for one another.

In a *New York Times* article, James Pagano, the chief marketing officer for Calyx & Corolla, one of the biggest U.S. buyers of Ecuadorean roses, had this slick nugget of compassion to impart: "'We buy what we think consumers will perceive to be a high-quality rose at a competitive price. The environment, he said, 'is not an issue we have any business being in.'"[5]

The "environment" was not an issue Columbus had any business being in, either. It did not matter to him how hard people worked to ferret largely nonexistent gold out of the earth. What mattered was the weight of his ship when he pulled into Queen Isabella's port.

Not unlike Mr. Pagano, her majesty wanted a high-quality explorer at a competitive price.

When someone's lover sends roses to the office, coworkers are known to react with envy. Roses on one's desk are a status symbol. They mean your lover loves you enough to send you roses. You are cherished by someone who can and will throw around the dough to prove it to "the world."

Ecuadorean plantation roses shine like red suns, do not bloom into old age, have no smell, and remain in their prime for much longer than garden-variety roses, which age and droop and fill the room with their stunning lifeforce scent, as a grand finale, when they turn toward death.

Yard roses are generally cared for by a human being who adores them.

Plantation roses poison and sicken the people who care for them, but they are, I gather, perceived by the consumer to be a high-quality rose at a competitive price.

While it is an utmost expression of truest love to order someone plantation roses, which will be delivered by an impersonal third party, it would probably be an expression of "bad taste" or "chintziness" to ask your garden-delight neighbor if you can barter some homemade chocolate chip cookies for a dozen of her roses and then carefully arrange them in a jar you found under the sink and hand deliver them to your beloved at work.

In our pathologically self-absorbed, brand-seduced culture, where people somehow maintain an illusory "status" through the act of purchasing, it is "high class" to buy plantation roses that cause miscarriages in the people who tend them, and "low class" to barter for your neighbor's, who loves them to life with ardor.

I find it so very interesting that most of the things that connote wealth and love in my country come at the astoundingly high and noncompetitive price of freedom, longevity, and life for so many people of color and indians on the planet.

White people too.

Not to mention foxes, minks, filets mignon to be.

Diamonds are forever causing misery in Africa.

Gold is wealth.

Roses, love.

Or so we are told.

And so it appears.

We could also dabble into why pro-life people aren't beating down Calyx & Corolla's door in outrage at the death to innocents that the rose plantation poisons perpetuate, and why the lives of Ecuadorean children aren't as important as the lives of (white) U.S. children, and why a woman choosing to terminate a pregnancy is somehow considered more murderous than the systematic occupational siege under which the rose plantation employees and their reproductive systems exist, and why environmental crimes against poor women are not included in mainstream feminist discourse about reproductive rights, and why the fuck we consciously and unconsciously attribute value to people's lives based on their religion, class, and/or skin color, but, alas, we need to get back on topic here.

If you have read *Fast Food Nation,* or indeed, have a job in almost any large factory, then you know that many people in this country work in grueling, draconian, unhealthy environments too, but our culture serves these horrors up in a way that not only reinforces survival of the fittest but coerces people to sanction things that are, in fact, morally repugnant. We are encouraged to listen to "arguments" and look at "both" sides of genocidal and ecocidal atrocities.

Like this:

Slavery

Well, see, the Africans believed in slavery too. If we hadn't enslaved them, they would have enslaved each other. We were just taking an active part in the world economy of the time.

Indian nations

They weren't farming the land. They were sitting on a goddamn cornucopia goldmine and just letting it go to waste. They died because they couldn't adapt to modern civilization.

Sharks

Look, we can't have them using our beaches for their feeding ground. We kill them in the most humane possible way, so don't worry about that. Would you prefer that one of your kids get mauled?

Trees

Forest fires only happen because there are too many trees, duh.

Mysteriously, it seems that a "genocide" is considered *a bona fide genocide* solely when the victims are not plants, animals, eco-systems, indigenous people, and/or people of color. The ongoing five hundred years during which this country has practiced war, slavery, colonization, ecocide, imperialism, and terrorism as a part of its culture and economy are never referred to as such.

47

Autobiography of a Blue-Eyed Devil

This centuries-long atrocity is palmed off as a series of doors steadfastly opened by and for brave white men, who have been willing to take almost insurmountable risks so that we could all benefit from their actions and live democratic, free Amerikkkan Dreamy lives, and it is only ungrateful, brash, unpatriotic, ignorant people who are not prayerfully grateful.

Kiss my ass, kiss my ass, kiss my ass.

A Noam Chomsky quote I found in *War Talk* resounded in my thoughts on how constructed perspective plays into the concept of genocide:

> During the Thanksgiving holiday a few weeks ago, I took a walk with some friends and family in a national park. We came across a gravestone, which had on it the following inscription: "Here lies an Indian woman, a Wampanoag, whose family and tribe gave of themselves and their land that this great nation might be born and grow."
>
> Of course, it is not quite accurate to say that the indigenous population gave of themselves and their land for this noble purpose. Rather, they were slaughtered, decimated, and dispersed in the course of one of the greatest exercises in genocide in human history . . . which we celebrate each October when we honor Columbus—a notable mass murderer himself—on Columbus Day.

Hundreds of American citizens, well-meaning and decent people, troop by that gravestone regularly and read it, apparently without reaction; except, perhaps, a feeling of satisfaction that at last we are giving some due recognition to the sacrifices of the native peoples . . . They might react differently if they were to visit Auschwitz or Dachau and find a gravestone reading: "Here lies a woman, a Jew, whose family and people gave of themselves and their possessions that this great nation might grow and prosper."[6]

People—and animals, trees, rivers, mountains, and oceans—*do* mind being killed so that white men can take up more space, have more power, and make more money.

They mind this very much.

They do not mind dying, for death is part of life, but they do mind dying in this way, for this reason.

My sleep is consistently disrupted by the spirits of those who do not want their deaths to have been in vain. They chant Patti Smith's lyric into my try-to-sleepyby head: "Jesus died for somebody's sins, but not mine." The spirits are also evidently familiar with the song "Open Your Eyes" by the Lords of the New Church, and intone, "'Cause meek inherits earth . . . six feet deep," over and over and *fucking over*. These spirits have, for all intents and purposes, taken over my life. Slaves, priestesses, moms and warriors, gangstas (also warriors, though unrecognized as such by mainstream society), witches, ancient goddesses, wrongfully incarcerated souls, and many, many more folks show me the world through their eyes, and it is not pretty.

It is not ugly either, but it is very complex and not at all relaxing.

I suppose somewhere herein lies the most self-serving quality of the chip on my shoulder about my culture's penchant for role-playing Columbus in day-to-day life—I would really like to get a good night's sleep.

I figure nice sleeps are more likely to occur in my life if folks start reckoning with the past, acknowledging and vindicating the very harsh and vivid reality of stolen lives.

Columbus is very important to the leaders of the New World Order because his "story" ideologically and symbolically justifies every coup they orchestrate, every corporation they allow to set up shop anywhere on earth, every civil war they have insinuated into being, and every dead body piled up on the doorstep of the United States of Amerikkka.

Without the Columbus card, the whole white house comes tumbling down.

I call that pretty dang important too.

However, not only—by the very standards set down by the U.S. alpha dog brand of survival of the fittest—was Columbus an abject, resounding failure at locating resources for King Ferdinand and Queen Isabella, he was only one of a seemingly infinite parade of explorers, colonizers, imperialists, and conquistadors who spent (and still spend) their time fucking shit up for animals, humans, and the environment. As Zinn says, "What Columbus did to the Arawaks of the Bahamas, Cortés did to the Aztecs of Mexico, Pizarro to the Incas of Peru, and the English settlers of "Virginia" and "Massachusetts" to the Powhatans and the Pequots.[7]

Columbus did not, and does not, by any means, exist within a vacuum. The lie of valor and courage he represents, along with the fact that we celebrate a day in his honor, are the only things compelling me to single his sorry ass out. Columbus was a dime a dozen, and not even a freshly minted first-edition dime, at that. By the time of 1492, when Columbus sailed the ocean blue, many populations of people on the planet had been conquered, enslaved, or otherwise brutalized by someone at some point.

Embracing an "us and them" mentality leads to worker-slaves who can be convinced to spend their lives constructing pyramids in Egypt, great walls in China, and hanging gardens in Babylon. Teaching one's children that "their" god is the best, only, and most just god in the whole wide world has led to the senseless murder, rape, and enslavement of beings whose spirits have continued to roam the earth since the term "civilization" was coined.

Enacting dominance over others is nothing new.

Been there, done that, got the t-shirt, let's move on.

I was in Manchester, England, not long ago and I tripped out on how many white Britons asked me about slavery and genocide—as if they couldn't imagine coming from such a *barbarous* country. Manchester is one of the cities where the cotton that slaves picked was woven by British or Irish worker-slaves into fine linens for the wealthy of the world to enjoy, and for England to cash in on.

Oh, and France? Germany? Italy? Spain?

Give a lady a muthafukkkin break.

People in many white-ruled nations are very comfortable passing judgment on people in the U.S. based on the conveniently misplaced criteria that the indigenous people *they* slaughtered have been dead or assimilated much longer, and also, they hardly ever meet the people they enslaved.

That is, until, for instance, the 1970s and '80s, when African, Jamaican, Indian, Kashmiri, and Pakistani people began immigrating to Britain. Once Britain was no longer composed of a light-skinned population, the vicious racism of the British people—previously reserved for Scots, Irish, and Welsh folks— was, and continues to be, enacted in a much more immediate space in people's lives.

It was on a British teevee show that I discovered the racist slang term "Pakis," referring to all people from South Asia, as well as the mysterious term "proper blacks." As in, "I don't mind proper blacks, but I hate those bloody filthy Pakis."

Also, enquiring minds want to know: Did Prince Harry get in so much trouble for going to a costume party dressed as a Nazi with a swastika armband because he did something morally repugnant, or because he revealed more about his nation than his nation is comfortable acknowledging to itself?

And I must say, even though I have paranormal love for

Canadians, part of Napoleon's territory, did, indeed, include Canada. Slavery is very much a part of Canada's history as well, and genocide is a topic that First Nations people can speak on with great eloquence.

It's like this:

I can hate on the U.S. because *I fucken love my country.*

But you all living in countries that come from an equally unexamined male-dominated white supremacist racist imperialism, you all need to step away from my people and look at your own shit.

Unless, of course, you have something positive and constructive to offer.

In my culture, white supremacist racist male domination and imperialism is rationalized as "normal."

On the *other* hand, my country has been successfully branded as the greatest democracy on the planet. This marketing brand is not bought by the hundreds of populations we've invaded and shit on for the past five hundred years, but at any rate, if this *is* somehow the greatest democracy on the planet—like my dear friend Alex Cleghorn always reminds me—we can do better.

Here is a sticker I saw on someone's bike the other day:

"I love my country, but I think we should start seeing other people."

⚔

As purveyors of alleged worldwide democracy, *we have no excuse* for utterly failing to take into consideration the thousands of social models based on cooperation that have existed throughout time. Our constitution was, in fact, inspired by a much more cooperative social model. Without the Iroquois confederacy, the founding fathers and pals would have been faced with quite the blank piece of constitutional parchment. The founding fathers carefully studied the Iroquois Confederacy's constitution and edited out all the pesky tenets that didn't serve white male domination. For instance, the ones about how very unquestioningly powerful and integral women, children, and elders are to a truly great democracy. Then they added doctrines about "ownership" and other things the collective Iroquois nations considered absurd, if not unthinkable. If this is, indeed, the greatest democracy on the planet, we have no excuse for wholly basing our existence on (white) male lore about how survival inherently involves domination. However, since we have, for the most part, been successfully taught to base our existence on lore such as this, I am forced to assert we have no *actual* claim on being a great democracy.

But I do concede, it is a wildly successful marketing brand.

In closing:

If we in this country are going to choose to begin U.S. history with Christopher Columbus, let's learn the truth about him, bridge this truth to the world we presently live in, and resist everything he represents, *especially* those things that live inside our own learned, pathologically self-absorbed hearts, and which we've been indoctrinated to condone or ignore, thus normalizing the denial of our own humanity.

Oh yeah, and let's boycott the sacred motherfuckall out of his holiday.

It is a blatant white supremacist racist propaganda community celebration where banks, schools, and post offices are closed, and parades honoring a known rapist/murderer meander down city streets. It is an annual jab in the heart for all sovereign indian nations and everyone who doesn't think it's a good idea to view the world like it is your personal home improvement, investment project, or business plan. It is a symbolic, historically based present-day backslapping gladfest for everyone who defines "the fittest" as the most unscrupulous, the greediest, the most racist and elitist white-identified alpha males in what is subsequently considered to be a dog-eat-dog world.

Fuck Columbus Day.

God Told Me to Kill You

Myth: God ordained the white man to be his overseer in this land. Expansion and progress are the exact same thing. There was no holocaust or genocide in the Americas. Indian nations just died off because they were not fit and we all know the unfit naturally do not survive. It's Just the Way It Is.

In the 1600s, folks in much of Europe were very busy leading clean, god-fearing lives and keeping on the lookout for suspicious witches in their neighborhoods.

This watchfulness generally resulted in the church

seizing the land/property of witches and burning them at the stake. You could tell a witch because she or he wasn't willing to trade a complex religion based on the goddess, earth, water, fire, and sky for one that worshipped nothing more than a single man-god. When you are of the earth and you know you are of the earth, it really confounds your brain when you are asked to attribute the ceaseless wonder and power of the earth solely to some white man-god.

Those wishing to shine in the eyes of this god—via church officials in their communities—denounced all suspicious neighbors for consorting with the devil. This is, if you think about it, rather an odd accusation to level at individuals who can't wrap their minds around all-powerful male entities, come what may.

Many people figured out that they and their children lived longer if they shined in the eyes of this god via church officials in their communities. And thus, the church amassed the possessions and property of countless suspicious witches.

I am directly descended from suspicious witches found in Ireland, where Catholics (colonized Irish) and Protestants (British-Irish colonizers) presently vie for power and control.

The suspicious witches remain underground.

For now.

Urban life during witch-killing times involved high instances of child prostitution, rich men sexually exploiting poor children, syphilis, poverty, and other nasty diseases. To many, these social ills were brought upon folks not by their own policies and beliefs, but by no lesser personage than the devil himself, who was a very busy fellow during this time.

Some demographics of people—many of whom were influenced by the ideas of a man named John Calvin—didn't think the church went *far enough* to force people to live sinless lives. Burning suspicious witches on the stake in front of their children just wasn't cutting the mustard. These folks were very unhappy with the rampaging godlessness and devilfulness. When they heard that there was a "New World" to which England wanted to open the door, they figured this would be a good chance to escape all the handshaking with the devil going on in Europe.

As far as I've been able to discern, the Pilgrims and Puritans were a joyless bunch who carried deeply ignorant, white male supremacist beliefs across the ocean with them, and didn't like sex. How they managed to procreate remains something of a mystery to me, but I've gathered that sheets with fancy flower-embroidered cuntholes helped out quite a bit.

It rarely occurred to these folks that "natives"—be they Mandinka, Chinese, Irish, or Seminole—had pretty good ideas about how to live that had served their people for thousands and thousands of years.

It did occur to them to feel sorry for "heathens" and "savages" who lived bibleless lives, and it also occurred to them—out of abject intolerance projected as unconditional charity—to wish to show these folks what "god" is all about and how to live without sinning. It didn't cross their minds, though, that people were living civilized, highly developed, and both harmonious and strife-filled lives before they showed up on the scene.[†]

This is directly related to the phenomenon where white imperialists decide something has been "discovered" based solely on the fact that they are suddenly able to perceive the "discovered" thing, on their terms.

John Calvin's concept of predestination lurked in the minds of our founding fathers' sons' sons for many years before formally making its debut as "manifest destiny" in 1845. That's the year John O'Sullivan, editor of the *United States Magazine and Democratic Review,* wrote that it was white settlers' "manifest destiny to overspread the continent allotted by Providence for the free development of our yearly multiplying millions."[1]

In his doctrine of predestination, Calvin espoused the idea that god blesses some people with eternal life and damns others to burn forever in hell, for no particular reason. The only way to tell who was blessed and who was damned was to check out how well they were doing in this life—"well," in this context, being a serious-ass value judgment. This is, after all, terribly similar to the secular philosophy of "survival of the

---

† I suppose, in fairness, it's not accurate to say this. It must have at least crossed Ben Franklin's mind, since he noticed that white people who lived with indians for any length of time were incredibly loath to return to "civilized" society and generally only did so on pain of death.

fittest," which is essentially a self-affirming theory: Whoever is on "top" is meant to be on "top" because those on "top" define whom the "top" comprises.

Mr. O'Sullivan used the concept of manifest destiny to justify the U.S.'s hijacking of "California," "Texas," "Arizona," and "New Mexico" away from Mexico, which had already been hijacked by Spain.

Manifest destiny came to provide a wonderful cover for people who might otherwise become kinda concerned about the decimation, enslavement, and overall bloodshed that had been taking place for the past 350 years, and that showed absolutely no signs of abating. The end result was a rather frightening population, soothed with a divine justification that killing and enslaving were the golden ticket into heaven.

Here is how my trusty, stuffy, patriarchal 1965 *Random House Dictionary* defines manifest destiny:

> The belief or doctrine, held chiefly in the middle and latter part of the 19th century, that it is the destiny of the U.S. to expand its territory over the whole of North America and to extend and enhance its political, social, and economic influences.[2]

I love how I can *always count on my dictionary* to obfuscate even the most well-documented instances of white man's bullshit. I love my 1965 *Random House Dictionary*!

Note how there is no mention of what "the U.S." did to "expand its territory." There's no mention of the smallpox-infested blankets that the U.S. government distributed to indian tribes and nations in order to expand its territories. No mention of the sixty million buffalo that were systematically slaughtered in order to starve the Plains nations to death. No mention of the forced, backbreaking labor of African people who were enslaved to "enhance political, social, and economic influences." And no mention of the individual white folks who perpetuated these, and many, many more, crimes against the earth and humanity. No one can be held accountable for something that is, quite simply, the "destiny" of "the U.S."

And I just *fucking adore* the part where manifest destiny is relegated to the past—"the middle and latter part of the nineteenth century," to be precise. Manifest destiny has most recently been renamed catchy things like "North American Free Trade Agreement," which sounds kinda hippie and community-based, and "full spectrum dominance," which, uh, doesn't. It is actually the exact same concept, normalizing and justifying the exact same genocide and enslavement.

"God" is, by the way, still evidently really involved in white supremacist racist imperialism. It was just yesterday, in the year 2004, that the allegedly thoroughly modern twenty-first-century Associated Press newswire carried an actual instance of reportage where an alleged minister said that "god" had spoken directly to him about the destiny of President Arbusto.

Yes. "God" spoke to one Patrick Robertson, and here is what "god" had to say:

> The Lord has just blessed him [Arbusto]. I mean, he could make terrible mistakes and comes out of it. It doesn't make any difference what he does, good or bad, God picks him up because he's a man of prayer and God's blessing him.[3]

This "god" character has allegedly been speaking to presidents at highly convenient times for a while. At the close of the nineteenth century, President McKinley got down on his knees and prayed for "god's" guidance when seeking a rationale for invading the Philippines. And "god" said unto his white kowtowing racist ass, "Kill them all and let me sort them out." And this was done. Countless people died, and a country already seriously molested by Spanish colonization was further traumatized and has been divided ever since.

Like so many things, this is really interesting to me.

See, I think there're only three sins: lying, cheating, and stealing. When I lie, cheat, or steal, god[†] strikes my ass down.

---

† My "god" is constantly evolving. At present, "god" mostly involves Mata Kali; Nuestra Virgen de Guadalupe; Holysacred Durga, Slayer of Ignorance, Shining Lady of Compassion; Kwan Yin; and Single Mother with a Knife Ezili Danto. More about this in my next book, *Are You There God? It's Me, Inga.*

I refrain from committing these three sins not because I am some, er, noble person, but merely because I got sick of getting my ass kicked every time I lied, cheated, or stole. For instance, when I was a Bad Teenager, everything I shoplifted broke, was stolen from me, or met some ugly, bad end. Every time I lied to my mom, the lie came back to haunt me and I'd get in even more trouble than I would have initially been in—though not necessarily with my mom.

Admittedly, I never had the courage to proclaim, "I am now going to do something really shitty in the name of god," so I don't know if that would somehow cover my ass or not.

I'm too scared of god's wrath to try it.

So, like, I wonder, who is this "god" who doesn't care if you do "good or bad," who "picks you up" even after you make "terrible mistakes"? This "god" sounds an awful lot like a rich man who dotes on his eldest son and will do anything to ensure his spawn's place at the center of the universe.

My god, on the other hand, wants me to be a person who can face herself in the mirror every morning and wonder, "How'm I gonna love the world today?"

Yet, I see the value judgment herein.

My idea of loving the world does not involve convincing people that my god is the only real and true god, yet for many Christians, this is the exact—and often, only—way in which they believe they *can* love the world.

※

In San Francisco, I was riding a bus down Mission Street, approaching 16th. It was a very busy sunny day, people everywhere.

I saw two pimply, pasty-faced young Mormon men talking at an elderly Mexicana matriarch. I wondered to myself, "Hmmm, why are two youngsters *talking at* an elder instead of *listening to* any wisdom she may wish to bless them with out of the potential sheer compassion of her heart?"

I pulled the cord and hopped off the bus, to better witness this phenomenon.

They were wearing their white shirts and nametags, their shiny new mountain bikes casually propped up on hips that, sadly, may very well never have the opportunity to undulate, shimmy, or shake.

The woman was wearing a cotton floral-print dress, thick beige stockings, a shawl around her shoulders, and sturdy black shoes. Her hair was coiled into a neat bun at the back of her head. She didn't speak much, but understood English quite well. Her bilingual status automatically placed her in a higher brain-usage bracket than most U.S. citizens—young, pasty-faced, and Mormon, or not.

But I digress.

She politely listened to the boys as they told her what god is.

I was in total awe at her graciousness. She smiled at the Mormon children and nodded her head from time to time.

I saw the deep brown and gold-flecked twinkling of her

eyes, which at one point during the exchange she rested on me, standing at the bus stop, well off to the side. From her eyes, I got the idea that she'd lived a rich life, much richer than any I had so far imagined, and subsequently had room in her heart for the Mormons. She did not feel compelled to slap them across the face for their impertinence in assuming that she—who, by the way, was standing on land that rightfully belongs to her people—was ignorant about god.

I mean, figure: If you manage to get old and retain a mad-ass twinkle in your eyes, it's a mathematical certainty that you're on intimate terms with god, whatever you perceive her to be.

I watched the boys wave their arms, explaining god, the kingdom of god, the hierarchy of god, the indisputable word of god.

No doubt inspired by the twinkle in her eyes, I began to laugh like a donkey let loose in the hay field.

The image of teenagers explaining god to an elder is, in most all contexts, hilarious. Once I managed to get past the rage—which, by the way, I am still only able to do when I summon the specific image of that lady's sparkling eyes—I saw the humor.

Maybe they didn't piss the lady off because they served as no reflection of herself. Maybe they were fifty million worlds away from her world, and maybe she experienced the Mormons as a visit from alien beings.

Me and my white ass, on the other hand, take things like Mormons kinda personally.

In the unconscious mainstream white/white-identified imagination, it makes perfect sense for a young white/white-god-identified person to explain god to anyone she or he can coerce or intimidate into listening. It is considered acceptable to send these teenagers and missionaries of many other stripes to the Americas, Africa, India, Asia, the Pacific Islands, the Caribbean, and now even the Middle East—anyplace where whites are not the majority of the population—to, in no uncertain terms, all-knowingly and patronizingly explain god to all these folks too.

How unutterably embarrassing.

So sure is the white, puritan, Jesus-hijacking imagination of its place in the center of the universe, people in the U.S. do not even approach acknowledging the unutterable global embarrassment of this reality.

At any rate, the lady on Mission Street—with room in her heart for patronizing teenage Mormons—has become quite the role model for me, but there remains little room in my heart for Mormons, so my life still ain't as rich.

Perhaps I will muster the compassion and wherewithal to negotiate this.

Perhaps not.

La, la, la.

And so.

If the 1800s were a prom, the theme would have been Killing Indians in All of the Americas.

The folks who lived in what, unfortunately, had recently been decided upon as the white USA were killed for their land. Those in the rest of the Americas were killed for raw materials that were of pathological interest to emerging Robber Baron Industries.

Here's how my soulmate in a past life, Eduardo Galeano, describes this time period:

> Adolescent capitalism, stampeding and gluttonous, transfigures what it touches. The forest exists for the ax to chop down and the desert for the train to cross; the river is worth bothering about if it contains gold, and the mountain if it shelters coal or iron. No one walks. All run, in a hurry, it's urgent, after the nomad shadow of wealth and power. Space exists for time to defeat, and time for progress to sacrifice on its altars.[4]

Laura Ingalls Wilder was born in 1867, twenty-two years after the term "manifest destiny" was coined—which was, evidently, plenty of time for it to become a rallying cry for white supremacist genocide.

Long before she started writing the *Little House on the Prairie* books, Laura and the fam moved from "Wisconsin" to "Kansas Territory," which was in the process of being **settled** by whites.

The *New Yorker* magazine crows, "Any boy or girl who has access to all the books in the series will be the richer for their first-hand record of pioneer life in the opening West and for their warm-hearted family values."

"Why don't you like the Indians, Ma?" Laura asked, as she caught a drip of molasses with her tongue.

"I just don't like them; and don't lick your fingers, Laura," Ma said.[5]

Laura is confused by this statement. It seems that her family, in fact, lives in a country that belongs to vast and varied tribes of indian nations. When she points this out to her mother, she is rebuffed with words of boundaries and lines drawn by the victors of history's new telling.

Any boy or girl who has access to all the books in the series will be the richer for their first-hand record of pioneer life in the opening West and for their warm-hearted family values.

Laura sits by the fire with her beloved Pa, and wonders aloud when she will get to view the spectacle of a papoose—one of her obsessions. She knows her Pa got to see Real-Live Savage Indians when he was a kid, and she knows that they are "wild men with red skins and their hatchets are called tomahawks," but she doesn't know if she will ever have the exotic experience of *actually getting to view one.*[6]

Any boy or girl who has access to all the books in the series will be the richer for their first-hand record of pioneer life in the opening West and for their warm-hearted family values.

One pretty day, Mrs. Scott pops in to the homestead to have a nice visit with Ma. Laura and Mary sit nicely and listen to the women converse pleasantly on such topics as the home decor, the new rocking chair, and the rationale of mass genocide. Part of this rationale involves something Mrs. Scott refers to as "common sense and justice," in which millions of people whose varied civilizations she knows nothing about are "wild animals" who "roam around over this country." "Treaties or not treaties," she says, "the land belongs to folks that'll farm it."

Mrs. Scott sincerely laments the fact that the government even bothers to *make* treaties. "The only good Indian," she concludes in the presence of two children," is a dead Indian."[7]

Any boy or girl who has access to all the books in the series will be the richer for their first-hand record of pioneer life in the opening West and for their warm-hearted family values.

Laura is having another earnest conversation with her Pa. She asks if the indigenous people of the ever expanding United States will—in an attempt to somehow outpace the thundering force of Manifest Destiny—move west. Pa assures her that this is precisely what will happen. He explains how "white settlers" come in and Indians move on. It's a natural thing, as is evidenced by the fact that white people *always* get the choicest parcels of real estate. Or as Pa says, "We get here first and take our pick."

Laura is only somewhat mollified with this answer, but when she presses for further information, Pa decides it is absolutely and sincerely time for bed.[8]

Little House on the Prairie is deemed reading that will enrich a child's life by a periodical that many in this culture hold with the highest esteem. In order for the *New Yorker* to get away with this shit, it must have a lot of readers who retain ignorance about—and justification for—genocide as a warm-hearted family value.

By the late 1800s, things weren't going the way the settlers and the government had hoped. Meaning folks were resisting their forced removal from the sacred land of their ancestors. Sometimes this resulted in white settlers being killed. There are numerous mentions of white massacres in Ms. Ingalls's text.

There were also numerous mentions of white massacres in newspapers. According to many sources from the time, "Savage Indians" liked nothing better than to kill white men, rape white women, and eat white babies. I can count on the media of the nineteenth century—just as I can count on today's media—to rewrite events in a way that reflects the ideology of Robber Baron newspaper owners.

The news sources people held in high esteem, like the *New Yorker* of today, were never, ever run by the Iroquois Confederacy, who were deemed quite intelligent enough to, as I mentioned, provide the forefathers with a framework for this nation's constitution.

Then as now, the murder/rape of a white person *because he or she is white* was one of the most punishable crimes in the annals of the U.S. judiciary system, but the true murderers, rapists, and baby killers are the ones who tell this country's children the story of history. I cannot sufficiently underscore the gravity of this situation. Whites are the ones who did the scalping. In fact, white men were known to cut the sacredholy cunts out of women and sew them onto their cowboy outfits. Soldiers routinely massacred people who showed up at their forts to sign peace treaties. The savagery we hear so much about is a projection whites created in order to somehow absolve ourselves for the sickness in our souls that we live in almost total denial of. Talking pictures and teeveeland took that shit and *ran* with it. Been running strong ever since.

The stories we're told as children plant little seeds of justification for white supremacist racism, ultimately providing an intricate forest of confusion and/or denial, making it difficult to discern between self-serving fantasy and undeniable reality.

Perhaps this could be viewed as a sort of depth perception impairment.

Yo Disney.

Take your *Indian in the Cupboard* and shove him up your big fat white ass to stop up all the other racist pieces of *Lilo & Stitch* shit inside of you.

Racist fucks got children's imaginations colonized, coercing highly intelligent people to pay money to see their evil shit.

Aladdin, Mulan, Pocahontas. Don't get me started.

I recently read an account of a woman in the Amazon whose people were not "contacted" (her word) by whites until the 1990s. She described how the world stopped talking when whites showed up with their cameras and guns to shoot everyone with. The animals, trees, and rivers all suddenly became mute.

Maybe I didn't read this at all.

It might have been a dream.

Probably not.

So yeah, where was I.

Back in pioneer times.

In the 1870s.

The whites were driven out of "Kansas" and the Ingalls clan took all of their learned fear of and ignorance about an entire population of human beings and moved east, to Walnut Grove, "Minnesota," where the weekly series and that little bitch Nellie Oleson were located.

But all that happens after this particular book in the series.

At the close of *Little House on the Prairie,* the family watches miles and miles of the enforced diaspora passing their home, on the way to a new "Indian Territory," a.k.a. "Oklahoma," via the Trail of Tears.

Laura has a temper tantrum because she is obsessed with "owning" a papoose, and her parents (magnanimously?) refuse to take a baby away from its mother for their child's amusement.

Dear Liz,

I know you love the teevee version of **Little House on the Prairie,** and have delighted in the antics of Laura Ingalls ever since you were a little kid. I know it bums you out to see that she was a product of a racist white society, but so are you and me, and pretty much everyone we know.

Love,
Your sister,
Inga La Gringa

Autobiography of a Blue-Eyed Devil

Whites are still taking up space, moving into other folks' territories. I see manifest destiny enacted every day of my life, only now it's called "gentrification," which, to the contemporary ear, sounds much "nicer."

Gentrification often starts with the artists, revolutionaries, freaks, transfolks, and queers (what I would call my people) moving into poor neighborhoods inhabited by people of color. Often—but by no means always—the people moving in are white. The artists, revolutionaries, freaks, transfolks, and queers of color are in a position of straddling a number of worlds—of ideology, race, ethnicity, sexuality, gender, skin tone, hair type, religion, and class, to name a few—whatever their race may be. In creative/political/sexual spaces populated by whites, everyone else has to consistently negotiate **unconscious whites**, and if not unconscious whites, then internalized and/or institutionalized white supremacist beliefs and power structures.

Even though this vanguard of gentrification often includes some pretty cool white people who have wonderful ideas and make amazing music and art that I would literally die without—by far some of the most conscious whites unconscious white society produces at this point in history—the denials and ignorance of white supremacist racism and imperialism still very much factor into our indoctrination. These denials and this ignorance take up an *enormous* amount of space. People of color, **off-whites**, and indigenous folks are expected to unquestioningly make accommodations for this, which is bullshit insult heaped onto already existing injury.

I, too, negotiate white supremacist racism, *but only because I have chosen* to look at the world differently than I was told to by my culture. I could choose to be in denial of the historic and contemporary ignorance my white ass carries into every room I enter but, for various reasons discussed in later chapters, this is not a viable choice to me.

The *only reason* this is a viable choice to any white or white-identified person is that we are taught from day one that it is a viable choice.

More on this later, too.

So, onward ho, gentrification.

For the past twenty years, I've lived in every major city on the West Coast, and this is how it happens in my neck of the woods:

The people of color and/or economically disenfranchised folks who live in the to-be-gentrified neighborhood are usually quite unhappy when the new people move in, but sometimes, the homo/artist vanguard ends up charming the folks in some ways because, well, homos and artists tend to be colorful characters.

They have parades and Giving Trees† and get permission

---

† A Giving Tree is where you hang up that gorgeous chrome toaster you never use since you stopped eating wheat, and that pretty yellow and red scarf you didn't wear one time last winter, and the rest of that box of oranges a secret admirer left for you that you will never be able to finish. Et cetera. All passersby are free to take from the Giving Tree.

for community gardens and patrol the police and stuff like that. I mean, these are people who *actually want* the world to be a more beautiful and loving place, and they are never shy about demonstrating this, with everything from drag queens run amok to imaginative proposals the city council just can't resist.

Overall, not the absolute worst people to move into your neighborhood.

So the two demographics abide with each other, and sometimes even get along.

But then (gasp!) the neighborhood is soon "discovered" by developers and becomes "cool" according to marketing firms and the local media.

And we all know what happens next:

"Artist" loft spaces that artists can never afford to live in, fratman nightclubs—replete with drunken groupthink date rapists—Starbucks, Banana Republic, the Gap.

A wave of asswipes representing (I guess) the "gentry" crashes to shore, raising property values and shoving all the original inhabitants—as well as the unintentional vanguard of artists, revolutionaries, freaks, transfolks, and queers—out to the fringes, where the process will start all over again and the end result is always, always, always white and/or white-identified people invading space and taking people's homes away.

Gentrification serves the exact same function as manifest destiny, only the ideology behind it is rationalized differently, as it *absolutely has to be* because we aren't necessarily as concerned with how to get into heaven as our forebears were. We are concerned with self-image, and we want people to think we are hip and cool, so we move into "newly discovered" hip and cool neighborhoods.

Like manifest destiny, gentrification is rooted in white supremacist economics. The exploitation of land, humans, and animals follows the same pattern whether we're looking at indian "territory," present-day northeast Portland, or entire economically disenfranchised countries. All of this land-taking is about the inability to see, respect, and value of color, indigenous, and/or poor communities, ideologies, local businesses, and institutions. This is made quite clear in my Microsoft computer dictionary's definition of gentrification:

> The process of transforming an unprosperous neighborhood of buildings needing repair into a more prosperous one, for example, through investment in remodeling buildings or houses.

I mean, gee, that sounds like a worthy enough practice. According to this definition, a poor neighborhood is magically transformed into a prosperous one by investing in it.[†]

There is no mention of the people who live in the poor neighborhood, nor does this definition convey exactly what happens to the people once their neighborhood has been "transformed." The fact that many poor communities have

---

† This is, by the way, also the definition of "globalization." Just switch the term "neighborhood of buildings" with "nation" and "buildings and houses" with "social, political, and economic infrastructure." My interpretation of both terms, however, remains exactly the same.

thriving local businesses that don't necessarily fit into the capitalist economic model—the barber who sells CDs and candy, the locksmith's wife who offers home-knit scarves and sweaters, the tiny café that doubles as an informal lounge and debate center for neighborhood Muslims—is certainly not worth mentioning.

The Microsoft definition of "gentrification" rather keenly calls to mind a local history book I recently came across in Galesburg, "Illinois." In it, I was informed that indian nations were "removed" before the various sects of Protestant "settlers" built the town. This was the sole mention of an entire population of slaughtered or displaced people in the whole book.

Just like earlier U.S. citizens, we don't stop to examine our historically entrenched motives, we just go with the white supremacist flow. Foisted upon us as this choice is, doing so feels perfectly natural. *This would not feel natural,* and folks would be far less organically inclined to repeat the atrocities of the past, if we did not learn a fully ridiculous version of U.S. history.

Which we do.

Five Hundred Years of Servitude

Myth: Slavery was a bad thing that happened because people weren't as smart as we are now, even though it is kinda true that white people just naturally rise to the top because we tend to be more naturally able than anybody else to understand freedom, wealth, and democracy.

In U.S. history classes, we learn that slavery was over as of January 1, 1863, when President Lincoln issued the Emancipation Proclamation. This seems like pretty important information to convey to the huddled masses, but the government didn't really go out of its way to let a lot of free black folks in on this.

It could, perhaps, be graphed thusly: The farther away you were from "Washington, D.C.," and the Civil War Propaganda Machine, the lesser your chances of finding out you were no longer the property of a white person. Consequently, many folks were not informed that they were free on January 1, 1863. If it had been *really important* to the United States that everyone knew slavery was "over," I am quite sure the government would have come up with the resources and wherewithal to clue folks in.

These are, after all, the exact same people who didn't have many problems rounding up entire indian nations during the same period and ushering them at gunpoint onto the Trail of Tears.

We don't learn that thousands of newly freed, wholly terrorized black people walked that wretched, sorrowful path too. Neither do we learn that state penitentiaries and large prisons were first being constructed while Lincoln's signature on the Emancipation Proclamation was still wet.

In any case, the U.S. government had *the capacity* (as opposed to the inclination) to inform slaves of their freedom.

Juneteenth is a celebration marking June 19, 1865, the day slaves in "Texas" found out they had, in fact, not been slaves for two and a half years.

The impersonal nature of historical factoids kinda cushions this.

Imagine that on January 1, 1863, you have a three-year-old child who is kept in a separate part of the plantation while you are working in the fields. You get to see your cherished child for a few hours each week, if you bust your ass really, really, really hard. By the time you find out that you have, in fact, been legally able to have an actual stab at family life for the past two and a half years, your child is almost six, and you gotta wake up one morning and face the lifelong trauma that the most formative years of your baby's life have been even more needlessly stolen from you.

This is a fairly Pollyanna-ish scenario, for in that span of two and a half years, thousands of "Texas" children were sold, and their parents were hard-pressed to ever find them again.

This is just one small, imagined reality.

There are millions more.

The system of perpetual slavery that was widely embraced in the U.S. involved torture, sexual humiliation, rape, and systematic breeding. The underlying objective was to destroy the will of human beings for many future generations.

In his seminal book *The Possessive Investment in Whiteness*, George Lipsitz discusses how the U.S. system of slavery was racialized by the founding father types in ways that other forms of slavery throughout world history were not:

> Although slavery has existed in many countries without any particular racial dimensions to it, the slave system that emerged in North America soon took on distinctly racial forms. Africans enslaved in North America faced a racialized system of power that

reserved permanent, hereditary, chattel slavery for
black people.[1]

I attribute this difference to white men's terror of economic and genetic annihilation. To this day, many white men,
either consciously or not, are driven by this fear.

They learn it from their fathers.

It is a very intimate thing.

Reproductively speaking, whites are the most vulnerable race.
If a white person has a child with a person of color, that child
will no longer be considered white. Imagine this terror for white
men: If their daughters and sisters were to decide that men
of color were more desirable mates, then sooner or later the
"pure" racial makeup of whiteness would be gone forever. White
women are still very much considered—by an extension of
identity—white men's prime biological real estate. As such,
there is a "value" attributed to white women that applies in
pretty much no other arena of consideration.

This fear explains why Operation Rescue's leadership is
almost entirely composed of white men seeking power and control over the bodies of their prime biological real estate.

It is also why the topic of "reproductive rights" for poor
indigenous women and women of color rarely enters mainstream feminist discourse, much less the media landscape. The
issues facing these demographics are far different from the ones
urban white women face. Black, Mexicana, Chicana, indigenous,

and poor rural white women deal with forced sterilizations and high rates of miscarriage from living in highly toxic areas polluted by nearby factories, refineries, or smelting plants. Huge polluting corporations, after all, aren't allowed to open shop upwind from Brentwood.

When environmental disease is mapped across the U.S., the areas most affected are *always* those with the densest populations of people of color, indians, and poor whites.

In slavery times, as relatively less directly now, women of color were not *allowed* to bring a white man to court for rape. White men like Strom Thurmond don't mind if their seed produces half-white children, so long as they're not considered "equal."

Most people know Thomas Jefferson owned and fathered slaves, but he still, somehow, seems like a rather decent sort. I mean what do I expect him to do, *buck the system?* The fittest do not survive by bucking the system that defines them as the fittest, and slave owners were, above and beyond all else, businessmen.

Fear underlies many of the historic and contemporary reasons why white men undermine, stereotype, and attack the masculinity of men of color and the chastity of women of color. Throwing men of color in prison, legally lynching them, or outright murdering them renders men of color unable to protect their loved ones from the physical, emotional, and economic threats of white supremacist racism. To this day, it is rare for a woman of color or an indigenous woman to bring a white man to justice for sexual violence of any kind.

Autobiography of a Blue-Eyed Devil

These white responses to the threat of genetic annihilation are deeply rooted in the slavery of our past.

There is an ongoing theme that our great and noble founding fathers beheld an otherworldly all-seeing wisdom in regard to the formation of the U.S. government, and we just need to get back on track. Supporting the views of this very limited sector of the population, however dead and gone they are at this point, condones the white supremacist racist undercurrent of slavery that, to this day, remains largely unquestioned in our culture.

The deeply grandfathered spirit and ideology of elite white men is alive and well in this environment. Any rationalization that the words of elite white dead men will somehow magically rein in the crazed actions of elite white living men is plain-as-fuck bad math.

I learned about slavery from my parents and their bookshelf, so when *Roots* came out, I wasn't the total tabula rasa yes-nancy that the U.S. public education system had set me up to be. I remember lying on my stomach for hours, reading about slavery times, raining a torrent of questions on my father's head, and generally trying to wrap my brain around the concept of human "ownership." I don't think I met with much success until I saw *Roots.* It was one of the rare non-PBS teevee shows our dad sanctioned, and we even got to stay up past bedtime to watch it.

One scene I have always kept with me features Kizzy, Cicely Tyson's character and a loathsome white lady. Slavery is "over," and the white lady pulls up in her fine carriage, interrupting our heroine in—what is now very much—her business. The lady is a past owner and is used to her bidding being done. She tells Kizzy to go to the well and get her some water.

My acute emotional response is probably responsible for this scene remaining in my heart all this time. I was all, "NO! NO! Please, world, make there be some way that Kizzy doesn't get water for that cow.[†] Please, please please."

My heart sank when she went to get the water, but then it *exploded* in my chest and I jumped off the couch and screamed in total joy, because Kizzy hawked a spitwad in the cup before taking it to the cow.

A feeling of deep satisfaction rushed through me as the woman drank the spitwad water.

The only other movie scene that has stayed with me in the exact same way is the one in *Thelma and Louise* when Thelma is about to be raped. As I watched, my heart sank because rape scenes are so damaging, and I wanted so badly for her to not be raped. I'd never seen a movie where a woman in this position doesn't get raped, so there was an acute feeling of inevitability in that part of my sinking heart, but then Louise came out and shot the piece of shit dead.

I jumped out my seat and screamed in total joy then too, even though Thelma and Louise both end up dying for this transgression.

---

† In my family, the worst thing to call a woman was "a cow." This does not mean a large woman. It means an odious one. If my mother said I was being a "cow," I knew I was a VIP on her shitlist. This is in the context of a household where cuss words were consistently deployed.

※

Throughout history, covert resistance has been a pretty good idea if you want to keep living. One of my favorite forms of covert resistance during slavery times is the quilts used to direct folks on the Underground Railroad. Strategically hanging them over fences or out windows, people "aired out" quilts with arrows or other directions painstakingly stitched in.

In the days after slavery "ended,"[†] however, when whites were enacting their deep-rooted fear of economic and genetic annihilation, any form of construed resistance brought on terror and violence. In response to the "humiliation" of the Civil War and the ensuing period of Reconstruction, Southern white men brainstormed the idea of wearing white sheets to commemorate all the men who died fighting for the Confederacy. Nighttime lynching raids, however, were nothing new. They came out of a long tradition of hunting down runaway slaves.

The KKK-inclined felt the need to cloak themselves, initially, because they did not want to be hassled by federal troops who were stationed in the South to maintain the new laws that resulted from the Civil War. When the troops left, however, the white hoods remained and became a symbol and means to frighten the bejesus out of not only black people, but anyone opposed to white supremacy.

When Northern troops were pulled out of the South, it

---

† I'm making an effort, for the moment, to set aside the reality that slavery persists today.

signaled the end of Reconstruction and the beginning of a new tide of white fear and hatred that flooded *the nation's* (as opposed to just the South's) consciousness, resulting in continued segregation, Jim Crow laws, ongoing lynchings, and many other horrors.

During the twelve-odd years of Reconstruction, a black middle class had formed, hundreds of black legislators (even a few women) had been elected to state and national offices, and Congress had passed two civil rights acts.

As part of the legacy of Reconstruction, people the likes of W. E. B. DuBois were talking more shit than Chuck D has ever dreamed of—for though DuBois was born during Reconstruction and lived through the horror of violence that followed, he also lived much closer to a time that beheld a relatively luxurious glimmer of hope and change than Mr. D has yet to glimpse in his lifetime.

In 1884, during the wake of Reconstruction, a white woman named Belva Ann Lockwood ran for president of the United States. More than a hundred years later, people in this country scoff at the idea of a presidential run by a conservative bible-thumping white woman whose erectile-disordered husband used to be a big man in politics—much less by an Anasazi sculptor and transgender activist mother of four, or an old-school Puerto Rican–Filipino American hiphop deejay/attorney.

Yes, Reconstruction was a truly "enlightened," if brief, time of possibilities.

In *Lies My Teacher Told Me,* James W. Loewen discusses

how much more progressive the period of Reconstruction was than anything since experienced in the United States:

> The facts about Reconstruction compel us to acknowledge that in many ways race relations in this country have yet to return to the point reached in, say, 1870. In that year, to take a small but symbolic example, A. T. Morgan, a white state senator from Hinds County, Mississippi, married Carrie Highgate, a black woman from New York, *and was reelected.* Today this probably could not happen, not in Hinds County, Mississippi, or in many counties throughout the United States. Nonetheless, the archetype of progress prompts many white Americans to conclude that black Americans have no legitimate claim on our attention today because the problem of race relations has surely been ameliorated.
>
> A. T. Morgan's marriage is hard for us to make sense of, because Americans have so internalized the cultural archetype of progress that by now we have a built-in tendency to assume that we are more tolerant, more sophisticated, more, well, *progressive* than we were in the past.[2]

As far as I can tell, the twelve or so years of Reconstruction were the closest this country has *ever* gotten to even approaching any kind of serious engagement with the possibilities of *anything* besides an elite-white-male-ruled agenda.

Aside, of course, from the time before Europeans showed up here on Turtle Island, nowhere in U.S. history have I found a more top-to-bottom questioning and recontextualizing of this nation's identity.

If things that went down over 135 years ago are now considered impossible pipe dreams, then there is something wrong with our image of ourselves and our ever-evolving "place" in history, don't you think?

Fucken, I do.

Let us spread our "we're so much more evolved now" ass cheeks and administer fairly traded Zapatista coffee enemas amongst ourselves.

The only reason the faint glimmer of light *existed at all* during Reconstruction was because people were going through some serious question-asking time. The present population that often struggles with economic survival, supports slave-economy businesses, and is informed by the teevee that making such choices is completely inevitable no longer asks such questions as:

How do we define freedom? Who is free? Who is not? Why are some people free and others not? How can a society implement and maintain equality of opportunity? Are all people created and sustained as equal, or just (heterosexual-seeming) white biological men? Are all these men created and sustained as equal, or just the ones who have a lot of money? How, exactly, do we define "equal"? What might a society look like where the concept of "equality" itself was inherent and completely unremarkable?

It is almost solely the rights of black people and white women that were considered during Reconstruction. Meanwhile, manifest destiny thundered into the west and none of the people who lived on that land benefited from this brief questioning in any way. As far as indigenous people—and those with Chinese, Japanese, Filipino, Hawai'ian, Mexicano, Sudamericano, Centroamericano, Puerto Rican, and/or Cuban roots—were concerned, there was no respite from subjugation and oppression, however fleeting and doomed by racist white imperialists.

During this time, the human rights of homos and transgendered folks could still be summed up in the playground chant "Forget you, forgot you, I never thought about you."

However, if Reconstruction had lived on, instead of being snuffed like a material witness at a busy intersection in broad daylight, I do believe it would have had the potential to evolve into a true opposition to white male imperialism.

But it was not meant to be, for whites still carried a learned fear of genetic annihilation in our Pilgrim and oppressed-immigrant DNA, and were unwilling to address our fears.

And we still are.

In school, we learn that Reconstruction more or less "failed" because black folks just couldn't get their shit together. They abused their power and the whites had to help them out, so, lah dee dah, the possibilities engendered during Reconstruction flowed their "inevitable course" because black people just couldn't hack the complex reality of freedom and democracy.

Not smart enough.

Too corrupt.

Genetically lazy.

Et cetera.

The "failure" of Reconstruction is dressed all nice 'n' passive-aggressive in our textbooks, but essentially, they all convey the idea that it was no fault of whites that black people weren't "able" to organize and be a part of "our" great nation. There's not much examination of how, exactly, in one short decade, ex-slaves gained literacy, ran for political office, embraced the concept of democracy through voting rights, procured college educations, organized fully functioning communities, and generally realized an astounding array of accomplishments, which are comfortably personified in folks such as George Washington Carver. The practice of white men guarding polling places and terrorizing blacks who showed up to vote, for instance, is rarely (if ever) factored into these textbook renditions of the "failure" of Reconstruction.

In *Faces and Masks,* Eduardo Galeano describes an event during Ida B. Wells's courageous and relentless campaign to end the ongoing terrorization of black people through lynching, two decades after Reconstruction's systematic and premeditated murder. In 1898, Ms. Wells sought out and gained an audience with President McKinley, protesting that ten thousand lynchings had taken place in the preceding twenty years.

This equals 1.4 lynchings a day, from 1878 to 1898. Ms. Wells asked President McKinley what gave the U.S. government the right to invade other countries in the name of national security when many of its own citizens did not enjoy national security here at home. She described to him the lynching deaths of young black men accused of raping white women and the celebrations that followed.[3] Meanwhile, white men raped black women with *total impunity*.

President McKinley evidently promised Ida B. Wells that he would look into it.

You might remember President McKinley.

He was the racist piece of shit who, sometime around his meeting with Ms. Wells in 1898, sanctioned the murder of thousands of Filipino people in the name of Patrick Robertson's "god."

When I imagine Ida B. Wells meeting with this man, my heart seizes up inside me. I think of this brilliant woman, fighting with all of the life inside her to meet with this racist dickcheney, and I think of the "sincere" smile on his face as he "deals" with this "rather uppity black woman," and I think of that smile turning into a smirk when she turns to leave, and how that smirk probably didn't leave his face for the rest of that day.

You can trounce Condoleezza Rice right now, if it somehow makes you feel better, but god spoke to me the other day, and He told me that He saw Ida B. Wells, Sojourner Truth, and Harriet Tubman sitting in a corner of heaven, rather balefully hawking loogies onto an autographed photo of Condoleezza Rice that had been sent to Him by the White House publicity department.

I said, "Gee, god, weren't you angry and wrathful about your property being destroyed in this manner?"

And god said, "No. In my all-seeing compassion, I understood the need to respond to the befoulment of one's entire legacy in the name of women such as Condoleezza Rice."

And I said, "Wow, god, that's deep. Amen, mother. I mean father."

And god laughed at my little joke.

Long after Reconstruction, many vibrant and highly effective black communities, cities, and towns were still in existence. In the 1920s, Tulsa, "Oklahoma," had one such vital black community, with lawyers, doctors, libraries, hospitals, shops, schools, and other great things that all communities should rightfully have. The average dollar stayed in the community for up to one hundred days, as opposed to now, when the average dollar stays in a black community for ten minutes or less. Every dollar in this community was black-owned, as opposed to now, when for every dollar a white person has, a black person has eleven cents.

These folks were so effective, in fact, the whites in Tulsa started getting uncomfortable. So a young black man was predictably, duly, and wrongfully accused of raping a white woman. Black men of the community—many of whom were World War I veterans—responded by surrounding the local jail to keep the young man from being killed. White folks responded to this by inciting a lynch mob mentality in a front-page editorial in the newspaper, deputizing—for all intents and purposes—the entire white population and dropping explosives from airplanes. Somewhere in the neighborhood of ten thousand white Tulsans took part in the systematic looting and destruction of the entire black community. At the end of the day, over three hundred folks were dead, and six thousand black people were later interred in a makeshift camp.

History calls this a "race riot," which subtly implicates the black population in its own destruction, instead of a "genocide," which does not.

So I'll tell you what.

If there is any truth in the notion that black folks in the past and present have had a difficult time embracing the Amerikkkan Dream, that truth lies utterly in the *thousands* of historical and contemporary incidents such as the genocide in Tulsa, "Oklahoma." The truth lies where justice is nowhere to be found: in segregation, in separate and unequal, in redlining, in miscegenation laws, in the KKK, in the elections of people such as David Duke, Strom Thurmond, and Jesse Helms, in racial profiling, in gang injunctions, in three-strikes-yer-out laws, in police brutality and murder, in the completely unquestioned incarceration (and loss of voting rights) of young people of color—mostly black men.

George Lipsitz puts it this way in *The Possessive Investment in Whiteness*:

> Whiteness has a cash value: it accounts for individuals through profits made from housing secured in discriminatory markets, through the unequal educations allocated to children of different races, through insider networks that channel employment opportunities to the relatives and friends of those who have profited most from present and past racial discrimination, and especially, through intergenerational transfers of inherited wealth that pass on the spoils of discrimination to succeeding generations.[4]

The truth is glaring, but in this country, the eyes of whites are wide shut.

Acknowledging lived, historical realities does not, by the way, constitute portraying a demographic of people as "victims." People the world over have resisted domination, since long before Europeans arrived on these shores.

Resistance has never stopped, nor will it.

"Victims" don't courageously fight the good fight with words, images, music, science, art, performance, brilliantly organized political movements, and yes, sometimes violence, for hundreds and hundreds of fucking years.

Conversely, and perhaps moreover, white people and institutions indeed *have* made every attempt to victimize everyone else, and until *we all* muster the collective courage to face this shit head-on, we'll continue to live within the media-induced confines of unconscious white supremacist racist domination.

And that, my friend, like so many things in this world, is a choice.

In my perfect world, Juneteenth is a national holiday, not only for black people to celebrate, but one of formal atonement and reflection on past and present crimes against humanity for whites and all U.S. citizens who take part in a culture and global economy that continues to enslave millions of people on the planet.[†]

While we're at it, we could institute a Trail of Tears Day, as a national holiday of Total Silence (except for babies and little kids) in the USA, to honor the lives of those who walked this harrowing path. On this day, everyone would eat *only* chocolate cake, which would symbolize dirt, but with the sweetness of facing the past.

People allergic to chocolate could substitute cinnamon cake *with* matching frosting, and some genius vegan baker-alchemists could come up with a diabetic/wheat-free alternative.

I swear, I should really be in charge of national holidays.

This country would be so much more fun.

---

† Due to the divide-and-conquer nature of white imperialism—along with the highly complex, chaotic tendency of history to come around full circle— this demographic presently includes people descended from slaves and decimated indian nations. Anyone who shops at Target or Wal-Mart supports contemporary slavery.

Manifest Destiny Variety Show

Myth: We are always the good guys. Our entire purpose is to spread freedom and democracy across the globe.

From the end of Reconstruction to the present, it continues to be the Manifest Destiny Variety Show!

Starring the United States of Amerikkka!

Costarring a couple world wars and a cold one!

With special guests the Yellow Menace and McCarthyism!
And highly convenient cameo appearances by an assortment of military operations and coups against sovereign nations!

(Applause loop runs now.)

Prologue

Leading up to World War II, people in the U.S. were in a fairly constant struggle for human, civil, and/or labor rights. It was one uprising after the next.

The Civil War–Winning Robber Baron Fittest had wasted no time in introducing their new, improved, revolutionary industrialized method of enslaving working people. Socialist, populist, labor, and many truly democratic parties had sprouted up all over the country, along with continued uprisings of indigenous nations, white women, blacks, and new immigrants. Hundreds of women and men—including whites—had been imprisoned, assassinated, and lynched for organizing unions, strikes, and other threats to the lords of industry's fiefdoms.

At the time, "whiteness" was more restricted than it is now.

In the eastern states, where the indians had been driven off the land hundreds of years ago and shiploads of immigrants arrived on a daily basis, Irish, Italian, and Eastern European immigrants were not considered "white." During the days when the Robber Barons came to power, though, many marginalized and oppressed immigrants realized (via, undoubtedly, the media) that since they had "lighter" skin, "straighter" hair, and sometimes, blue, green, or violet eyes, they were also "white" people—even though they generally lived in abject poverty and were looked upon with total disdain by the larger Protestant-descended "traditionally white" population. This did not stop them from waging war against black people for low-paying jobs and other meager leavings the Robber Barons' system of economics tossed off their grand dining table.

Giving two dogs one bone is a great way to control a population of people who have been beaten down into believing that they are dogs. Dividing and conquering has set people against each other in so many contexts, for so many years, it is presently a cornerstone of our indoctrination. At this point, we think of it as "normal" to compete, backstab, and engage in trite internecine—oftentimes violent—warfare within our communities and intimate family spaces.

At any rate, despite the continued and evolving horror of white supremacist racism, back in the day, people were *involved,* and talked shit *frequently.* There were thousands of newspapers, magazines, and organizations dedicated to overthrowing the capitalist Lucky Sperm Club puds who insinuated the survival-of-the-fittest work and family ethic into everyone's lives.

The intelligence level of people who lived in pre-teevee times was, one is rather compelled to surmise, much higher than it is now.

Autobiography of a Blue-Eyed Devil

At some point, the Robber Barons more or less became the U.S. government, and it was discovered that when there is a *war* people lose focus on their real enemies.

Another great way to control a population.

Adolf Hitler truly did suck, but in the long run, he came in so handy, they've been casting others in his role ever since.

At one point, Khrushchev, Castro, and the Phantom of Communism were leading men. Now, it's Osama, Saddam, and the Phantom of Terrorism. Creating and vilifying an enemy offers a population a location upon which to focus its confusion, anger, and unmet ambitions.

Act I: World War II

And so.

Once Upon a Time.

World War II was about a really evil man who had an evil plan to kill all the Jewish people in Europe and then move on to kill everyone in the world who wasn't a blond-haired blue-eyed heterosexual Aryan.

Maybe this story could be called "Xtreme Manifest Destiny."

The evil man got people to believe that Aryans were the supreme race—it didn't take much to convince them—and many prominent white men in the U.S. effusively supported the Nazi regime, including a certain grandfather named Prescott Arbusto.

But that's not part of "the story."

If we talk about Prescott Arbusto, and how he got bankers to bankroll Hitler and how the U.S. government had to rein him in after joining the war, we'd be going off message. We'd be going really, really off message if we wondered why Prescott Arbusto was—through the legal machinations of his lawyer, Allen Dulles—not nailed for collusion with the enemy and how *exactly* he continued to amass money and power after such insanely treasonous acts.

However, if you were to *choose* to incorporate the Arbusto family ties with Nazi fascism as part of the story, here is a good place to start: www.guerrillafunk.com/thoughts/doc545.html.

The *story* is that brave (white) G.I. Joe men in the U.S. helped to defeat the evil of this one man, and all the (white) Rosie the Riveter women went to work in factories or became nurses to the help the cause and it was a time when the nation (with a smattering of help from the rest of the world) came together to overcome pure evil.

Yeah, right.

Righty, right, right.

Scene 1: In Which Things Are Translated

I am not a soldier, so I really don't know what it would do to my spirit to go into battle with the intention to combat genocide while wearing the uniform of a country that is responsible for committing genocide against my people and countless other tribes. Yet, many indigenous people did volunteer to fight for the United States and the Allied forces.

"We" would not have won the war if our intelligence networks hadn't been able to communicate. This was made possible by Navajo warriors, who developed a code the Axis powers were unable to decipher. Besides a medal here and there and a movie made "in their honor" fifty-odd years after the fact, the Navajo warriors are not much mentioned in the story of WWII because in the white-identified U.S. imagination (and in the movie made fifty-odd years later), only white men can be the *real* heroes.

It is a fanatical obsession amongst white men.

This phenomenon is also on glaring display in the hero representations of the 2001 World Trade Center attacks. All the action figures in Wal-Marts across the land are white men, and all the "victims" depicted in the media who received 1.8 million dollars in "compensation" are white heterosexual widows who had to sign away their right to sue the U.S. government in order to get the dough.

I, however, personally know only one hero: a Puerto Rican police officer who, while pregnant, ended up losing one of her lungs from breathing the air while pulling bodies out of the wreckage. There is no action figure representing her, no honor or tribute for the miraculous birth of her healthy baby girl, and she has had to fight tooth and nail for any kind of financial compensation.

Scene 2: In Which a Director Resigns

The concept of a pure-blooded race of Aryan people was just too much for people in this country to *accept*. According to the message we receive, the Nazi doctrine crossed a line of human decency in our freedom-loving, completely democratic way of viewing the world. Galeano points out Amerikkka's racial and ideological hypocrisy:

> U.S. soldiers embark for the war fronts. Many are black under the command of white officers.
>
> Those who survive will return home. The blacks will enter by the back door, and, in the Southern states, continue to live, work, and die apart, and even then will lie in separate graves. Hooded Ku Klux Klansmen will still insure that blacks do not intrude into the white world, and above all into the bedrooms of white women.
>
> The war accepts blacks, thousands and thousands of them, but not the Red Cross. The Red Cross bans black blood in the plasma banks, so as to avoid the possibility that races might mix by transfusion.
>
> The research of Charles Drew, inventor of life, has finally made it possible to save blood. Thanks to him, plasma banks are reviving thousands of dying men on the battlefields of Europe.
>
> When the Red Cross decides to reject the blood of blacks, Drew, director of the Red Cross plasma service, resigns. Drew is black.[1]

The spring 2004 edition of *Stay Free!* magazine features an article on eugenics that I found incredibly contextualizing on the matter of the alleged self-righteousness U.S. citizens fondly entertain vis-à-vis the evilness of the dreaded Nazi regime. The concept of breeding a pure white race of "highly intelligent" do-gooders was all the mainstream rage in this country from the 1880s (not long after the concept of manifest destiny swept the white nation's consciousness) well into the 1930s. This belief lay almost entirely in the seemingly inescapable terror of genetic (and economic) annihilation. As eugenics logic (if that's not an oxymoron) goes, if the U.S. could free itself from the burdens of "unintelligent" people, there would be fewer societal burdens on taxpayers. This sounds almost uncannily similar to the Reaganomics that has led to many present "economic" ideologies entertained by present-day Republicans, but it would be, er, *un-American* to call any of these folks Nazi fascists, huh.

Actually, it would be more accurate to call Nazis Amerikkkan wannabes.

The eugenics movement finally started to crumble with the rise of Nazi Germany. *Partly inspired by eugenics efforts in the United States* [my emphasis], Hitler's government began a national program to round up and sterilize the unfit. Many leading eugenicists in the States watched in awe. A prominent Virginia doctor, dismayed at the rapid growth of undesirables, urged the state legislature to broaden its sterilization laws by warning, "Hitler is beating us at our own game!" Such true believers

held to their guns with the passage of the Nurem-
burg Laws in 1935, applauding Hitler and seething
with envy as their utopian fantasies played out
across the Atlantic.[2]

Scene 3: In Which I Humiliate a Student

All that effort paid off, and "we" crushed evil under the heels of
our freedom-worshipping combat boots. It's so great that we're
the good guys! We've defeated Hitler and everything's *the bees
knees* again. Well, wait. One more thing. We have a new technology we're itching to try out. We can't let this opportunity pass.
President Truman muses on *exactly how much* evil one must
enact in order to eviscerate *all evil* from the planet. (While a
bipartisan cross-section of all mathematicians asserts that a
negative plus a negative will never, ever, ever result in a positive, presidents and mathematicians are completely different
personality types.) Galeano describes how the U.S. responds to
Truman's soul-searching query:

> A sun of fire, a violent light never before seen in
> the world, rises slowly, cracks the sky open, and
> collapses. Three days later, a second sun of suns
> bursts over Japan. Beneath remain the cinders of
> two cities, a desert of rubble, tens of thousands
> dead, and more thousands condemned to die little
> by little for years to come.

Autobiography of a Blue-Eyed Devil

The war was nearly over, Hitler and Mussolini gone, when President Harry Truman gave the order to drop atomic bombs on the populations of Hiroshima and Nagasaki. In the United States, it is the culmination of a national clamor for the prompt annihilation of the Yellow Peril. It is high time to finish off once and for all the imperial conceits of this arrogant Asian country, never colonized by anyone. The only good one is a dead one, says the press of these treacherous little monkeys.

Now all doubt is dispelled. There is one great conqueror among the conquerors. The United States emerges from the war intact and more powerful than ever. It acts as if the whole of the world were its trophy.[3]

I've had a lot of interesting jobs in my life, and one of them was teaching English as a second language to wealthy kids from South Korea, Japan, Hong Kong, Taiwan, Thailand, Saudi Arabia, Oman, and sometimes China. On the first day of class, I generally got them talking about the towns they were from.

One day, a young Japanese man quietly said he was from Hiroshima. All the other Japanese kids leaned away from him—their bodies literally slanting as far from him as possible, as if trying to distance themselves from a part of history they'd learned not to discuss in polite society. The look of misery on his face when he said this instantaneously painful word almost cut me down like a scythe.

"I am from Hiroshima," he said, and the room was silent.

No, the room was more than silent. It was a vacuum-packed airlocked minefield of memories and emotions no one was prepared to wade across, perhaps ever, and certainly not in the context of the first day of an ESL class.

Even the garrulous Saudi boys—who had the devil of a time wrapping their entitled minds around a woman who nicely told them to shut the flying fuck up while others were talking—were eerily hushed.

At that moment, I wondered if I'd had other people from Hiroshima or Nagasaki in previous classes who opted out of saying either of these words out loud, and instead told everyone they were from Osaka or Kagoshima.

I wondered about how I learned to perceive these two words. They signified the end of World War II. I knew they meant two bombs that killed everything, but I grew up knowing I live in a country that drops such bombs. It's kinda like being a kid who gets fucked by her or his dad every night before bed; it seems normal until you learn not all kids have this experience. "Hiroshima" and "Nagasaki" didn't mean thousands of dead people, the survivors and their great-grandchildren poisoned for life. They didn't mean wondering how the people from these two cities lived on, and how they were viewed by the larger Japanese population. In that moment, I clearly saw the terror my country has unleashed upon the world in my name.

In the ESL classroom, history stood before me, pointing a finger at my ignorance, shedding light on the shame of not knowing—of not fully comprehending—what my country has done.

Never again did I ask students what town they were from. I learned that in the vacuum-packed airlocked minefield of history, even the most innocuous queries can stir up deadly memories and emotions.

After that, I tried my luck with the subject of everyone's favorite meal.

Scene 4: In Which My Grammy Surprises Me

I am in my Grammy's house, sitting by her chair, listening to her reminisce. She says, "I know you might not understand this now, but I think we were right to put Japanese people in camps. I was very close friends with some people who got in trouble for transmitting radio signals to Japan. I felt so betrayed by them for doing that. It was a terrible time."

I am shocked.

My Grammy is *all about love.* She's a lover *and* a fighter. She *rails* against injustice, oppression, racism, imperialism, and corrupt politicians. I've joyfully listened to her bitch about all of these things for hours and hours. I mean, christ, when I told her I was a homo, her immediate concern was that the only recourse I'd have for meeting people she referred to as "nice women" was going to "those gay bar places."

I am not prepared to hear her justify the internment of Japanese nationals and Japanese Americans.

I start a harangue about how people were targeted by authorities and neighbors so their property could be seized, just like what was done to suspicious witches during the Inquisition and Crusades. How does she *know* for a fact that those friends of hers were really and actually sending radio signals to Japan? Was she *there*? Did she *see* them? And what about all the young Japanese American men who came "home" from the hell of war only to be interned in a goddamn camp? Couldn't she place herself in the context of being at the mercy of Hearst newspapers on the west coast of "California" during the media-manufactured "Yellow Peril"?

But my Grammy anticipates a harangue from me, and its content held no significance for her. She lived the majority of her life believing that her friends had betrayed her and there was nothing I could say that would change her experience. It was a very intimate and painful conclusion she chose to carry in her heart long before she ever held baby me in her arms.

I took a measure of solace in the fact that the granddaughter of a woman who learned to begrudge an entire race of people through war propaganda has lived to see through the lies. However, this provides an exceptionally wan comfort during the present Guantánamo times, when anyone who looks remotely "Middle Eastern" in the limited U.S. mainstream imagination (mysteriously, this includes Hindus, Sikhs, and "swarthy" Christians) can be illegally socked away for an indefinite period of time, without being charged or tried for any crime, and without having access to legal advice. But then again, what good would "legal" advice be for someone who is being illegally detained, tortured, humiliated, and interrogated?

Scene 5: In Which an Austrian Is Intolerantly Tolerant

I am living in Los Angeles when my friend Steve Flusty gently chides me for wanting to visit the Museum of Tolerance. He insists it should be renamed the Museum of Intolerance. I am shocked, as he expects me to be, but he then provides a context, and I quote:

> My main beef with the museum is its deep-seated homophobia. From the time of its foundation, the museum was steeped in conservative religious prejudices that manifested as an adamant refusal to explicitly address the victimization of homosexuals during the Holocaust. This was despite persistent efforts by queer groups to have this rectified (although such efforts were eventually successful, albeit with significant limitations).
>
> The other problem I have with the museum is that the focus on racist hate groups excludes any consideration of the ingrained and pervasive racism that structures our society—it makes contemporary racism look like an unfortunate aberration instead of the pervasive norm we damn well know it to be.

In solidarity with all of the victims of the Holocaust, in solidarity with the definition of the word "tolerance," and in solidarity with my dear pal Flusty, I forgo a visit to this museum.

The poetic irony of Arnold Schwarzenegger donating

money and face time to the Museum of Intolerance as a symbolic machination to politically distance himself from his Nazi roots might be lost on some, but not me.

Act II: Trophy Collecting

So yeah.

We're the winners of the world. The Cold War rides in on World War II's coattails, and brings a bit of dread and paranoia, but by and large, it's Happy Days! Rock 'n' roll music is here to stay! Milkshakes, malt shops, jukeboxes! Those fabulous greasers-vs.-jocks high school years leading into the crazy college daze when coeds wore their sweaters tight.

What a blast!

Or at least—not unlike all the other messages that constitute the mainstream U.S. story of history—these are some of the 1950s realities we're generally presented with.

While the Amerikkkan Dream Sockhop led to the first formal demographic who modeled their lives after stereotypes and sitcom plots found on teevee, where profoundly oppressive problems such as ring around the collar insinuated their ways into the public imagination, the 1950s were the beginning of a very unhappy period for most everyone who resisted the concept of the world being the U.S.'s trophy.

It turns out that the dawning of a post-Hitler planet was an incredibly busy time for the United States government. You'd think they'd have had their hands full with the McCarthy hearings that lashed Hollywood into a propaganda apparatus, and with the continued lynchings, treaty-bashings, and "race riots" that lashed indigenous people and people of color into fomenting a civil rights movement, but a number of "operations" were nonetheless needed to make sure the rest of the world fully comprehended whose trophy it was.

The main difference between a "war" and an "operation" is that during a "war," the public is more or less led to believe that we have some kind of "say" in matters, via Congress. An "operation" yields the exact same results as a "war," but without all the annoyance of seeming to procure the blessings of the people whose taxes pay for it.

We Amerikkkans let the boys do what they need to do to run the country, and rejoice in our freedom and democracy.

Here is a partial listing of the locations and dates of overt and covert U.S. operations in the past six decades:

China, 1945–46
Korea, 1950–53
China, 1950–53
Iran, 1953–1979
Guatemala, 1954
Indonesia, 1958
Cuba, 1959–60
Guatemala, 1960
Congo, 1964
Peru, 1965

Laos, 1964–73
Vietnam, 1961–73
Chile, 1973–1990
Cambodia, 1969–70
Guatemala, 1967–69
Grenada, 1983
Libya, 1986
El Salvador, 1980s
Nicaragua, 1980s
Panama, 1989
Iraq, 1991–present
Sudan, 1998
Afghanistan, 1998–present
Yugoslavia, 1999

Most of these operations were/are invariably justified under the guise of protecting democracy from communists/drug traffickers/terrorists. I think the U.S. government's handmaiden, Augusto Pinochet, did a great job of summing up this rationale when, after brutally snuffing Chile's 150-year-old democracy at the bidding of the United States, he stated, "Democracy is the breeding ground of communism."

I am not sure if he made this assertion before or after executing, torturing, and disappearing tens of thousands of Chilean citizens, but it was definitely in the wake of the assassination of President Salvador Allende.

Oh, and if you ever wonder why Mr. Pinochet has not yet been tried in the International Court of Justice for crimes against humanity, you could write a letter to the U.S. government and ask.

Scene 1: Operation Ajax

I've been blessed with the friendship of a number of Iranian Americans—some whose families fled the shah, some whose families fled Ayatollah Khomeini. Through these friendships, I've patched together a perspective or two from subjective oral histories. Most of what I semicomprehend of Persian history, however, is from *Shah of Shahs*, by Ryszard Kapuscinski, a Polish Press Agency investigative journalist who spent his time nosing around revolutions, wars, and coups going down in poor countries.

Shah of Shahs is a lovingly composed volume. At just over 150 pages, it is all the more poetic for its brevity. I recommend *Shah of Shahs* to anyone who is interested in understanding how deeply the U.S. has been involved in repressing the democratic will of the wildly diverse population of people known (at least in the U.S.) as "Middle Easterners."

On the back of the book, the *New York Times* extols Mr. Kapuscinski's work:

> Insightful and important . . . a readable, timely and valuable contribution to the understanding of the revolutionary forces at work in Iran . . . the reader almost becomes a participant.

The *Los Angeles Times* calls it "a supercharged particle of a book."

It never ceases to amaze me how reviewers—and by proxy, many readers—in the U.S. can read books like this and somehow stand aside from our culpability, and at the same time, remain wholly condescending.

It's quite the masterful exercise of deeply entrenched denial.

The "reader" would become *a lot* more of a "participant" if the "reader" realized that whenever they mention Dulles International Airport in "Washington, D.C.," they are, in fact, honoring some of the individuals who were responsible for, among other atrocities, sundering any chance of democracy in Iran. "Understanding the revolutionary forces at work in Iran" takes on a whole new meaning when one realizes that the "revolutionary forces" would never have coalesced into the momentum of political Islamic fundamentalism without the U.S. government fucking shit up for the Iranian people—who are, on the whole, not religious fundamentalists. Yes, this cute "supercharged particle of a book" will atomically bomb your perception, if—unlike culturally myopic fools who blurb books—you choose to read it in the conscious light of accountability.

In 1925, Shah Reza Khan came into power through a British-orchestrated coup. His whole title was: Shah Reza the Great,

King of Kings, Shadow of the Almighty, God's Vicar and the Center of the Universe.

Whatta guy.

The King of Kings made absolutely no distinctions between leadership and ownership. As his power grew, so too did the demarcation lines of his vast estate. He bought thousands of villages, becoming a landlord of Wal-Mart proportions. In Shah Reza Khan's imagination, every living being had a responsibility to consciously recognize the power structure of his dominion. Mr. Kapuscinski dug up this historical anecdote:

> One day there is a public execution: On the Shah's orders a firing squad kills a donkey that, ignoring all warning signs, entered a meadow belonging to Reza Khan. Peasants from neighboring villages are herded to the place of execution to learn respect for the master's property.[4]

Compared to some of the sadistic, bloodthirsty psychopathic rapists who have terrorized under European or U.S. thumbs, the Shadow of the Almighty seems a relatively tolerable sort. He built schools, roads, and hospitals, and displayed semblances of genuine concern and love for his people.

But Persians were literally "his" people.

In his lust for glory, however, Shah Reza Khan forgot to keep licking the feet of those who put him in power. (This is a pattern I have noticed with dictators. They hardly ever leave well enough alone, which will also be Arbusto's downfall.)

During World War II, Shah Reza Khan seemed to have discovered that Hitler was his ideological pal, and screwed himself over by refusing to allow the Allies to use his railroad to get supplies to the Russians.

And so, as Ryszard Kapuscinski says, "Empire giveth; empire taketh away."

Russia, the U.S., and Britain kicked Reza Khan's military's ass for this transgression. Since the shah ruled solely through his beloved, well-equipped, and well-fed military, he was nothing without them. In September 1941, the British nicely asked him to abdicate power to his son, Mohammed Reza Pahlavi, who was a twenty-two-year-old playboy about the globe at the time. This new shah had a lot of better things to do than run Persia (his father had renamed the nation "Iran" during his reign). It was important for the new shah to ski, fly his private airplane, organize fancy dress balls, and play soccer.

This left government officials, such as Dr. Mohammed Mossadegh, the informal job of running the country. Dr. Mossadegh was formally elected prime minister in 1951 and was the first democratically minded leader of Iran in a long, long time.

Ever, actually.

Three days after he became prime minister, on April 28, 1951, parliament passed his bill nationalizing oil. This meant that the Iranian people would actually benefit from the vast resource that the U.S. and other industrialized nations were completely and utterly dependent upon.

How long do you think this lasted?

Let's look at how Kapuscinski contextualizes this event:

> We have to enter into the spirit of that epoch . . . the
> world has changed a great deal since. In those days,
> to dare the sort of act that Doctor Mossadegh just per-
> formed was tantamount to dropping a bomb suddenly
> on Washington or London. The psychological effect
> was the same: shock, fear, anger, outrage.[5]

All of a sudden, the playboy shah was a very important
man to everyone whose last name was Dulles.

If you fly out of Dulles Airport in Virginia, ever wonder
what the word Dulles means? It stands for the Dulles family—
Secretary of State John Foster Dulles and his brother, CIA
Director Allen Dulles (during President Eisenhower's
administration).

They were responsible for the overthrow of the democratically elected leader of Iran.

As was President Theodore Roosevelt's grandson, Kermit
Roosevelt, the CIA agent who traveled to Iran to pull off the coup.

Now why should we be concerned about a coup that happened so far away almost fifty years ago this month?

New York Times reporter Stephen Kinzer put it this way:

> It is not far-fetched to draw a line from Operation
> Ajax through the shah's repressive regime and the
> Islamic revolution to the fireballs that engulfed the
> World Trade Center in New York.

The shahs throughout history had, by and large, been a bane of the Persian people's existence. Collectively, the various shahs were more or less viewed as an annoying, potentially violent male relative who shows up at important events, dominates the conversation, smokes the stinkiest cigars imaginable, and openly steals the silverware. Persians were resigned to this relative showing up from time to time, but they certainly did not want to interact with him on a daily basis.

The people made this very clear by—among other acts of resistance throughout his regime—pulling down the numerous monuments the newest Shah Reza almost immediately had erected for himself and his father.

The U.S., however, thought their li'l preoccupied and easily manipulated shah was just the greatest, and ordered him to yank Mossadegh off the stage. To his credit, I will say, the shah did this with a modicum of reluctance—if only because he did not see how running a country might fit in with his tight polo schedule.

In 1953, after surviving an unsuccessful assassination attempt or two, Dr. Mossadegh was put under house arrest and the shah came back full force. He started digging the whole concept of power, and eventually developed an obsession about how to keep it. The Iranian people, on the other hand, were kinda digging the whole prospect of what democracy might look like, and were quite disinclined to relinquish this vision. The shah found out that the best way to hold on to power was to silence any form of dissent. Everyone smart and arty disappeared. College students were encouraged to study abroad, and for the most part, never returned. The mysterious, amorphous police force known as Savak enforced total allegiance to the shah. People who were taken by Savak disappeared. Their families had nowhere to file a report, no office in which to inquire, no one to appeal to. They could look for them in one of the six thousand prisons,[†] but this would take a great deal of time. If Shah Reza Khan was the omniscient corporate officer of his vast dominion back in the day, his son utilized Savak to micromanage the entire population. With over sixty thousand agents and over three million informants, Savak infiltrated and controlled schools, workplaces, media, everything. Like a virus tearing through a crowded bus, there was no escape from Savak.

Imagine maintaining personal relationships in such a milieu. All talk—for around fifteen years—was kept to platitudes, between husband and wife, parent and child, lovers, siblings, and best friends. No one spoke of their inner thoughts or experiences because no one wanted to have any information that could in some way implicate a loved one during the highly possible occurrence of being tortured by Savak.

Two of my Iranian American friends are Peri Heydari Pakroo and her cousin, Parisha. Peri was born and raised in Milwaukee. Her father left Iran in the early 1960s because he opposed the shah and, like many young people at that time, did not see much of a future for himself in Iran.

Parisha's father—that is, Peri's dad's brother—was a general in the shah's army. When Parisha was nine years old, she

---

† Iran is a little more than twice the size of "Texas."

was awoken in the middle of the night, told to pack up a bag, shuttled into a helicopter, and whisked away. Her family fled the 1979 revolution and eventually landed in Milwaukee, where Parisha, who spoke not a word of English, met her cousin, Peri, who spoke not a word of Farsi.

I mention this because the relationship between Peri and Parisha's fathers calls to mind what Iranian democracy might have looked like. Though the two men existed on completely opposite sides of the political belief spectrum, they got along fine. They debated, argued, and loved each other. Peri's father helped his brother's family acclimate to life in the U.S., and the two remained close until the passing of Parisha's father, a couple years ago.

My uncles Bruce and Allen, on the other hand, raised here in the U.S., have not had a civil word for one another in almost three, count them, *three decades,* since they had a big falling-out over abalone hunters, who kill seals, which eat abalone. Allen thought the seals should fuck off, Bruce thought the abalone hunters should fuck off, and there has been no peace in my family ever since.

I shit you not.

In fairness to my uncles, the hunters vs. seals and abalone argument merely represented the breaking point of a much larger ideological divide that exists between most hippies (Bruce) and rednecks (Allen).

I've never met Peri's dad, and did not have a chance to meet Parisha's, so I do not know exactly why they got along. From what I have gathered, however, it seems that they put great value on their freedom to disagree with one another, and understood what a huge luxury this is. In the much-heralded "democracy" of the U.S., my uncles take this precious luxury for granted. Perhaps this nonchalance about our rights and freedoms is why we allow our government to gallop around the globe, trouncing on every democracy they can get their bloody hands on.

As *New York Times* reporter Stephen Kinzer noted in a *Guardian* article by Russell Mokhiber and Robert Weissman:

> "Imagine today what it must sound like to Iranians to hear American leaders tell them—'We want you to have a democracy in Iran, we disapprove of your present government, we wish to help you bring democracy to your country.' Naturally, they roll their eyes and say—'We had a democracy once, but you crushed it,'" [Kinzer] said. "This shows how differently other people perceive us from the way we perceive ourselves. We think of ourselves as paladins of democracy. But actually, in Iran, we destroyed the last democratic regime the country ever had and set them on a road to what has been half a century of dictatorship."[6]

Unlike many *New York Times* "investigative" reporters of today, Stephen Kinzer seems to be someone who *actually inves-*

tigates the world in which we live. He has written a few books concerning the U.S. government's role in sundering various democracies. Besides *All the Shah's Men: An American Coup and the Roots of Middle East Terror,* he also cowrote *Bitter Fruit: The Story of the American Coup in Guatemala.* The *Guardian* article, about how we destroyed the only democracy the Iranian people ever glimpsed out of the corner of their eyes, reports that Mr. Kinzer noted he is "thinking of putting together a boxed set of his books on American coups."

I would be very happy if Mr. Kinzer were to make these volumes available.

I would be stoked out of my mind if they were procured by high school history teachers all over the United States.

I would be ecstatic if Oprah put them on her book list.

Barring that, I'll be content if readers of this book apprehend just how *busy* our government was in the 1950s. This busyness inspired me to think up a little something I call the Formula for Subjugation.

Scene 2: Operation Guatemala

Let's call 1492 "1953," and let's call Christopher Columbus "Sam Zemurray," and let's call Spain "the United Fruit Corporation" (now Chiquita) and let's call "Hispaniola" (Haiti and the Dominican Republic) "Guatemala."

If these four factors all share the exact same corresponding and relative values to one another, then they will all add up to the exact same corresponding and relative result.

Let's see if it works.

1492 + Christopher Columbus + Spain + "Hispanola" = white people killing/enslaving indian people and taking their land.

1953 + Sam Zemurray + United Fruit + Guatemala = white people killing/enslaving indian people and taking their land.

Hmm. It seems to add up.

The Formula for Subjugation can be applied to pretty much every coup, imperialistic orchestration, and military occupation in the history of the United States (and Britain, Germany, Italy, Spain, Holland, and Portugal, for that matter.)

Here is Galeano's telling of the man who inspired Truman and Eisenhower to foment Operation PBSUCCESS, using, of course, our grandparents' tax dollars:

> Throne of bananas, crown of bananas, a banana held
> like a scepter: Sam Zemurray, master of the lands
> and seas of the banana kingdom, did not believe it
> possible that his Guatemalan vassals could give him
> a headache. *The Indians are too ignorant for Marxism,*
> he used to say, and was applauded by his court at his
> royal palace in Boston, Massachusetts. . . .
>
> Sam Zemurray's troubles began when president
> Juan José Arévalo forced the company to respect
> the union and its right to strike. From bad to worse:
> A new president, Jacobo Arbenz, introduces agrar-

ian reform, seizes United Fruit's uncultivated lands,
begins dividing them among a hundred thousand
families, and acts as if Guatemala were ruled by the
landless, the letterless, the breadless, the *less*.[7]

Before Presidents Arévalo and Arbenz were chosen by their
people to lead, United Fruit ruled Guatemala with impunity.
Under the previous administrations of Manuel Estrada Cabrera
and Jorge Ubico, the entire nation of Guatemala was, for all
intents and purposes, little more than a division of the United
Fruit Corporation. The company could take whatever land it
wanted, no matter how large, small, or thoroughly inhabited
since the beginning of time. It owned *the entire infrastructure* of
the country, the military, the media, and of course, the politicians who, under United Fruit's payroll, ruled the country.

Every nation in the world exists to serve the United States of
Amerikkka. Germany, Japan, Russia, Cuba, Libya, Palestine,
Iraq, China, North Korea, Iran, and Venezuela served/serve
Amerikkkans by representing an "evil" that allows the
population to ideologically consider themselves to be "good."
Canada and the white European countries—except for, as of
this moment, France—generally serve Amerikkka by kinda
like being our pals, so we can think we're part of a "global community." Everyone else—that is, the "poor" countries that are
often, coincidentally, filled with riches and resources, to which

Amerikkkans are somehow naturally entitled—serves as fully subjugated worker-slaves to supply us with our sneakers, MP3 players, "quaint" or "exotic" vacation locales, coffee, legal and illegal drugs, oil, and many other things.

Oh, and bananas.

In a CIA-generated memo, Mr. Arbenz's courageous attempt to secure some of his nation's wealth for the people who lived there was referred to as "an intensely nationalistic program of progress colored by the touchy, anti-foreign inferiority complex of the 'Banana Republic.'"[8] Although the tone of this memo is "mean" instead of "nice," this is more of the same racist condescension that can be found on the back cover of books like *Shah of Shahs*.

Besides Sam Zemurray, a number of other people were directly or indirectly responsible for sundering democracy and installing a long string of nationalist-resistance- and indigenous-slaughtering dictators in Guatemala. Eduardo Galeano's *Century of the Wind* gave me insights into some of these notable personages, who were eager to add more trophies to the U.S. government's display case. Among these were: Mr. Dwight Eisenhower (well, of course); the Dulles brothers, John Foster and Allen (both huge proponents of white supremacist racist imperialism. You might recall Allen, from when Prescott Arbusto needed to get off the hook for funding Hitler's fascist

Nazism); the Cabot brothers, John Moors and Thomas (the latter being president of United Fruit); U.S. Senator Henry Cabot Lodge (a United Fruit shareholder); Spruille Braden, Robert Hill, and John Peurifoy (all three used their diplomatic connections to advance United Fruit's interests); and finally, just in case President Eisenhower might have somehow, miraculously, momentarily forgotten how important it was to keep United Fruit happy, his personal secretary, Anne Whitman, was always on hand to serve as a reminder. Her husband was employed by United Fruit.[9]

What does 2001 + Arbusto + Halliburton + Iraq and Afghanistan equal?

The names change.
　　The song remains the same.

Langston Hughes wrote a poem that always reminds me of this. Except for some of the names and places, Mr. Hughes might have written "Merry Christmas"[10] from his grave in 2004, instead of from his consciousness in 1930.

　　　　　Merry Christmas, China,
　　　　From the gun-boats in the river,
　　　　Ten-inch shells for Christmas gifts,

Autobiography of a Blue-Eyed Devil

And peace on earth forever.

Merry Christmas, India,
To Gandhi in his cell,
From righteous Christian England,
Ring out, bright Christmas bell!

Ring Merry Christmas, Africa,
From Cairo to the Cape!
Ring Hallehuiah! Praise the Lord!
(For murder and for rape.)

Ring Merry Christmas, Haiti!
(And drown the voodoo drums—
We'll rob you to the Christian hymns
Until the next Christ comes.)

Ring Merry Christmas, Cuba!
(While Yankee domination
Keeps a nice fat president
In a little half-starved nation.)

And to you down-and-outers,
("Due to economic laws")
Oh, eat, drink, and be merry
With a bread-line Santa Claus—

While all the world hails Christmas,

While all the church bells sway!
While, better still, the Christian guns
Proclaim this joyous day!

While holy steel that makes us strong
Spits forth a mighty Yuletide song:
SHOOT Merry Christmas everywhere!
Let Merry Christmas GAS the air!

In the words of Eduardo Galeano, here is how the Formula of
Subjugation was explicitly implemented and rationalized during
Operation Guatemala:

1954: Boston
The Lie Machine, Piece by Piece

The Motor
The executioner becomes the victim; the victim, the
executioner. Those who prepare the invasion of Guatemala from Honduras attribute to Guatemala the intention to invade Honduras and all Central America . . .

Gear I
News and articles, declarations, pamphlets, photographs, films, and comic strips about Communist
atrocities in Guatemala bombard the public. This educational material, whose origin is undisclosed, comes

from the offices of United Fruit in Boston and from government offices in Washington.

Gear II

The Archbishop of Guatemala, Mariano Rossell Arellano, exhorts the populace to rise *against communism, enemy of God and the Fatherland.* Thirty CIA planes rain down his pastoral message over the whole country. The archbishop has the image of the popular Christ of Esquipulas, which will be named Captain General of the Liberating Brigade, brought to the capital.

Gear III

At the Pan-American Conference, John Foster Dulles pounds the table with his fist and gets the blessing of the Organization of American States for the projected invasion. At the United Nations, Henry Cabot Lodge blocks Jacobo Arbenz's demands for help. U.S. diplomacy is mobilized throughout the world. The complicity of England and France is obtained in exchange for a U.S. commitment to silence over the delicate matters of the Suez Canal, Cyprus, and Indochina.

Gear IV

The dictators of Nicaragua, Honduras, Venezuela, and the Dominican Republic not only lend training camps, radio transmitters, and airports to "Operation

Guatemala," they also make a contribution to the propaganda campaign. Somoza I calls together the international press in Managua and displays some pistols
with hammers and sickles stamped on them. They
are, he says, from a Russian submarine intercepted
en route to Guatemala.[11]

Though Mr. Galeano doesn't go into Gear V, it doesn't need
a lot of explanation.

Gear V is rape, torture, imprisonment, and death to innocents.
And so.

Precisely, how is it that our population has learned to relate
the *uninvestigated attacks* on New York's World Trade Center in
2001 (Gear I) with, for instance, the slaughter and rape of Fallujah in 2004 (Gear V)?

If you are a person who listens closely to the news, you might
notice that the Lie Machine has presently been configured to
take down the government in Iran. As of this writing, Gears I
and II have successfully been deployed. Some incarnation of
Gears III and IV will hit the ground running sometime in the
spring and summer of 2005.

The resistance in my heart for what my country is doing to
people in the Middle East consumes every moment of my life.

I woke up in the middle of the night when we allowed,
nay, commissioned, the looting of ancient treasures in
Baghdad's museums. I woke up, blood racing through my

body like I just ran five miles, and I knew something had been irreparably damaged.

I stayed awake in bed, sobbing quietly for a few hours.

Then I got up to find out what was broken.

After I read eyewitness accounts of prison soldiers affixing pornographic images and photos of pigs on cell walls facing Mecca, I did not sleep for three days.

There were also dark circles under my eyes after learning that our soldiers wear their boots into mosques that have never, in hundreds or thousands of years, been touched by the soles of shoes.

And then my friend Peggy told me about her brother who is stationed in Fallujah. He called home on Thanksgiving and talked to his four-year-old daughter. She asked what he ate for dinner. The meal he had eaten was the first hot food he'd had in three weeks, but he did his best to make it sound good. His little girl said, "But Daddy, didn't you have pie?" He forgot to make up a slice of pie, and maybe he already felt bad having to lie, so he said, "No, baby. I didn't have any pie." So his daughter said, "Don't worry Daddy, I'll save you a piece."

Heart. Fucking. Break.

I do not know how a U.S. soldier in Fallujah might contain his grief, knowing there is a piece of pie sitting in the refrigerator, placed there by his four-year-old child, who wants her daddy to come home and eat it.

I do not know how I might contain my grief if my government manages to shift into Gear V in Iran.

Or North Korea.

Or Venezuela.

Or Cuba.

Blessings be upon these nations and our soldiers, and may our people rise up in their—and our own—defense.

Postage Stamp Redemptions

Myth: White supremacist racism and imperialism ended with the Civil Rights Movement, which is over and was just a smashing success.

I am one of millions of people who grew up in the post–Civil Rights Movement United States of Amerikkka. According to my schooling and socialization, racism was in its final, ghastly throes of life right around the time I was born, thank goodness. I mean, it was *so hard* for all the "coloreds" back when there was racism. The pre-civil-rights era was a *dark time* in this nation's history, and it's just great that all that's over and we've since moved on.

As a white person, of course, I have never really suffered from racism, but I'm a Benevolent and Good White Person, and it matters to me that other people no longer have to deal with horrible things like not being served in restaurants and STUFF LIKE THAT anymore.

Yay!

And it's great that sexism also happens to be over because I am a woman and even though I have never experienced sexism—thanks to that offshoot of the Civil Rights Movement, the Women's Movement—I have heard horrible things about how difficult it used to be for women to be looked upon as equals.

It's so *grand* to have been born when all of THAT STUFF was already in the past. I got to begin life in this country with a clean slate, a clear conscience, and equality for all.

Hip hip hooray for me and all the other people born after Martin Luther King's collective-consciousness-shifting speech, "I Have A Dream," not to mention Betty Friedan's culture-altering book, *The Feminine Mystique.*

I get nervous just *thinking about* imagining what life might be like if these crucial social movements hadn't changed everything for the better.

Whew!

I mean, I know there are still some totally workable problems, like hate crimes, police brutality, marginalization, and ghettoization; whitewashed history (pun intended); poverty, rape, violence, wholesale destruction of the planet, disease, hunger, and racial profiling (which leads to legally sanctioned lynching); continued debasement of indigenous, Chicano, Mexicano, Central American, and South American populations, cultures, traditions, and lands; black voter disenfranchisement; and religions, social norms, and economic models based on the hatred and fear of and all women, children, and men of color, indigenous folks, trannies, white women and girls, and homos. Of course, there's all that pesky racial, sexual, and gender ignorance espoused in ads, sitcoms, books, the media, and movies, not to mention rampant tokenism—oh, and also, white male domination of the planet, with its attendant white supremacist ideological infiltration of the global status quo, but things sure are better than they used to be.

Aren't they.

Aren't they.

Aren't things better now that we sometimes get to affix on our envelopes a one-inch-by-two-inch piece of paper that has Malcolm X's picture on the other side.

At present, the Civil Rights Movement has been completely co-opted. It is employed as a beacon in the night, guiding this country into the belief that things have changed for everyone, and that we now live in a free and just society.

This fills me with a deep sense of loss for all of the people who struggled in this movement, for their efforts to be absorbed and used against their children and grandchildren by the very forces they so courageously and vehemently opposed.

As a nodding triumph to "civil rights," the United States now celebrates the birthday of Dr. Martin Luther King Jr., as if this posthumous honor somehow atones for, sanctifies, and magically overrides the continuing legalized murder, incarceration, and disenfranchisement of hundreds of thousands of women, children, and men.

Wait, I am getting ahead of myself.

In *most* of the fifty states, there is a Martin Luther King Day.

In "Virginia," where white people were evidently terrified out of their minds at the prospect of a day honoring a black man, the state government came up with a *compromise*.

In "Virginia," they celebrate Martin Luther King, Jr./ Robert E. Lee Day.

Local folks call it "King-Lee Day" for short.

To contextualize, this would be kinda like honoring people who have died from violent crimes with a Jeffrey Dahmer Day.

It seems that people in power have also figured out that designating certain months of the year as times to "honor" history provides further evidence that "we" have courageously faced the past head-on, so what the fuck are "you" all still bitching about? These annual exaltations include a semi-innocuous list of his-

torical "celebrities" that rarely veers course: George Washington
Carver, Harriet Tubman, and Sojourner Truth for Black History
Month; Elizabeth Cady Stanton, Amelia Earhart, and Sally Ride
for (white) Women's History Month. Asian American History
Month is a time when everyone feels kinda bad about Japanese
internment during World War II, and reads Amy Tan's books.

As ever, the original inhabitants of Turtle Island are
entirely overlooked. Mysteriously, the only time indigenous
people are guaranteed a mainstream Amerikkkan mention is on
Thanksgiving.

Again, to contextualize, this would be kinda like someone
busting into your home and robbing you blind, then sending you
postcards once a year to remind you how much they are enjoying all of your stuff, and getting annoyed with you if you don't
respond with appreciation for their thoughtfulness.

The same formula that led John F. Kennedy to co-opt the 1963
March on Washington has been successfully employed to control historical perception of what the Civil Rights Movement
really was. Two months after the march, in a speech in Detroit,
Malcolm X described this co-optation tactic:

> This is what they did with the march on Washington.
> They joined it . . . became part of it, took it over. And
> as they took it over, it lost its militancy. It ceased to be
> angry, it ceased to be hot, it ceased to be uncompro-
> mising. Why, it even ceased to be a march. It became

> a picnic, a circus. Nothing but a circus, with clowns
> and all. . . .
>
> No, it was a sellout. It was a takeover. . . . They
> controlled it so tight, they told those Negroes what
> time to hit town, where to stop, what signs to carry,
> what song to sing, what speech they could make, and
> what speech they couldn't make, and then told them
> to get out of town by sundown.[1]

In the context of resisting white supremacist racism and imperialism, every time an oppressive demand—no matter how seemingly insignificant—is considered or even acknowledged, adversaries carve themselves up a little more space in one's heart and imagination.

People of a mind to oppress others do not deserve this space.

In "Freedom Sings," a *brilliant* interview by Sarah Ruth van Gelder for *Yes! Magazine,* Harry Belafonte offers up a perspective on why—I am venturing—this was an important point to Mr. X:

> **Sarah**: Having survived McCarthyism, do you have
> any advice on how to survive this period of political
> repression we seem to be entering and to keep the
> movements for positive change alive?
>
> **Harry**: Do not submit. It is extremely critical that
> repression be met full head-on and that it be resisted
> with every fiber in our being. There is just absolutely

> no compromise that can be made with it. As a matter
> of fact, compromise is what oppression feeds on.
>
> Without compromise it would be defeated. Just
> as some cancers feed on hormones, compromise
> becomes the hormone of oppression.[2]

That master of procuring compromises, John F. Kennedy, is treated with a reverence unparalleled by any other U.S. president. Lyndon B. Johnson is not. But it was Mr. Johnson whom President Kennedy sent to Norway during the March on Washington because of his alleged ardently pro-civil-rights stance. Kennedy evidently didn't want the occasion marred by Johnson's presence. One of Kennedy's buds, Arthur Schlesinger Jr., once said, "The best spirit of Kennedy was largely absent from the racial deliberations of his presidency."[3] Schlesinger is, by the way, the same man who in 1990 stated that Afrocentrism in U.S. history is "psychotherapy" for blacks—as James Loewen phrases it, "a one-sided misguided attempt to make African Americans feel good about themselves."[4]

I think there might be some truth in this assessment because "normal" history sure as fuck is psychotherapy for whites, and we get really bent out of shape when anyone wonders why we feel so one-sidedly, misguidedly good about ourselves.

Kennedy, furthermore, didn't care enough about "racial deliberations" to rein in the rabid, psychotic, sexually deranged, racist head of the FBI, J. Edgar Hoover. During the Civil Rights Movement, the government tested and employed various new formulas to suppress resistance to white supremacist racist imperialism. To many, this was a time of hope and possibility, but to Hoover's FBI, it was a decades-long experiment in how best to control, divide, and conquer the population.

The FBI's COINTELPRO tactics involved a veritable gamut of illegal acts: murder of various leaders, gleeful character assassinations—such as spreading rumors of extramarital affairs and venereal disease to sabotage people's most intimate relationships—and wrongful incarceration based on elaborate sting operations.

The result was stolen lives and terrorization of black, indian, off-white, Puerto Rican, Chicano, and Mexicano individuals and communities.

Many individuals, such as Leonard Peltier, Sundiata Acoli, and Mumia Abu-Jamal, have spent decades in prison for their contributions to the Civil Rights Movement, and they are still there as of this writing.

I imagine their freedom every day.

I realize that I should define what the Civil Rights Movement is in my mind.

First of all, I suppose the term itself doesn't totally sit well with me. It seems to me that people must acquire human rights before moving on to procuring civil rights, but the name of the movement does nothing to negate the massive, collective power of imagination behind it, so I don't quibble too terribly about this.

Many white and white-identified people are comfortable looking at the Civil Rights Movement as a job well done, and relegating it, with a multicultural sigh of relief, to the "tasks completed" sector of their conscious reality of justice. African American people are generally portrayed as the only faction of the population who were demanding human and civil rights.

When PBS shows documentaries about the Civil Rights Movement, you get shots of Selma, "Alabama," and of evil old white policemen with their fire hoses trained on good young African American children. You see reenactments of Rosa Parks sitting at the front of the bus, speech excerpts from Dr. King and Malcolm X, and sometimes, interviews with their widows.

In reality, however, the Civil Rights Movement was the Deacons for Defense, the Young Lords, the American Indian Movement, the Gay Liberation Front (which, in the beginning, included transgender folks), the Brown Berets, the Street Transvestite Action Revolutionaries, Yuri Kochiyama, Shirley Chisholm, the Black Panthers, the Women's Movement, the Black Liberation Army, and many, many other groups and individuals who were fighting for the exact same thing, at the exact same time—only, with few exceptions, they were all fighting separately instead of together.

The Chicano and Puerto Rican Civil Rights Movements in Los Angeles, New York City, and Chicago are largely ignored in mainstream narratives. El Movimiento, the Brown Berets, and the Young Lords are not acknowledged in historical hindsight as the Black Panthers are—who themselves have only been mentioned with anything approaching objectivity in the past decade.[†]

The American Indian Movement's takeover of Alcatraz Island, the second battle at Wounded Knee, fish-ins, and many other acts of resistance for stolen land and broken treaties are, if not entirely ignored, regarded as "separate" issues.

Women demanding equal rights, and the outpouring of activism from transgendered people and queers, are likewise relegated to their own ghettoized (and often, sub-ghettoized) corners of history. The vast continuum of human and civil rights was not then, and is not now, viewed as one and the same thing.

My deepest feelings on this subject were stated, and moreover lived, by the author, poet, activist, genius, and academic June Jordan (may she rest in peace). In the following passage, Ms. Jordan is discussing her response to Buford O. Furrow Jr.'s 1999 hate-crime spree in a Los Angeles neighborhood, when he shot up a Jewish daycare center, wounding three children

---

[†] I mean, now that "Muslim terrorists" have taken the place of "black militants" in the lexicon of today's mainstream white media, it kinda seems safer to say things about the Black Panthers that don't necessarily incite terror about white-hating murderers. If you think I am exaggerating, go to your public library and read up on media characterizations of Black Panthers up until the mid-1990s.

and two adults, and then went on to shoot a Filipino American postman nine times.

> And maybe the unity of resistance to hatred that will stop that hatred seems improbable. Maybe an orthodox Jewish congregation will never stand in protective vigil outside a gay and lesbian community center, or the clinic of an abortion provider. Maybe a Black student organization will never rally for Asian American rights. And maybe gay and lesbian activists will not bodily interpose themselves between a synagogue and a "Phineas Priest" [white supremacist bible thumper].
>
> Maybe none of us will ever recognize that all of us are wrongfully, equally, condemned: The Spawn of the Devil.
>
> Maybe. But meanwhile, I am moving on an irrepressible wish that all of us will: All of us will build that circle of our common safety that all of us deserve.
>
> I'm saying "Are you hunting for Jews? You're looking for me!"[5]

It is in the interest of the white men who have been in power to create the illusion that the Civil Rights Movement was a racially isolated segment of society demanding what, in hindsight, certainly appear to be "well-deserved" rights.

It would be devastating for the powers that presently be if

folks openly acknowledged that the Civil Rights Movement was represented by pretty much every segment of the population that was not elite white men.

It would be devastating for those running this country if folks acknowledged that the Civil Rights Movement never truly ended, but instead morphed into something much, much larger.

It would be just incredibly devastating for the white men and those on their payroll if folks acknowledged that the Civil Rights Movement may presently have no name, but has nonetheless swelled to include an international coalition of environmental, hiphop, and antiglobalization activists, in addition to indigenous people, disgruntled white women and off-white folks, people of color, homos, and transgender people.

When I was born, Vietnamese people were digging intricate tunnels and bunkers. In order to survive, they subsisted on a starvation diet underneath the earth.

Millions of people did not survive.

Babies learned silence.

Toddlers knew it.

Children enforced it.

Young men from the U.S.—a disproportionate percentage of whom were previously involved in, or were demographically potentially involved in, the growing movement to overthrow elite white men in power—were coerced into a psychological nightmare of racial sabotage,[†] peer pressure, and unspeakable fear that led them to witness and/or perpetrate crimes against humanity. Then they came home and everyone hated them, and they were our fathers and brothers, nephews, grandsons, lovers, and now grandfathers, and there was no more talk of resistance to white supremacist racism from them anymore.

Not after that.

Not after the things they did, survived, and witnessed while I gurgled happily in my crib.

Millions of people did not survive.
Millions of people did not survive.

How do you think it affects a culture when millions of people are senselessly murdered? Millions of women raped. Millions of children slaughtered. How does it affect a child to grow up in a culture that is grieving from loss and heinous sexual and psychological abuse?

In Vietnam, children learn about the American conflict.

[†] A significant number of black, Chicano, and indian soldiers did not come home because of racist white soldiers and officers conducting lynchings or setting soldiers up on suicide missions. Vietnamese, Laotian, and Cambodian people were not necessarily the most pressing enemy to all U.S. soldiers. For more information on this, read Wallace Terry's *Bloods: An Oral History of the Vietnam War by Black Veterans*.

Autobiography of a Blue-Eyed Devil

There are no Vietnamese children who are not somehow intimately affected by this brutal occupation.

And how does it affect children when these losses and abuses resonate deeply in their culture, but no one ever speaks of them?

I did not learn about the Vietnam War—at home or at school. Yet, like all children in the United States, I was—and continue to be—intimately affected by this brutal occupation that is called a war.

The brutal occupation in Vietnam silenced an entire generation of people in the United States.

In this silence, I was born.

I did not learn silence like Vietnamese children did. I learned silence in the deafening roar of history that was quelled throughout my life. The silence I learned comes from having no words, no vocabulary, no frame of reference.

I cannot speak of things I do not perceive.

And did I want mashed bananas or rice cereal for breakfast in the morning, when an Agent named Orange spilled out over Vietnam, singeing the skin, fur, flowers, and leaves

off

of

everything.

I remember the word "Vietnam" from when I was a kid. It was a very strange word. There was none other like it, not even the curious "Watergate," which I was content thinking of as a broken-down theme park. "Vietnam" was a tenuous specter, always hovering somewhere in my world, but always just outside my reach.

Queries about what, exactly, Vietnam *was* met answers categorized along with the ones concerning how I was to believe that Jesus died on the cross for my sins two thousand years before I ever lived to commit them.

Shrouds of mystery.

Vague reassurances.

Too young to understand.

At Some future point in your brain's cognitive development.

Wait and see.

"Vietnam" was a bad place.

Bad things happened there.

The end, go back to your desk and study for the spelling test on Friday, go to bed, go play outside with your cousins, don't you have some CHORE you should be doing, stop pestering people with questions.

That's what "Vietnam" meant.

One time, not long after a kindergarten friend told me about the existence of someone named the devil who lived in a place called hell, I asked my dad if Vietnam was something like that.

Maddeningly, he didn't answer directly, or even look up from the newspaper he was reading. He just apologized for putting me on the planet, as he often did while buried in the *Los Angeles Times*.

I was here a solid nine years before I figured out that "Vietnam" is both a country and a "war." It was another decade before I got a pretty clear idea of what this word meant.

My boyfriend, Reuben, and I had moved into an apartment in Seattle together.

The managers, Chuck and Irene, were two of the loveliest adults I'd ever met. Irene was a journalist and Chuck was a veteran who dealt antiques and collectibles. I knew that Chuck couldn't have any kind of "normal" job, and I knew this somehow had to do with his time in the country and the "war" of Vietnam, but I didn't pry.

By this time, I suppose—not unlike the Japanese students in my ESL class—I'd learned not to delve too deeply into certain subjects.

I often called Chuck and Irene on the phone or hung out at their pad when I wanted to know about history, meanings of words, or their take on current events.

Chuck and Irene always had the time of day to give, and I loved them for it.

One day, as I left my apartment to go be sexually harassed at the restaurant where I waited tables, Chuck was vacuuming our hallway. I walked up behind him and tapped him on the shoulder to say hello. He spun around lightning fast and executed some intricate lickety-split military maneuver on me. In the flash of an eyelash, and without hurting me, he had somehow bent me backward over his leg and was poised to snap my neck.

I stared at him, somehow knowing he meant me no harm, but nonetheless jerked well into the fear of seeing that ending my life is a very simple task.

The military does a really good job of training soldiers to kill.

I did not know I could be overpowered and murdered so quickly, so effortlessly. I would not have had time to scream. There would have been no loud noises, no blood.

2:47:01 = living Inga, 2:47:04 = dead Inga.

It wasn't but a moment, and Chuck almost immediately came to himself, tears welling up in his eyes, straightening me back up, and apologizing, apologizing, apologizing, telling me about something called post-traumatic stress disorder and how he had it and it made him crazy and never, ever, never come up behind him or any veteran who was in Vietnam during that time and he was so sorry, so sorry.

I was not upset with Chuck, but I was kinda peeved at myself for not getting off my ass and figuring out what "Vietnam" meant, besides a country and a "war." I felt like an ignorant, spoiled little fuck who cashed in on other people's pain through my (painstakingly indoctrinated) choice to be deluded by my culture.

More than anything, I wanted to console Chuck, but there was no possible way to do this.

None.

None.

Not one.

In his horror-filled eyes, I saw the answers to all my questions about what "Vietnam" was. I saw why my questions were rebuffed when I was a child. I saw that people wanted to protect children from that pain. And I saw that there is no such way to protect us.

I was late for work, blinded by tears and a profound grief that I immediately recognized I had inherited a long time ago, and would carry with me for the rest of my life.

Dearest People of South, Central, and North Vietnam; Dearest Cambodians; Dearest Laotians;

Is it any consolation to you that the young men who went to your countries and ruined everything have been pretty much whacked out ever since?

Does that bring back the laughter of your grandmother as she chopped green chiles in the family garden? Does that bring back the huge trees you climbed as children? Does that bring back your sister's sanity after losing all three of her children in one afternoon? Does that bring back the beautiful boy you were flirting with the very evening he was shot in the head at point-blank range?

The young men are old now, and images of what they did, witnessed, and condoned have haunted their lives. They do not sleep well, have a difficult time loving, and often abuse various substances. They've gone insane, lost their families, their homes, committed crimes, lan-

quished in prison. Many of their children have been raised by fathers who can often no longer open their hearts. Many of their children have been abused, abandoned, and neglected on a scale that sociologists haven't even begun to examine.

Some of these men opted for total denial, and, if they happen to be in positions of power, they often commit even more crimes against humanity and the earth, because to do otherwise would involve facing themselves and their past.

Which you figure into quite significantly.

In ways that are not always obvious, but are nonetheless pervasive and insidious in my country, these men pay dearly for what they did to you, and generally do so in silence, shame, nightmares, deep-rooted sadness, and isolation.

None of this brings anything or anyone back.

My country is still committing crimes against you, only now they are imperialist economic ones.

We add insult to injury.

We are taught to forget.

We repeat the past.

We learn not to delve or pry.

Love,
Inga M.

I believe the Vietnam Brutal Occupation served—amongst other geopolitical and economic machinations—as a systematic exercise in demolishing the powerful foundation of young people rising up against the Manifest Destiny Variety Show.

See, I am a person who enjoys looking at the outcomes of things. I learned this from reading Agatha Christie mysteries, which my mom turned me on to when I was a kid, and which I continue rereading to this day. No matter how many extenuating circumstances surround a given murder, Ms. Christie's detectives, Hercule Poirot and Jane Marple, never lose sight of the all-important *end result*.

One of the outcomes of the "war" in Vietnam was—in conjunction with some key assassinations—the complete disruption of the momentum of the Civil Rights Movement. COINTELPRO targeted the leaders and organizations, and the brutal occupation in Vietnam absconded with the rank and file.

Suddenly, with this crime against humanity looming in our destiny, the fight for human and civil rights at home had to share the stage with the fight against U.S. imperialism. In many ways, they segued together quite nicely, like when Muhammad Ali went to jail instead of going to Vietnam. He had absolutely no beef with Vietnamese folks and gave up his freedom to illustrate this fact.

But

    the result,

        the outcome,

            the reality,

was that black, Chicano, Puerto Rican, and indigenous young men were carted off to war in numbers almost as disproportionate as those we see today in U.S. prison populations.

✗

Hercule Poirot likes to list how things transpired, so I some-times do that too.

This is how it went:

The Vietnam War disrupted the Civil Rights Movement.

Severely traumatized soldiers came home when the war ended.

Crack cocaine was introduced and guns were distributed into ghettos and barrios by our government, via pro-imperialism Centroamericanos, who had relocated to the U.S. when the Sand-inistas took over the government of Nicaragua.

Economic recession hit.

Gang violence increased.

The War on Drugs began.

The three-strikes law filled state and privately owned prisons that were, and continue to be, built with the exact same tax dollars that would otherwise be used to build colleges and universities.

In that order.

Future anthropologists will have few problems seeing the logic in a white supremacist racist male-dominated imperialist cul-ture placing a great priority on keeping (young) people of color oppressed, divided, and conquered.

When considering prison populations and gangs, there is one thing to keep in mind: *Everything* you have not *directly learned* from those who have been victimized by the U.S.

criminal justice system, or family members, advocates, or activists fighting for justice for those who have been victimized by the U.S. criminal justice system, *indoctrinates you and manufactures your consent into believing that certain people deserve to be oppressed.*

In Los Angeles, dating back to the 1920s and '30s, there were many black clubs and social groups, often based around family. There were jobs, too, and South Los Angeles was populated with whites as well as blacks.

The earliest black social resistance groups—which evolved into gangs—in Los Angeles arose in the mid-1940s, from the generations of kids whose parents moved there from the South.

By the 1950s, there were many neighborhood gangs that had formed up as a response to white hatred. These young people's fathers and grandfathers were World War II veterans who relocated their families from southern states where lynchings were common occurrences. If moving west was about dreaming of a better future, then getting one's ass kicked by whites would be just incredibly unacceptable.

Chicano gangs had already formed by then, for Chicano kids had a bit more time to experience white hatred. In the 1943 zoot suit riots, for example, servicemen stationed in the area poured into East Los Angeles and, with the tacit approval of city authorities, beat the hell out of every Chicano teenager who crossed their path. Then the police swarmed in, arresting any young Chicano male they found—whether he was lying in a pool of blood or not.

Having been born and raised in "California," I really trip out on how people in the rest of the country freely entertain the stereotype about "California" being about wheatgrass juice, love, and liberal good vibrations. The corner of Haight and Ashbury takes up very little historic and geographic space in "California," and is now a Gap 'n' Jamba Juice jungle anyways.

White people in "California" are just as prone to racial ignorance, hatred, and violence as white people anywhere. Back in the day, black and Chicano kids growing up in Los Angeles had to deal with white boys who wanted to kick their asses, an LAPD that wanted to kick their asses and throw them in jail, and a "justice system" that would (and continues to) fully sanction all of this ass-kicking and stolen life.

In a research article on his brilliant website, Streetgangs.com, Alejandro A. Alonso writes about how white racist violence and unjust economic and judicial laws tie into early gang history:

> Several of the first black clubs to emerge in the late
> 1940s and early 1950s formed initially as a defensive
> reaction to combat much of the white violence that had
> been plaguing the black community for several years.
> In the surrounding communities of the original black

ghetto of Central Avenue and Watts, and in the cities of Huntington Park and South Gate, white Angelenos were developing a dissatisfaction for the growing black population that was migrating from the South during WWII. During the 1940s, resentment from the white community grew as several blacks challenged the legal housing discrimination laws that prevented them from purchasing property outside the original settlement neighborhoods and integrate[d] into the public schools. Areas outside of the original black settlement of Los Angeles were neighborhoods covered by legally enforced, racially restrictive covenants or deed restrictions. This practice, adapted by white homeowners, was established in 1922 and was designed to maintain social and racial homogeneity of neighborhoods by denying non-whites access to property ownership. . . .

In Huntington Park, Bell, and South Gate, towns that were predominately white, teenagers formed some of the early street clubs during the 1940s. One of the most infamous clubs of that time was the *Spook Hunters*, a group of white teenagers that often attacked black youths. If blacks were seen outside of the black settlement area, which was roughly bounded by Slauson to the South, Alameda Avenue to the east, and Main Street to the west, they were often attacked. The name of this club emphasized their racist attitude towards blacks, as "Spook" is a derogatory term used to identify blacks and "Hunters" highlighted their desire to attack blacks as their method of fighting integration and promoting residential segregation. Their animosity towards blacks was publicly known; the back of their club jackets displayed an animated black face with exaggerated facial features and a noose hanging around the neck. The *Spook Hunters* would often cross Alameda traveling west to violently attack black youths from the area. . . . Raymond Wright was one of the founders of a black club called the *Businessmen,* a large East side club based at South Park between Slauson Avenue and Vernon Avenue. He stated that "you couldn't pass Alameda, because those white boys in South Gate would set you on fire," and fear of attack among black youths was not, surprisingly, common. In 1941, white students at Fremont High School threatened blacks by burning them in effigy and displaying posters saying, "we want no niggers at this school." . . . White clubs in Inglewood, Gardena, and on the West side engaged in similar acts, but the *Spook Hunters* were the most violent of all white clubs in Los Angeles.

The black youths in Aliso Village, a housing project in East Los Angeles, started a club called the *Devil Hunters* in response to the *Spook Hunters* and other white clubs that were engaging in violent confrontations with blacks. The term "Devil" reflected how blacks viewed racist whites and Ku Klux Klan

members. The *Devil Hunters* and other black residents fought back against white violence with their
own form of violence. In 1944, nearly 100 frustrated
black youths, who were denied jobs on the city's
streetcar system, attacked a passing streetcar and
assaulted several white passengers. . . . During the
late 1940s and early 1950s, other neighborhood clubs
emerged to fight the white establishment. Members
of the *Businessmen* and other black clubs had several
encounters with the *Spook Hunters* and other white
clubs of the time.[6]

After the great white flight in the 1950s, black gangs
started fighting each other. The West Side was perceived as
wealthier and "softer" by the East Side, and violence often
ensued, but it involved hand-to-hand combat, knives, and tire
irons, not guns. The six reported gang-related deaths that
occurred in 1960 were considered astronomical. This relatively
mild (by today's standards) but still very damaging gang rivalry
stuff went on until 1965, when the Watts riots—a massive and
unified response to police brutality—exploded during the height
of the Civil Rights Movement. After the Watts riots, people in
gangs turned their imaginations to forming into resistance
groups. The black community in Los Angeles immersed itself
in political awareness, pride, new community resources, and
uncompromising resistance to white supremacist racism.

For the next five years, there was *no reported gang activity*.
No longer fighting the whites who attacked them, and no

longer fighting one another, people rose up together to face the social structure of white supremacist racism head-on.

Some say "Crip" was originally an acronym for Continuous Revolution in Progress. This was probably more of a catchy afterthought than an actual reality, but the political ideologies of resistance groups such as the Black Panthers informed the founders of the Crips.

Instead of continuing, the revolution in progress was co-opted and pillaged by white men in power, who used more systemic methods—such as taking away all of the jobs and replacing them with an illegal drug economy that maintains a self-sustaining system of autogenocide—than were used against past resistance organizations.

Crack cocaine assisted in creating the present framework of autogenocide that is now rampant in many ghettos and barrios in Amerikkka.

In *The Isis Papers*, Dr. Frances Cress Welsing discusses the connection between illegal drugs and the white man's fear of genetic annihilation:

White supremacy domination and oppression of all non-white people is essential for global white genetic survival. The prevention of white genetic annihilation is pursued through all means, including chemical and biological warfare. Today, the white genetic survival imperative, instead of using chemicals in

> gas chambers, is using chemicals on the streets—
> crack, crank, cocaine, ecstasy, PCP, heroin and
> methadone (all "designer chemicals"). Ultimately,
> these chemicals are produced by whites and made
> available through urban Blacks, particularly Black
> males—upon whom the future of Black people is
> dependent. The core dynamic of white genetic sur-
> vival eventually leads whites to major acts of geno-
> cide (destruction of the genes of non-white people),
> or toward *genocidal imperatives*.[7]

Here is a business scheme I thought of recently.

Say you want to provide weapons to various folks in the world whom you want to arm. Let's say these folks are Nica-raguan contras, who are fighting against the Sandinistas. The Sandinistas believe in stuff like nationalizing their country's resources, but you call this "communism" and everyone knows "communism" is from empires of evil. But see, you can't let all your shareholders *know* that you are arming anti-"communist" forces because they might want their invest-ment shares to go to other things, like education, welfare, healthcare, social services, and environmental protection. So you buy drugs from, oh, let's say, Colombia. Maybe you don't even actually *buy* the drugs. Maybe you do some kinda barter deal where you agree to train Colombian death squads at the School of the Americas. But whatever. Somehow or other, you get the drugs. Then you sell the drugs to people who will sell the drugs to people that you don't give a fuck about, like perhaps young people of color who might otherwise rise up against you because they certainly have in the past, and there's certainly no less reason for them to do so now. You also sell them semiautomatic weapons of mass destruction at rock-bottom wholesale prices.

For a song.

Once the drugs are sold, you use the money to buy weapons from ooo, I dunno, maybe Iran.

Then you arm your contras and have a happy day.

Meanwhile, you happen to have a lot of friends who want to get into the private prison business, and lord, there's some money to be made there, what with slave labor and all. You *could* take all the shareholder cash for building universities and instead build prisons for your friends to run.

Problem is, there's not enough criminals to fill all the prisons you have in mind.

This, however, can be worked out if you can rely on your media to fill people's heads with racist lies about the adversaries. Yes. It turns out you can count on your media, because you always, always have.

Now what you do is you make really harsh, totally unjust laws for people possessing the particular drug you are selling, but no other kind of drug.

This is a win-win business scheme from many vantage points:

- The drug you sell is a special kind of drug that makes

people paranoid, jittery, and in the long run, insane. By providing this drug to demographics that you collectively view as adversaries unworthy of regard in any manner, you seriously destabilize the entire population.

- Providing drugs for distribution and semiautomatic weapons to gangs who already war with one another does, indeed, amount to genocide. But it *appears* as a self-inflicted form of genocide in the media, which, with few exceptions, is just as racist as you are.

- The majority of shareholders are white people who just can't bring themselves to believe you would do something so evil because you are nice enough to them. They don't see that side of you because they won't see that side of themselves.

- Entire nations—which you view in the exact same way as you view the adversaries you sell the drugs to—are also destabilized, but on a larger scale. Instead of a slow trickle dying and being arrested every day, entire villages can be decimated with total impunity.

- You are in a great position. Everyone is fighting, you're making money (for you get a cut during every transaction), you're in power, and your adversaries are fighting each other at home and abroad.

This is just a rough overview, but not only do I think it could work, I think this business scheme could be applied in an endless array of contexts.

And you see how this flows?

It flows no matter who is in charge of the business. It flows into laws where if someone gets arrested, oh, like four—no, that's too many chances . . . say, if someone gets arrested three times, then they get put into a private corporate prison to do slave labor for the rest of their days on this earth.

Yes, it is *mean,* but it will be a constant source of share-holder income for the prisons, not to mention all the money to be made by "contracting" the prisoners to pave state roads, make airline reservations, and manufacture various goods.

No one will really complain, because the self-sustaining environment of autogenocide that you created is called "gang violence" and everyone knows what *that* means.

Well, enough of my harebrained business schemes, let's get back to reality.

Crack destroyed the lives and minds of thousands and thousands of young people who might have otherwise helped to organize and resist the out-of-control racism in this society. Hiphop artist, activist, and real estate investor Paris talks about the effects of crack in an article on his kickass website, Guerrilla Funk:

> The introduction of crack cocaine by the CIA into our
> communities during the 1980s made black youth gangs
> bigger and more dangerous than they had ever been

before. The illicit profits of drug trafficking provided, and continues to provide, vicious incentives for those of us without direction, immediate opportunity or hope to murder ourselves. In fact, much of the recent escalation in the murder rates can be directly traced to busted drug deals, competition over markets, disputes over turf and bruised egos.[8]

In 1998, Donna Warren sued the CIA for its role in bringing crack to and keeping crack in South Central Los Angeles. She lost her son to crack-related violence, and decided to fight back.[†] Ms. Warren's case was never brought to trial, even though the CIA admitted culpability in this matter.

The War on Drugs—a carefully plotted crime against humanity, much like the War on Terrorism—was designed to decimate and incarcerate communities of color, consuming barrios and ghettos indiscriminately. When you take away all the jobs and leave an illegal economy in their wake, everyone who works in the new, illegal economy is subject to arrest whenever it is convenient.

As a friend of mine who has worked in this illegal economy once told me, "It would be nice to have a job where I can assume I will come home from work every night without being shot at or arrested."

[†] She is still fighting. Most recently, she ran for political office with the Green Party.

✗

Norwin Meneses, one of the men who supplied drug dealers
with large quantities of cocaine, was in tight with the dictator of Nicaragua, Anastasio Somoza, who was overthrown by
the Sandinistas and assassinated by a poet, which is, in itself,
eternally poetic. Mr. Meneses was very well known to the FBI,
the CIA, the DEA, and every other federal crime organization
in the United States, yet there was no effort to keep him out of
this country after Somoza's ouster. If you think he wasn't a paid
employee of the CIA, you, my friend, are a **coincidence theorist** bar none.

Norwin Meneses supplied cocaine to Oscar Danilo
Blandón—another one of Somoza's pals, and also assuredly on
the payroll of the CIA. Mr. Blandón supplied cocaine to
"Freeway" Ricky Ross, the first ever crack dealer in South
Central. The Nicaraguans used the cocaine money to fund the
fledgling contras. That is, crack and cocaine users paid for
the movement to overthrow the nationalist Sandinista
government in Nicaragua. A government, I might add,
that opposed the usual U.S. policy of raping countries for
their resources.

In July 1979, a Republican congressman, Tennyson
Guyer, in his capacity as chairman of the cocaine task force
of the House Select Committee on Narcotics Abuse and Control, held a series of cocaine hearings in our nation's capital.
Amidst a majority of testimonies extolling the virtues of
coke, the classiness of coke, and the untouchable nature of

the *kind* of people who could afford to use coke,[†] Dr. Robert Byck, a drug researcher from Yale, testified. He talked about some of the things he learned at a conference in Lima, Peru, just two weeks prior.

Dr. Raul Jeri, a professor of clinical neurology at the National University of San Marcos, did a presentation at the Lima conference and had written numerous academic articles about a "new" kind of cocaine—known as paste—which came into existence somewhere around 1974. The most addictive drug ever known to civilization tore across Peru like chicken pox at a daycare center, and within two years had spread to Ecuador and Bolivia. Mr. Jeri had spent the previous five years studying the effects of paste—which was cocaine prepared as a smokable substance.

Some of Mr. Jeri's observations:

"When seen, these patients were generally very thin, unkempt, pale and looking suspiciously from one side to the other," Jeri wrote. "These movements were associated. . . . with visual hallucinations (shadows, light or human figures) which they observed in the temporal fields of vision."

Many of the patients bore scratches from trying

[†] Cocaine was outlawed in 1914. This came about at the behest of sheriffs in the South—and the ever-racist media of the U.S.—who linked black men on cocaine to the rape of the white man's prime biological real estate. Now that the drug was linked to wealthy white people, it seems the government was being pressured to ease up on cocaine laws.

to dig out the hallucinations that they felt crawling under their skin. . . .

"It is hard to believe to what extremes of social degradation these men [sic] may fall, especially those who were brilliant students, efficient professionals, or successful businessmen [sic]," he wrote. "These individuals became so dependent on the drug that they had practically no other interest in life."[9]

Nils Noya, a Bolivian psychiatrist, was amazed at how addictive paste was. Some people in his studies would gladly smoke sixty to eighty paste cigarettes in one sitting.

So our intrepid Dr. Byck was there at the cocaine hearing to send a red flare warning to the U.S. government. Paste was a form of cocaine that completely demoralized individuals, made them no longer functioning members of society, inspired them to care for nothing else in the whole wide world aside from where their next hit would come from, and eventually, caused irreparable brain damage.

The timing alone between this conference and when crack hit the streets of South Central Los Angeles gives a cynical person such as myself the impression that Dr. Byck's much-considered words were taken not as a grim warning, but, rather, as advice on how to make sure black people in the U.S. kept their asses in line.

No more worries about Watts riots and Civil Rights Movements if the community is dealing with a viciously addictive drug that makes otherwise intelligent human beings into manic zombies.

Ricky Ross didn't see the connection between his business and the U.S. government until he was serving life in prison and *San Jose Mercury News* journalist Gary Webb[†]—who was investigating Oscar Danilo Blandón for an article, which eventually led him back to the whole Iran-contra scandal—went to interview him.

Here's part of Webb's recounting of this exchange:

I spent hours with Ross at the Metropolitan Correctional Center. He knew nothing of Blandón's past, I discovered. He had no idea who the Contras were or whose side they were on. To him, Danilo was just a nice guy with a lot of cheap dope.

"What would you say if I were to tell you that he was working for the Contras, selling cocaine to help them buy weapons and supplies?" I asked.

Ross goggled. "And they put me in jail? I'd say that was some kind of fucked up shit there. They say I sold dope all over, but man, I *know* he done sold ten times more than me. Are you being straight with me?"

I told him I had documents to prove it. Ross just shook his head and looked away.

"He's been working for the government the whole damn time," he muttered.[10]

[†] Who "committed suicide" in December 2004. RIP.

Oh, lordisa, the sickness of this nation's soul is so grotesque, I really don't wonder at the phenomenon of living in denial. I set out to write this book because all my life, I have felt an acute Jekyll and Hyde misgiving about the culture I was raised in. But to see it, to look deep into it without flinching, without averting my eyes from the horror, this has irreparably taxed my belief in both monstrosity and humanity.

A friend of mine who was raised in South Central Los Angeles says, "You know, I probably would have been a lot like you if I grew up somewhere else." But I guess attending your five hundredth funeral before you reach the age of thirty kinda mars your ability to be affected by humanity's monstrosity. When my friend celebrates one of her homies' twenty-fifth birthdays, it is with deep sadness that she could be so happy that someone she loves has made it to such a ripe "old" age.

On numerous occasions throughout my friend's childhood and adolescence, she unloaded wooden crates of semiautomatic weapons. These crates were invariably stenciled with the words "U.S. Marine Corps" or "U.S. Army Corps."

How does it come to pass that U.S. military-issue weapons arrive in the hands of young people of color in South Central Los Angeles?

Lots of coincidence theorists seem to think that putting guns and uncannily addictive drugs that represent one of the only sources of viable income into the hands of young people who often have no hope for the future because the community has no resources to put behind them would not result in high death rates if *only* we were talking about whites.

White kids don't kill each other and go to jail all the time, so there must be something just inherently *wrong* with young people in ghettos and barrios. It's prolly something genetic that white kids don't have.

I know!

We're just a kinder and gentler people.

That's it.

The energy and momentum of young people of color resisting a white supremacist racist culture has been turned in upon itself, with the active guidance of police, the media, the criminal justice, entertainment, and economic systems, the CIA, and the U.S. government, along with an entire population of people who are willing to abide life with white supremacist racism unquestioningly lording it over our hearts.

At this point, all a newspaper article needs are the words "black," "gang," and/or "crack cocaine" in the same sentence for mainstream Amerikkkans to completely, unquestioningly sanction the death, beating, or incarceration of a young person.

And the result,

the outcome,

the reality,

is young people of color enacting autogenocide, being killed and brutalized by the police, and/or spending years of their lives in prison for crimes white kids get community service for.

I can't help but feel this is some kind of horrible mass retribution for the various triumphs that the Civil Rights Movement did manage to painstakingly glean from the U.S. government. Even more likely, however, the government just doesn't want anything like that to ever happen again, so youth are nipped when they are buds.

The chances of COINTELPRO not having anything to do with the final destruction of black resistance groups, as well as the formation of what are now deeply entrenched rivalries between gangs, are about as good as my ass not having anything to do with the shit I had a couple hours after dinner this evening.

In September of 2001, just before the World Trade Center attacks, representatives of the U.S. government *walked out* on the World Conference on Racism. Congresswoman Cynthia "For President" McKinney, however, didn't mind sticking around. She had a few things on her mind, and as it turns out, COINTELPRO tactics against the black U.S. population was one of them.

Ms. "For President" McKinney presented United Nations High Commissioner for Human Rights Mary Robinson with two documents to serve as evidence of the U.S. government's violation of not only U.S. law, but also the International Convention on the Elimination of Racial Discrimination.

The first document was written by National Security Advisor Zbigniew Brzezinski, dated March 17, 1978. Entitled "confidential memorandum 46," this document detailed how the federal government planned to destroy functioning black leadership in the United States. Memo 46 provided many insights into the government's abject terror of the influence black resistance and political movements and organizations might have on the hearts and minds of the population.

The second document, a report entitled "Human Rights in the United States [The Unfinished Story—Current Political Prisoners—Victims of COINTELPRO]," highlighted the U.S. government's extensive efforts, from the 1950s to the 1980s, to target political activists and organizations.

After presenting these documents, Ms. "For President" McKinney spoke on the crimes of the U.S. government:

> From as early as the 1950s and right up until the 1980s the U.S. government directed the machinery of state against the African American political movement and, in so doing, effectively put an end to the civil rights movement inspired by Dr. Martin Luther King. COINTELPRO was in clear violation of the U.S. Constitution and a wide range of U.S. laws, as well as in clear breach of internationally accepted standards for human rights and fundamental freedoms. That our government would turn its full resources against its own law-abiding citizens is unforgivable and ranks us among those rogue nations of the world who have chosen to kill hope and sow misery in its place.[11]

How might it be possible that a government willing to commit crimes against humanity to sunder a political resistance movement could have nothing to do with creating the self-sustaining framework for mass autogenocide that defines the present state of gang warfare dividing and conquering young people of color nationwide?

How many times have you read about someone dying in a gang-related death, wondered why "those kids" are so violent and fucked-up, sighed condescendingly, and turned the page?

"Those kids" are living in warfare, and negotiating many of the exact same realities as Palestinian children, who have also experienced the horror of warfare for entire generations.

"Killing hope and sowing misery" are two of the hallmarks of any form of warfare. So are funerals, police brutality, explosive incarceration rates, and drugs as one of the only viable economies. The byzantine origins of all of these hopeless and miserable realities have *never* been accurately reported, considered, or discussed in the media.

Rather, *COPS* blares in the laundromat when I am doing my wash. I ask the lady to change the channel and she kinda—but not quite—sneers, and asks why. "I don't enjoy watching black people being humiliated and brutalized by white cops. It seems like racist pornography to me," I say. She rolls her eyes, and says, "A perp's a perp, christ," as she smacks the remote button.

In awe at her comfort with police terminology, I turn to go back to my business.

Do I need to mention that the laundromat lady was not a black woman?

Probably not, but I will anyway because people of all races

make complex and incredibly unfortunate choices in order to survive in a white supremacist racist culture.

Some, however, are more aware than others that they *are* making every effort to survive in a white supremacist racist culture.

After the Rodney King riots, life insurance salespeople canvassed South Central Los Angeles, hawking policies to parents for their teenage sons. While this hopefully resulted in a number of life insurance salespeople getting their asses kicked, it is also evidence of the complete lack of respect and regard white society is willing to accept as some kind of "norm."

What are the chances of a life insurance company setting up canvassing operations in Littleton, "Colorado," after the Columbine massacre? Why would this appear "unconscionable" in a white neighborhood but perfectly acceptable in a black one?

I am reminded of something a Wall Street commodities trader said in the movie *The Corporation*:

"In devastation,
There is opportunity."[†]

In places densely populated by indigenous people and

---

† Carlton Brown said this. He was one of the only people of color featured in *The Corporation*. I found it poetic that it was a black man working in the white corporate world of capitalist economics who made, in my opinion, the most stark and direct statement in this film.

people of color, there is much devastation and many opportunities for the white man's economic system.

People in the U.S. thought of slavery as "normal" at one time.

Things have changed.

Slavery has taken on a different guise.

And to many, many people in my society, it still appears "normal."

Bruce A. Dixon, associate editor of the *Black Commentator*, points out another aspect of this normalcy:

Much as black Americans of two and three generations ago adjusted to pervasive segregation as a 'normal' condition of life, many in our communities have learned to treat the phenomenon of mass incarceration like we do the weather. It's hot in the summer, cold in the winter, and a third of the black males between 18 and 30 are in jails and prisons, on parole or probation. It's life. Get over it.[12]

Here are some mathematical insights from *Black Commentator* magazine:

Although it is true that few inmates are "political prisoners" in the narrow sense of the term, America's rise as the world's prison superpower was certainly the result of calculated political decision-making. "Mass

incarceration was the national response to the Civil
Rights and Black Power Movements, a white societal
reaction to Black intrusions onto white 'space,'" wrote
Black Commentator, March 18. "White society clearly
approves of the results: massively disproportionate
Black and Latino incarceration."

Since 1971, U.S. prisons and jails have grown ten-
fold—from less than 200,000 inmates to 2.1 million—
while whites have dwindled to only 30 percent of
the prison population. With only five percent of the
world's people, the U.S. accounts for 25 percent of
the planet's prisoners—fully half of them Black. One
out of eight prisoners on Earth is African American.
That's race politics with a vengeance.

The U.S. broke with historical patterns of
incarceration—a little over 100 prisoners per
100,000 population—in the mid-Seventies. Then,
with roughly equal fervor, Presidents Reagan, Bush,
Sr. and Clinton and each of the states methodically
assembled the world's largest Gulag. As the Justice
Policy Institute reported in 2001, the Black prison
population exploded.

"From 1980 to 1992, the African American incarceration rate increased by an average of 138.4 per
100,000 per year. Still, despite a more than doubling
of the African American incarceration rate in the 12
years prior to President Clinton's term in office, the
African American incarceration rate continued to

increase by an average rate of 100.4 per 100,000 per year. In total, between 1980 and 1999, the incarceration rate for African Americans more than tripled from 1156 per 100,000 to 3,620 per 100,000."

The Institute notes . . . "In 1986 and 1988, two federal sentencing laws were enacted that made the punishment for distributing crack cocaine 100 times greater than the punishment for powder cocaine." No, Black crack dealers and users are not "political prisoners"—but they are imprisoned for long stretches and in huge numbers for what are clearly political reasons.[13]

Just as the United States of Amerikkka does not admit that many of its prisoners are there for political reasons, it also does not admit that its prison system is inherently political. Not only does it create an entire class of people who are often no longer eligible to vote, but the location of prisons affects the electoral districts in this country, which are decided upon by population. When large numbers of people are in prison instead of in their communities, their political representation in the nation's capital decreases. Private prisons are often built within districts of white Republicans, thus increasing their population and representational power. A small town with twenty-five thousand inhabitants and a prison containing ten thousand people is thus considered a town of thirty-five thousand inhabitants.

Paul Street, an urban social policy researcher, wrote an

article entitled "Those People in That Prison Can't Vote Me Out:
The Political Consequences of Racist Felony Disenfranchisement," which provides more context:

> In a disturbing re-enactment of the notorious three-
> fifths clause of the US Constitution, whereby 60
> percent of the ante-bellum South's non-voting and un-
> free (slave) black population counted towards the con-
> gressional representation of Slave states, 21st century
> America's very disproportionately black and urban
> prisoners count towards the political apportionment
> (representation) accorded to predominantly white
> and rural communities that tend to host prisons in,
> say, "downstate" Illinois or "upstate" New York. Thus,
> if a Chicagoan like me takes a one-year position at
> Southern Illinois University in Carbondale but main-
> tains a residence on the predominantly black and
> Democratic South Side of Chicago, I still contribute
> to the likelihood that Chicago and the South Side will
> have a large number of state representatives and Con-
> gresspersons. But if I get arrested and then sentenced
> to 2 years in the Big Muddy correctional facility in
> very predominantly white far-southern Illinois, I'll
> count towards the political representation of whiter
> and more Republican Southern Illinois.[14]

Can you hear the echoes of slavery? In case it's still a little
fuzzy, maybe the people of "Oregon" can help you out.

※

In the May 1, 1998, issue of *Prison Legal News,* Dan Pens wrote
an article entitled "Oregon's Prison Slaveocracy." Mr. Pens
opened the article with a 1981 (just a year or two after crack
cocaine hit the streets of Los Angeles) quote from Reagan-era
Supreme Court Chief Justice Warren Burger:

> What I propose is, that as we embark on this mas-
> sive prison construction program, we try a new
> approach[:] convert our "warehouses" into factories
> with fences around them. To do that we must change
> our thinking and change the reactionary statutes that
> stand in the way. I believe the American people are
> ready to do that.[15]

By the time the1994 election rolled around, people in
"Oregon" were evidently ready to do that. Here is the ballot
wording of Measure 17, presented to the voting public:

> QUESTION. Shall constitution require state prison
> inmates to work or train 40 hours per week, (and)
> allow public (and) private sectors to use inmate work?[16]

Seventy-one percent of the population voted for Measure 17.
By 1995, it was *constitutionally mandatory* that people in prisons
work for private industry without compensation. Measure 17,
however, was so eagerly written—one can almost see the drool

stains that ended up splattering the finished version—it could not be enforced. Two problems stood in the way: First, there were not enough jobs or other qualifying activities for all prisoners in the system to work a forty-hour week; it also seems that "Oregon's" prisons were not originally set up to be "factories with fences." Second, federal law required that prisoners keep at least 20 percent of what they earn in order for the goods they produce to be sold across state lines. Under Measure 17, prisoners received nothing for their work.

So two years later, Measure 49 came on the ballot. It addressed Measure 17's weak points by further gutting the rights of prisoners.

Among the motivations behind both these measures was the desire to attract Nike factories back to the state. Proponents figured domestic prison slave labor might be more attractive than foreign sweatshop labor. This way, the state attracts industries (which fled after NAFTA passed) and makes money directly, and industry can produce all their goods for just one flat fee, without having to hassle about wages, healthcare, or other such bothersome things.

> "This is strictly about good business," says corrections administrator Larry Herring. "We're using their labor to get the highest possible return while they are incarcerated. . . ."
>
> There are some, like Oregon State Rep. Kevin Mannix, sponsor of both "get tough" ballot measures, who think the Oregon Department of Corrections can

offer a high enough return on investment and low enough labor costs to compete with any Third World sweatshop. Mannix is lobbying hard to lure Oregon-based Nike shoes to come back home.

"We propose that [Nike] take a look at their transportation costs and their labor costs," says Mannix. "We could offer [competitive] prison labor right here in Oregon."[17]

The "Oregon" public obviously agreed. Although the idea was framed differently and called something else, the population embraced Burger's "factories with fences" plan and passed Measure 49 with a staggering 91 percent approval.

"Oregon" is not alone in its embrace of prison labor. Across the country corporations employ the forced labor of prisoners. Among them are Lee Jeans, Boeing, Victoria's Secret, and Eddie Bauer. When natural disasters strike here in the U.S., if you look closely at the "rescue workers," you may notice that many of them are wearing orange jumpsuits.

I do not understand how a country can base its identity on freedom when so many of its people are not now, and have never been, free.

Reckoning

$\mathfrak{I}$ am thankful to Immortal Technique for writing one of the most beautiful quotes I have ever seen on the subject of freedom. In the liner notes for *Revolutionary 1*, he wrote:

If you were given freedom by the same people who
made you into a slave, then do you really know
what freedom is, and have you ever really experienced it at all?[1]

If we are given words, anecdotes, messages, and stories
about the U.S.'s historical role in the domestic and world theater
by the very people—and airport namesakes—whose self-interest
is best served by our unquestioning ignorance, then what do you
think they're inclined to say when they refer to our nation's past?

Besides lies, I mean.

If someone's *entire life* is invested in a lie, then that someone would be pretty committed to lying.

As the dearly cherished Ms. Arundhati Roy posits:

In the "free" market, free speech has become a commodity like everything else—justice, human rights,
drinking water, clean air. It's available only to those who
can afford it. And naturally, those who can afford it use
free speech to manufacture the kind of product, confect
the kind of public opinion, that best suits their purpose.[2]

Throughout the rise of western civilization, when liars in power
say someone is "evil," "a terrorist," "a communist," "a guerrilla,"
"a conspiracy theorist," or "an insurgent," that means the someone, somehow, poses a threat to the liar's lie.

When liars talk about "discovering," "exploring," "combating gang violence," "helping set up a free market," "liberating," "spreading freedom," or "creating democracy" somewhere, it generally means the place in question has a population that must be controlled, or resources the liar wants, or the people in the place are discussing the possibility of nationalizing their resources and cutting off some of the profits that Unocal, Dow, DuPont, Adidas, Disney, Coca-Cola, Microsoft, Halliburton, or General Electric are vampiring off of them.

I marvel at the hidden-in-plain-sight truths in the liars' terms, such as the "War on Terrorism" or "War on Terror." The Arbusto liars are terrorizing the U.S. economic and social structure and the world right now. They are, in fact, riding on a wave of terrorism that their lies have created and sustained. I see a truth in this by looking at their chosen phrase to incite patriotic terror in the U.S. population as *a description of their actions*.

In the Amerikkkan media, I read the words of these murderers (for I cannot stomach hearing their voices on the radio or teevee) from the vantage point that everything they say will be a lie that comes from a lie that comes from a lie that somehow got finagled into seeming like the truth.

In this kinda labyrinthine manner, one can develop a practice of discovering the inalienable truths in the lies of liars.

It is a fascinating pastime, 'cause their lies are at this point so deeply embedded in their hearts, the liars often come around full circle and end up inadvertently and unconsciously telling the stark, raving truth.

Autobiography of a Blue-Eyed Devil

❊

It is daunting to realize the enormity of lies we, as citizens of the United States, have accepted in our hearts, and I say this with careful consideration, for I am speaking to everyone who abides life in this culture. This cultural milieu does not, however, free white people into being somehow magically exempt from facing how we perpetuate white supremacist racism toward our fellow citizens every moment of our unconscious white lives. There is no sidestepping the reality that white people have cashed in on this horror for over five hundred years, that this country was founded on stolen land and constructed by the labor of an enslaved people who have never been spiritually, symbolically, or economically compensated.

Neither can we sidestep the reality that our collective willingness to accept what we are told about the real intentions of "progress," "globalization," and various military operations has led us to where we are right now, and right now, everything sucks.

It is really quite overwhelming to wrap one's mind around the fact that most everything we learn in school and from the media is complete and utter white supremacist racist bullshit. In order to begin accepting this, one must be willing to completely reeducate, which is a tall order. However, in light of the reality that most everyone in the world suffers because of our willingness to accept lies as truth, and we therefore continue to allow our corporate government to act with wanton impunity, I have little compassion for the difficulties one encounters when facing this shit head-on.

Mass ignorance kills, rapes, tortures, brutalizes, enslaves, incarcerates, diseases, and starves people of color and indigenous people at home and across the globe.

I don't believe this is some kind of situation where powerful liars sit around and decide how best to kill people of color in the world. I believe that most of these folks are moneyed white people, and they inherited a worldview from their parents and grandparents just like the rest of us. What, exactly, compels them to be racist fucks is open to conjecture, but there is no denying the fact that the moneyed class, which has such a huge influence on the worldview of everyone else in my country, are, indeed, racist fucks.

I may have developed a mild crush on Harry Belafonte. In his interview with *Yes! Magazine,* Sarah Ruth van Gelder asked if he saw any opportunities arising from the World Trade Center attacks. Mr. Belafonte's thoughts on this ring deep and true into my heart:

> Not since the early days of the civil rights movement
> has America been given an opportunity as great as
> the opportunity we have now. It's one thing for us to
> avenge our pain, our anger, and our rage by targeting
> bin Laden and a handful of men who have wrought
> this villainy. But one should be wise enough to ask,
> What fueled all this? What continues to sustain the
> possibility that this will not go away? I think the
> answer is poverty.

Dr. King once said that when we reach this kind of crisis, this kind of terror experience, that we should stop long enough to look at ourselves through the eyes of our detractors and find what wisdom we can glean from understanding how we have directly contributed to that tyranny. What have we done to humanity that brings us to this place of inhumanity? Terrorism is in many, many ways the final utterance of voices unheard.

We have the opportunity now to look at the two billion people in the world who suffer from the most abject poverty, hunger, disease, and devastation. Add to that another two billion people who are just plain poor. If you look into the world of those caught in economic oppression, illiteracy, disease, and sexism, then you'll understand more clearly what we have to do.

The problem has always knocked at the door; we've just never been attentive. And I think now, with our technology, our capacity to grow food, our ability to stop raping the Earth and destroying the ecology and killing off fellow creatures, we have a chance to bring a new harmony and a new path to human development.

America can no longer afford to be as arrogant as we've been. We can no longer exempt ourselves from the global family of concern. We can no longer exempt ourselves from conferences on racism like the conference in Durban that we walked out on, or concerns about trade, or global warming.

So this is a great opportunity to take a good, hard look at these things. Because now we're more vulnerable than we've ever been. The only thing that can put that to rest forever is to abolish poverty. To eradicate preventable diseases. First and foremost to get rid of ignorance.[3]

We live in a time when the crimes against humanity that have taken place for the past five hundred years are coming home to roost. We can choose to ignore this and continue to live in denial. In order to do this successfully, we must wrap our lives in Amerikkkan flags, accept arguments that are framed by the U.S. government, and swallow every single lie espoused in the media and the history books. Our imaginations must also remain completely colonized.

We can make that choice.

Or we can choose to face the past, present, and future, and take an active part in the reckoning that is happening, regardless of which choices we make.

Part 2 Branches of Oppression

If you do not understand White Supremacy (Racism)—what it is, and how it works—everything else that you understand will only confuse you.

—Neely Fuller,
*The United-Independent Compensatory Code/
System/Concept*

Introduction to Part 2

It's so big, this thing.

It's bigger than I can really say.

How's a crow tell what the sky is to her and her clan—her "murder," we call it,

in a sundry manifestation

of our terror

of magnificent sentinels

of holysacred things.

Autobiography of a Blue-Eyed Devil

How do you describe the sky when it is an inseparable, fundamental part of your existence. You don't say "blue" when there are sixty-eight billion different blues in your world, and you don't say "gray" for the same reason. You don't think about "high" and "low," because these things are matters of constantly shifting relativity. And you know, when the wind determines how you move your body on any given day, in any given moment, you undoubtedly experience it as an extension of yourself.

And so on.

There are two places:

a.) the environment you are born into, which varies enormously, depending on who constructed it, and why and how.

b.) the world, of which there is only one, though it exists in millions of fractalized continuums.

Crows are born into this world.

I was not.

I was born into an environment of white supremacist racism, imperialism, and male domination.

It is what I have experienced all my life. The big difference between my environment and the crow's sky is my environment was not created by god, in all her wisdom. Or maybe it was and I'm just not smart enough to discern the divine purpose of five hundred plus years of systematic geno-, femi-, and ecocide in the Americas, on top of multiple millennia of similar horrors occurring in most every culture on the planet.

Racism-as-environment *certainly appears* to have been constructed by wealthy white men who have seemingly unlimited access to:

- money and grandfathers
- history's presentation
- (via) literature, music, art, science, math, media, and eventually, film, telecommunications, and computers
- the inevitably high-ceilinged rooms of commerce, legislation, and war

My environment was painstakingly constructed by conquistadors, explorers, slave traders, imperialists, bible writers, capitalists, strikebreakers, Puritans 'n' Christians, military heroes, politicians, Jesus hijackers, blockbuster movie producers, ad cats, CEOs, masters and slaves, hunters and prey, victors and victims, and one mustn't forget the endless variety of civic propagandists, coincidence theorists, and yes-nancies who toe this massive, massive line of historic and contemporary oppression.

But this book isn't just about white supremacist racism and imperialism.

It is about the choices we make in this environment.

Many of the biggest choices we make are directly influenced by white supremacist racism and imperialism.

This is a big distinction.

Most people in the U.S. support economic slavery by unquestioningly giving their money to corporations that fully suck the lifeblood out of entire demographics in Mexico, El Salvador, Vietnam, Haiti, India, China, and many other countries where whites don't much factor into the head count.

People from all ethnicities, races, religions, genders, and classes freely give their money—their own lifeblood—to these suckers.

There are many ways to procure goods in satisfying ways that do not require money. Knowing this, however, requires a shift in perspective, a slight—yet crucial—movement into the world, utilizing the vastly underestimated biological gift that can never truly be taken away from anyone: *the glorious human imagination*. Admitting that your imagination has been colonized and then doing something about it is by no means an easy thing to do, but it is very much a thing that can be done, no matter how little economic latitude you may have.

If you shop at Wal-Mart, you are giving your money to full-on Arbusto-supporting right-wing activists who treat their employees like total shit and buy their goods from plantation-states who "employ" economic slaves. If you pay federal taxes, you are funding the brutal occupations in Iraq and Afghanistan. If you eat Domino's pizza, you are giving money to right-wing

antichoice activists who also fully support the Arbusto administration. All of their ingredients come from big agribusiness corporations that make fake tomatoes and hormone-infused sausage.

If I were on *Fear Factor* and they said I had to eat one slice
of Domino's pizza, I would enthusiastically skip down their
walk of shame.

There's also the rather large problem with how we think
plants and animals are "lower" life forms, to be used by us, the
fittest. And then there are the widespread and varied retardations
of how men view women; how people view "god," diff-abled folks,
and homos; how women view ourselves and allow men to rule our
lives and the lives of our babies, which also results in a smorgas-
bord of—often highly manipulative—pathologies; how gender is
policed with hatred and fear; how young folks treat old ones; and
how pretty much everyone somehow magically forgets the complexities and pain of childhood, and consequently underestimates
and refuses to see the innate wisdom of children and teenagers.

So, no.

This isn't just about white supremacist racism and imperialism, but these two things live deep in the hearts of everyone
who was raised in this environment, and detrimentally affect
our lives, destinies, and worldviews.

In my experience, once we can open ourselves up to our
own learned racist, imperialist tendencies and/or responses,
all the other unconscious choices we make start getting caught
in the light.

꒰

Autobiography of a Blue-Eyed Devil

And now it is time for a poetic interlude with your effervescent hostess, whose imagination does not compel her to shell out wads of cash every time a need or desire for something arises in her life:

Somewhere, Someone Can Hook You Up
By Inga La Gringa

If you're gonna eat meat, then raise chickens.
If you can't raise chickens, then have a chicken co-op with someone
    who has the space. If you don't know anyone who has the space,
    put up flyers or advertise online and find them.
Somewhere,
someone
can hook you up.
Knit winter wear and sew clothes for the kids in your neighborhood.
Exchange this for music lessons for your children, for help putting in
    a garden, for expertise on canning.
Do manicures and style hair.
Exchange this for new interior decor.
Fix cars or broken appliances.
Exchange this for help with your taxes.
Teach young people the history you have lived.
Exchange this for new slang words.
Offer self-defense classes in the park.
Exchange this for help fixing up your house.
Counsel someone with their finances.

Exchange this for a gorgeous eight-tiered wedding cake for your sister.
Make a website.
Exchange this for childcare.
Mentor someone with your chess skills.
Exchange this for poker expertise.
Paint someone's front porch/stoop.
Exchange this for a year's worth of homemade candles.
Make sure all the kids in your neighborhood know how to swim.
Exchange this for the love and gratitude of parents who cannot
*   afford swim lessons for their children.*
Somewhere,
someone
can hook you up.

In the interest of survival, I have found it necessary to step
into the world, outside of this environment. On bad days,
when new, improved racist human-rights abuses are passed
into laws, when a lynching is palmed off as a suicide, when my
email inbox (but not the newspapers) fills up with word that
the Shenandoah family and other Oneida wolf clan mothers
are under siege again, when the Navy presses on with its sonar
that is exploding the brains of dolphins and whales, when
years of a young black man's life are stolen by police who set
him up in a sting operation with a bike, *a fucken unlocked bike
left on the street corner,* I say:

> "This is an environment, it is not the world."
> I say this over and over and over.

Maybe it is a chant, maybe it is a prayer.

"This is an environment, it is not the world. This is an environment, it is not the world."

It is an environment that is *threatening* the world, yes, but when choosing life in these dark times, razor-thin distinctions are often the only viable solace.

This particular razor-thin distinction means that I have choices in the face of seemingly unopposable power.

If I open myself up to this world, this world opens itself up to me.

If I base all my thoughts, beliefs, and perceptions on the environment I was born into, cultural constructs will dictate my life and destiny.

This is a choice.

Here is story about choices:

Once upon a time, Nazi Bob led a gang of mean skinheads that you steered clear of if you knew what was good for you.

Boys like Nazi Bob hated girls like me—little bleeding heart punk rock race traitors who probably "sucked off beaners and niggers" when we weren't too busy "munching carpet."

I steered clear of Nazi Bob good as gold.

One night my friends 'n' me went to an all-ages dance joint. When the club closed, all the kids from inside stood outside, smoking cigarettes and cloves and laughing. I was sitting on a bench, watching everyone.

It was quiet and nice.

Suddenly, the air seized in and up, upon itself.

One moment, you have here the vivacious hum of kids visiting pleasantly, and in the next heartbeat, tension charged the air sphincter tight. The awful, awful sound of human bone hitting plate glass filled the world.

Forty feet away from me, a shop windowpane shattered and people scattered like they too were shards of glass. I stood up on the bench I'd been sitting on to see what was happening. Nazi Bob and all his buddies were kicking the living shit out of this older Rasta guy who was known for minding his own mellow beeswax and playing a wicked sax.

An earsplitting scream came up into my throat and got caught there because terror clapped a fist over my esophagus.

Choked.

The scream wouldn't come out.

I looked around for my friends.

All was confusion, everyone was running.

Why weren't we a group of kids who armed ourselves with rocks and bricks and attacked the skinheads en masse? We outnumbered them seven to one, easy. Everyone knew this was wrong. Everyone knew someone was being hurt in a grisly, totally fucked-up manner.

Our reaction—our choice—was to flee.

We chose fear.

It was a fear rooted in the grim reality of living in an

environment where if Nazi Bob wanted to find out where you lived or worked, he undoubtedly could and, indeed, would. If you were a woman, and a gang rape wasn't the plan for you, then there was an auxiliary group of skinhead girls who would beat the living shit out of you. Seven of these girls had cornered me in the bathroom of this same club just a few weeks prior, and the only thing that saved my ass was an irrational tendency to go psychotically ballistic when cornered. This reaction bought me the split seconds I needed to career out of the bathroom.

Nazi Bob was not afraid to hurt people, or to see to it that people were hurt.

It had been proven time and again.

I was not exempt from this fear, and it hit me like the ton of bricks we did not throw—*I was too scared to think of anything irrational or ballistic to help this man.* A chick whose boyfriend's name is "Reuben" asking eight skinheads to stop beating a black man equaled severe retaliation. Hell, even if my boyfriend's name were "Tom Metzger," I woulda gotten my ass kicked.

If not then, later.

In my concept of time—as opposed to the mellow Rasta gentleman's—it was over very quickly.

I stood there, a slack-jaw dumbass, until the sounds of sirens arrived and the skinhead boys bolted. Then paramedics and four (white, legendarily racist) policemen were there.

The tight-ass air slumped in on itself.

I was still standing on the bench, staring into nothingness, when one of my friends came and got me. I didn't do *squat* to help that man. The sound of his body breaking the store window has never left my heart.

He is black, and so he took that beating, got steel-toe kicked within inches of his life. He is black, so he knew the feeling of all those boots hitting his flesh.

I am white, so I had the choice to keep attention away from myself. The scream got caught in my throat. My skin color and fear camouflaged me into the background.

Nazi Bob *might* have regarded me if I *provided* a stimulus, but I did not choose to do this. I don't know the feeling of Nazi Bob's steel-toed boot in my face because I had a choice.

I chose to do nothing.

The Rasta dude did not have that choice or any other.

As an adult thinking back on that night, I see how the dynamics of one single human being's ignorance and fear swirled up into a tornado of violence that nearly destroyed another single human being's sacred and glorious life.

Yet, wishing I had a different, superhero reaction that saved the Rasta gentleman from being hurt does not alter the reality that he was hurt in a horrible manner. Feeling guilty about myself for standing on that bench like a fool does not magically disappear the Rasta gentleman's lacerations, internal wounds, scars, and memories. Nothing, in fact, changes the inescapable reality that I live in an environment with skinheads who terrorize people, or that I was too afraid to think of finding a big rock, and beaning Nazi Bob in the head with it.

From that moment on, however, it has been impossible for me to remain unconscious of the luxury and power of choices.

Making unconsidered choices throughout one's life contributes to the collective perception that a constructed environment is the world.

A woman named Jhaleh once told me a story that also helped me to understand the power and luxury of choices.

One time, Jhaleh took a woman visiting from Uzbekistan to the grocery store, just a few hours after the woman had arrived in the U.S. Their first stop was the pet food aisle. Jhaleh made her selections, and headed toward the dairy section, but the Uzbek woman stood rooted in the middle of the aisle, staring, mouth open, eyes agog.

Suddenly perceiving the incomprehensible plenitude of a U.S. grocery store to this woman from Uzbekistan, Jhaleh realized it would be overwhelming for her to witness the endless aisles of opulence. Entranced, the woman nodded when Jhaleh told her to stay right there while she finished up her shopping. She quickly got the items she needed, and made her way back to the pet food aisle. The woman was still standing in the exact same spot, scanning the shelves slowly. Jhaleh asked her if she was all right and the woman, never tearing her gaze from the wall of Meow Mix, Fancy Feast, and Kitten Chow, replied, "I want to be an American kitty."

This sentence comes to me often.

It flits through my head when I turn on a faucet and water comes out, when I flick a dial and heat pours through the vents in my home, when I go to thrift stores and find brand-new clothes and blankets, when I walk down the street and see flowers and trees and birds and butterflies instead of tanks, rubble, the severed limbs of dead people, or yellow-taped areas filled with crime scene investigators and coroners' vans.

I could make the choice to believe that the USA is the land of abundance and freedom, and that the people who live here are inherently better at flourishing and thriving than people in poor countries. This choice, of course, would require that I also choose to remain completely ignorant of the realities of people in ghettos, barrios, prisons, the sex work industry, and rural coal mining/farming/logging towns, and on reservations here in the USA.

Or I could make the choice to believe that the victors of history's present telling have constructed a self-sustaining environment, which they present as the world, that is easily palmed off on a population whose imaginations have been colonized ever since the bible, U.S. history, and Hollywood were allowed to define what is considered to be sacred, celebratory, and beautiful.

I tried the first choice when I was younger, and I never met much success with it, largely because it bored me to tears.

The second choice, however, serves me well.

It inspires me to seek knowledge, to listen closely, to imagine, and to dream of existing in an environment that is an engaged aspect of the world.

The world is beautiful.

The more I see this, the more the world shows itself to me, and the more I see this.

Here are some beautiful things I've noticed in the little tiny itsy bitsy part of the world that I have seen so far today:

- The iridescent sparkle of morning dew on a blade of grass that splashed to the earth when a swallow's low-flying wings jarred the stillness.
- The way swallows always start showing off and doing devil-may-care loop-dee-loops the second they notice that they have an audience.
- The caring smile of an old woman who saw me stumble on a crack in the sidewalk.
- The vegan pumpkin stew that my dear carnivore friends Ariel and Maria made last night with me in mind.
- The four-year-old nephew, hollering to his poop, "Bye-bye! See ya tomorrow!" every time he flushes the toilet.
- The lavender, the rosemary, the roses.
- The distant sound of traffic, moshing with the wind and sounding exactly like the ocean on a semiangry afternoon.
- The neighbor's chicken that escapes from the pen almost

every day and no one can figure out how. It is a magic chicken, or maybe a very crafty tunnel-boring chicken.

No environment can take away the billions and billions of beautiful things that compose this endlessly complex world.

Making the choice to be present in the world offers me the wherewithal to thrive in the ugly, mean-spirited, fearful, pathologically racist, homophobic, sexist, ableist, classist, ageist, two-gendered human supremacist environment I live in.

I've learned to practice seeing the powerful force of the world. It is the goddess, Bre'r Rabbit, the Matrix, the hobbit with the golden ring, the fruit on the tree of knowledge, the Holy Grail, the thundering down under rumbling deep inside a volcano. It is much, much stronger than any man-made environment, but it is difficult to believe this when you don't learn to step out of this environment and into it.

It is beautiful, the world.

Do not get me wrong.

No one's being a Pollyanna over here.

The world is also a horrifying place. It contains many environments filled with racism, pain, and brutal death. Hunger, rape, and poverty. Stolen lives, stolen land, and stolen stories from the past. Meanwhile, entire populations learn to rationalize and sanction all this horror by keeping the collective gaze averted.

Autobiography of a Blue-Eyed Devil

To be present in the world is to also live with these realities upon your heart, and to closely examine the environment you were born into, and every repercussion of white supremacist racism and imperialism that your perception can seize upon, all together, as one.

In the world, all the horror is one.

Like seemingly everything else, the horror of the world is reflected into endless demographics in endless contexts. It's still all one horrendous horror, with the velocity of manufactured history and consent hurling it into every curvature of the global marketplace.

And there are many, many choices involved with how a person might negotiate one's life in the midst of all this horror.

An acquaintance and I were talking about this just the other day. He was telling me that he hunkers down into his daily life scheme of things because he cannot deal with all the horror in this world. I told him that I cannot live like that. He thought I was full of shit. "You can't take in all that stuff," he insisted. "It will drive you insane."

But I disagreed. I hear this sentiment often, in a variety of forms.

Your average pissed-off citizen in the U.S. is willing to fight for three or four "causes," maybe, but the line's gotta be drawn somewhere.

When you're present in the world you don't just see one or the other. The horror and beauty go hand in hand. Even as this environment breaks your heart, the world fuels, protects, instructs, inspires, guides, and gently humors you.

So things balance out.

That conversation reminded me of a story I'd heard just a few days prior. I believe it comes from the Cherokee nation, but is told around many peoples' sacred fires:

> An old Grandfather said to his grandson, who came to him with anger at a friend who had done him an injustice. . . .
>
> "Let me tell you a story. I too, at times, have felt great hate for those who have taken so much, with no sorrow for what they do. But hate wears you down, and does not hurt your enemy. It's like taking poison and wishing your enemy would die."
>
> "I have struggled with these feelings many times. It is as if there are two wolves inside me; one is good and does no harm. He lives in harmony with all around him and does not take offense when no offense was intended. He will only fight when it is right to do so, and in the right way.
>
> But . . . the other wolf . . . ah! The littlest thing will send him into a fit of temper. He fights every-one, all of the time, for no reason. He cannot think because his anger and hate are so great. It is helpless anger, for his anger will change nothing."

"Sometimes it is hard to live with these two wolves inside me, for both of them try to dominate my spirit."

The boy looked intently into his Grandfather's eyes and asked, "Which one wins, Grandfather?"

The Grandfather smiled and quietly said, "The one I feed."[1]

To be present in the world, it is also important to shake your butt to the beat of sirens and car alarms. And, obviously, always dance while a sound system on wheels passes you by.

If you look at something, like a low-limbed old oak tree or a ladder leading up to an easily recontextualized billboard, and you think, "Gee, it would be so easy to climb up there," and you then do NOT climb up there, you are not being present in the world.

The thing that tells you to climb up there is your body in the world.

The thing that tells you that's a ridiculous and dangerous thing to do is your mind in the environment.

Climb up there.

My job has been to spend six years arranging a lot of words in such a way that they might speak with honor and respect to the people who take time out of their lives to read my book. I have learned that it is deeply humbling to know that a person spends many hours with my words—which is partly why I spend so much time arranging them.

The trouble with this book is I know that many people reading it experience the detrimental effects of living in a white supremacist and imperialist environment a fuck of a lot more than I ever will. And too, I know many people reading this book will have never in their life stopped to consider how white supremacist racism and imperialism affects every facet of their existence. Moreover, I know that the vast majority of people reading this book will have experiences all over the vast universe of In Between.

In light of this, I have three offerings.

Offering #1: Defensiveness, guilt, blame, denial, resentment, anger, jealousy, bitterness, mean-spiritedness, and the need to compete all feed the fucked-up wolf inside you.

Offering #2: Compassion, listening, accountability, patience, courage, open-mindedness, focus, imagination, creativity, and the desire to cooperate all feed the cool wolf inside you.

Offering #3: On my website, www.ingalagringa.com, there is the Imagination Reclamation Resource Guide, lovingly compiled by the brilliant valkyrie writer Mel Kozakiewicz and your effervescent hostess Inga La Gringa.

It is difficult to write about this environment while living in the midst of it.

I suspect it could be difficult to read about it too.

I thank you for taking the time.

Tiptoeing around Noah's Big Drunk Ass

𝕴 was not raised with organized religion. My mother is a witchy, indifferent Irish Catholic, and I probably would have been instructed in Vague Catholicism if my father had been of a similar mind. He, however, vociferously opposed organized religion of any kind. Since Mom wasn't invested enough to argue the point, I got my ideas about god and religion mostly from my weird parents, the earth, and the sky. Throw into this mix Grammy, Aunt Genie, and Uncle Bruce, who insisted my cousins, my siblings, and I fully apprehend the sentience of every being. Whether we were plunging down waterfalls, fishing for crawdads, or picking berries in the woods, my family made the rule of absolute respect for all living beings very clear.

Not to sound like some rainbow child—which I guess, alas, I always will to people who jauntily abide life in a violently white supremacist, racist, woman-earth-transgender-and-queer-hating culture. If a kid does not have organized religion shoved down her throat, it's likely she'll turn to her world for spiritual teachings. I suspect a deep awareness of the world is, if encouraged, an organic occurrence.

My childhood world was, by and large, the central coast of "California."

Most of my earliest lessons about power, respect, the passage of time, change, miracles, and the infinite wonder of being alive came from the times I spent at beaches stretching from Point Sal, to the south, up to Port San Luis.

This part of the "California" coast has, up to the recent past, largely been left alone. It is hours away from both Los Angeles and San Francisco, with no major airports or tourist attractions. Interstate 5, the fastest, most convenient freeway, was laid down a couple hours to the east. There are more and more corporate hotels opening in Pismo Beach and the people of Cambria have been valiantly and relentlessly fighting against William Randolph Hearst's descendents, who want to erect a huge resort 'n' golf course right on a cliff overlooking an otherwise pristine coastline. Since Arbusto came into power, more and more oil rigs have sprung up on the horizon, and in 2003 a gigantic refinery appeared seemingly overnight *right on the beach* in Mariposa Reina.

On the whole, however, when I was a kid, there wasn't much shakin' on the central coast of "California."

In the dunes I learned the earth could swallow me up in one chew, like a blueberry. But I also learned that when I paid attention to the world around me and watched where the sun was, I could keep from being swallowed up by the dunes, and heedlessly romp in them for hours.

In the caves in the cliffs I listened to ocean opera in total surround sound, the arias of the earth pounding into my heart and salts misting in my nose.

The tide pools, in their endless drama, showed me how many worlds there are. Millions and millions of worlds inside this one.

One time, my dad took my siblings and me to the beach during a huge storm, and we stood on the cliffs, watching the waves take huge bites out of craggy rock walls. Chomp, chomp, chomp, and entire segments of cliff were gone.

This display of power staggered my mind.

The ocean almost killed me once, but it was just messin' around. It wanted to be sure I knew who was boss. I was seven and listened very, very carefully when a huge wave I was trying to dive under crashed right into the small of my back and at first kinked me into a V-shape, and then *churned* me into the white foaming mass of chaos. The ocean slammed me to the sandy floor and sucked me back up over and over, only to jettison me like a wet sock onto the shore at the very instant that my brain said, "Okay. For reals. Air now or truly no more thinking."

I landed belly down, spread-eagled on the sand, water spurting out most of my orifices, gasping for air, totally spent and laughing.

This wasn't a "frightening" experience.

It was exhilarating and life-affirming. I knew and trusted the ocean. At that point in my life, we had shared many intimate and wonderful moments together. The ocean is a goddamn backslapping jokester with a sense of humor as big as it is. This wasn't the first (or last) time it gave me a good ribbing. Throughout the whole ordeal, my body was completely relaxed, and it *felt so superlatively good* to be an inseparable part of the infinite mass of power that the ocean is—regardless of the fact that I had no breath to augment the experience. While my life or death was up to it, I was fully cognizant that it was just havin' its idea of a little fun.

Lettin' me know who's who in the grand scheme.

But still, this isn't the kind of fun one, uh, *seeks out*.

If I had chosen fear instead of awe, if my body had been tense instead of relaxed, if a deep respect for the ocean hadn't been instilled in me since the day I was born, my mom never woulda put eight candles on a birthday cake for me.

As I lay on the sand laughing and gasping, I knew all that too.

I have never forgotten this feeling of being totally at the mercy of an infinitely stronger force, where my actions and choices nonetheless influence my destiny. That experience has helped me to contextualize myself in this life countless times, and in fact is probably one of the forces driving this book.

Tiptoeing around Noah's Big Drunk Ass

It was, verily, a hands-on religious experience. Punk rock baptism in the name of my life.

So, you know, don't talk to a child about some old white man named god sitting on a throne in a castle in the sky and don't talk to a child about some bright red guy named satan sitting on a throne in the fiery center of the earth when she has already met the ocean face to face.

Or, at least, you can talk to her, but she will not be able to attribute any meaning to your words.

Rainbow child, my ass.

When I got to be an adult, the religions people organize—as opposed to the fully relative, universal, organically occurring one that's divined from living life in this world—made little sense to me.

To this day, I do not understand the concept that Jesus died on the cross for my sins. It has been explained to me by many people, and I am still unable to wrap my mind around this tenet.

Jesus lived in a culture that thought it was a good idea to *nail people to wooden crosses* for punishment. Doesn't this strike you as a pretty grotesque way of controlling a population? What was going on in the culture that *dreamed up* this form of punishment?

With all the "Jesus-loving" going on in my country, I have a difficult time understanding how people don't see that the culture we abide life in conjures up no less grotesque means of control.

I mean, I have learned a lot about Jesus and I think he was a truly wonderful person. I love Jesus like I love everyone who is all about love. So if all these alleged Jesus-lovers in my country *really* love Jesus, then how come they don't notice that they abide life in a culture eerily similar to the one that decided it was a good idea to nail him to a wooden cross in the first place?

I mean, do y'all think Jesus *enjoyed* that shit?

To this day, it confounds the brain that threatened to quit when I was seven.

In my life, I have met two True Christians. One is a woman aptly named Harmony Glover, and to the day she passed on from old age, Jesus inspired her to unconditionally love every living being she came into contact with.

The other is my friend Riz Rollins, who is also inspired to love in this way. He went to theology school to become an evangelical minister, but he dropped out because organized religion started seeming like a crock of shit to him.

I thank both of them because they have taken the time to teach me about the dominant religion in my culture.

It was Riz who first told me about Ham. Or more specifically, Riz told me about his grandmother's relationship with the story of Ham.

According to this interpretation, Ham is the biblical justification for slavery. He defied and "brought shame" upon his father, Noah—the ark guy. There-ever-after, all of Ham's children were to have "dark" skin and were to be subservient to the children of Ham's two older brothers—Shem and Japheth—who "stayed" white.

That's why white people get to kill, enslave, brutalize, incarcerate, impoverish, and rape everyone else. Because thousands of years ago, Ham allegedly fucked up.

End of story.

To Riz's grandmother the myriad injustices of being black in Amerikkka are *Just the Way It Is*.

Lay low, swing low, whatever it takes.

Just keep the fuck out of white folks' way.

And I wonder from whose white mouth Riz's grandmother's mother's grandmother's mother first heard this story, because she sure as motherfuckall did not hear it from her grandmother in Africa.

When I read Derrick Jensen's *The Culture of Make Believe*, I saw another aspect of the Ham Reality. Mr. Jensen was raised with religion, and the Ham story never sat well with him. Here's his rendition of what Ham did "wrong":

Noah got drunk and passed out naked in his tent.
Ham came in, saw "the nakedness of his father," and
went outside to tell his brothers. His brothers picked

up a garment, walked backward into the tent, covered their father, and made their way out, the whole time keeping eyes averted from the sight of Noah's naked body.[1]

What a couple of brownnosers they were, huh.

This Ham story actually cracked me up a lot, because my dad refused to wear clothes at home. In my father's mind "home" extended to the front yard, where he would retrieve the morning paper. All family, friends, neighbors, mail deliverers, and meter reader types had the opportunity to see the nakedness of my father pretty much every day.

It was a source of great embarrassment, especially if one of us couldn't beat him to the door when someone knocked.

Conversely, it is also why, when the policeman who lived around the corner invited a neighbor friend and me into his home while his family was gone, and chased us around the house and then wagged his ugly pink dick through the bathroom door at us, I suffered no feelings of confusion.

This action was straight up, totally wrong and fucked.

My naked dad never pulled any bullshit like that. He did regular stuff like read the paper, drone on and on about what chores we should be doing, and remain steadfastly unmoved by our dire need for sugar-sweetened cereals.

Because of the well-known nakedness of my father, I slammed the bathroom door on the cop neighbor's dick.

He howled like an evil demon trapped in goodness and crumpled to the bathroom floor. My friend was horrified at what I had done to a grownup and would not leave his house with me, as if perhaps I were the problem.

Obviously, her father wore clothes at home.

I was only a kid, like I say, and it is a pretty sound assumption that I didn't know much at that point. Still, there was no question in my mind about whether or not grown men were supposed to wag their dicks at little kids. I saw the policeman in a *much* different nakedness than the nakedness of my father.

These instances were not, in fact, the only nakedness or the only dick-wagging that I witnessed as a child. Dad's beach of choice was Pirate's Cove, the nudie beach. My cousin, Dawn, my best friend, Hannah, and I spent many an hour with stomach-aches from laughing at the dicks 'n' balls flopping around when the men played frisbee down by the water.

It was a form of entertainment, like poking our fingers into the center of sea anemones. After a good swim, one might say, "Hey, let's eat grapes and watch the frisbee dicks!"

What *fun* that was.

It is horrifying and hilarious to look at this.

My father's open, literal nakedness caused problems with our neighbors, visiting Jehovah's Witnesses, the papergirl, most of our friends, and their parents. The policeman's unseen and perverted nakedness was really just fine and dandy with all and sundry.

Many parents probably even felt "safer" knowing a cop lived nearby.

Fuck, man, I wouldn't be surprised if a few of our neighbors took their complaints about my dad's nakedness directly to the wag-his-dick-at-little-girls cop around the block.

He was a respected member of the community.

My pot-smoking, atheist, hippie father absolutely was not.

Derrick Jensen spent a lot of time thinking about the Ham story, and it wasn't until he was a totally grown-up adult that he finally put together what, exactly, Ham did wrong:

> I now understand that it's not so important to this story what happened—if it happened at all— thousands of years ago in what has since become a godforsaken desert. What's more important is the lesson that can be pulled from this cautionary tale, which is that in order for a system of domination to be maintained (remember, Noah had the power and will to enslave one of his sons and all of that son's descendants to his two others and theirs) rigid protocols must be maintained, which include first and foremost that one must never see those in power as they are—in this case, naked—nor especially to perceive them as vulnerable—in this case, passed out.

To see them at the same time naked and vulnerable
is to find oneself no longer susceptible to any power
of theirs *save physical force*.[2]

Growing up as a white child in the post–Civil Rights Movement USA, I was encouraged to believe certain things about the
police:

- They got robbers, murderers, and other "bad guys."
- They solved crimes and came to our school and taught us
  how to cross streets when we were in first grade.
- They were good and nice and if you were ever lost, you
  should find them and they would give you a lollipop and
  take you home.

Except that when I was eight, I saw a policeman in his
nakedness, and it had quite an impact on what I later recognized as my perception of power and control.[†]

The cop moved a few years later, but until then, we
regarded each other with leery sidelong glances. I watched him
be a policeman and a dad. I'd see him in his uniform, coming
home for lunch in his flashy patrol car, and although "fucken
piece-of-shit pedophile hypocrite" was a number of years away

---

† I do not know exactly why I did not tell my parents about this incident. I
remember thinking it would cause problems, but I did not consider how it
would likely result in my father and uncles being incarcerated for beating a
cop with baseball bats.

from my vocabulary, the spirit of this term was alive and well in my perception of him.

I don't know what he thought of me, but I'm fond of imagining that his dick ran for his scrotum whenever I was around.

I have no memory of trusting the police.

I have no memory of assuming they were necessarily up to good.

While I've met many police officers who really do try to serve their community in beneficial ways—the vast majority women, transgender, queer, and/or of color—my perception of the police was formed around a memory of a white man who figured wagging his dick at little girls was somehow conducive to his idea of a happy life.

The police weren't merely nice folks who dropped by our school to teach us bicycle safety and to tell us to watch out for "drug pushers." (People who, I was sure, lurked in the J.C. Penney parking lot, on the watch for kids they could shove into their vans—if you read my first book, you might remember that vans were something I was repeatedly told to avoid. The "drug pushers" would then hold the kid—uh, me—down and "push" drugs into her veins with hypodermic needles.)

I thought the police had good ideas about bicycle safety, and I certainly avoided van drivers and all other people who looked like they might be "drug pushers." (I could tell "drug pushers" by the creepy, furtive expression in their eyes. I think I probably mistook garden-variety pedophiles or off-duty cops for "drug pushers" a lot.) Regardless of where I got my (dis)information and (mis)perceptions, I also felt it was a good idea to steer clear of the police with comparable gusto.

As an adult, I see this was a complex reality for a kid to negotiate. It was presented to me by the environment I grew up
in. I knew "good" guys were also "bad" guys, but I still honored their wisdom about certain survival tactics. I also knew
that this meant "bad" guys necessarily must also be "good"
guys. I knew some "bad" things were talked about and others
were better left unsaid.

 This is the kind of place I grew up in.

 You too.

The Ham Reality describes a belief system where "dark-skinned"
people are descended from a man who saw his "father" for what
he was, which greatly contrasted with the way he presented
himself. This Reality has been transfused into the ideological
under- and overtones of our culture ever since Ham first came
in handy for the white man's rendition of *The Way Things Are*.

 The police represent civic, street-level maintenance of the
corporate and larger government interests that they protect
and serve.

 The police are employed by the institution that enforces
the will of the powers that (are generally perceived to) be—that
is, the all-powerful white man father, who maintains control

through male domination, white supremacist racism, and imperialism, sustaining poverty and illegal local economies within a "haves" and "have-nots" environment, and obsesses over "proving" to nature and the earth that he's boss.

In order for this system to work right, everyone who resists any of these things must be assimilated, oppressed, silenced, killed, incarcerated, and/or enslaved.

Entire cities and neighborhoods throughout this country know to fear and/or despise the police because the police shoot their children dead, shake people down, deal drugs, extort, brutalize, and coerce the population into abusing itself.

Cops know people of color see them in their nakedness because *they display their nakedness* to people of color.

On graphic view here is the spectacle where white and white-identified people—who have been indoctrinated to avert our eyes and cover up ugly stuff that we don't want to see—live in a completely different constructed environment, and do not understand what almost everyone else is dealing with.

Elaborately and unconsciously choosing to make Shem and Japheth one's role models does not magically make white supremacist racism *Just the Way It Is*. This choice does not absolve anyone from responsibility. Choosing to avert one's eyes from the nakedness of those in power nearly always results in widespread poverty, death, incarceration, homelessness, and destruction of innocent people. What this means is that "harm-

less" and "law-abiding" folks who opt for inculcated, unexamined choices throughout life are, in fact, overseers, murderers,
prosecutors, landlords, and pillagers.

In August 1998, an LAPD officer named Rafael Perez was
arrested for stealing six pounds[†] of cocaine out of the police
department evidence room. He was a member of the Rampart
division's "anti-gang" CRASH (Community Resources Against
Street Hoodlums) unit.

   I've spent many hours reading from a huge archive found
on Streetgangs.com about what is now generally referred to
as the "Rampart scandal." Before going into it, here are some
things to keep in mind about the relationship between the
police and the media:

- The police use the media to **manufacture consent** and
  to create a particular, widespread perception of a situation or group.
- The media almost always allow the police the focal narration and bend-over-backward benefit of the doubt.
- The media hardly ever, ever step out of line with a
  negative story about the police, but they *will* look into
  particular nastiness until the police provide a remotely
  believable cover-up.
- Individual reporters who pry too much are silenced or

---

† This amount fluctuates in media reports. Six is mentioned most often.

> demoted, or sometimes, as with James Hatfield and Gary Webb, they conveniently "commit suicide."
>
> • There is an overall agreement that the public should only know certain things, none of which involves the police being seen in their nakedness.

The saga of Rafael Perez and the LAPD is a very complex story, with ambiguous demarcations between "good" and "bad" people.

Uh, much like reality.

Mr. Perez, along with a number of other black LAPD officers, was branded as a "gangsta cop" by either the media or the LAPD. As will be discussed later, there is no denying that the CRASH unit specifically, and the LAPD in general, is just another gang in the streets of Los Angeles. This particular branding, however, had very specific racial overtones. The arrest of Rafael Perez was supposed to lead people to discover and latch on to the idea that "gangstas" had infiltrated the otherwise good and noble LAPD.

Many of the black cops in the CRASH unit grew up in Los Angeles, and some of them had allegiances with certain gangs, as well as with some rather famous people in the rap and hiphop community—in much the same way that the larger, white LAPD police force has close ties with people in the white mainstream entertainment community, which is populated with equally as unseemly, corrupt, and violent individuals as those allegedly found in the "gangsta rap" community.

Denzel Washington's character in *Training Day* is inspired by Rafael Perez, but if you want to watch an "inspired by actual events" movie about the white LAPD's crimes, you gotta pretend you're back in the 1950s and watch *L.A. Confidential*.

I believe that the reasons Mr. Perez was singled out for wrongdoing had to do with the fact that some white members of the LAPD (or the city, state, or federal government) were growing uncomfortable with and threatened by the power accruing from black entertainment/law-enforcement allegiances, and because Mr. Perez and his cohorts were not necessarily loyal to the "traditional" (white) power structure of either the LAPD or the entertainment industry.

So a sting operation with the six pounds of cocaine was set up. The LAPD knew that Rafael Perez knew things about some well-known crimes, and decided that, given a good shove between a rock and a hard place, Mr. Perez would tattle on people in the rap and hiphop community. He was *supposed* to get scared and start harping about the murders of Tupac Shakur and Biggie Smalls, implicating, among others, Suge Knight, of Death Row Records. The media was *supposed* to pounce on how "gangsta cops" had infiltrated the LAPD, and it probably would have, if only Mr. Perez had not fully embraced the reality that he would likely be killed if he told the stories the LAPD wanted him to tell. It seems there was also a widely embraced assumption that Mr. Perez's ultimate loyalties lay with the larger (white) LAPD.

On the whole, Mr. Perez seems to have looked at the hand

he'd been dealt, and decided to play it in quite a different manner than was (unbelievably unimaginatively) expected of him. He never said a word about any of the people he was *supposed* to talk about—except his partner, Nino Durden. Perez couldn't confess to his own crimes without implicating Mr. Durden.

It was thought that Mr. Perez would uphold the blue wall of silence over everything else. When it came down to it, however, Rafael Perez said, "Fuck your blue wall and fuck your silence."

Mr. Perez seems to have decided that if certain members of the LAPD were gonna use him as a means to corroborate that "rogue gangsta cops" had set up operations in the midst of an otherwise forthright and community-serving LAPD, then he was gonna open his mouth wide, and implicate, instead, the entire police department.

Chief among the crimes sitting on Mr. Perez's heart was the shooting of an innocent young man named Javier Ovando, planting a rifle on him, and testifying against him at his trial. Mr. Ovando, who was paralyzed after being shot and will tool around the rest of his life in a wheelchair, was sentenced to twenty-three years in prison. At his trial, Mr. Ovando's obvious "lack of remorse" was commented on. So was the fact that he lay on a gurney throughout his trial. By the time Rafael Perez confessed to framing him, Mr. Ovando had served more that two years of his sentence, and was immediately released. However, because he is what people in "California" refer to as an "illegal," he was held in INS custody until they figured out whether or not to deport him.

His civil trial against the city of Los Angeles taught me this:

Two years of stolen life + losing the ability to walk ever again after being shot three times + being terrorized by the police and the criminal justice system + a cop (miraculously) admitting that this was done to you + being further held in illegal INS custody, long after the Treaty of Guadalupe Hidalgo was violated = fifteen million dollars.

Some people might think of this as "fair," but ask yourself: If, instead of being Mr. Ovando's destiny, this were a long-term reality teevee show, would *you* audition?

Mr. Perez not only decided to toss a big fuck-you the LAPD's way, but also seems to have gone through a serious soul-searching after he got popped for the cocaine. In one *Los Angeles Times* article, he talked about what was going through his head after being busted:

> "I feel this is one of the best things that's ever happened to me," Perez said. "I definitely believe I was on a road to destruction. I was on a road to a place that no one should be. This experience has opened my eyes, opened my heart to a lot of things."
>
> Six days after his arrest, Perez was sitting in the county jail when another inmate came up to him and asked him what it felt like to be a cop behind bars. The inmate said he wished all police officers would have to spend 30 days in jail before they work the streets so they know how their job affects the people they arrest.

"When he told me that, it hit me to the bone," Perez said. "It made me think: Absolutely right. If an officer was forced to spend 30 days just to get a feel of the isolation and what jail is like, I'd have to tend to believe that things would be a little bit different."[3]

I have no idealistic visions of Rafael Perez. I think he was an asshole for terrorizing a community of people and abusing his power. I have to say, though, I got a kick out of Mr. Perez's big LAPD-bashing motor mouth. Rafael Perez talked and talked and talked, oh how Rafael Perez talked. Mr. Perez just could not stop talking (and plea-bargaining) about all the horrible things he did and saw while employed with the CRASH[†] unit. Evidently, Mr. Ovando was not the only person Rafael Perez shot, framed, or terrorized. He talked about how cops routinely sell drugs and coerce prostitutes into fucking cops for protection from, uh, cops. He talked about how meetings with supervisors largely involved brainstorming sessions about how to cover up CRASH unit crimes, plant evidence, and frame innocent people.

Reports surfaced about the FBI's encouragement of CRASH to turn people over to the INS under the guise of "gang membership."

Immigration and Naturalization Service agents

---

† Remember, this stands for Community Resources Against Street Hoodlums, which itself quite calls into question the LAPD's ideas about what a community, a resource, and a street hoodlum might actually be.

ordered to deport immigrants detained by anti-gang
officers in the Los Angeles Police Department's Rampart Division told investigators the assignment was
"rammed down our throats" over the objections of
the U.S. attorney's office after pressure from the FBI,
according to federal documents.

The 27 INS agents, who were interviewed for an
internal immigration service report, create a com-
posite picture of an unpopular program launched
by overzealous INS managers over the objections
of agents in the INS' own Organized Crime Drug
Enforcement Task Force—known by the acronym
OCDETF. They said they repeatedly told John McAl-
lister, the INS assistant district director for inves-
tigations, that their involvement in the program
did not conform to their congressional mandate to
combat large-scale drug trafficking. LAPD's cooperation in the effort may have violated a special city
order that restricts police inquiries into residents'
immigration status.

Moreover, the task force coordinator, John Del
George, raised moral objections to its operations,
saying that "only a very small portion of those
arrested were actually hard-core gang members."
According to the report, Del George "recalled interviewing one 'gang member' who was actually an assistant manager at McDonald's, was married, had kids,
and had been out of 'gang' life for years."[4]

Autobiography of a Blue-Eyed Devil

Luis J. Rodriguez also grew up in L.A. He was involved with gangs back in the 1970s. His book *Always Running: Gang Days in L.A.* backs up Mr. Perez's many statements about police activities, even though Mr. Rodriguez was living this reality well before Rafael Perez was even born, before crack and guns were introduced into the community by hirelings of the U.S. government:

> In the barrio, the police are just another gang. We even give them names. There's Cowboy, Big Red, Boffo and Maddog. They like those names. Sometimes they come up to us while we linger on a street corner and tell us Sangra [a rival gang] called us *chavalas,* a loose term for girls. Other times, they approach dudes from Sangra and say Lomas is a tougher gang and Sangra is nothing. Shootings, assaults and skirmishes between the barrios are direct results of police activity. Even drug dealing. I know this. Everybody knows this.[5]

Dropping gang members off in a rival gang's territory is just one tactic in the systematic terrorism that was, and continues to be, employed against gang members. Almost three decades later, Ronald Chatman, a.k.a. O/G Madd Ronald, corroborates Mr. Rodriguez's experience:

> I grew up in a neighborhood where L.A.P.D. would drive through with a blue rag tied to the antenna of

their police car. L.A.P.D. use to pick up Bloods and drop them off in Crip neighborhoods, just as well as they use to pick up Crips and drop them off in Blood neighborhoods, and this was always done where ever the rival gang hung out. Right in front of them so you were left to fend for yourself. I have been beat up and set up by the same people whose job it is to protect and serve me.[6]

By the end of 1999, more than seventy LAPD officers were implicated in similar crimes and the legality of over three thousand cases was called into question. Hundreds of people were set free from wrongful imprisonment.

This is right around when the LAPD dug into its treasure trove of smut on Rafael Perez (doubtless, there exists one on pretty much any police officer in any major city), and the media started calling his "credibility" into question. If you point out the drunken nakedness of the white father, you become instantly unpopular in the family. Prior to this, Mr. Perez was portrayed, more or less, as "a good cop gone bad," but when he got on a roll with the media's undivided attention focused on him, the narration around him began to change. He was henceforth referred to as a thief, drug dealer, rogue cop, and all-around "bad apple."

After the extent of wrongdoing started spiraling out of control, I noticed that the *Los Angeles Times* articles also stopped referring to Javier Ovando as an "unarmed young man." He was called an "unarmed gang member" in every article after the first year's worth. Mr. Ovando had no prior criminal record, and even if he had, even if he *had been* an active gang member, this does not exonerate anyone for the miscarriage of justice he and his family endured.

As Congresswoman Maxine Waters is often wont to point out, "Just because you're in a gang doesn't mean you bang."

And even if you bang, it doesn't mean you deserve to be shot, paralyzed, framed, incarcerated, and further detained.

The media[†] *chose* to use the term "gang member" to describe Javier Ovando because it draws attention away from his humanity, and allows readers to decide that, really, when you get down to it, it's not like we're talking about a "good" kid or even a "promising" one.

It's just some illegal immigrant "gang member."

Rafael Perez laid it all out for the community, and while the initial response was a bit of outrage, the city government of Los Angeles came to the assessment that the costs involved with not averting eyes and not covering up this nakedness were, on the whole, too exorbitant. Addressing and rectifying this problem would involve tearing down and reconstructing the overall view of gang members and their families, of justice, the police, poverty, and ultimately, the nature of white supremacist racism.

Too close to home, too close to our hearts, really it's not so

---

† In fairness to Matt Lait and Scott Glover, two of the *Los Angeles Times* staff reporters who did an exemplary job of covering this story, they have to answer to editors and publishers, who answer to city officials, who answer to state officials, who answer to federal officials. From what I've read, these two journalists were completely invested in keeping the community abreast of this situation. I don't doubt that Mr. Lait and Mr. Glover *actually* know a lot more about police corruption than they were allowed to report.

bad after all, we can live with this, those kids really do cause an awful lot of problems over there in those neighborhoods.

Averting our eyes and covering up nakedness is always found to be the best course of action.

The bible says so.

Since the media's role is to sustain a negative perception of "gangstas," rather than offering gang members a voice in the community, there is no examination of why mainstream society does not consider "them" as on par with "us" or "our" children.

The media allegedly represent the truth, and what they say is generally considered the impartial, objective voice of reason. Any other perception stems from absurd conspiracy theories. Amerikkkan society takes the media's word for exactly "who" this complex and diverse demographic "is" because doing otherwise—not averting our eyes—would expose altogether too much. "We" might not be able to maintain the difference between "gang members" and "our" children anymore.

Nowhere was this sentiment more clearly espoused than on the allegedly and traditionally "liberal" PBS. *Frontline* aired the documentary *LAPD Blues* on May 15, 2001. It was supposed to be, I gather, some kind of exposé of the Rampart scandal, timed perfectly for "closure" and consisting mostly of interviews with white cops. This show is, in fact, how I came to the conclusion that Rafael Perez was set up in the first place. Viewed in this light, these interviews are composed of perspectives from the very people who framed Mr. Perez.

Read this excerpt from the interview with detective Frank
Lyga and see if you can put together a motive for creating the
perception that there were a bunch of rogue black "gangsta"
cops in the LAPD:

PETER BOYER: One day in the spring of 1997, Detective Frank Lyga was in plainclothes, driving back to
the stationhouse.

DET. FRANK LYGA: I was stopped at a light, number
one car, sitting there minding my own business. And
then I heard rap music, and I looked over to my left
and saw a green Montero with a male black in the
driver's seat.

And then our eyes met. You know, he threatened
me, "Punk, I'll put a cap in your ass." And I said,
"Excuse me?" And then—then the hand motions. You
know, he starts doing this. He said, "Yeah, well I'll
kick your motherfuckin' ass, punk," you know? And
I'm going—he goes, "Pull over. Let's"—you know, he
wants to fight. He was a stone-cold gangsta. In my
training and experience, this guy had "I'm a gang
member" written all over him.

So at that point, the light turned green. I pulled
forward, and we went through the intersection.
And I'm watching him in the mirror. I look forward,
and I'm now going to be stopped in traffic. And he's
coming. And I remember going, "Shit!"

I got on my radio and I announced, "Hey, I got a

problem. I got a black guy in a green Montero, and he may have a gun, and I need help. Get up here." And then I unbuckle my seatbelt, and I take my gun out and put it on my waist, just right against the door and on my lap.

He pulls up alongside of me. He stops, and he comes across and he leans over the passenger seat and extends his arm and points the gun at me and yells, "I'll cap you, mother!" I bring my right arm over my left shoulder. I fire a round at him. I look back at him, and he's—the gun is still pointing at me. And I fired a second round.

And after I fired the second round, I almost could hear the impact, the thud of the round hitting him. But I definitely saw it in his face. We were only nine feet away, nine feet apart. And his eyes got really big, and he got this grimace on his face. And his arm went from this position here, right straight to the steering wheel. It didn't do one of these deals, it went right to the steering wheel, and he accelerated.

I could tell by the look in his eyes that I hit him, and I hit him hard. And as he pulls into the gas station, the car just—the momentum just stopped. It went "Vhhhum."

BOYER: The driver was dead.

LYGA: You know, not to be callous or cold or anything, but I kind of thought, "Good." I mean, you know, that's the nature of the beast.

BOYER: Three hours later, Detective Lyga's superior officers told him who he'd shot.

> LYGA: And they got this stupid look on their face. And
> Dennis walks up to me and puts his arm around me,
> and says, "You're going to have to suck this one up. The
> guy was a policeman." I says, "What?" He says, "The
> guy was a policeman." I says, "From where?" "One of
> ours. Worked Pacific." I says, "You're kidding me." At
> that point, now—now the world was crashing down.
> NEWSCASTER: LAPD officer Kevin Gaines was gunned
> down by one of his own, killed on Tuesday afternoon in
> North Hollywood by an undercover officer.[7]

Kevin Gaines was one of the alleged "gangsta cops," and
his murder occurred not long before Rafael Perez was nailed for
stealing cocaine from an evidence room.

The *only* time in this PBS show that you ever hear *any* perspective
from the South Central Los Angeles community is through a rap
song flitting around in the background of a few scenes. The filmmakers also had the weird audacity to ignore the LAPD's diverse
history with police brutality by encapsulating the spirit of the
LAPD via old teevee images of Pleasantville cops.

Still looking for documented perspectives of people who
actually live in the Rampart area, I eventually found an *LAPD
Blues/Frontline* auxiliary section called "The Streets of Rampart
Today" on PBS's website. *Frontline* interviewed members of the
Coalition to Improve the Quality of Life in Rampart. It says in
the introduction that *Frontline* "also spoke with a number of

Rampart gang members, including some falsely arrested by Rafael Perez. Most of the gang members spoke off-the-record; some described a police unit that terrorized gang members and engaged in criminal conduct well beyond what even Perez has alleged."[8] However, only one gang member is recorded on the web page I was reading from.

But I'm getting ahead of myself.

The first perspective is from Carmen Vaughn, who raised four kids by herself. Carmen Vaughn lived in the Pico-Union neighborhood for thirty years, and led a Neighborhood Watch group—which means, for better or worse, the cops are nice to her and her group. She lauds Los Angeles's gang injunctions—arbitrary restraining orders that amount to people being thrown in jail if they breach a myriad of dictates, like having a cell phone or being on a certain block.[†] Mrs. Vaughn's greatest desire is to live in a safe community. She has suffered greatly from all the violence, and so have her children. One can understand that fully backing the LAPD appears to her the best option.

Next up we have Father John Bakas. He is introduced as an "unapologetic supporter of the LAPD," and has these words of wisdom to impart:

> Yes indeed, CRASH did bring some fear into some of the so-called gangsters. And you know something my

---

† The ACLU has brought several lawsuits against the LAPD on gang injunctions. I really wish human rights organizations would get more involved in U.S. ghettos, reservations, and barrios.

dear friend? Fear is a legitimate emotion. It's a legitimate emotion. And we need a little bit more of that.[9]

I agree. Fear is a legitimate emotion. It is there to tell you
that you are in danger and something must change in order for
you to stay alive. Living in fear, however, is living in danger,
without change.

Then we move on to Dr. Mary Ann Hutchinson, a psycholo-
gist who concedes that she grew up in the generation that called
cops pigs, only she doesn't say the actual word, "pigs." She says
"the 'P' word." She supports the LAPD and the gang injunctions.

And lastly, but not leastly, we have the token gang
member. Was he *really* the only one willing to speak on the
record, or just one who was specifically fucked over by Rafael
Perez and Nino Durden?

Ruben Rojas does offer a perspective on gangs that we
don't hear too often in the media, but alas, warrants only a few
sentences on *Frontline's* website.

"A lot of people have misconceptions on gangs, but, I
mean, my friends, all we'd ever do was just have a good
time. Party and stay to ourselves," he says. "We were
young. And we never planned on hurting anybody. In
the course of time, of course it happened, you know,
but it was never our intention to harm anyone."[10]

He says that CRASH was just a gang like any other gang,
but with more power, and he solely implicated Perez and

Durden, who framed him and got him thrown in jail with a three-year sentence for possession of cocaine. Mr. Rojas was released from jail and got one million dollars in a settlement. He implicates no one else besides Perez and Durden. It may very well be true that these two officers were the ones he witnessed abusing their power the most in his neighborhood. It seems to me, however, that his perspective was consciously chosen because it served the eye-averting "bad apple" theme.

In general, gang members would probably be more willing to go on the record if they felt they were being treated with respect and their perspectives would be presented with dignity. Since this almost never happens in mainstream society, it is not surprising to me that *Frontline* couldn't get anyone to go on the record.

Every one of these voices from the community supported the LAPD, and the draconian, completely unjust gang injunctions. In fact, this entire documentary package seems like little more than an infomercial for the "new, improved" LAPD and the gang injunctions. These injunctions are, mysteriously, the city's answer to the problem of police corruption and brutality.

The logic goes something like this:

If a community of people is victimized by the police and the public somehow finds out about it and starts asking questions that will, in the end, cost the city a lot of money, the best course of action is to step up and further legalize the terrorization of the community being victimized by the police.

At the end of the day, the whole unfortunate scandal was just a few "bad apples."

The Rampart "investigation" was stonewalled, sidetracked, and underfunded every step of the way, pretty much in the exact same manner as the September 11, 2001, "investigation" was. The investigation nailed a few cops, and ultimately removed Bernard Parks, the LAPD's black chief of police, maybe kinda like how the Iraq occupation was machinated into becoming Colin Powell's undoing.

And so, with no real conclusions, the whole nightmare was banished to the background chatter of humanity's consciousness. It was defined and filed away under the heading "The Rampart Scandal." Parks was fired and the pasty-faced Chief William Bratton stepped in. His first decree was to crack down on rich kids who tear around L.A. in their fast cars while high on alcohol and drugs.

Ha, ha, ha.

Joke.

Chief Bratton wasn't in office for fifty-two minutes before announcing his new zero-tolerance plan for graffiti and "gang" violence. Injunctions have been enforced to the fullest under his rule.

The moral of this story: A few bad apples can cost a lot of money, so don't point anyone out as a bad apple unless you are sure that they will never speak about the true nature of rot.

In the summer of 2002, the "California" section of the *Los Angeles Times* featured a front-page photograph of Congresswoman Maxine Waters. She was holding up two checks to

publicize a legal defense fund for a down-on-his-luck rave
DJ named Mitchell Crooks, who was jailed in Placer County,
"California," in connection with a five-year-old petty theft
(stealing two VCRs from his mother) and drunk driving
charge. He had previously been sentenced to seven months in
prison, but rather than serve his time, Mr. Crooks absconded
to Los Angeles.

"We will go to Placer," Ms. Waters declares in the article.
"We will stand with him. We will help to pay his lawyers. We
will support his bail."[11]

Why such interest in and support of a young man who
was irresponsible enough to get behind the wheel of a car while
intoxicated, thus endangering the lives of others (personally,
I don't have much sympathy for drunk drivers, as my younger
brother might be alive right now if it weren't for one), and disrespectful enough to rip off his own mama and not serve the
measly seven months he got in the first place?

Ms. Waters's work for human and civil rights movements is
the stuff legends are made of. For the past few decades, she has
been actively engaged with the needs of her constituents, and
Mr. Crooks is not even eligible to vote for her.

It was, however, Mitchell Crooks who was staying at
the Econo Lodge in Inglewood, "California," on July 6, 2002,
when he heard a commotion outside his motel, peered out the
window, and saw Inglewood cops beating the shit out of a
sixteen-year-old youth named Donovan Jackson-Chavis.

Mr. Crooks was thus inspired to grab his video camera and
film a white officer named Jeremy Morse hurling the young

man onto the hood of a patrol car and punching him in the face. After recording this two-minute episode of police brutality, Mr. Crooks sat on the bed in his hotel room and weighed his options. There was a warrant out for his arrest. The police would be able to locate him if he turned in the video, and handing the footage over to the media would certainly not endear him to his future captors. Nonetheless, Mr. Crooks decided to start phoning television stations. By the next afternoon, the two minutes of heart-wrenching footage was on the air. I call this footage "heart-wrenching" not merely for what it captures—which is, indeed, heart-wrenching—but for what it does not capture. For the scenes Mr. Crooks must have witnessed from his window at the Econo Lodge before he gathered the wherewithal to grab his camera and hit the record button. But mostly, for the thousands of similar scenes that occur on a daily basis in this country, and go undocumented by citizen videographers.

It leads me to wonder how many people are terrorized by the police when a camera is not around.

On July 11, Mitchell Crooks was arrested by police officers and taken away in an unmarked black SUV with tinted windows. Witnesses reported him screaming for help as the police shoved him into the SUV. In a radio interview the previous afternoon, Mr. Crooks had expressed his fear of what the police would do to him while he was in custody.

✺

There are many terms to describe Congresswoman Maxine Waters, and "goddamn fool" will never be one of them.[†] She was fully aware that the police and other authorities were sending a message by so ardently going after Mr. Crooks. The message is (ahem):

"If you have ever been in trouble with the police and you document us kicking someone's ass like we often seem to do, you will be beaten and jailed without further ado."

To this message, Ms. Waters answered, "We will do whatever is necessary to say to citizens, when you come forward, when you are willing to stand up, when you see abuse by the police department or anybody else, we are gonna honor you."[12]

Her way of honoring Mr. Crooks was to raise money for his legal defense and announce that he had a big party to look forward to after he got out of jail: "We are going to ask the mayor to block off a whole block. And we are going to invite the entire community. We are going to have the biggest welcome party you have ever seen."[13]

The genius of this statement is that it serves as a graceful, self-fulfilling prophetic threat to the police that Mr. Crooks *will* get out of jail alive and well.

⚘

[†] After the U.S.-supported coup against President Aristide, it was rumored that Congresswoman Waters smuggled a cell phone to him. Aristide's voice went out to the world media, and that's a pretty dang good reason why he is still alive.

Autobiography of a Blue-Eyed Devil

In August, Mitchell Crooks was sentenced to serve 110 days, which means, I suppose, that in the long run, his absconding strategy prevailed. He was held in twenty-two-hour-a-day lockdown to protect him from white racist prison groups. While certainly not optimal conditions, this probably wouldn't have happened without Ms. Waters's highly publicized support.

The police, their attorneys, and the media portrayed the situation as one in which Donovan Jackson-Chavis was somehow squeezing the officer's balls, and so the officer punched the child in the face. If true, which I know like the color of my peachy ass is not the case, but anyway, if true, this account does not explain why Officer Morse hurled Donovan from a prone position on the ground onto the hood of the police car in the first place. The young man was slight of build and looked like he had never in his life considered the possibility of being dangerous, much less armed. Police do not treat people this way, with looks of abject hatred and rage on their faces, unless they are being, uh, "brutal."

At the first meeting of the Donovan Jackson-Chavis Justice Committee, held at Faith United Methodist Church in Los Angeles, the legendary civil rights activist Mr. Dick Gregory proclaimed, "We've got to explain it like this to white people. Police brutality is just as real to me as sun cancer is to you."[14†]

---

† I read the transcript of this meeting on Los Angeles's Indymedia website. When I read about the exact same meeting on the "mainstream" KTLA website, this quote was not mentioned, and Mr. Gregory was described as a "comedian." Referring to Mr. Gregory as "a comedian" is kinda like calling Bill Clinton "a saxophone player." When such instances of disrespect are pointed out, they often sound like "nitpicking" to the unconscious ear.

⚡

After Donovan Jackson-Chavis was assaulted by the police, the media was given orders to stand down. I have no evidence to substantiate this statement, but there is no other reason why, all of a sudden, news of abducted little white girls *deluged* the mainstream media. It was very much as if the media was asserting the idea that little white girls who get stolen from their homes at night are much more newsworthy victims than young black men who get beaten by the police. The stories of little girls taken from their homes, sexually assaulted, and killed plays on the emotions of the population.[†]

While research authorities stated over and over that child abduction rates had actually *gone down* in the past few years, news stories featuring Elizabeth Smart and Samantha Runnion flooded the front pages, handily usurping the momentum of anger that people in Los Angeles were experiencing over the beating of Donovan Jackson-Chavis, and thus diverting another potential riot.

In Los Angeles, the memorial service for Samantha Runnion rivaled that of Princess Diana. It was televised live for two hours.

I mean no disrespect to the memory of Samantha Runnion, her family, or anyone victimized by violence. However, I question a community and media that orchestrate such a grand

---

[†] I deeply resent the fact that white women and girls are used in this way. Sexual violence is a real aspect of life and history for all women (and many men) in this culture of rape warfare.

display of remorse only when the perpetrator of a heinous
crime is not someone who is allegedly supposed to be protecting
and serving the community. Have you ever heard tell of a two-
hour-long televised extravaganza memorial service for a young
person of color who was murdered by the police? I certainly
have not. Yet, there are *many* more victims of police brutality
and murder than there are victims of stranger abduction.

In a compassionate and truly just society, people would
have much stronger reactions to these atrocities.

On July 15, 2002, America Online's "News" site featured the following item:

> AOL News: Rodney King Poll
> "Has there been progress in **minority** treatment by
> police since the Rodney King beating?"
> 45% (17,376): Yes
> 37% (14,392): No
> 15% (5,676): Not Sure
> 4% (1,511): Other
> Total Votes: 38,955

Abner Louima was sodomized with a broom/plunger
handle (reports on what was used vary) by Officer Justin Volpe
after the Rodney King beating. Amadou Diallo was senselessly
murdered in a hail of New York City police bullets after the
Rodney King beating. Hundreds of youth have been killed or

assaulted by police in Portland, Jersey City, and Cincinnati since the Rodney King beating.

These events, and many, many more that went unreported, undocumented, and unwitnessed, occurred well after the Rodney King beating.

The correct answer to this poll, therefore, is a definite, resolute, irrevocable, unambiguous, cut-and-dry, crystal clear, absolutely factual NO. It is the only correct answer, yet it was not deemed so by the majority of respondents.

"Not sure" and "other" are morally equivalent to "yes," because, like I just mentioned, NO is the *only* mathematically corroborated answer.

In this view of the poll results, 24,563 people—that is, 63 percent—were unable to provide the correct response.

I do not allege that this is some hard-core scientific poll, but that is also the beauty of it. AOL polls are things people do quite willingly, in the privacy of their own homes or work-places, during their leisure time. No one comes knocking on the door, interrupting dinner, there's no voice or person to identify with, and you can't respond to the same poll more than once. These polls troll the collective unconscious in ways "scientific" polls do not.

And in this country, white and white-identified people avert our gaze rather than face the fact that indian folks and people of color are systematically victimized and brutalized by the police.

⚡

There has *never* been a time in this country's history that people of color have not been in overt danger of being brutalized by the police.

Exactly when did this dramatic paradigm shift where people of color are no longer brutalized by the police take place?

Maybe back in the 1950s, when the combination of "juvenile delinquent" with either "Negro," "Mexican," or "colored" was a surefire recipe for a status-quo-sanctioned ass-kickin', if not lynching?

In the 1960s and 1970s, when all the law had to do was spit the word "militant" at the press and no one asked questions about folks dying in custody?

In the 1980s and 1990s, when the terms "drug dealer" and "gang member" were (and continue to be) employed in a similar manner?

Or now, when "terrorist," "enemy combatant," or even "Muslim" is employed to ensure mainstream acceptance of racial profiling, deportation, capital punishment, and/or incarceration?

The *ideology* that rules over the criminal justice system is exactly the same as it was back when slavery was first deemed "illegal." Big fucking deal if, in most parts of the U.S., police are no longer openly associated with the Ku Klux Klan. Big fucking deal if there are more police officers of color now than there were in the 1950s. People come to the conclusion that this white supremacist ideology is no longer in place just because police generally no longer terrorize individuals and communities during their "off" hours wearing white sheets and pointy hoods over their police uniforms?

This is considered an "improvement"?
Improvement, my **ofay** cracker ass.

In Jefferson Parish, "Louisiana," Mr. Lawrence Jacobs went to court one day because his son was being tried for murder. Imagine his horror when he saw that the prosecuting attorney's tie had a noose printed on it. On another day, he saw two prosecutors whose ties were emblazoned with a dangling rope and an image of the Grim Reaper. "That's when it really hit me," Mr. Jacobs said. "These guys are out to kill my son. And they're making light of it."[15]

How do you think the white man punished himself for this grotesque display of power and control, or "prosecutorial machismo" as the (white male?) *New York Times* reporter calls (condones?) it?

"Totally inappropriate," said Paul D. Connick Jr.,
the district attorney of Jefferson Parish, a suburb
of New Orleans. "And unprofessional. I told them:
'Don't wear those two ties to work. No nooses, no
Grim Reapers.'"[16]

Wow.
What a cutting reprimand.

Autobiography of a Blue-Eyed Devil

In East Baton Rouge, "Louisiana," the DA rings in each new death sentence with office parties, steak, and whiskey. In "Texas," there's a club called the Silver Needle Society, and one DA has a noose hanging over her office door. In "Mississippi," one could find a toy electric chair buzzing in a former assistant attorney general's office.

In the *New York Times* article where I read about these happenings, the author referred to this sickness as a "relish for capital punishment." This "relish" is due to the fact that prosecutors gain prestige when they "get" death sentences.

Unlike serial murderers, they are rewarded for killing people.

Question time:

How does one find a way in one's heart to condone the brutal televised police beatings of young men of color? How does one avert one's eyes from a criminal justice system that has legalized a new brand of lynching? How does one isolate all of these incidents, instead of viewing them as an historic continuum of whites' treatment of people of color and indigenous people? How does one divorce this from illegal detention of "terror" suspects and the sadistic brutality our soldiers are inflicting on a population thousands of miles away? How much humanity is one willing to sacrifice in order to maintain this system of control?

If the true occupation of the police is to protect and serve the interests of the great white male father on a civic level, then certainly our military's true occupation is to protect and serve his interests globally.

One of the Abu Ghraib "bad apples," Charles Graner, previously worked as a prison guard here in the U.S. Let's take a look at Mr. Graner's on-the-job training, according to an excerpt from London's *Daily Mail* newspaper:

> . . . Graner learned his "psychopathic torture techniques" at Pennsylvania's Greene state prison where guards employed a policy of "adjusting the attitudes" of inmates with beatings and sadomasochistic sex.
> . . . [Graner] was a junior guard at the jail in 1998 when a scandal erupted.
> New prisoners were stripsearched and clubbed as they stood naked and handcuffed. A torture chamber was set up in a windowless cell block called "the pad", covered with red cushioning to absorb blood and human tissue. Inmates who resisted were forced into homosexual acts. Guards would then use their blood to scrawl hate symbols from the Ku Klux Klan on the floor.[17]

According to other reports I read, Mr. Graner evidently looked forward to going to Iraq because there he would find many opportunities to kill—in Mr. Graner's parlance—"sand niggers." I imagine he was very excited about having a whole country filled with a new and improved kind of enemy "nigger" that most of our population was/is willing to perceive as terrorists

obsessed with destroying our wonderful democracy and sundering our plethora of free, free, freedoms.

If you are one of the people who were "outraged" about the
crime against humanity at the prison in Iraq, please strike up
a correspondence with any prisoner here in the U.S. She or he
will undoubtedly share personal experiences that echo those of
occupation prisoners.

In my name,
        in your name,
                with our money,
                        these things are done.

The "War on Drugs"—a term not at all different from the "War
on Terrorism"—laid down a red carpet for mandatory minimum
sentencing laws, such as the Three Strikes, Yer Out law. That's
right, get popped for stealing *a fucken apple* from the corner grocery store three times, and it's life in prison for your previously
two-striked-ass.

In the summer of 2004, I came across an article by Silja
J.A. Talvi, entitled "The New Plantation." Here is what Ms. Talvi
said on the absolute unjust implementation of Three Strikes:

> The law was supposed to take care of the "worst
> of the worst," but it has been bad news all the way
> around. Men and women have gotten life sentences
> for shoplifting, for repeat petty offenses, and out of
> the very nature of their persistent and untreated

drug habits. By the end of 2003, it had cost the cash-strapped state ["California"] about $8.1 billion in incarceration costs.

When the Justice Policy Institute decided to take an even closer look at the situation in a March 2004 report, Still Striking Out, they found something that made my head reel. The African American incarceration rate for Three Strikes was no less than *12 times higher* than that of European Americans.[18]

As a result of this "drug war," people of color and poor people have been systematically targeted by police and the media. How people are treated by the criminal "justice" system depends on their connections, privilege, wealth, power, and race.

More or less in that order.

In her song "Every Ghetto, Every City," Lauryn Hill sings about how the streets that nurtured her made sure that she'd never get too far.

In contrast, the streets that nurtured known substance abuser Noelle Arbusto made sure that she'll always get real far. Laws will be broken to see to this.

Ms. Arbusto, the daughter of Jeb, has been arrested multiple times for charges stemming from prescription-drug fraud. She was sent to rehab and stole prescription drugs while there. The judge, in essence, told her that she really needed to make some effort, young lady. Ms. Bush was sentenced to a whopping three days in jail before returning to rehab.

All of this occurred *before* she was caught in a rehab facility with crack in her shoe. This was substantiated in a 911 call, as recorded verbatim:

CALLER: I am located at the Center for Drug-Free Living, and I would like a police officer to come out, please.

[ORLANDO POLICE DISPATCH] OPERATOR: What address are you at, ma'am?

CALLER: [gives address]

OPERATOR: OK, can you tell me what happened?

CALLER: This is basically a treatment center for women with children.

OPERATOR: Yeah.

CALLER: And one of the women here was caught buying crack cocaine tonight. And a lot of the women are upset because she's been caught about five times. And we want something done because our children are here, and they just keep letting it slip under the counter and carpet.

OPERATOR: Your name?

CALLER: I'm anonymous.

OPERATOR: Well, we're going to have to meet with someone.

CALLER: OK. Can I put all the girls? Because we're all here; we're all here wanting to talk to someone.

OPERATOR: Who was she caught buying the drugs by? Who caught her buying the drugs?

CALLER: The staff.

OPERATOR: Pardon me?

CALLER: Staff. They said, you know, because it's basically Noelle Bush. And she keeps getting out of it. Because every—she does this all the time and she gets out of it because she's the governor's daughter. But we're sick of it here 'cause we have to do what's right, but she gets treated like some kind of princess. And everybody's tired of it, you know. We're just trying to get our lives together, and this girl's bringing drugs on property.

OPERATOR: OK. And the staff caught her?

CALLER: Yes.

OPERATOR: They caught her today?

CALLER: Yes. This is just about 30 minutes ago.

OPERATOR: And she's still there, though.

CALLER: Yes. And she is on probation, I guess. And all kinds of stuff. I don't know what all that is. But. And procedure is that they would call the police, but they're not doing it here, because of who she is.

OPERATOR: OK. So the staff is refusing to do anything about it.

CALLER: Because of who she is.

OPERATOR: OK. OK. OK, if you don't want to leave me your name that's fine. But somebody needs to meet with the officers when they get there.

> CALLER: OK, we'll be out front. Do you know how
> long . . .
> OPD Operator: OK. All of you will be out front?
> Caller: Yeah. There's 24 of us.[19]

Under a recently passed federal law, people in public housing can have their home seized if anyone who resides therein is convicted of using or dealing drugs. *It doesn't matter if the "crime" occurs on public housing premises or not.* If your dumbass sixteen-year-old gets busted with a bag of weed at the local library, then *you can lose your home*, which you are busting your ass working two jobs to keep.

I am still waiting for officials to apply this law to Mr. Arbusto, for if the governor's mansion isn't considered public housing every bit as much as a tax-funded low-income project is, then I don't know what else it could possibly be called.

Due to Mr. Arbusto's policies, over ten thousand *nonviolent* drug offenders have specifically been denied rehabilitation over incarceration.

The streets that nurtured this population of imprisoned individuals made sure that they'd never get too far, either.

Dear Noelle,

I apologize if it hurts your feelings that I am picking on you in my book. I imagine it is incredibly difficult to deal with the obligations and expectations that are forced upon you because of the family you were born into.

*There are, however, thousands of bright, imaginative, vibrant, and dearly loved kids and young adults being subjected to brutal prison environments for **years and years**. Many of them are serving time for lesser offenses than those you have committed.*

I would like you to know that—inasmuch as I am not personally acquainted with you—I have a tremendous amount of empathy for you, and I hope that you will put your mind to realizing your power to help the people whose lives are being stolen by the "Florida" criminal justice system.

With love,

Inga La Gringa

And what might be the fate of privileged children who do not accept the mythology of the streets that nurture them? Kids who see the nakedness of the father despite all the luxuries and material trappings that are designed to keep their eyes averted?

What follows is an excerpt from an interview I found on Portland's Indymedia website on August 23, 2002, the day after the protests that greeted Arbusto, who had just announced that the way to fight forest fires was to cut down the trees, and the way for him and his friends to control the oil resources of the planet was to—again—carpet bomb the people of Iraq back into the Stone Age.

I am here today because I don't believe what my parents' society is doing. They are rich. They sent me to a private school last year and thought they could keep me from thinking about all this. I know that rich people in the country are killing other people to get their money. When I ask my parents about why the trees are being killed or why people in other countries are our slaves they get really mad and send me to a private school. So here I am. And maybe someone here will answer my questions and maybe I have to run away and find other young people who don't believe in having money made in the wrong way.

It's all connected you know. The way women are treated and the way people in other countries are treated. They treat us like children and say we should not ask questions. Then if we do ask questions they reject us. I used to try to be accepted by everyone. I tried to be cute and pretty. I starved myself, I was bulimic and anorexic. I had to go to this private school to learn to eat again. Now, I am back in Portland and I want to feed myself the truth. I hope that I find other people who will speak the truth.[20]

This narrative broke my heart in exactly the same way as when I hear of young men and women killing each other, or being beaten or killed by the police, or being sent to prison for "crimes" that rich, privileged, often white youth are merely slapped on the hand for. (Although Noelle Bush, for instance, is neither a youth nor, for that matter, white.)

White and white-identified children who question the culture of wealth from which they and their parents have sprung are pretty much left to their own devices, in terms of survival.

In this context, less privileged kids are in a slightly better position. They more often have friends, family, and community who tend to also be dealing with a similar fight to survive in a racist and violent society.

This is, however, a slightly better position in a very specific context.

The corpses, disrupted families, and jailed lives do not belong to wealthy white kids.

The other day, a friend and I were talking about the highly organized aspects of Mormonism. I have had a big beef with— we could even call it a prejudice against—Mormons for many years. My friend was making an attempt to better inform me. She told me about how she went to Salt Lake City with her band one time, and was amazed to find contingents of disgruntled punk rock Mormon kids. They were very organized, and procured permits and venues for shows and fun events, and other resources from their community. Many of them were preparing to go on missions—a requirement in the Mormon church—and lamented the thought of having to shave off their orange mohawks.

I listened to her story, and thought about Mormon kids vs. kids in ghettos, in barrios, in poor rural communities, and on reservations. Mormon kids are sent out on missions to see the world; they're given money, clothes, a bike, a nametag, and an entitled view of exactly who and what god is. Gang members are given guns and an illegal drug economy, and left to sink or swim. I wonder what this world would look like if poor kids of color and indian kids were accorded resources similar to Mormon kids'. I am quite sure it would result in a huge drop in criminal activity, incarceration rates, and drug abuse, and a transformation of the way gangs are perceived.

I often fantasize about how my cultural environment would be different if white supremacist racism were consciously examined. I think I do this because explicit imaginings are nice mini-holidays from reliable despair.

A recent fantasy involves a real-life game show called, um, "The Manifest Destiny Extravaganza." It is an over-the-top game show, with lights, podiums that rise up from the stage floor in festive-colored fog, and scantily clad trannies, men, and women dancing around, maybe also serving as a kind of choir or chorus at certain times. The show's emcee— a B-boy/flygirl drag king genderfucker—is smarmy in the best possible way. S/he breakdances while contestants are thinking or writing down answers, dresses super flashy, and has big hair.

There are three contestants. They have to prove their intelligence about the true history of our nation. They gotta be up on slave rebellions, indian nation uprisings, treaties, and other legal machinations that were/are of sole benefit to whites, assassinations, wars, brutal occupations, and deep biographical information about politicians, industry bosses, and labor unions. Or maybe each contestant will have a specialty, such as the history of Scotch Irish slave ownership in Edgefield, "South Carolina."

Whatever.

The point is, they gotta know their shit, right.

So people watch this show and learn history, and the winning contestants get to Manifest their Destiny. They get to go to film school or learn how to play the piano. They get a kickass independent publishing or recording deal. They get to go to a high-class baking school anywhere on earth. The prize is any resource they need to manifest their hearts' most passionate destiny.

Another fantasy of mine is "Gang 'n' Gay Pride Day," when all the gang members, queers, and their families and allies in any given community get together and march through the streets in unity and mutual respect, and then have a big day in the park with rap 'n' disco music, drag queens, everyone's flags waving in the sky, and happy barbecue-sauce-stained kids running all over the place.

Okay, fantasy time's over.

That was a nice little holiday.

Let's get back to reliable despair.

If you perceive the police, the "justice" system, prisons, or any other white or white-identified male power structure as an entity made up of individuals who are focused on maintaining a system of white male domination and control—rather than accepting the various projected images of protecting, serving, rehabilitating, educating, or governing—then you see them in their nakedness.

Your eyes are no longer averted.

The only power you are then susceptible to is physical force.

This interests me greatly, for in the story of Ham, I see a great divide between how unconscious white and white-identified people perceive these institutions and how everyone else on the planet perceives them.

First nation people and people of color in the Americas, and entire populations in so-called third world countries, are more likely to see white or white-identified men of power in the context of maintaining a system of control because these folks represent populations the white men must control in order to maintain their power.

With the majority of the population willing to look away, this machination feeds upon itself and culminates in lived realities where racist blowhards like Rush Limbaugh colonize *space* inside our imaginations *regardless* of whether or not we "agree" with them.

Like Ham, and unlike Shem and Japheth, a lot of people in the U.S. see no point in tiptoeing around Noah's big drunk ofay ass.

Absolutely none of these millions and millions of people in the United States of America, however, are Rupert Murdoch, Roger Ailes, Bill Gates, Michael Eisner, Steven Spielberg, David Geffen, or indeed, Rush Limbaugh.

But because most of these millions and millions of

people do not address the reality and overall pattern of white supremacist racist male domination, we do not see each other struggling. We do not perceive ourselves as having choices that affect our destiny.

The collective practice of averting eyes maintains itself in much the same way as globalization, illegal drug economies, and autogenocide do in poor nations and communities.

Think of this in terms of abuse in a family:

If you know in your heart that something is wrong, but you are coerced into acting as if nothing is wrong, then you are taking part, and you know this. Maybe you are taking part in your own abuse, or maybe you are taking part in the abuse of someone else, but you are, nonetheless, taking part. And since you know in your heart how fully wrong and fucked it is, but you don't see a way out, you choose to continue to take part because it might kill you inside for a while to admit to yourself that you are doing this.

That is how Amerikkka (dys)functions.

What Amerikkka does not seem to grasp is that after you die inside for a while—which is, indeed, incredibly painful—you get reborn.

Which is, indeed, incredibly healing.

The first time is always hardest, but it gets easier with practice.

There are a lot of white people who experience the rigid protocols maintaining this system of white male domination.

The environmental forest spirit warriors whom I love and

adore and give thanks for every day of my life have been legally killed, beaten, incarcerated, or threatened with death by logging industry thugs and the police.

The warriors see the white man in his nakedness.

The largely white group of anti-Arbusto protesters in Portland who witnessed a policeman pepper spraying a ten-month-old baby and her father, then, according to eyewitness accounts, saying something to the effect of, "That's why you shouldn't bring kids to protests," and hucking it up with his buddies as the child screamed in pain—they have seen the white man in his nakedness.

The hospital workers who were dumbfounded at such an act of cruelty while treating this tiny patient's horror-filled eyes, nose, and throat have seen the white man in his nakedness too.

Dock workers on the West Coast saw the white man in his nakedness when he locked them out of their jobs and told the lapdog media mouthpieces that the workers wouldn't meet the "generous" negotiations they were offered.

People of *all races* see this shit go down.

By and large, however, white people have to *be engaged in a specific context* that is perceived as threatening to the descendents of Noah's favorite sons before we *experience* the maintenance of these rigid protocols. Even then, we often choose not to educate ourselves about the historic struggle and daily reality of so many of our fellow citizens.

All people of color and first nation folks evidently have to do in order to pose a threat to the white man is get born.

Indigenous children and children of color—those not

raised in privileged, heavily sheltered, imperialist, or white-identified environments—are much more often the recipients of oral histories describing the police in their nakedness, because their families are the ones to whom the police most often display physical force.

As a means of survival, I've learned to craft my countenance when dealing with the police. Because of the color of my skin, I have had the luxury and opportunity to learn to transform my face and manufacture emergency calming pheromones when the police are around. I also project many accepted stereotypes for white women in this culture. I act lost, worried, neurotic, confused, scared, and/or super, super, super sorry for inconveniencing a police officer. I consciously cash in on my whiteness because I do not want my freedom taken away. For many people, this is not an option, and so their freedom is taken away.

The police generally assume people of color see them in their nakedness, but they can *sense* it, regardless of their perception of you and your race. They can smell the attendant fear of knowing that, in their nakedness, they might just kick your ass and craft a reason to take away your freedom if they damn well please. If they know you know these things, they will fuck with you for the exact same reason that a dog licks his balls—because he can.

So I learned to make it look and smell like I do not know these things.

I cannot possibly understate the breadth of this luxury.

I have, like I say, been leery of the police since I was
a kid, but figuring out a formal, totally conscious survival
tactic was inspired soon after my seventeenth birthday, when
I punched a cop in the face. During my ride to jail, I was
informed at least eleven times that I was a nasty little whore
who needed, more than anything else on god's good earth,
to be anally fucked.[†] My whiteness—and possibly my last
name[‡]—protected me from being raped in my holding cell at
the San Luis Obispo Men's Colony.

I realized I can *pretend* I don't know the police are not what they
present themselves to be, and not be harassed by them, or I can
let it show in my eyes and countenance that I know they are up
to very little good, and be hassled all the fucken time.

My days as a punk rocker provided ample opportunity to
develop this perspective.

When I was a teenager in Santa Maria, "California," all the
cops knew me and my friends. They pulled us over whenever
they saw us, busted our parties, threw us in jail, and beat us up

---

† If I had been a seventeen-year-old Chicana or black woman who
punched a cop in the face, my chance of being raped would have increased
dramatically. Also, I might very well have written my first book from the
confines of a prison cell, if at all.

‡ The cop's wife and my mom were nurses together. My mom knew that this
cop beat his wife, and I do believe a combination of late-night phone calls
and a bit of blackmail had something to do with the decision to leave me be.

if we were boys—this latter tendency was what inspired me to punch that cop in the face in the first place.

Through these teenage experiences, I developed a practice of attracting the police, and I had problems with them in every town and city I went to.

After spending a solitary night chained to the wall in a holding cell, not knowing if someone was going to walk in and rape me, I started looking at the way I comported myself around the police.

I was *afforded* this moment of clarity by my white supremacist, Noah-lovin' society.

In my twenties, I learned exactly how to make the police not see me.

It was rather an emergency situation then too, during an interview with a white policeman. I wanted to interview him because he seemed like an arrogant asshole, and I thought it would be interesting to find out where he was coming from.

I told him it was for a "school project" (which it was, more or less).

One thing I've learned from interviewing others and being interviewed is that people (including myself) love to talk about their lives.

People love, love, love to open up and tell their stories.

So he said yes and we met at a diner.

By listening closely to the policeman's characterizations

of himself as well as his (for reals) drunken father, which came to me through a very odd stream of consciousness that I prodded along with a comment or question here and there, I came to the horrifying realization that this cop was responsible for the murder of a young white kid a number of months prior.

He confessed to me through a series of strange anecdotes and repeated mentions of the death of this young man, which I had in no way connected to him, much less brought up as a topic of conversation. At one moment in our conversation, I suddenly *knew* he was living with the reality of murdering someone's beloved child, friend, brother, lover.

My heart pounded like a jackrabbit's in an osprey's shadow.

I got a crash course in not being "seen" while I sat across the table from that man. I became a doe-eyed actress, filled with breathless wonder at his ever-so-interesting life. I raised my eyebrows in stupidity and crafted questions that confirmed his courage and masculinity: "Do you ever get scared when you pull over cars?" "Why do you think people commit crimes?" "How long does it take you to put on your whole uniform?"

He was an entitled psychopath, employed to protect and serve his community.

I knew this like I know exactly how much distance I need to get my bike brakes to work on a rainy day.

So yes.

I have been granted *hugely luxurious choices*—perhaps even the choice to interview a white cop who finds me unthreatening enough to unconsciously unburden his mortal sin upon—by my society, because of how I am perceived.

I could fuck these choices up, by becoming a huge forest activist. I could certainly *attract the attention* of Shem and Japheth's descendents, so they'd feel like it was a good idea to plant a bomb in my car and then blame it on me, like the FBI did to Judi Bari, RIP, but the vastly larger point here is:

Many people are not,
at any time in their lives,
afforded
any
of these
hugely luxurious choices.
Period.

In cooking terms, "to coddle" means to cook something at a temperature just below boiling point.

This definition interests me greatly because white and white-identified people are cooked just below the boiling point. They can live their whole lives without realizing they're being cooked. As long as this population is kept at a comfortable temperature, they will go along with the lies.

Everyone else is heated at a rolling boil. They know they're being cooked, and with that comes a certain sense of bittersweet freedom, which is where the imagination brews up rebellion and dissent. Which is also where white society knows it's gotta focus its overt domination if it wants to keep the coddled folks from feeling the heat.

I understand what white people have to go up against in realizing the part we play in a system of domination, so I can also vividly imagine the blue wall of silence that police officers (don't) face. And I understand the red, white, and blue ocean of denial that U.S. citizens (refuse to) face.

It is easier for everyone to live in denial, but everyone at the receiving end of this denial gets shafted. Since, in some context or another, everyone is at the receiving end of someone else's denial, then sooner or later, everyone gets shafted.

On and on and on.

My friend Cedric is one of the most peaceful, kind, loving, and warmhearted people I have ever been blessed to know. He is a Taurus bass player, which is the best sign for a man to be and the best instrument for anyone to play. He has long dreadlocks and drives something like a Volkswagen Passat.

He *gave* me money so I could go on a national book tour when *Cunt* came out.

We sat across the table from one another in Seattle's Café Septieme, where the bathrooms are always spicy sweet smelling, and I told him I needed money to go on tour.

He was quiet for a moment, and his chess player eyes went somewhere else, maybe peering into his bank account, minusing this from that, transferring the one to the other. He comes back and goes, "I can help you. How much do you need."

I didn't answer him for a while.

My heart exploded in my chest, and I started crying.

I am, for the most part, a crybaby.

But I did not cry out loud when he told me about the period in his life when his car still appeared shiny and new and he kept getting pulled over by the police on his way home from late-night gigs, and the time he placed his hands at two and ten o'clock on the steering wheel, to lessen his chances of being shot, and when the cop came up to the window, Cedric said, "I am going to reach for my wallet now and retrieve my driver's license."

This particular cop was black too, and told Cedric not to tell the cops about reaching for anything. "Just get your wallet out," he said, "don't make announcements. That will only make them wonder about you."

He was giving my friend brotherly survival advice.

I do not want my friend to need to be given such advice.

I do not want my friend to wonder if he will be shot every time the police decide to wonder why a black guy with dreads is driving a nice, new car.

I do not want my friend to live with the reality of potential certain death.

When he told me this story, I cried inside, secret quiet.

I couldn't cry out loud like in Septieme when he gave me tour money, because this is his fucking reality.

This is his life.

I didn't want Cedric to see my terror. He has grown up with his family's eyes upon him. He does not need to see me looking at him with this same fear.

I asked myself why my friend's reality made me cry inside and the answer, as recorded in my journal, was this:

> I am crying for myself and everyone who abides life
> in a culture where people who mirror images of what
> "criminals," "gangstas," or "terrorists" look like in the
> existing mainstream white supremacist imagina-
> tion face possible legal execution whenever they get
> behind the wheel of a car.

Cedric's anecdote—one of millions—inspired feelings simi-lar to those I experienced when I realized the effect rape had on my mother's life, on my life, and on the lives of millions of people in this world. There is nothing I can do to alter the lived reality of this long history of violence, humiliation, and hatred.

Not in my family, and not in the world.

I know what has happened, and continues to happen, and inside of this intimate and cultural history and present night-mare is me and my childhood.

Inside of this churning mass of power—a giant wave of white supremacist racism—is still me. And just like that time the ocean almost killed me, how I choose to react to the situa-tion dramatically affects my destiny.

It is interesting to look at my two main Ham sources.

When I heard about Ham from Riz, there was a certain amount of personal pain involved. He grew up on the receiving end of this bullshit story, and spent many years of his life deconstructing it. It hurts him that his grandmother still believes it. She loves her religion, and she is an old woman and there is just no place for deconstructing and recontextualizing her beliefs. The story of Ham lingers in the undercurrents of Riz's upbringing. Whenever he goes to visit his grandmother—in this deeply personal and intimate setting—Ham and his "shame" are present.

When I read about Ham in Derrick Jensen's book, there was a certain amount of personal pain involved too, but Derrick grew up at the victor's end of this bullshit story. He spent years of his life deconstructing it because *it didn't sit well with him.*

Derrick's pain arises from a place similar to my own. We both knew we were being told lies, but we did not know what the truth was. Lie after lie after lie was shoved down our throats, and there was no recourse for negotiating all of this falseness. I mean, when you're eight, you aren't gonna meet much success going up against the police and the bible because you have neither the vocabulary nor the experience to communicate your disbelief in such huge, huge lies. You are supposed to grow up and take the lies on, wear them like a second skin.

Maybe this bullshit story hurts you intimately, or maybe it has never sat well with you, or maybe you are perfectly content with it, but no matter what, it is absolutely a bullshit story.

Eenie, Meenie, Miney, Mo, Catch a Cracker by the Toe

Once, when I lived in *la corazón* of the Mission in San Francisco, I was washing clothes at the local *lavandería*. After loading my washers, I noticed a businessman-on-his-day-off gravitating toward me, trying to make eye contact. I glazed my expression so it looked like I could only see the walls behind him.

Mr. Business was the kind of (white) man who looks at me disdainfully—if he acknowledges my presence at all—when I am in his elevator at his office building (which is probably a case of me creating my own reality, for I am almost guaranteed to disdain being in his elevator as much as, if not more than, he disdains me being in his elevator). There are thousands of social contexts in which I would have been completely baffled as to why this man was seeking me out.

This, however, was not one of them.

After all, I've been living white with whites for over thirty-five years.

Everyone in the room was of Chicano, Mexicano, Guatemalan, and El Salvadoran descent. It was a huge, lively family scene, with moms, dads, kids, bachelors and bachelorettes, grandmothers and grandfathers all running around tending to their chores, just like me and Mr. Business.

But see, our buddy was threatened to find himself being the *minority*. He didn't like this one little iota. His response was to seek out the only other white person in the room, in a woefully impaired effort to somehow form a *group* of white people.

Eventually, I guess out of sheer desperation, he gave up on the passive-aggressive eye-contact approach, and directly tried to engage me in conversation.

I pigsnorted loudly and went outside for some fresh air.

I was not into Mr. Business.

Preoccupied with learned fear-based racial designations, he not only alienated himself in this happy, busy setting, but did so in a completely entitled manner. His anxious insecurity at the sudden, horrifying realization that he *is a white person* did nothing to endear him to me. I was furthermore completely offended by his attempt to include me in his ignorance based solely on the color of my skin.

And white people say they don't experience racism.

I experience racism *all the fucken time,* and it is most often perpetuated by other whites, who extort me in millions of subtle ways to be complicit.

Ooo, didn't Mr. Business think I sucked when I left him high and dry, hanging there to deal with his own shit. And don't go thinking it was his masculine virility that I offended, because he was not flirting with me. He was attempting to create an alliance based solely on our alleged racial kinship. He knew I knew this and it made him uncomfortable as fuckall.

Next up, he decided to passive-aggressively "punish" me with low-level hostility. From that moment on, his body was stiff and he took every opportunity to stalk past me, tense and seething.

Consumed by his fragile identity that was only supported in the context of a white majority, he had to somehow assert his position to himself. At first I was viewed as a potential ally, but ultimately, I became the antagonist he chose for his obsessive drama.

The really fascinating thing about this interaction was how the entire saga unfolded almost silently. He said maybe "Hi," and I pigsnorted, which counts as verbal communication.

Other than that, no sounds were exchanged.

If someone had videotaped the entire episode, it would have been completely uninteresting. Just a bunch of people washing their clothes. Yet, a totally intense, racially charged communication buzzed in the room like an idling chainsaw.

I realize that it was, indeed, *my fault* that Mr. Business made that compelling display of insecurity and fear, *for it would not have appeared* had I not pointed it out by pigsnorting at his projected characterization of me and everyone else in the *lavandería*.

If I had agreed to go along with it—that is, entered into a conversation with him—he would have never been faced with his own white supremacist racism, and moreover, I would have felt as if I had deeply betrayed myself.

Not that it even approached that point.

The moment I saw the look of relief in his eyes when I walked in with my dirty clothes, I knew what he was up to, and never considered corroborating his identity at the expense of my own.

Like I say, I've come to understand that unconscious white people are quite adept at herding and corralling their perceptions into great stretches of denial to keep from discovering the magnificently unrealistic reality they and our culture have constructed for what would otherwise be glorious and sacred lives.

I want no truck in this.

My friend Steve Flusty hooked me up with a term to describe phenomenona such as this. When I first started working on this book, he asked about my "thesis" (as he academically called it), and I groped for words, describing the endlessly various, often highly innocuous, manifestations of white supremacist racism in our culture. Somewhere in these ramblings, Flusty said, "Well, that sounds *awfully* similar to heteronormativity, so maybe you are talking about something we could call 'white normativity.'"

Church bells announcing the resurrection jangled in my heart as I lunged across the table and planted a kiss on Flusty E. Coyote's supergenius forehead.

Armed with this term, I was much better equipped to articulate the environment in which I was born.

Thank you, Flusty. Thank you ever most kindly.

And so.

White normativity is a debilitating and widespread condition/affliction where the assumption of whiteness and the overall goodness of whiteness is, uh, normal. Not unlike cancer or poverty, white normativity manifests in fractalized, endless scenarios. Racism, hate groups, legal and illegal lynching, tokenism, and economic, sexual, and legal slavery all exist *within* white normativity. It gives these forms of oppression an environment in which to thrive. White normativity itself, however, is generally an innocuous, day-to-day, moment-by-moment assumption that whiteness is the accepted standard of worth for everyone on the planet.

It is the foundation, the framework, the house that Jack built. And we all live in it together.

Autobiography of a Blue-Eyed Devil

Almost every day of my life, I witness white people enacting learned normative racial ignorance and fears.

White normativity is everywhere: The white gas station attendant's body stiffens when three saggy-pants Filipino American teenage boys come laughing into the store late at night. I watch him watch them as he fumbles around ringing up my sunflower seeds and water. I know precisely where the young men are in the store by following the man's eyes. For a time, in his mind, I am gone. He ceases even the pretense of ringing me up. I do not harrumph to get his attention so he'll hurry up with this piddly transaction so I can continue my drive up I-5. This experience becomes a part of my long night ahead—an opportunity for me to see a total stranger in his nakedness. I know it is because I am a white woman that he unconsciously feels safe unconsciously tuning me out.

I watch him watch the kids.

He is so afraid, I almost feel sad for him.

I fantasize about the look on his face if I were to whip out a semiautomatic weapon and train it on his forehead. I momentarily lament the fact that I believe guns attract bad situations and it is therefore against the grain of my being to have one in my possession.

He emerges from his racially based fantasy of terror, right as I emerge from my gun fantasy, when the young men get in line behind me. For the first time since they've entered the store, their laughter and joking subsides. I know they sense me and the man and our weird fantasies, but, so immersed were they in their own happiness at hanging out together, they truly had no idea what was going on up at the cash register.

All of this has taken place in less than four minutes.

I say nothing about this to anyone because it is just too ordinary.

The white cop turns, puts his hand on his hip, fingers lightly caressing his billy club like it is a lover he hates to leave in the morning, when he sees a black male friend and I enter the coffee shop and get in line behind him. I wonder if the cop is aware that he did this when he saw my friend. I wonder how many times my friend has—even peripherally—seen a cop do things like this, and how many cumulative hours of his sacred, glorious life he has spent, either consciously or unconsciously, learning to deflect and ignore such grievous-bodily-harm-threatening, potentially life-endangering police actions.

I say nothing about this to my friend because it is so fleeting, and if, perchance, he missed seeing the cop's almost imperceptible movement, I certainly don't want to point it out to him.

Unlike me, my friend lives in this environment with fearful, racist, armed (white) cops physically noting his existence every day of his life.

❧

Autobiography of a Blue-Eyed Devil

On *The Oprah Winfrey Show* a black man and a white man discuss a film they have made together called *Two Towns of Jasper*. The white man filmed the white people of Jasper and the black man filmed the black people of Jasper. This is the "Texas" town where James Byrd Jr. was chained to a truck and dragged for miles into the darkness and, oh lordisa, killed.

(A moment of silence, please, for Mr. Byrd, for his family and community, and for everyone who lives with the shadow of violent white hatred hanging anywhere near the vicinity of their lives.)

Oprah interviews the filmmakers, and I learn that the two men have been friends for over twenty years. She asks them if they were surprised that a horrifying crime like that could take place in "this day and age." ("What day, what age?" I whispered to myself.)

The black man says no, he was not surprised.

The white man says yes, he was surprised.

And I freak out because how could this white man be friends with this black man for *over two decades* and NEVER, NOT ONCE, see the ignorance and fear white people perpetuate toward his friend and relate that to the three men who decided it was a good idea to drag a man to his death?

I scream into the dreaded teevee, "HOW IS THIS POSSIBLE?"

But the teevee has no answers for me.

In *Venus Boyz,* a brilliant documentary about drag kings and gender variance that everyone should see, MilDréd Gerestant describes how difficult it is for her to hail a cab when she is dressed as a man.

Eenie, Meenie, Miney, Mo, Catch a Cracker by the Toe

In stark contrast, Del LaGrace Volcano is astounded at how "men" watch out for one another, and how much more respect he gets living as a "man." Conditioned as he has been— and how most white people are—he does not feel the need to qualify his experience as that of a "white man" instead of just a general "man."

MilDréd's experiences passing as a black man are much, much different than Del's experiences passing as a white man.

While Mr. Volcano's insights are every bit as valid as Ms. Gerestant's, I found it nonetheless disheartening that his perspective as an extremely marginalized individual was completely devoid of acknowledgment of white normative racism.

Even in one of the most oppressed demographics of U.S. culture, where the social constructs of sexuality and gender are examined, challenged, and totally resisted with stunning abandon and otherwise autonomous imagination, the social construct of white normative racism is alive and well, festering in our hearts.

I am in Walla Walla, "Washington," staying at a big old house that has been converted to an inn. All of the other rooms branch off from the upstairs landing, but my room is accessed by a short hallway.

When I arrive, I am tired and don't notice much about the place, other than it is just fucken out of control on the Halloween decorations, like Martha Stewart jacked on meth has had her way with every balustrade, doorway, nook, and cranny.

Autobiography of a Blue-Eyed Devil

It isn't until the morning that I notice the two "picka-ninny" reproductions on the wall in the little hallway leading to my room.

The first, entitled *Watermelon Kiss*, portrays two coal-oily, unkempt, knotty-haired five- or six-year-old children, with huge red lips half the size of their faces. With one arm, the little boy is hugging a watermelon larger than he is. In his other hand, he grips the little girl's face, causing her lips to pucker up, in what can only be described as monstrous red labia.

As things turn out, this is the least offensive of the two.

In the second reproduction, *Loves Me, Loves Me Not*, the same children are featured. The little girl has her back to the boy. She is holding a black-eyed Susan in her hand, plucking off the yellow petals and dropping them on the ground. Behind her, the boy is leaning against a hillock. A dazed look on his face, he smiles vaguely. In one hand, he holds a nicked and rusty straight-edge razor, poised at his jugular. In the other, a sawed-off shotgun, finger on the trigger, pointing toward his head, via his lower jaw. I am given to understand that if it turns out that she does not love him, his just-past-toddling life will end in a blood-splatteringly gruesome suicide.

I reel.

I look around the plush, overly adorned inn. Everything is in its place, sparkling and thoughtfully situated to achieve the calming effect of warm hearth and home. I feel like I am slog-ging through a physical metaphor—a huge can of Amerikkka concentrate—as I drag my ass down the stairs and outside for some blessed fresh air.

Eenie, Meenie, Miney, Mo, Catch a Cracker by the Toe

When I ask Jacked-on-Meth Martha how she rationalizes these fully offensive, morally repugnant images, she gives me the blankest look I have ever in my life seen, exactly like a freshly gessoed canvas. I watch her eyes as she tries to wrap her mind around why I, a fellow cracker, might be so enraged, but I guess she can't think of a reason.

Pupils dilated, lips pursed like drawstring sweats.

Says nothing at all.

I walk away, wondering how many years it has taken Jacked-on-Meth Martha to herd and corral her perceptions into this great stretch of denial in her heart.

In the *New York Times,* in a fully run-of-the-mill, dime-a-dozen ad promoting a new book, the following blurb appeared:

> I'm a white, urban reader whose imagination was
> seized by a black author writing about a black cowboy
> coming of age in 1871. That's a tribute to the power of
> a fine novel.
> —Bob Minzesheimer

Wow.

A *black* author wrote a novel about a *black cowboy* and the story seized the imagination of *the white urban reader,* Bob Minzesheimer. Based on this information, I am utterly convinced that this book, *Gabriel's Story,* by David Anthony Durham, must be a really, really amazing work of literature. It is, after all, *a feat of tremendous literary prowess* for a black writer to seize the imagination of a white reader, even more so a savvy urban one who has seen it all by now.

Would the publishing company have included this blurb in an ad for one of its books if the races of the reviewer and author were switched around? And would the *New York Times* ad proofreader have let it run?

Let's see how it sounds:

I am a black urban reader whose imagination was seized by a white author writing about a white cowboy coming of age in 1871. That's a tribute to the power of a fine novel.

In this way—while the book still sounds amazing—the reviewer becomes kinda ignorant and racist to the white normative mind. A white reviewer's ignorant and racist critique about a black author, however, is considered perfectly acceptable copy in one of the most "respected" daily newspapers in the country.

Another way of looking at this, in the post–Toni Morrison, post–James Baldwin, post–Langston Hughes, post–Zora Neale Hurston, post–Alex Haley, post–Ntozake Shange, post-Sapphire, post–Jacqueline Woodson, post–Sanyika Shakur (a.k.a. Monster Kody Scott), post–Martin Luther King Jr., post–Neely Fuller, post–Malcolm X, post–Edwidge Danticat, post–bell hooks, post–Octavia Butler, post– Jamil Abdullah Al-Amin (a.k.a. H. Rap Brown), post–Richard Wright, post–Frederick Douglass world we

Eenie, Meenie, Miney, Mo, Catch a Cracker by the Toe

presently live in, is: Bob Minzesheimer is embarrassingly ignorant, yet his thought process is honored by mainstream Amerikkka. He is allowed, and moreover financially compensated, to
critique the creative work of other human beings.

This, and the millions of other similar slights that are perpetuated on reality teevee shows, music videos, news reporting,
advertisements, and award shows, is logical (or rational, plausi-
ble, meaningful, realistic, attractive, moral, or just) only within
the construct of white normativity.

When a population's hearts and imaginations are colonized, the
collective sense of humanity is shepherded by their colonizers.
Those who colonize imagination do not have the population's
best interest at heart.

Some populations in the world resist this, some do not.
We do not.

A *few* of the *many* well-known imagination colonizers in the
U.S. are Disney, McDonald's, Coca-Cola, Viacom, MTV, VH1,
Time, Newsweek, the *New York Times, Los Angeles Times, Wash-
ington Post,* and *Wall Street Journal,* DreamWorks SKG, Universal
Music Group, KFC, Nestlé, ABC, BET, CNN, Univision, Clear
Channel Communications, Aaron Spelling, Steven Spielberg,
Jerry Bruckheimer, Ridley Scott, *People* magazine, Microsoft,
Wal-Mart, Warner Bros., *Entertainment Tonight,* Geffen Records,
Burger King, *COPS,* Nintendo, and Starbucks.

In my country, these are some of the "nongovernmental organizations" that assist in constructing a reality in which whiteness is the polestar and everything else revolves around it.

In washrooms all across the country, hand-washing and CPR charts displayed on walls feature (often cartoon) images of white hands killing germs and saving white lives. Everything from driver's education manuals and swimsuit calendars to nail polish sample posters in drugstores features white bodies.

Mickey Mouse's face is Caucasian, even though he is, otherwise, a black mouse.

Billboards depict white people, sometimes with a friend or two of color, unless the product is being marketed *strictly to* people of color. Then you see ads for Miller High Life showing a group of carefree, heterosexual (usually light-skinned) black friends gathered around the table at their friendly neighborhood bar. Asian and Pacific Islander people sometimes figure into ads for computer stuff and cars, but not much else outside of vacation posters to Thailand and Hawai'i.

As a general rule, and perhaps in unconscious reaction to the fact that this nation is the result of genocide, indigenous people are rarely seen in advertising, unless they are the explicit subject, as in college fund advertisements featuring fully assimilated-appearing Cherokee attorneys and Seminole Cree doctors trained in Western medicine. In ads such as these, whites are presented as soulful benefactors, though we are not necessarily present. We are there in spirit, putting forth the idea that indians really can achieve "success" if they try hard enough, and if white people "help" them.

Stripped of white normativity bolstering one's perceptions, places such as Squaw Valley, team names like the Cleveland Indians, and playground chants like "Eenie Meenie Miney Mo, Catch a Nigger by the Toe," sound racist, vicious, and meanspirited.

Look around our world, and see all the smiling white, white-defined, and white-identified faces.

They are selling more than sunglasses, alcohol, movie tickets, and charity.

They are selling whiteness too.

In the interview "Bamboozled by Ads: Politics, Propaganda and Advertising," Jean Kilbourne discusses the phenomenon of people in the U.S. thinking we are immune from cultural indoctrination by those who colonize space in our minds:

> The only reason that Americans might be more vulnerable than people from other countries is that we believe we're not vulnerable. There's such a widespread belief in America that we're not influenced by anything really, that you know, we're not culturally conditioned. And in a sense, that makes it more difficult for us to really see the kind of conditioning that does go on all around us. So it's a way in which—and I think the advertisers really count on this—that we

believe we're not influenced, and therefore we're less
alert, in a way. . . .

I'm sure that most Americans would say they
want to be talked to as thinking people, but the evidence is clear that in fact we tend to be very susceptible to being sold stuff. And one of the things that's
alarmed me the most as I've studied advertising over
all these years, is the extent to which our political
system has really been hijacked by the advertisers.
That it's all about advertising, commercials, spin,
hype, and not at all, really, about the issues anymore. But it's very difficult to get people to really see
that and understand it.[1]

Whiteness is not an organic state of nature. It is carefully created and maintained, and it, as well as the "race" of white
people, is but a minuscule fractal within the universe.

Furthermore, as Flusty E. Coyote points out in the foreword, "whiteness" is not defined by either skin color or the
absence of skin color. Jewish, Arabic, Irish, Italian, Chicano,
and Hispanic people, and many people of Asian descent,
often have very "white" skin, but are not considered "white"
by WASP, Aryan, or media standards. Brazilian, Belizean, or
Mexican people who are considered "white" in their countries of origin will not necessarily be considered "white" in the
United States. Some Jews I know (mostly on the West Coast)
identify as "white" and some (mostly on the East Coast) identify as "Jewish," which is not "white." My Iranian friends mark

Eenie, Meenie, Miney, Mo, Catch a Cracker by the Toe

"Asian," "Caucasian," or "Other" on official forms because there is no appropriate designation.

White "purity" racists look at me and *see* a perfectly acceptable-looking version of whitey, but I know from experience that when they hear my *last* name (which is, evidently, a big letdown after learning my first name) and find out I am a hybrid Irish Italian (both "mud races"), I instantly transmogrify into dirt white filth twice over.

Whiteness is a mind-set, a "way of life," a series of elaborate choices.

It's social and breezy and debonair.

It's cocktails after work and pillow-baby-soft toilet paper.

It's restaurants that tinkle with silver and crystal, bustle quiet with waitstaff.

It's clean clothes and clipped lawns.

It's hunting and fishing and skiing and golfing.

It's a college fund for the kids and tailgate parties before the big game.

It's the proposal, the engagement, the wedding, the cake.

It's *lovely* children.

It's sex, drugs, and rock 'n' roll.

It's a promise to accept a white man as your lord and personal savior.

It's baseball, hot dogs, apple pie, and Chevrolet.

It's *Friends*.

It's celebrity lifestyles and haute couture.

It's presidents and senators.

It's a lot of things, whiteness is.

But mostly it's invisible.

It's everywhere and nowhere, always lurking somewhere.

Interestingly, white supremacist, separatist, and nationalist groups are generally, for better or worse, far more evolved in their understanding of race politics than the general population of unconscious white people.

There are conscious off-whites in this culture who are highly aware of what whiteness is, what it historically means, and what it presently represents. Some, such as William Upski Wimsatt, author of *No More Prisons* and *How to Get Stupid White Men Out of Office,* are found in the hiphop community. Michael Moore's views are available to a very mainstream audience. Mab Segrest and Tim Wise have been writing about this shit for years. Stan Goff mixes his antiracist and feminist ideologies with his vast military experience in his antiwar activism. All of these folks also have huge audiences. And one mustn't forget the blessed Quakers,[†] who remain present and accounted for in resisting this nation's crimes against humanity for the past three hundred years.

Aside from these folks (and at the opposite end of the spectrum), one of the few demographics that have earned the distinction of knowing they are white are the white supremacist types. They think about race, and it matters to them.[‡]

This particular brand of racial awareness, however, is a direct result of consciously embracing abject fear and ignorance.

Eenie, Meenie, Miney, Mo, Catch a Cracker by the Toe

So where does that leave the general unconscious white population?

Nowhere, that's where.

An extension of white people's unconsciousness of whiteness is the common, conversational designation of race *only* when someone is not white.

When telling a story, a white person will say "a girl," "the clerk," "some man," and "that little kid down the street," and it is taken for granted that whites are being spoken of.

As in: "There was one guy who was very straightlaced and I'm not sure why he was even there, and then this Japanese drag queen with a bouffant hairdo, it was fabulous, oh my god! And some skater kids and a black emcee and a bunch of other homos."

In this made-up description of an event, I am to understand that the straightlaced guy was white. The skater kids may have been a mixed brew of ethnicities, but I know they were not predominantly Cambodian or Somali American, and I can

---

† Who are, last I heard, being investigated as a "terrorist" organization for their proactive stance against the occupation in Iraq. Quakers are often getting into hot water with the U.S. government, lordisa bless them.

‡ On the (albeit rare) occasions that white supremacists dig their heads out of their asses, they have a penchant for becoming some of the most virulent and articulate white antiracist activists in their communities. Kinda like how some soldiers who took part in various U.S. occupations evolve into some of the most kickass antiwar activists our nation readily cultivates.

safely assume the homos were probably so overwhelmingly white as to not be designated anything else.

Daily and weekly newspaper and magazine articles specifically, and the media in general, are also great sources for viewing this phenomenon.

In the aftermath of the Columbine shootings *never* did the white mainstream media refer to the race of Dylan Klebold and Eric Harris. And every time there was another school shooting, the newspapers and -casters trumpeted headlines: "What's Wrong with America's Schoolkids?" The gun-toters were, without exception, referred to as "students," "kids," and "children." Yet, in every single case, it was *white boys* behind the massacres.

If boys of a single, specific race *other than* white were perpetrating these crimes, newspapers would blare headlines like "Another Samoan Youth Charged in School Shooting." CNN would have an in-depth investigation called "Samoans: What Are They Teaching Their Kids?" There would be a rise in hate crimes against Samoan Americans (or anyone who appears of Samoan descent in the mainstream media-influenced imagination), and the police would crack down on Samoan American gang members (or anyone who looks like a Samoan American gang member to the police), whether or not gangs had anything to do with the school shootings.

Any kid of color who took a gun to school would be (and is) described by his or her race, first and foremost. If this trend involved only girls, then gender would assuredly be designated. But since it's white boys, you know, *normal, general people*, they are described as "schoolkids." No mention of gender, much less race, ever enters the white mainstream public and media discussion.

And this poses a *serious* problem for white boys, and those of us who live in the world with them. If a pattern like this exists in our society, and no one is interested in finding out why white boys are freaking out, then no one is helping them, or, ultimately, loving them. Nowhere in the media is the very real condition of White Boy Rage discussed.

When I see photographs of Iraqi prisoners being terrorized, sexually humiliated, and tortured, there are often white male and female soldiers milling around or taking part. I have never ever seen an image of a person of color in a U.S. military uniform doing degrading things to other human beings. The person who wrote the report on these activities in the Abu Ghraib prison, General Antonio Taguba, is Filipino American. Many of the people working to cover up these kinds of atrocities with the tired-ass "bad apple" theory are also white or white-identified.

As with the Columbine massacre, nowhere in the mainstream media has it been acknowledged that *white* soldiers evidently feel compelled to sodomize Iraqi people with foreign objects—not at all unlike Officer Justin Volpe's desire to sodomize Abner Louima in a similar manner, and under similar conditions. To make a deep foray into this topic, one must discuss the nature of white supremacist racism in our country, and, well, that's just not considered normal.

A broadening concept of normalcy is often mistaken for "progress" in this culture—particularly in mainstream pop culture. The ongoing perception that the Civil Rights Movement was just a smashing success has led to a wider variety of representations of people of color in the movie, teevee, and music industries, but never to the point that white people's level of comfort is trespassed upon.

Nowadays, unconscious white people seem to mirthfully enjoy *looking back on* those crazy times when people were still experiencing, as Arbusto might say, "the habit of racism."

In an ad for a "comedy" called *Not Another Teen Movie,* the only person of color in a crowd of white girls, fraternity boys to be, and a naked female foreign exchange student was a character described as "the token black."

On *South Park*, the only black kid in the town is likewise named "Token."

Pwa, ha, ha, don't I get it?

It's *irony.*

It's white people laughing at how *in the past* we adopted this thing called "tokenism" to make us feel like we weren't a bunch of pieces of racist shit, and now that time in history is *over* and *we* have fully integrated—that is, included—people of color into *our* society so we can now laugh at how misguided we were when we needed tokenism.

Pwa, ha, ha, we used to be so silly.

But ya gotta love us, huh?

Eenie, Meenie, Miney, Mo, Catch a Cracker by the Toe

And then there are all the entertainment industry ghettos for people of color, which are often just as pedestrian, uninspiring, and offensive to the intellect of conscious folks as white normative entertainment is.

Black women appear on teevee and in movies more now than ever before, and are no longer constantly cast solely as prostitutes or mammies.

Big whoop dee muthafucken doo.

Why would anyone feel like "racism has disappeared" in Hollywood and in the media just because a couple of specific suck-ass stereotypes are no longer foisted onto the shoulders of a deeply complex and highly diverse demographic? Now there are a truckload of stereotypes instead of just two.

What a goddamn stellar improvement.

Hollywood slapped itself on the back when Hattie McDaniel won an Oscar in 1939 just as wholeheartedly as it did when Halle Berry won one in 2002.

Does it mean there is no more racism because black actresses, newscasters, show hosts, and journalists *exist at all* in this society? Because Oprah is so successful, racism no longer occurs?

This fully ridiculous sentiment was quite clear when the newspapers announced that Oprah had bought a home in Montecito, a very exclusive suburb of Santa Barbara. One excited longtime neighbor was gushing in the *Los Angeles Times* about what a wonderful indication this was that racism was absolutely finished in Amerikkka because back in the day, when Lena Horne wanted to move to Montecito, the residents *immediately and unanimously* stated, "Over our dead, rich, honky bodies."

I loved Oprah before she fawned over Laura Bush and Arnold Schwarzenegger.

Now I only like her.

Oprah does a lot of cool things. She does not talk as much shit as I like to hear, but that is (as my dear friend Harperetta would remind me) a value judgment, and Oprah is a very powerful woman who, I believe, truly wants the world to be a nice place for everyone.

If I want to hear a conservative retardist white or white-identified man or woman talking shit on the teevee, I am presented with a veritable plethora of choices. But if I want to hear even *one* revolutionary-minded black woman talking shit on the teevee, I am fresh the fuck out of luck.

I want to watch *Late Night with Joycelyn Elders*.

I want to watch the *Ramona Africa News Hour*.

I want to watch the variety show hosted by everyone's favorite spiritual healer and drag king, MilDréd Gerestant, where she calls all the shots and multigendered young people of all races perform spoken word and hiphop, sing, dance, lip-synch, and otherwise have a good time with their truths.

None of these folks have shows on teevee because of white normative racism, so don't "Oprah" me.

Eenie, Meenie, Miney, Mo, Catch a Cracker by the Toe

The former U.S. Commission on Civil Rights chairwoman Mary Frances Berry, Congresswoman Cynthia "For President" McKinney, and former Surgeon General Joycelyn Elders all have deeply compelling stories about what happens to powerful women of color who step outside the carefully demarcated constraints that white normativity demands.

Congresswoman Cynthia "For President" McKinney, for instance, wants to know exactly what happened on September 11, 2001, is fomenting plans for new black leadership in the U.S., and constantly speaks out on human rights. Consequently, much to the dismay of her constituents, careful machinations were employed to fraudulently vote her out of office in 2002. However, due to an overwhelming 2004 election victory, she's back in office.

Secretary of State and Oil Tanker Namesake Condoleezza Rice will never step outside of the constraints of white normative and/or supremacist racism. Her rise to power has been utterly steadfast and magnificent.

Although I can escape white normativity by rarely watching the teevee or opening any major magazine or newspaper, most instances of white normativity I encounter take place in everyday, mundane interactions, or in profoundly intimate emotional and psychic milieus.

I frequently experience frustration around truly, openly addressing the phenomenon of white normativity. I remember one time when I was on a plane that this frustration ruled my heart.

Autobiography of a Blue-Eyed Devil

Most airports have only corporate food, so if I don't plan ahead and make myself a sandwich at home, I am generally hungry during my Airport Experience. Though I do enjoy cheese pizza, few forces on earth[†] could get me to eat one from a Pizza Hut. Ditto vegetarian Subways. The only reason I enter a McDonald's or Burger King is I travel a lot and have learned their bathrooms are usually reasonably clean.[‡]

But the Portland airport seems to give local businesses a first shot over huge corporations at retail spaces. (The Columbus, "Ohio," and Denver, "Colorado," airports are also notable for this.) There's this one great Japanese bento place in the Portland airport, and they have fresh (possibly even locally grown, organic!?) vegetables and tofu, so fucken right on, you know what I am saying here.

I was pretty stoked when I got on the plane with my happy plastic rectangle of noodles, tofu, hot sauces, and veggies, including fresh-off-the-cob corn. Food's a big event for me on the airplane—I can stretch out a good meal to last for a big chunk of the flight. Enjoying a nice meal is a damn fine way to pass the time in any context, and I looked forward to my happy plastic rectangle from the moment I stepped into the plane and found my seat between an elderly Japanese American man and

---

† Starvation, for instance, is an incredible force that often inspires people to do things they would never otherwise do, such as eating death to stave off death or selling drugs that kill and enslave others.

‡ Something I cash in on due to tyrannical and inhumane labor practices. Read *Fast Food Nation* if you haven't already.

a white woman in her mid-fifties. By the time we got altitude and I forced myself to wait until the flight attendants brought the drinks around, I had worked myself up to almost drooling in anticipation of this wonderful meal.

I opened the happy rectangle and started whittling the splinters off my chopsticks. The man was napping, but the smell of the food woke him up. He looked with interest at my happy rectangle for a moment, elbowed me a little, smiled, nodded, and went back to sleepyby land.

The lady, however, stared with great interest as I whittled my chopsticks. I knew—from her body language and the way she cleared her throat—that she wanted to discuss this activity, but I put up a psychic wall and she couldn't find her way past it.

I rarely desire conversation on an airplane, and certainly not when I am hungry and about to eat a highly anticipated meal.

Oh, lordisa, it was so good.

In my town, I would have considered it straight up satisfying, so on a plane it was an epicurean fantasy on my fold-down table.

The lady couldn't get past her wonder at the "strangeness" of my meal. It became her entire focus. I started getting really annoyed because I knew good and goddamn well if I had been eating a hamburger she would have found some other place to settle her boredom.

I managed to keep the psychic wall up until I got through all the big vegetables and was setting to work on the gorgeous corn. I guess I got so swept up in Corn Excitement that I kinda let the psychic wall down, because that's when she broke into my space with this little niblet, and I quote: "What do they call that?"

I set down my chopsticks, turned to her, and said, "Who is 'they'?"

She stumbled over her words for a moment, perhaps realizing, finally, that she had been totally invading my quiet eating space for the past twenty minutes, or perhaps wondering, indeed, who she meant by "they," or perhaps she was merely jarred by my non-whitepleasantry response.

Finally, she decided to pretend like I just did not understand her question. Enunciating each word very clearly and loudly, as if I didn't speak the language but would understand it if she put forth the ol' college try, she went, "Oh! I Mean What Is That Food Called?"

"It is noodles. And tofu. And vegetables. With hot sauce."

She said, "Ahhhh!"

Then she piped down and left me alone.

In this situation, I verbally responded to in-the-moment white-normative racism, but I didn't muster the presence of mind and wherewithal to articulate what I truly think. Namely:

"Hey, you know what? Lemme tell you. You are a white woman. You have grown up white in a white-dominated society. Since I, too, am white, I know from firsthand experience that you have learned to view the world as a place created for you to view through the filter of your abject, unexamined assumptions. A direct manifestation of this reality is found in the present context, where you seem to believe you have a right—that is, the white normative entitlement—to view my 'ethnic' lunch as a form of entertainment for you. I am eating something 'different' and perhaps you are marveling at how 'exotic' and 'mysterious' this lunch of mine is, and though you are evidently quite unwilling to set aside your own limited view of reality, I am nevertheless a hungry Taurus† person who actually does exist in the world when you are not around to view me, and I would like to eat my meal in peace. Do you think you could imagine some way to set aside your completely unquestioned and unconscious indoctrination as a white U.S. citizen long enough for me to enjoy my food? Thank you."

I'm a writer, and it's nice to think about what I would have said in my idea of a perfect world. I have, however, very rarely met success in addressing these myriad and highly complex occurrences in the thousands of daily and mundane racial ignorance/fear-based interactions I have with folks.

Like when a novelty shop in my neighborhood decided to make a display in its window showcasing Homies—plastic collectible figures representing characters in (primarily Chicano) gang and urban culture. Every Homie known to humankind was perfectly arrayed, including "Willie G," a large-version Homie in a wheelchair. There is a fairly high probability that Willie G is in a wheelchair because he was shot in autogenocidal gang warfare or by the police. I have no problem with Homies, but they do rep-

---

† Tauruses are people who say things like, "*Of course* I remember you. We met eight years ago at that party with those fucken kickass heart of palm, bamboo shoot, and grilled tempeh finger sandwiches."

resent a lot more than "cute li'l hiphop generation" collectibles. I did, however, have a huge-ass problem with the little white boy mannequin in the window, dressed as a "gangsta," lording it over what I imagine was his complete collection of Homies. A life-size white child, co-opting the dress style of people he knows nothing about, standing amid all his little brown-skinned toys.

I really thought that sucked.

I went into the store and explained to the white woman behind the counter that the window was disrespectful to the rap and hiphop communities, gang members, real-life homies, or anyone who has grown up in a poor urban environment. She told me that "we" *actually* had a meeting about that very window, and "everyone" decided that it wasn't offensive.

"And, uh, how many gang members were at that meeting?" I asked.

"None," she said, as if I were being, um, silly. "It was an *employee* meeting."

"Well, I am standing here before you, and I am telling you that almost anyone who grew up in an environment similar to the one represented by Homies would be outraged at that window."

She reiterated the point that it had been "thoroughly" discussed.

I asked her to take the white boy out of the window.

She said she would tell the manager about my "complaint."

The white boy mannequin stayed in the window for a month and my entrenched vandal fantasies could not override my general karmic support for locally owned businesses.

Eenie, Meenie, Miney, Mo, Catch a Cracker by the Toe

I fumed without thinking up a response that might inspire conscious reckoning and evolution in my neighborhood.

Which, on balance, sucked even more than the window itself.

So even on occasion when I do figure out how to directly respond to the phenomenon of white normative racism, it still does not come near to touching upon the root of the matter. And even if it *did*, how could that *possibly* address the reality of living in a country founded on continuing slavery and (auto)genocide, and how could *that* ever be tied in to the individual, fully incorporated white normative reality of the person I am trying to communicate with?

No one is saying this is simple.

No one is saying that reading a book or two will make everything "better." This shit runs deep and we hafta be willing to *go* deep to even begin to wrap our minds around the pervasiveness of white normativity within our environment of white supremacist racism. The level of historical and personal accountability is staggering, and I do not fool myself into thinking any of this can be truly acknowledged in mundane, everyday interactions with people who are invested in unquestioned assumptions about whiteness.

Or at least I haven't figured out how.

If you have learned how to consistently address the low-level torture of everyday white normativity, please write to me and I will make sure your insights appear in a future edition of this book.

✺

I did see Steve "Mr. Rad" Harvey do a wonderful job with this on his teevee variety show, but it was also a Do-or-Die Face-Saving Situation.

On the episode I viewed, one of the acts was three white women from, like, Petaluma, "California." They were showing a bunch of rats dressed up in different costumes. There's, oh, you know, a punk rock rat, a devil rat, a fair maiden rat, et cetera. They don't do any tricks, just twitch and waddle around in their custom-made rat outfits.

Steve Harvey is not into the rats.

One of the women—let's call her Dumb Ass—keeps trying to get Mr. Harvey to hold a rat, and he just isn't having it. She really, really persists, and finally he says something like, "Fuck, man, where I come from we don't have a lot of positive associations with rats. So step away from the Steve Harvey with the fucken rat, lady."

Of course, this is my interpretation, but, uh, sans the cuss words this was the general gist of his response, right?

So, far from *actually listening* to what this highly intelligent man who can morph serious statements into lightning-strike repartee is fucken *saying,* far from looking at him and seeing a human being with memories, history, and very real issues, much like herself, Ms. Ass decides that Mr. Harvey *is displaying prejudice toward her rats.* She says—and I actually dove for an ATM receipt and a pen on my friend Ariel's coffee table to write this down—*she says,* "We all know how hard it is to overcome prejudice."

Eenie, Meenie, Miney, Mo, Catch a Cracker by the Toe

She is *so sure* that she is not capable of being a racist, this certainty actually protects her from objectively viewing both herself and Steve Harvey. Her construction of Post–Civil Rights Whiteness creates a gulf that surrounds her, and nothing else can get in.

It's truly a spectacle.

There is a sucking vacuum in the whole theater and the cameraperson finds some black people in the audience and films their reactions.[†] The people the camera finds are, of course, aghast. Almost without missing a beat, however, Steve Harvey (and I wrote this down too) says, "If you were that concerned about prejudice, you wouldn't have put the devil costume on the black rat."

The theater explodes in laughter and relief, and Ms. Ass pretends like everything is still just cool and nothing amiss has taken place at all, other than maybe Steve Harvey was a little "rude" to her. How can she afford any other reaction? Any other reaction would force her to look at herself, and since there's no problem here and the Civil Rights Movement ended injustice and racism in this country once and for all, why should she bother with that?

I mean, she can celebrate multicultural diversity with the best of 'em.

꙰

---

† This also happens a lot during award shows. Whenever someone says something racist at the Oscars, for instance, the camera finds someone like Denzel Washington or Halle Berry to note his or her reaction. I find this a very curious practice—least of all because Ms. Berry is half white.

White people are not the only ones who unconsciously buy into and perpetuate this lame-ass shit. *Everyone* who grows up in this culture is indoctrinated in white supremacist racism and white normativity. I strongly, consciously *identify* with the endlessly complex nature of this reality. I have, however, most consistently *experienced* this indoctrination as a white person born during the Civil Rights Movement, and bred on the west coast of the U.S.

While white supremacist racism and white normativity are at the root of, for example, beefs between Korean Americans and black people or traditional indians and progressive indians within the same or neighboring tribes, I did not grow up in communities where this dynamic was present. Instead, I have some experience and insights on the racism perpetuated against Mexicano and Centroamericano immigrants and seasonal workers by whites and Chicanos, and even more information on the white people who make no such differentiations and wish *they would all* go "back" where they came from. This is such a hilarious sentiment, for the town I grew up in is still legally in Mexico, and someday, a class action lawsuit will be filed against the U.S. government, and we'll all have a rousing good time talking about the new retroactive status of illegal immigrants.

Living in a dog-eat-dog culture that creates and encourages racial divisions, assigns constructed racial identities, and makes unexamined assumptions based on a person's perceived race (or ethnicity, class, gender, age, sexuality, et cetera) takes a toll on pretty much everyone.

The unexamined and logically retarded term "reverse

racism" is supposed to be some way to explain how people of color can be prejudiced toward whites. This term is problematic on a number of levels. In my experience, much of the "racism" that people of color entertain toward whites is based not *necessarily* in prejudice, but in deep resentment of the fact that whites refuse to acknowledge the present and the past. Growing up in a white-dominated society provides ample opportunity for fostering such resentment. Therefore, before approaching any authentic racism a person of color might have against a white person, this absolutely valid resentment must first be acknowledged, addressed, and cleared from the air. Since there is no place for such dialogue in our culture, there is also no way to gauge the *actual racism* people of color might have toward white people.

Furthermore, white people do not "own" racism—though we are incredibly adept at perpetuating it. There are millions of racisms in this world, and the concept of something being racism in "reverse" makes no mathematical sense.

In general, people who grow up in Amerikkka learn to, at best, distrust *anyone* who is not from their specific social group.

This is the state of nature of survival of the fittest via divide 'n' conquer.

I get on the bus and sit down toward the back. A few seats away, four young girls are laughing and chatting it up. I watch the city out the window. Then I hear, "Hey white bitch! White bitch, move! Our friends are getting on at the next stop. Move your ass!"

They're, like, fourteen. I am more than double their age, and they are calling me something that cholas and black girls never called me in high school. It was, "Inga La Gringa, how goes it, ese," or if people wanted to call me something shitty they'd say "weird punkrock-ass bitch," or something like that, which sucked, but was still a far cry from being a "white bitch." White bitches were the girls who sneered at everyone who was not them or whom they did not want to fuck, and talked loudly, excitedly, and/or obsessively about their boyfriends and/or horses and/or Journey.

I was thinking all this in the split second of wondering how to react to the situation at hand, but as luck would have it, across the aisle, a grandmother-aged lady turned in her seat and goes, "You children sound just like the Klan. Now hush up."

The girls' silence was ebbing, but still deafening when their boisterous friends joined them at the next stop.

I quietly said my thanks to the woman when I got off the bus, but I knew she wasn't sticking up for me, per se. She was sticking up for herself and for the kids and for humanity, in general. She nodded, and smiled, eyes sparkling with a warm, yet smug, satisfaction.

I am in San Francisco's Chinatown. I stop in front of a store and admire a full-length coat that I cannot afford. The dot-com bubble has burst, times are hard, and the shopkeepers are being more aggressive than usual. A young Chinese American woman walks up to me and asks if I want to see the coat in my size, as she dexterously leads me by the elbow into the tiny shop. Two black women are standing at the rack, looking at the exact same coat I was admiring. The shopkeeper nudges into their space to pull the coat off the rack for me, white-ass Inga La Gringa.

The women look at me accusingly.

I hate life in this moment.

Nothing will erase the reality that the shopkeeper deemed me a better source of money than she did the two women who were already in the shop. Evidently, in this shopkeeper's imagination, I am a more promising customer than two well-coiffed, well-dressed black women carrying shopping bags, who, judging by their jewelry, shoes, and purses, probably drive nice cars and have credit cards (all things I do not have), and in general are giving off every surefire signifier that they are dedicated shoppers. I am wearing baggy men's pants that are too long for me, a wrinkled sweater, and very ugly maroon slip-on shoes that are so old, Goodwill probably wouldn't take them. I hang the coat back up and leave the store, right on the heels of the two ladies, who are furious.

This was a lose, lose, lose situation all around, and it would not have happened if the shopkeeper had simply assisted the customers in her store.

While white normativity resonates in everyone's life, I have always, obviously, experienced it from the perspective of a white girl or woman.

In the normative white imagination (via movies, ads, the teevee, magazines, etc.), I represent not only one of the least threatening demographics in society, but also the one most often depicted as a rape or murder victim—thus my lifelong obsession with knowing how to protect myself. This is generally, on some level, the angle from which I am viewed, and my identity has been greatly informed by this widespread perception of me.

Other than the basic fact of my whiteness—which itself can be extremely threatening to people directly oppressed by white normative racism—I am not generally perceived as a threat. Therefore, I do not have the experiential comprehension of the myriad ways it impacts people's lives when they *are* perceived to be threatening in the dominant white normative imagination. I mean, I could move to Japan, East Los Angeles, or Jamaica and experience *the rest* of my life as "different," "other," or a "minority." I could don a military uniform and walk around Iraq or Afghanistan with a big gun in my hands, but even given those circumstances, I *would still* have the frame of reference of the first three decades of my life living as a white girl or woman in Amerikkka.

I can never truly know how it is to *grow up* in a society that has constructed a reality where I do not positively factor in. I know how it feels to be perceived as stupid, ignorant, irrelevant, and/or under the protection of the white man, but I do not know how it feels to be perceived as a menace to society. It is too late for any other reality. I have already grown up white in the post–Civil Rights Movement USA.

Within the social construct of white normativity, I have only my perspective. It is a perspective I have spent much of my life developing, and I know it contains many unspoken truths.

Eenie, Meenie, Miney, Mo, Catch a Cracker by the Toe

I do not purport to know "how it is" for first nation people and people of color, any more than I expect never-incarcerated bio-logical males to *truly understand* the moment-by-moment reality of living in a predatory rape culture.

And at the same time, to further illustrate the complexity of humanity, many never-incarcerated biological men *do* know the experience of being raped quite intimately, but live in denial of this because to do otherwise would threaten yet another soci-etal construct: their masculinity.

Everyone is deeply affected by white normative racism, and only through looking at your historical and present place in this environment—at the deep truths inside your own heart and imagination—can you negotiate your way through the morass of white fears and ignorance. This applies to *everyone* living in *any country* where white normative and supremacist racism and imperialism affects the destiny of the population.

It's just that some people know it and live it and some people choose not to.

I usually feel a tad ill at ease when I am at events like wed-dings or birthday parties, when a heteronormative social setting distinguishes my queerness. In such situations, I am sometimes considered a threat—an intimate one that involves the sexuality of unconscious (and frequently, sexually repressed) heterosexual folks.

Sometimes unconscious heterosexual women think I am automatically, magically sexually attracted to them, based on the criteria that I am generally intimate with women. The rationale, *I think,* is that since I am sexually attracted to women, and they are women, then I am sexually attracted to them.[†] The fact that I would probably not want to have sex with someone whom I am not deeply attracted to, who has never eaten pussy or wielded a dildo, never enters their minds. Further away is the possibility that being a homo does not inherently involve frequent sexual encounters with complete strangers.

Unconscious heterosexual men either edge around me as if I were surrounded by barbed wire or make attempts to engage me in conversations designed to assure me that they are very open-minded—which *can* indeed involve telling me that they have no problem with women getting it on. It's gay *men* who seriously gotta fall off the face of the earth.[‡] As further evidence of this startling open-mindedness, I have been repeatedly informed that it has always been a fantasy to watch two women having sex.

Puke.

When I am around queers and transgendered folks—and this includes homosexuals, heterosexuals, asexuals, bisexuals, omnisexuals, transsexuals, polysexuals, pansexuals, intersexuals, and all other people who tend to be aware of the highly com-

---

† Might this be not only a heteronormative response, but also a heterosexual projection? Are unconscious heterosexuals automatically attracted to the entire opposite sex? Hmm.

‡ An almost certain indication of repressed homosexual desires, childhood sexual abuse, and/or time spent in prison or the military.

plex nature of human sexuality—I take it for granted that I can be free to have normal conversations about things that interest me. Unlike when I am in heteronormative settings, I am never forced to make my sexuality a topic of conversation, though I am free to talk about facets of my sexuality if I want. So I find it trying to be in situations where something so innate and deeply personal as my sexuality sets the tone for all interaction and is fodder for small talk and endless, annoying, passive-aggressive projection and innuendo.

So I think about how this must be for people who have to consciously deal with unconscious white society all the time.

I wonder how this must be for people who speak with a "foreign accent."

I perceive how this must be for people in wheelchairs.

I envision how this must be for turkeys and christmastrees.

I imagine how this must be for people without jobs, for ex-felons, for war veterans, for people in prisons and ghettos and living in poverty on reservations.

I educate myself about as many realities as I can, because this frees my imagination from the white normative environment in which I live.

Queer and transgendered indigenous women and women of color must tangle with every major bullshit constructed reality that composes the mainstream U.S. cultural environment: heteronormativity, white supremacist racism and normativity, and male domination.

White heterosexual males may bask in the unconscious luxury of these—and all attendant—constructions, if they so choose.

Somewhere in between is everyone else, negotiating all this bullshit that very few people—including many, many white heterosexual males—actually experience as fulfilling, life-enriching, loving, conducive, bolstering, and enjoyable.

I *could,* feasibly, pass as a heterosexual if I tried really hard. This holds true for all queers—though passing for anything other than what you really are generally leads to suicide, severe depression, criminal behavior, drug or alcohol addiction, or just general weird and creepy perversion. Passing as a traditional heterosexual is, however, within the realm of physical possibility.

Likewise, given the right amount of mind-numbing prescription drugs and mild lobotomies available, I could fit into indoctrinated, unconscious mainstream society without anyone taking much notice of me.

These are fucked-up choices that would render me dead inside my soul, but they are, nevertheless, choices. Many people in this country and this world do not have even fucked-up choices. Aside from the passive-aggressive low-level hostility of white normativity, the wrath of white supremacist racism and imperialism crashes into homes in the dead of night, killing or arresting everyone in sight.

When one can discern the *overall pattern* of freedoms,

choices, and luxuries that one may or may not have, a space inside one's imagination is reclaimed from the colonization we all experience in this country.

It becomes patently absurd to avert our eyes.

This is, by no means, just about white people seeing the world outside unconscious white normativity. We accept as "normal" so many forms of injustice and inhumanity: in abiding the brutal treatment of animals and the earth, in the economic slavery of factory workers in U.S. prisons and poor nations, and in the sickening rape statistics of people—both in and out of prison.

The rape statistic for women in prison is the same as for the unincarcerated mainstream population: one in four. This is staggering, given the male-to-female ratio we're talking here.

Could it be that sexual predators are attracted to employment in places where they will have unquestioned power over their prey, and we, as citizens, do not demand that prison rape—of all genders—be punished totalitarianly?

Do we make concessions in our hearts?

Do we condone this crime against humanity by prejudging people who serve time?

If laws are unjust, then what is *the precise definition* of a criminal?

What if, *just what if*, you were to wake up one morning and realize that—just as one person's freedom fighter is another person's terrorist—someone in a U.S. prison might very well be one of two million court cases that needs to be reviewed by an all-grandmother tribunal? If, after such a review, a person was still deemed to have committed a crime, and sent back to serve out their time, does anyone, in fact, "deserve" to be sexually terrorized with impunity?

These are a few of the many questions I ask in my heart, the ones that keep me awake at night, the ones that call up spirits who tell me they do not want their deaths to have been in vain. Questions such as this assist me in deconstructing normativities I've learned during my indoctrination as a U.S. citizen.

Since the "threat of terrorism" has jingoistically swept the country, I have noticed that when I pose questions like this during public speaking engagements, there always seem to be a few people in the audience inspired to challenge my love of country. My patriotism—or perceived lack thereof—is sometimes confused with my deep yearning to live in a nation that negotiates its present by reckoning with its past. The kaleidoscopic, complex nature of my country is largely responsible for this yearning of mine.

After fielding a number of challenges to my "patriotism," I wrote the following ode. I was surprised at how healing it was for me to list some of the many reasons I love my country. Writing this gave me a deeper understanding of what motivated me to ever sit down and write this book in the first place.

And so it goes.

Eenie, Meenie, Miney, Mo, Catch a Cracker by the Toe

Why I Love America[†]
By Inga La Gringa

I love America because Malcolm X is from here.

I love America because Malcolm X, Audre Lorde, Paul Robeson, Diamanda Galás, Robin D.G. Kelley, Noam Chomsky, Howard Zinn, Paris, my Grammy, Missy Elliott, Yuri Kochiyama, Oscar the Grouch, Ho Che Anderson, Janeane Garofalo, Cookie Monster, Maxine Waters, Cynthia McKinney, Jan Schakowsky, and Gore Vidal are all from here.

They all grew up in America, just like me.

I love America because it's where I've had Iranian rosewater syrup ice cream and Indian cardamom ginger ice cream too. America feeds me vegetarian kung pao chicken, rich Ethiopian stews, and Boca Burgers with organic tomato slices, fat and juicy and salt-and-peppered. I love the food of America. It is the best of the whole wide world.

I love America because there are so many voices here. There is Neil Diamond and Talib Kweli. Ann Coulter and Lisa Tiger. Bill Cosby and Louis Farrakhan. Colonel David Hackworth and General Tommy Franks. When I think of all the voices in America, I almost lose consciousness with the breathtaking whirling in my mind.

I love America because each state is a different country and when I am all bundled up in "Minnesota" when it is a

---

† If you write an ode to America and email it to me, I will post it on my website.

bone-numbing fifty-two degrees outside, *total strangers* chide me and tell me to *take off my hat,* and in "Ohio," a group of young Amish people told me I was English, and I said, "No, I am Irish and Italian," and they laughed at my ignorance, because to them, everyone who is non-Amish—including Neil Diamond, Talib Kweli, Ann Coulter, Lisa Tiger, Bill Cosby, Louis Farrakhan, Colonel David Hackworth, and General Tommy Franks—is "English," and in "New York" it is totally against the law to dance in a bar and you can get in big trouble, and if you tell people in "Louisiana" that you don't eat meat, they will feel sorry for you and express their sincerest condolences. One of my favorites, I think, is when I am in "Michigan" and if I ask someone where they are from, they will hold up their right hand and point somewhere on it.

I love America because almost everyone I hold dear to my heart and share memories and history with lives here.

I love America because it offered a home to my immigrant mother, gave her a place to raise her children.

I love America because there is a festival here for every conceivable occasion, celebrating the strawberry harvest, the antique motorcycle, the first day the mall opened, the most poised six-year-old girl in a specific geographic region, and the go-cart. There are Greek Orthodox festivals, hippies run amuck festivals, black nationalism hiphop festivals, Sun Dance Warrior festivals, Japanese cherry blossom festivals, lunar new year festivals, gang truce festivals, and Mennonite quilting festivals here in America.

If I did not love America, I would do what the bumper sticker says and leave it in a heartbeat, but I cannot imagine how sad I would be living somewhere that is not America. How could I survive without radical cheerleaders and Dave Chappelle, without loud-mouthed assholes like Howard Stern, without pampered doggies in cashmere sweaters, without Margaret Cho and Alix Olson, without deep plush golden velvet interiored lowriders and flamboyant homos prancing down the street in ball gowns aglow with little white lights in the tulle?

I love America because it describes every aspect of my identity, humanity, and complex ideology.

It is a beautiful place and I am deeply honored to have been born here.

I love America.

Cards on the Table

$\mathcal{D}$uring my life, I have lost many white friends. It is a recurring experience, where a white friend will say or do something that creates an unbridgeable gulf between us. I had no idea how to diagnose this the first time it happened—or the second, or the third, or the fourth, but maybe by the fifth or twelfth time I started to catch on. I do remember that first time quite vividly, however.

One of my dearest friends and I were cutting high school and smoking pot. We were shooting the shit, and suddenly, she said, "I am so happy I was born white." "Why?" I asked. "Because," she informed me, "it is great to be white and it would suck to be anything else." I was all, "Are you serious? You seriously believe that?" With the very conviction that I had always cherished in her, she said, "Absolutely. No doubt about it."

We got into an argument, but nothing constructive came from it.

I did not know that our friendship was over at that point. For many years, we remained "friends" based solely on the fact that we had been friends for so long. It took me some time to realize that my fundamental (racial) identity and her fundamental (racial) identity had nothing in common, and our friendship consequently never flourished or grew past that day.

This conversation impacted my life in other ways too. I remember wondering if I was "lucky" to be born white, and if so, then would that mean that everyone who did not have white skin could be considered "unlucky"? Was it a "blessing" to be white?

Over time I pieced together a metaphor to address questions like these.

Ahem.

There are fifty-two cards in a big deck in the sky.

When we are born, we get dealt a hand from this deck.

Sometimes it is a hand with love and abundance and security and no war raging outside our home. Sometimes it is a hand with lots of trappings and gourmet food, but not much caring

and communication, or maybe there aren't so many meals
and financial comforts, but there is a lot of love and affection.
Sometimes it is a hand with wealth and luxury, but also GREAT
WRONGS inherited from the family ancestors, which you have
no control over but nonetheless possess. Sometimes it's a hand
where adults rape you and beat the fuck out of you, or there is
insanity, ill health, or physical disability, or your family is torn
apart by violence and unjust laws and despair and everywhere
you look, you see the exact same gaping abyss vacuum of NO
HOPE, which always threatens to suck you into it like it sucks in
everything around you.

Here is a secret I found out not too long ago:

You can *play* the hand you were dealt and get more cards.

It does not matter what this hand is. The *act* of playing
your hand entitles you to another one, and as an added bonus,
when you get good at playing your hand, you sometimes get to
throw away cards you don't like.

If you do not ever look at the hand you were dealt, then
you will probably never play it, and not only will you be stuck
with that first-ever hand, you'll have to lug around all the other
cards that will eventually come your way.

This choice generally leads to despair, frustration, anger,
depression, feeling like you have no control over your destiny,
and dying a miserable death after living a preoccupied life,
because no one can possibly be a happy, free person if they are
lugging around all these fucken cards.

Many people I know and love are still holding on to the hand they were dealt at birth.

To my family, I say, "Fuck, are you crazy? Play those old-ass cards in your hand."

And they say, "I am used to them. I know them. It's *Just the Way It Is*. I'll figure out a way to be happy and free without letting go of them."

And I say, "Well, give my regards to Mr. Roarke and Tattoo. I'll be waiting for you at the airport when you come home from Fantasy Island."

I say there are fifty-two cards in a big deck in the sky, and like so many things, that is both true and false. It is true because I have added up all the various cards I've been dealt and fifty-two sounds about right. It is false because the particular fifty-two cards in my deck do not exist in anyone else's.

Everybody has their own fifty-two cards, and this, too, is true but also false.

Many cards appear in everyone's deck. But the exact same card may have vastly different meanings and values. A death card for a wealthy white kid in Cincinnati, "Ohio," may mean alcohol or drugs were involved, or maybe someone was riding too fast on a jet ski. A death card for a poor black kid in Cincinnati, "Ohio," means that *no matter how the kid dies,* his or her death exists on a *continuum* of violent deaths at the hands of an aggressively racist police force.

You cannot look at a card in your hand and automatically

assume that it means the same thing to someone else holding the exact same card.

If you choose to live a conscious life, you must first play the hand you were dealt at birth and then develop a practice of looking at every single card you are dealt throughout your life and figuring out ways to play them as you go along. There is no happily ever after end to this, and at no point will you experience anything other than a fleeting sense of accomplishment, which will almost immediately be replaced by the reality of another card that must be played.

Being accountable is not an action; it is a state of mind. Consciously examining and playing the cards you are dealt is one way to operate in this state. Conscious accountability, however, requires time, patience, and a willingness to look deep into your heart. The Amerikkkan environment, for the most part, provides only examples of living in a state of unconscious unaccountability.

In the very early morning of December 3, 1984, every single person within a forty-kilometer radius of Bhopal, India, woke up at the exact same time. This moment marked the beginning of the next three days—and also, the rest of their lives—when forty tons of toxic gas leaked out of the Union Carbide plant, located near the heart of Kali Grounds, the poorest area of Bhopal.[1]

How much would it suck to wake up with fluid in your lungs?

How filled with terror would you be to see your little sister clawing at her throat, gasping for breath, and crying hysterically because, I mean, what the flying mother fuck? How's a kid supposed to wrap her mind around this kind of wake-up call?

By the time the sun hit the horizon, five hundred thousand people were poisoned. Come dinnertime, thousands of people were dead. When we think of cardiac arrest here in the U.S., we generally imagine individuals in their forties or seventies who are maybe overweight. In Bhopal, however, people know that given the right amount of toxic gas in their systems, theretofore-healthy toddlers are quite likely to experience sudden heart failure.

The final death toll reached as high as thirty thousand in the immediate aftermath. Since then, hundreds of thousands have lived with and/or died from chronic illnesses brought on by exposure to the toxic gas. Now, twenty years later, there is a demographic known as Second Generation Bhopalis, born with severe birth defects and illnesses.

This atrocity occurred because one man made the decision to save some money. Warren Anderson, CEO of Union Carbide, realized he could save hundreds of rupees a day by shutting down safety systems at the plant in the heart of a slum, and so, this was done. The maintenance crew went through a serious downsizing, and Union Carbide's profit margins increased exponentially. This means a handful of people had slightly better-looking investment portfolios because of Mr. Anderson's decision.

In our culture, improving investment portfolios is looked upon as an act of heroism.

It is one of the ways CEOs cut swathes for themselves.

In India, on the other hand, Mr. Anderson is considered a criminal.

Perhaps because of the aforementioned hero factor, the U.S. government has not honored India's extradition request, and Mr. Anderson continues to live a luxurious, seemingly care-free life, albeit in the semiseclusion that the Hamptons provide.

I know how it feels to make a decision I later deeply regret, and how important it is to face what I have done.

In December of 1988, my siblings, Joe B., Liz, and Nick, asked me to come down to "California" to take a group photo portrait to give to our mom for Christmas. I was living in Olympia, "Washington," at the time and had a lot shaking there. I told them sorry, I couldn't make it for Christmas that year.

Four months later, Nick died in a car crash.

I have lived my life since then knowing it was my selfish-ness that kept this precious gift from our mother. It is difficult to face this, even now. There is nothing in the world I can ever do to put a photo of all four of her children into her hands.

Never.

I robbed my mother—and my entire family—of this gift.

This reality has the power to haunt me for the rest of my life. I could get an enormous amount of mileage feeling guilty about this. But I don't want some heinously stupid shit I did to have that kinda power over the rest of my life, so I decided to be conscious of the fact that I am an incredibly selfish person.

Autobiography of a Blue-Eyed Devil

Coming up as I did in this culture that has reminded me all
my life to look out for number one, I had to teach myself
how to listen to the needs of others and seize upon every
possible opportunity to express my love. I have transformed
this grave mistake of mine into a lifelong commitment to be
a conscious, loving human being. It does not atone for what
I did to my mother and siblings, but it has nevertheless produced a more caring and responsive family member for them
to have around.

And so, I think about the Mr. Andersons of this world a lot.

Certainly, deciding not to go home for Christmas isn't comparable to being responsible for destroying the lives of hundreds
of thousands of people for twenty years running, but that is also
precisely why I wonder about men like Mr. Anderson.

How does he live with himself?

How do you smile and laugh and think simple, happy
thoughts when you have not reckoned with the fact that you
have had an inescapably detrimental effect on hundreds of
thousands of people's lives?

Is your smile false?

Is your laughter hollow?

Do you ever get to experience the joy of simple, happy
thoughts?

All I have come up with is Mr. Anderson must have a profound, learned disrespect for life—based in white supremacist
racism and imperialism—and *truly think* that the heart beating

in the chest of someone in India is somehow less worthy of life than the one beating in the chest of, say, his grandchild.

I saw a photo of him golfing with friends a couple of years ago.

Unlike the sobbing Bhopali man I saw pictured carrying his dead four-year-old son in his arms, Mr. Anderson was smiling in the golf-course sunshine.

Warren Anderson is not, by any means, the only such person sheltered and housed in mansions by us. Miami, "Florida," for instance, is one place where ex-dictators from South and Central America are welcomed to make happy homes for themselves. Evidently, if you serve the interests of white male domination on a grand enough scale, you will be taken care of.

In this context, perhaps the punishment meted out to violent and destructive individuals in our society can be viewed as a kind of *class* issue. It is not deemed enough to merely destroy the lives of your family or immediate community. If you do that, you're a monster. That is a shameful way to proceed through life and you might eventually get punished for it, especially if you're not white. Likewise, it is not okay to rape and/or kill only two or fifteen people. You have to have the manpower behind you to victimize *at least* five thousand human beings in order to qualify for the mansion-in-hiding retirement plan.

While Mr. Anderson kept living the life he knows after overseeing the deaths of tens of thousands of people, he could have easily made the conscious decision to commit his life to social justice and human rights—if not in the world, then at least in Bhopal, India.

He did not make that choice.

He did not play that card.

He still holds it in his hand, and it will be passed on to his descendents until someone plays it.

That is one of the things I have noticed about those cards from that big deck in the sky. GREAT WRONGS of many kinds are passed down from generation to generation until someone in the family decides they're sick of seeing the resonations of long-past evil deeds every time they look deeply into the eyes of their elders.

The media in the United States has made the choice to keep people ignorant of what took place in Bhopal twenty years ago.

And the people of the United States have chosen to avert our gaze from the damage our fellow citizens, such as Warren Anderson, have wreaked on the rest of the world.

When I was working on my first book, I never really talked to any of my friends about it. I didn't *know* this was my policy until *Cunt* came out and my friends started calling me and saying things like, "What the fuck??? I had no idea you were writing a book like this. I thought you were working on a science fiction novel or something."

Also, while working on *Cunt,* I felt (duh) extremely isolated and alone. Being a profoundly private person in ways that aren't at all clear even to those closest to me, I decided that I would alter this policy while working on this book. I made an effort to discuss it with people I love.

And the thing was, with this book, I was forced to do so anyway.

Autobiography of a Blue-Eyed Devil has been an extremely painful undertaking. There've been times when I have been so utterly despondent, many of my friends couldn't help but notice and ask what's wrong.

This, too, led to discussions.

At one point I had been extremely depressed for three months. I was deeply involved in this book, and reading nothing but history. The history of Haiti. The history of the United States. The history of Nicaragua. The history of Mexico. The history of El Salvador, Brazil, Bolivia, Uruguay. On and on, I immersed myself in the bloodshed, rape, torture, and assassination of so many beautiful people who fought for their lives and land. It killed me to wake up every day and look at my little world, at how I have benefited from all this horror.

My mom called, all annoyed because her computer had crashed. I love my mom, and care about what is stressing her out, but a part of me was like, "I am living life so fucken large to have the luxury of my mom calling me on the phone, upset because she can't get online."

My friends complained about problems with their lovers, their cars, their plumbing. I was having a very hard time being present for the people I love, and one of my closest friends really needed me during this time.

Autobiography of a Blue-Eyed Devil

The week before the World Trade Center devastation, this friend called, angry that I wasn't being present. I explained to her that I was all fucked up and it was difficult for me to live my life in the face of so much horror. In an effort to shed light on what I was tripping on, I described some of the things I'd been reading—about how blood-red raw-heart hard people fight for their dignity and freedom, and how it is glossed over, and how people are still fighting, and how they now also fight economically, with 24 percent interest rates.

I described a scene in Edwidge Danticat's *Krik? Krak!* where U.S.-backed Haitian soldiers tear into people's homes and force fathers to have sex with their daughters, and sons to have sex with their mothers, and then the men are arrested for "moral crimes" and never seen again.

I was all, "I mean, this shit happened. It is happening now. It is real and it is taking me a while to figure out how to negotiate my life, this book, reality, and history."

And my friend, one of my closest friends, she sighs in frustration and goes, "Well, Inga, none of that stuff *affects you.*"

As in, I am making the choice to concern myself with the business of "other" people and my friendships are suffering for it.

It tore my heart at the roots to hear my friend say such a thing. An unbridgeable gulf came between us in that moment, and all of the deepest love I have for her splattered like it caught a bullet at point-blank range.

My friend's distant words, in fact, reminded me very much of one of the blurbs on the back of *Krik? Krak!*:

> Virtually flawless. . . . If the news from Haiti is too
> painful to read, read this book instead and understand
> the place more deeply than you ever thought possible.
> —*Washington Post Book World*

Oh, okay.

So I, the reader, am here in a civilized, wonderful, totally free democracy, which, if you minus every barrio, reservation, devastated rural community, and ghetto, is *absolutely nothing* like a "third world" country, and maybe it is just *a little bit too much* for me to handle what is *actually going on* in Haiti today, so aren't I lucky that a virtually flawless writer has taken the time to edify me with her stories so that I can more deeply understand the faraway plights of underprivileged people who also, by the way, practice an exotic and mysterious religion.

So I will be enriched by the stories of this virtually flawless storyteller, and I will glorify her for giving readers like me a chance to peer into the history of her country, as if it were a series of macabre fairy tales. They won't actually *affect* me or my worldview because it is all, all, all so far away from free me in my wonderful democracy filled with intelligent, fairly balanced folks who never need to resort to violence to solve our differences.

None of that stuff actually impacts *my* life.

It's happening "over there."

Sometimes "over there" is far, far away, and sometimes "over there" is just a few feet away from you, but if the wool is pulled tighty-tight over your eyes, it does not matter how far away "over there" really is.

Plane travel with my lady is almost always guaranteed to put me in a crabby mood. Airports are inescapably rife with white normative heterosexuality. I know I live in a kind of denial of my overall environment, and I consciously forge this by doing things like keeping a CD player and headphones on hand whenever I might be subject to overhearing people's cell phone conversations.

When I am alone in an airport, it's not so bad. With head-phones on and blaring, I bury myself in subversive readings. Or if I don't have subversive readings, I buy a U.S. government compendium of press releases, such as the *New York Times* or *Newsweek,* and subvert those readings through critical analysis.

Yes, since you asked, I am a barrel of laughs.

When I am with my girlfriend, however, I often negotiate a constant low- and high-level hostility that does not allow me to let my guard down, even for a split second. I maintain surveil-lance of the area around us like a military strategist.

And this trip—occurring just a few months after September 2001, when god-fearing, fag- and Muslim-hating jingoism swept the country like a swarm of locusts—was particularly trying.

On a layover in Chicago, while we walked to our gate

amidst sidelong stares and baleful glares, a white businessman elbowed me as he passed and spat, "You fucken weirdo."

My girlfriend felt my body stiffen up for the ol' velocity-empowered flat-of-my-palm-upward pile drive into the base of his skull, and put a death grip on my arm. This action spoke to the blinding red rage at the back of my eyes, and I whispered to myself, "Breathe, breathe, breathe. Don't start a melee in the airport, please. Breathe, breathe, breathe."

So this was my mood when I got on the plane.

As we found our seats, I noticed a white man two rows ahead of our seat stare at us in a most hate-filled fashion. I was not in the mood for this man, but I was tired. As anyone who defies the narrow field of what is acceptable to white "mainstream" society can confirm, it takes an enormous amount of energy to be the object of unconscious people's fears.

I did my best to ignore him, and sat down. I scoped him out after we settled into our seats. He was a retiree type, sitting with his wife. They were dressed well enough to be in first class, and I wished they were.

I sighed.

The plane took off, got altitude, I read.

Calmed down.

About an hour into the flight, I noticed two children sitting in front of the retiree couple, a brother and a sister, around nine and eleven years old, respectively. They had those stickers on their chests that designated them as children traveling without parents or guardians. They kneeled on their seats, facing the retirees. I watched them interact with the older couple, and as time wore on, I became increasingly uncomfortable. I noticed that most of the interaction was between the man and the girl. At some point, the wife got up and asked to hold the baby of the woman seated across the aisle.[†] When the wife got up, the man started really going overboard talking to the little girl. I noticed that whenever her brother piped into the conversation, the man rebuffed him.

He was not interested in the brother.

For her part, the girl was happy to have the attention of this man. He was "charmed" by her, and she knew it— inasmuch as a child is able to perceive the motivations of a sexual predator. I felt sorry for the little boy. He kept getting rejected, but he didn't understand it was because the man was a fucken pervert. This, need I remind you, is the *exact same man* who *had the gall* to glare at us when we got on the plane.

At some point, the little girl got up from her seat and the man pulled her onto his lap. I looked at the wife, who was smiling indulgently at the baby. As I got up to talk to a flight attendant, I saw the man touch the little girl on her flat chest.

I was incensed enough to take action when I first noticed the man's focus of attention and his body language and the hangdog look on the little boy's face, but I was worried that the

---

† I don't know why people think it's okay to touch or hold strangers' babies, but that's another topic, and one, I might add, that almost exclusively pertains to unconscious white women.

flight attendants would see me the way I am accustomed to being perceived in airplane culture—as an "indecent" homosexual. I was frightened that the flight attendants might take one look at that "decent" man and—like his wife—refuse to see what he was doing.

What would my choices be then?

Would I take matters into my own hands? Stand in the aisle and stare him down? "Accidentally" pull luggage down on his head and spill hot coffee on him? Sit on his wife's lap and tell her I have a crush on her?

I mentioned all this to my girlfriend right before I left on my quest to find a flight attendant.

"If they don't listen to me, maybe I will go insane."

I went to the back of the plane and found a flight attendant who looked like a mom. I told her I had been watching this man, and he was focusing on the little girl in a completely predatory way. Far from not believing me, the flight attendant gathered a few members of her crew around and asked me to repeat everything I saw. With a huge surge of relief that I should never, ever, ever have experienced, I repeated my story and returned to my seat. Two flight attendants walked up the aisle and I watched this whole dramatic sting operation go down. My girlfriend and I were the only ones aware of it. They watched the man, who, absorbed in his totally fucked-up seduction of a child, had pulled the little girl onto his lap again. The wife had retaken her seat and was heavily involved in her latest embroidery project while her husband all but fondled a child next to her.

This is when it hit me: This woman has no interest in her husband's criminal penchant for small girls. She does not want to see it. And so, hold a stranger's baby. Embroider.

A few minutes later, the mom flight attendant escorted a sleepy woman to the children's seats. She told the kids to come with her, and gave the seat to the sleepy woman, who immediately went back to sleep. I watched the retiree as this exchange took place, and his body stiffened like he just got dipped in plaster of paris, hands clenching the armrests.

Red hands, white knuckles.

He looked around 180 degrees, but I—the homosexual aberration responsible for degrading the moral character of our fine nation—was at the 270-degree marker, gleefully watching him make his realization.

The wife continued to embroider.

She *failed to notice* that the children were moved, but the man, oh yes, he was suddenly painfully aware that he was being scrutinized.

Later, the crew thanked me for ratting out the pervert. The mom flight attendant had tears in her eyes. She said, "If those were my kids, I would do anything for someone like you. We try to keep an eye on things, but we can't see everything. Thank you so much."

This little shout-out on an airplane put me in a much better mood, but I would have been truly happy if I lived in an environment where it was perfectly acceptable for me to make a citizen's arrest, and a crowd of cops were waiting for the bastard when we landed.

He was, after all, brazenly committing a heinous crime right in front of everyone.

For the rest of the flight, I watched the wife.

I was utterly, utterly fascinated with her.

The man was a writhing piece of wormy dogshit. Fuck his ass with a red-hot poker. He should be tarred, feathered, drawn and quartered. Men like this will never be held accountable for their actions in an environment that sexualizes children and offers twenty-five-year prison sentences to nonviolent drug offenders who harm no one and three- to five-year sentences to unarmed rapists who psychologically maim and terrorize entire communities. Powerful men the world over flock to countries where child prostitution is perfectly legal. Teens are presently excoriated to "wait until marriage," while movies and ads feature kids in overtly eroticized poses and situations. Children are abducted, raped, starved, prevented from having medical care, sent to schools run by corporations, murdered, sold into sexual slavery, shunted through abusive and corrupt foster care systems, neglected, married off for the price of two cows, and turned into porn stars across the motherfucken planet.

His existence is a minute circumstance, naturally occurring on a global continuum of child abuse. A continuum, in fact, that allows him to feel perfectly safe sexualizing a child right in front of an airplane full of people.

So I don't want to talk about that piece-of-shit man.

But the wife.

I could *not* get over the wife.

While the husband lavished his grotesque attentions on a child, she sat there, smiling happily. When the energy of his interaction with the child became more intense, she decided it was a good time to stretch her legs and get a look at that *adorable* baby across the aisle, maybe make some "mom" conversation with the new mother. Maybe she could offer some hard-learned advice on how to raise kids. By the time the flight attendants relocated the children, she was off in her own world with needle, thread, and quiet, happy thoughts.

How could she have missed all that activity right fucken next to her on a crowded plane?

This woman helped me solve a mystery that, until then, I'd been unable to wrap my mind around. She was willing to close off her perception to pretty much any atrocity that did not fit into her idea of the life she and her husband had created together. Likewise, the reason people in the U.S. are willing to avert our eyes from the crimes against humanity our government commits is we are completely seduced by the idea that "we" (and therefore, by extension, our government) are "good," and we choose not to see what is done in our name.

Just as the wife would be "shocked" to hear anyone accuse

her husband of being a pedophile piece of shit, so too would many U.S. citizens be "shocked" to hear anyone accuse our government of being pathologically entitled, autogenocidal, white supremacist corporate fascists, bent on ruling/destroying the world.

Like the wife on the airplane, we will justify, rationalize, or plain ol' not see horrors that are being enacted right under our noses.

Embroider, embroider, embroider.

South Central Los Angeles is right under our noses, and we don't spend much time considering, or even seeing, the lived realities of people who reside there.

A friend of mine grew up in South Central Los Angeles. At a very young age, she figured out that the best way to insure that she'd wake up in the morning was to sleep with a pit bull curled up at her feet and a .38 under her pillow. She learned to shoot a gun when she was eight, started carrying one every day when she was eleven, and can't presently imagine life without one in her home, even if it is fully dismantled and locked away.

She once asked me if I had a heater.

"Yeah," I said, not understanding why she was asking me about how I kept my home warm in the context of the discussion we were having, "but I prefer to use my woodstove."

After a pause in which she momentarily wondered if "woodstove" was a slang term she wasn't familiar with and promptly rejected this possibility, she cackled over in a fit of laughter.

"A heater is a gun," she said.

Autobiography of a Blue-Eyed Devil

With this bit of lexiconic confusion all cleared up, I answered her question. "No. I don't have a gun. My cousin insisted I learn to shoot one once, but it made me cry."

I can still hear Roger's voice in my head: "Just hold tight, watch the kick, and empty the fucker, blam, blam, blam!"

I did what he said, but every time I pulled the trigger, I felt the force that has killed millions of people and animals stabbing into my heart. Every time I pulled the trigger, a parade of the shot-dead marched through my mind's eye. Every time I pulled the trigger, I heard endless, earsplitting screams of mothers begging that that please, please, please not be their baby lying in a pool of blood.

Holding the heavy metal of seemingly infinite death in my hands was not, as it turned out, my cup of tea.

My friend would not have survived her childhood if she had entertained this reaction to guns. By the time she was seven years old, a terror of guns was laughable to her.

My reaction to guns is a direct byproduct of the luxury of having a childhood where my innocence was not ripped out of my soul by the harsh realities of racism, poverty, hunger, violence, and autogenocide.

My friend has post-traumatic stress disorder, which is frequently exacerbated by the need, just about every weekend of her adult life, to attend funerals of friends shot down in gang warfare.

She was in her late twenties when she realized that, when asked, most people who did not grow up around gang violence will say *of course* they have attended funerals.

When their grandparents died.

Which roughly adds up to about the same number of funerals my friend has attended on any given month of her life.

"What does it do to a person's psyche," she wonders aloud from time to time, "when they spend almost every weekend at a funeral."

I do not know how to respond to this statement, which is never meant to be a question, but she knows I am listening.

That is very often all I have to offer my friend who grew up in South Central Los Angeles.

My listening, I mean.

There is much evil in this environment we mistake for a world.

While evil certainly engenders realities where it seems like a good idea to sleep with a pit bull and a .38 every night, gang violence itself is not the truly evil thing we're dealing with here.

Evil is the fact that this kind of violence and terror takes place global inches away from people who *actually want* the world to be a better place, but cannot bring themselves to truly examine what is going down under their noses.

Evil is walking around with a full belly of food and already imagining what your next meal will be, while children are starving all around you, and meanwhile, never wondering how hunger can shape a person's identity, just like war and rape.

Evil is thinking that poverty is some elaborate form of "laziness" and/or "stupidity," instead of an inherited, socio-inflicted disease, appearing on a card dealt from a big deck in the sky.

Autobiography of a Blue-Eyed Devil

Evil is those muthafucken ads that show up in newspapers and on city buses every "holiday" season, simpering on about how "No One Should Be Hungry on Thanksgiving." So if we include Christmas, that leaves 363 days a year when it is perfectly fine if people are hungry.

That is some evil-ass shit, and people are patted on the back into believing that they are "good" because they fork over $14.62 to feed a family of four some bioengineered, USDA-approved, hormone- and steroid-infused turkey dinner once or twice a fucken year.

Evil is a society that deals with this violence and poverty by pretending that the kids who are dying and the people who are starving are somehow less human, less worthy of life. Unlikely to contribute much to society because they obviously have no wherewithal to make use of the plentiful Amerikkkan Dream resources available to every citizen in the United States.

In an interview in the beautiful photo/essay book *East Side Stories*, writer Luis Rodriguez offers keen insight into how some people might develop the idea that all people in this country have an equal stab at the good life, if only they would go to the trouble of *applying* themselves:

> I went to Bryn Mawr, Pennsylvania; I did a poetry
> residency at five schools there—all private schools.
> Parents pay $17,000 a year for their kids to go to those

schools. Almost 90 percent were white kids. There were some black kids, some Asian, some Puerto Rican kids, but most were white.

Great kids, lovely kids. I had no problem with these kids. They were creative. They were expressive. Their art was all over the walls, and they were learning. They had a 100 percent graduation rate and a 100 percent college entrance rate. And I'm wondering, "What's the difference? Are they better than you and me? Are they better than our kids are?" The difference is that *they are not allowed to fail.* [my italics] Nobody will let them fail—even when they want to fail, even when some of them are suicidal. Some of these kids are on drugs. Some of them are alcoholics. They've got problems like anybody. But, man, they put resources behind them so that they will make it. Our kids don't have these kind of resources.

You know, the only time anybody got up and said, "Why don't you inner-city people pick yourselves up by your own bootstraps?" was at one of those Bryn Mawr schools. Some kid, a white kid with glasses—a smart kid. He thought he was making it because of his own efforts, and we poor folk weren't making it because we weren't willing to work at it. . . . It was kind of odd, but he didn't realize that all his life someone's taken care of him. He didn't even think about this. He thought that it was all his doing.[2]

Autobiography of a Blue-Eyed Devil

✄

In James Diego Vigil's book *A Rainbow of Gangs: Street Cultures in the Mega-City*, I learned that ten thousand kids of color in Los Angeles—mostly young men—have died from gang violence in the past two decades.[3]

This isn't a nationwide statistic.

This isn't a global statistic.

In the city of Los Angeles.

Twenty years.

Ten thousand dead young people.

Almost forty-two youth have died, on average, every single month between 1982 and 2002 in Los Angeles.

Every day, 1.4 families bury their beloved child. (You might recall that Ida B. Wells's statistics on lynchings also averaged out to 1.4 a day, and I wonder so much at the concept that "things" have gotten "better.")

I relayed this statistic to my friend who grew up in South Central. She laughed, and said, "Eh, they were prolly only gathering data from a coupla hoods."

I remember when everyone was on a big *Beloved* kick a few years ago. Oprah hailed Toni Morrison, made a movie, and everyone was very touched by how things used to be so horrible that a woman could be driven by terror to kill her beloved child, back in the day, before whites stopped dominating the world.

And my friend, who used to sleep with a pit bull and a .38,

was telling me they were talking about *Beloved* in her ethnic studies class.[†] And when she got out of class she couldn't stop thinking about one of her homies.

He showed up at a funeral wearing a gorgeous red suit, red shoes, and a red hat. After the services, people commented on how divine his outfit was, and he said, "Yeah, I want to be buried in this suit."

Not long afterward, he killed his two-year-old son and himself and was buried in the red suit, shoes, hat.

He used a heater.

The note he left explained how he didn't see any hope and just couldn't take it anymore. He didn't want to see his beloved child grow up in this environment we consistently mistake for the world.

And my friend wondered, "How is that any different from *Beloved*?"

And you know, you gotta admit through whatever veil of ignorance you may choose to wear in order to protect yourself from the "evils of this world," there's just no fucken difference.

And that *the evilest thing of all* is the elaborate choices we make to protect ourselves.

When I was a teenager, all the kids in the neighborhood would meet in front of my house after the parties were over. We'd hang out and debrief about the night's events.

One night, when my friends dropped me off at home, I was

---

† Anything other than the "normal" study of whiteness is always qualified.

deliriously drunk. I lay on the front lawn, trying to keep the world from spinning long enough to get inside my house. One of my neighbors—a young man I'll call Frankie Ray—sauntered up. We'd been friends since elementary school. He sat down next to me on the lawn and we shot the shit for a bit. He realized how drunk I was and offered to help me get into bed. I thought this was a good idea, so he stood me up, opened the front door, and led me into my room. I fell onto my bed, mumbled thanks and goodnight. But Frankie Ray didn't leave. Instead, he got on top of me and messed around with my panties and tried to stick his dick in me. I was deliriously drunk, like I say, but to me, "deliriously drunk" means three beers. I can't *physically* handle alcohol, so I can rarely manage to get drunk enough for my *thinking* to severely cloud.

So I was all, "Frankie Ray, you piece of shit, what the fuck, get off me you asshole."

I think he was shocked at the force in my voice.

He got off me and left. I waited to hear the front door close and his feet on the porch outside. Jolted back into control of my motor skills, I got up, made sure the front door was locked, and went to sleep.

I never wavered about my decision on how to deal with this situation. I simply knew I wouldn't say anything to anyone about it.

People would have come down on Frankie Ray because I am white and he is black—not because he deeply betrayed the boundaries of his power, and of our trust and friendship.

I have thought about this many times over the years, about

how if Frankie Ray had it in him to try to fuck me when he thought I was blotto out of my mind, then maybe he did that to other girls too. But I could never get past the reality that if I opened my mouth, Frankie Ray would be punished for my race and his race, rather than just his bullshit action.

I saw no justice there, and never even told my siblings or closest friends.

I did not know then about Emmett Till, or the truly horrifying munificence of historical lynchings, rapes, and unjust laws related to situations where the white man uses white women as justification for the sickening disease of his racism, but I knew in my gut that speaking out against Frankie Ray would be a GREAT WRONG, and I guess I just didn't feel like answering his wrong with my own.

I do not think this is "right."

It is how my seventeen-year-old imagination played a card I got dealt.

There was a lot more going on in my bed that night than Frankie Ray wanting to get laid. If he were one of my white neighbors, no one would have believed me if I'd ratted him out. If I were a young black, Chicana, or Mexicana woman, no one in the larger white community would have truly cared. It is convenient for a white society to punish black men for raping white women, though rape itself is usually overlooked when a white man rapes a woman of any race—especially, though, if he rapes a woman of color.

I have no idea exactly where Frankie Ray was coming from that night, but when I look back, I do wonder if his action was a byproduct of the dynamic where a white woman can be viewed as a really great conscious or subconscious vehicle for getting back at the white man. When convenient to white men, white women are upheld as pillars of goodness, and the point of vulnerability in the white race that must be protected at all costs. We are, consequently, often viewed as a good *location* for men of color to say, "Yeah, fuck you, crackkka-jack oppressor-ass muthafucker."

Eldridge Cleaver voiced his perspective on this manifestation of white supremacist racism in *Soul on Ice:*

> I became a rapist. To refine my technique and
> *modus operandi*, I started out by practicing on black
> girls in the ghetto—in the black ghetto where dark
> and vicious deeds appear not as aberrations or devi-
> ations from the norm, but as part of the sufficiency
> of the Evil of a day—and when I considered myself
> smooth enough, I crossed the tracks and sought out
> white prey. I did this consciously, deliberately, will-
> fully, methodically—though looking back I see that
> I was in a frantic, wild, and completely abandoned
> frame of mind.
>
> Rape was an insurrectionary act. It delighted
> me that I was defying and trampling upon the white
> man's law, upon his system of values, and that I was
> defiling his women—and this point, I believe, was the
> most satisfying to me because I was very resentful
> over the historical fact of how the white man has used

the black woman. I felt I was getting revenge. From the site of the act of rape, consternation spreads out in concentric circles. I wanted to send waves of consternation throughout the white race. . . .

After I returned to prison, I took a long look at myself and, for the first time in my life, admitted that I was wrong, that I had gone astray—astray not so much from the white man's law as from being a human, civilized—for I could not approve the act of rape. Even though I had some insight into my own motivations, I did not feel justified. I lost my self-respect. My pride as a man dissolved and my whole fragile moral structure seemed to collapse, completely shattered.

That is why I started to write. To save myself.[4]

You know, this is fucked on so many different levels, it's difficult to really zero in here, but I'll give it a go. I don't know how to put order upon a reality that is corrosively insane—however, it's no less insane than the reality that we really and truly *do* place a fluctuating value on various lives.

Eldridge Cleaver "practiced" his rape technique on black women.

The U.S. military "practices" first aid techniques on goats.

As a military spokesperson recently conveyed, "Goats save human lives," and so, for this, there is a specific value placed on them.[5]

Somewhere, there are goat farms whose sole function

is to produce mass quantities of goats. They don't necessarily have to be ambulatory goats. It doesn't matter if the goats are healthy, for humans won't eat them. They just have to be bodies that will get cut badly and bleed profusely. Somewhere, there is this place, and, in concentric circles similar to those Mr. Cleaver spoke of, the horror of it infects the entire surrounding community, causing great depression among the population. Many people in that community are already traumatized because they're related to soldiers in Iraq, and these young soldiers are coerced into rationalizing the murders of many thousands of innocent people, children, babies, and the soldiers are also injured and killed in huge numbers, and in order to treat the horrendous wounds of these soldiers, medics train on goats.

After medics treat the goats' willfully inflicted shrapnel wounds, they are killed, a.k.a. "destroyed."

The goats, not the medics.

The medics are worth much, much more than the goats.

I mention this to qualify my definition of "corrosively insane" when viewing Eldridge Cleaver's actions in this environment where we all abide life.

Mr. Cleaver viewed, and millions of people indoctrinated in our culture view, black women's bodies and lives as expendable. Prior to his awakening, this indoctrination actually led Mr. Cleaver to believe he was exacting vengeance in the name of black women, and their mute role was to be raped by him for "practice." Women who live in ghettos, in barrios, in poor rural communities, and on reservations are valued much less than women who live in townhouses, mansions, and suburbs. This is not to say that wealthier women are *necessarily* treated better by their husbands, fathers, sons, and associates. Wealthy (white) women, when correctly sheltered, are merely *legitimate targets* for fewer predatory demographics of society.[†]

I appreciate Mr. Cleaver's viewpoint because through his experience, he came to a deeper understanding of our culture and wrote about it. I do not appreciate what he did, or how he once justified his actions, but I do appreciate that he put a critical analysis of how he played his cards into the world for people to consider.

I am a woman who wrote a book about living in a rape warfare culture, and I don't particularly enjoy confessing that I let someone slide for doing something fucked just because of our races, but I did indeed do this.

I do not condone the actions of rapists. I look at the environment I was born into, and I try to figure out what appears to me to be the *least corrosively insane* response I can think of.

So, yeah, that's how I played that card.

I didn't narc Frankie Ray off.

At the time, the punishment I conjured up was to close my heart to him. By the time my drunken teenage sleep settled in

---

† I made a graph illustrating who can get away with raping whom in this environment, which can be viewed on my website (www.ingalagringa.com).

that night, our friendship was around twenty minutes into irrevocably being a thing of the past.

He never apologized for this, and even if he had, it would have meant nothing to me. I can't think of one time in my life that an apology has changed the course of past events.

I once read about a tribe of Inuit people who never say, "Oh shit, I broke that glass, I'm sorry." In this cosmology, everything happens for a reason, within the rhythm of the world. If you break a glass, it can mean that the universe is trying to get your attention, that you are not focused on the space you are occupying, or that your body is telling you not to drink at this time. Breaking a glass can mean many things.

So when someone breaks a glass, the person will say, "I allowed that glass to break," and then maybe wonder why.

After I read about that, I started to think about taking responsibility for my choices and actions in ways that I had never before considered. And I started to notice that when I broke something, it was usually because I wasn't present, or was thinking about something that angers or frustrates me.

Be that as it may, I no longer break things as much as I did before reading about Inuit folks' perspective on this.

Saying "I am sorry" has no meaning. It communicates the sentiment of self-sorrow. I hear people say "Sorry," almost every day of my life, but it was back when Clinton "apologized" for slavery that I noticed an upswing in the everyday use of this word.

A recurring interaction I have with the word "sorry" is when I am in the grocery store. Someone will reach right in front of me, sometimes even jostling me or my cart, to grab something. People will say "sorry" as they do this, as if this utterance magically erases their rude behavior.

I mean, if you're gonna be a rude fuck, then just be a rude fuck.

I remember *the very instant* that I saw the endless horror of my own incredibly stupid and entirely offensive ignorance.

I was a student at the Evergreen State College, chatting with three other students. One asked the other two if they were going to the black nationalist meeting that night.

They both answered in the affirmative.

I asked what a black nationalist was, and was briefly informed that black nationalists want to separate from white Amerikkka.

At this point in my life, I thought white people were evil and black people were good, period. I entertained an over-the-top ideological view of black people, partially based in my lack of understanding of history and how deeply complex humanity is.

It never occurred to me that black people could "hate" white people like we "hate" them.

So I said, "Black nationalists hate white people?"

And I believe my three scholastic contemporaries, who assuredly fielded ignorance of this kind every single day of their college-going lives, were nonetheless taken aback at my pointed stupidity.

The young woman who'd brought up the subject said, "Well, uh, it's not quite that simple, but essentially, yes."

So I go, "Do you hate white people?"

And, stunned, she said, *"My father* is white."

She pretty much hated at least one white person after that, and it didn't take me too terribly long to understand why.

During the course of her college education, she vetted the ignorance of an infinite parade of white students on campus.

I was one of many.

And I felt like such a fucken ass after that.

Such a total, total ass.

Every time I saw this woman, I was very aware that she could not stand me, and I learned to honor this. I could have pretended that nothing was wrong and we were still friends. I could have decided that she was a "bitch" for "overreacting." I could have felt guilty and tried to somehow "make it up to her." There's an infinite number of things that I could have done to somehow rationalize my pointed stupidity, and maybe try to convince myself that I was not a total ass, but that wouldn't have meant shit, now would it, because the fact of the matter is, I was a total, total ass.

It seemed to make the most sense for me to look at myself, and wonder why my thoughts occurred to me the way they did, and why this was so hurtful, and how, in one short instant, I managed to completely sunder a casual friendship.

So that is what I did.

So yes, I am an asshole.

Furthermore, everyone is an asshole.

Including you and everyone you love.

No matter how "nice," "polite," or, if white, "well inten-
tioned" you are, you will undoubtedly fuck up repeatedly
throughout your life.

Big hoop dee doo.

Every time you fuck up, you are presented with an opportunity to examine and lay down a card you've been dealt.

For years and years I have thought it's a bad idea to wear
shoes in the house. Shoes have the chaos resonations and
physical filth of the outside world on the bottom of them. The
inside of my home is a sanctuary from All That Craziness
outside, so it's always made sense to take my shoes off at the
front door.

We're talking twenty years I've believed this shit, right.

When I go to the homes or temples of folks who don't wear
shoes inside, I am always comforted by the area at the front
door for taking off one's shoes.

When I was moving away from Los Angeles, my now-
ex-girlfriend's Hindu in-laws invited us over for dinner. This
was always a huge thing to look forward to, her sister-in-law's
mother, Prema is not only one of the most amazing cooks on the
planet, but she is beyond completely down with vegetarianism.

I had packed up a bag of food that wasn't coming with us
on our move, for Rupa, Prema and Raj's youngest daughter, and

put a pair of sandals I thought Nalini, my ex-girlfriend's sister-in-law, might like on top of the bag of food.

When we arrived, I set this package down in the foyer, and took off my shoes.

This is when Raj politely and wordlessly pointed out my utter *crime* of placing a *fucken pair of shoes* on top of a *bag of food*.

I understood this to be a spiritual crime, as opposed to a hygienic one. None of the actual foodstuff was being touched by the shoes, just the various cans, bottles, and packages.

It was no less very, very wrong.

After warmly greeting me, and noting the package I'd set down, Raj went into the kitchen and came back with a plastic bag. He picked up the sandals, placed them in the bag, and set them back down on top of the food. He did not say a word to me, and was, in fact, not really saying anything to me, per se, at all. Having no idea about my own feelings on shoes, he saw no reason to point out what I had done wrong. If I were his niece, Raj might have chided me gently, but he knows I'm not Hindu and assumed I don't think about the filth of shoes. He wasn't being dogmatic, wasn't teaching me a lesson. He merely saw something out of place and fixed it.

The lesson was there if I wanted to learn it.

I did, and was disgusted at what I had done. I thought to myself, "No matter how much I learn, I will always fuck up. There is simply no circumventing this reality."

There is nothing wrong with being pointedly stupid, making mistakes, displaying ignorance, fucking up, failing. These are some of the things that make people interesting and endlessly complex—which, to me, seems kinda the whole point of having opposable thumbs, kickass motor skills, and an interestingly endowed brain. Being a big enough person to say, "Dang, I fucked the fuck up. I will learn from this one, and think about it and hold myself accountable and look into the larger cultural and historic dynamics going on here. Cool. I'm great, I suck, I'm alive."

So I ask myself, If you can't admit that you're a fuckup, are you still human? Are you interesting or endlessly complex?

I laugh to myself, at the gigantic maw of ignorance that will always be inside me, no matter what, because I am a human being and human beings are bigger fuckups than everyone else on the planet, combined, and *not* forgetting locusts.

In this environment, we wake up every day, and some of us know that crimes against humanity are taking place, and some of us only know where we gotta be and how we're gonna get there, but no matter what you know when you wake up, there are places where stolen childhoods and broken bodies nourish the earth. And we walk upon their bodies, and pass the memories of their lives, and sooner or later, this is gonna take a toll.

Waving
to Stevie

On March 6, 2002, the *Washington Post* carried a story about a gala held at Ford's Theatre. Stevie Wonder was the star attraction. When Mr. Wonder took the stage, Arbusto could not contain his gleeful excitement that, in his fraudulent capacity as one of the most powerful people on the planet, he was about to be entertained by the venerable Mr. Wonder.

So Arbusto enthusiastically waved to him.

Bouncin' in his seat, smiling like the sunshine, waving to Stevie Wonder.

I was amazed but not amused.

No, actually, I was amused too.

At the time, I was thinking about the billions of ways that white supremacy is reinforced in the thought and language of my country. I was feeling very defeated about my ability to nail any of this shit in a good way, without writing just a big litany of complaints. Sometimes, I've wanted to crawl under a rock and die, but in that moment, I laughed and laughed and saw the whole funny enchilada of life again.

As it came to pass, when I read about Arbusto waving to Stevie Wonder, I felt quite clearly that god was talking directly to me.

Here is god's message:

Dear Inga,
Refusing to see is a lot different from being blind.
Love,
God

Blind people often smell, taste, feel, and/or hear the world with a profound clarity unaccessed by most sighted people. Refusing to see, on the other hand, results in behaviors such as gamely waving to a blind man on national television.

The environment we abide life in is filled with, indeed, led by, those who refuse to see.

According to my 1965 *Random House Dictionary*, myopia is "a condition of the eye in which parallel rays are focused in front of the retina, objects being seen distinctly only when near to the eye."[1]

My 2004 Microsoft Word computer dictionary defines myopia as "a common condition in which light entering the eye is focused in front of the retina and distant objects cannot be seen sharply."

Both definitions say pretty much the same thing, with the notable difference that, in thirty-nine years, the frequency of myopia has evidently increased so much the 2004 definition felt the need to qualify it with the term "common."

This physical affliction is—and you all know where I'm going with this—also a concurrently existing cultural affliction. As such, it has become so "common" few recognize it *as a condition* at all.

Cultural myopia, as an affliction, then, could be defined as a common condition in which information entering the colonized, unconscious imagination is focused solely through a limited worldview, and anything existing outside that limited worldview cannot be seen with clarity. This affliction leads to a perceptual habit of refusing to see events, experiences, or ideas that are not presented authentically, or at all, in the mainstream corporate media.

Sexuality, beauty, and fashion, for instance, are completely relative, mutative constructs that vary fantastically throughout the world and this country.

Focusing on sexuality, beauty, and fashion through a myopic lens provided by white, male-generated role models, such as Britney Spears, leads to the cultural phenomenon of eleven-year-old girls waxing their barely grown-in pubic hair so they can wear low-down ho pants.

I do not have a teevee, rarely listen to the radio, almost never read mainstream magazines, and mainly view news and analysis websites, and *still,* I know exactly who Britney Spears is. I know what she looks like, and I know what she is presented as thinking. I know who Britney Spears is presently married to, and I know that he is a low-down ho who ditched his pregnant girlfriend and child to cash in on a relationship with Ms. Spears.

These minutiae, which do not enrich my life in any way, colonize space inside my mind because I live in an environment where the choice of looking at the world myopically is constantly presented in my lived experience.

I dodge, duck, run, and hide, but it is always there, waving enthusiastically.

According to a January 4, 2005, AOL News headline, giving aid to tsunami survivors bordering the Bay of Bengal and the Indian Ocean actually *helps us* ("us" being Amerikkkans). How, exactly, does it "help us" to give money? Well, silly, according to the headline, it "proves" to the world that Amerikkka is not "anti-

Muslim" because a lot of the people whose lives were destroyed are Muslim (and Buddhist, Hindu, and many other religions).

So this is as if you and all your friends beat up some guy with baseball bats because he is driving a Ford Mustang, and you and your friends think all people who drive Ford Mustangs are the filth of the earth. But then, you see someone with a Chevy Impala by the side of the road with a flat tire. So you and your pals, you stop and help the Impala driver fix the flat. You *then* hold a press conference, explaining to your community that because you helped the Impala driver, what you did to the Mustang driver can, really, no longer be held in an unfavorable light. As an added bonus, you might go visit the Mustang driver in the intensive care unit at the hospital, and tell him about the Impala driver with the flat tire too, so that the Mustang driver won't have any hard feelings about the fact that you destroyed his kidneys and he will need to wear adult diapers for the rest of his life.

Makes sense, huh.

That's cultural myopia in the US of A.

I have found a few family-fun practices for examining the cultural myopia in the U.S. Developing practices of critical examination assists in constructing a frame of reference for truly seeing the millions of pathologically myopic word and thought choices perpetuated in our culture.

This makes you free.

One opportunity for analytical fun 'n' games is to gather all 'round and watch a teevee program together. Everyone has a pen and paper, noting instances of racism, sexism, and anything else that is, on balance, highly oppressive to one's own humanity. List nothing but stereotypes, including those in commercials. When the show and its attendant ads are over, turn off the teevee and compare notes with each other, and talk about it.

It is also greatly—if somewhat morbidly—instructive to get a photo of Dick Cheney, cover his left eye, and peer into his right one. Then cover his right eye and peer into the left one. If you do this with Arbusto, you will note that his eyes are rarely, if ever, matched up. Most people's eyes are not quite the same. In Arbusto's case, one looks like that of a little boy who enjoys strangling bunnies and the other looks like a semicomatose orb floating in a netherworld of entitlement.

But Cheney. Ooo.

His eyes both almost always have the exact same look in them: cold, calculating, and utterly reptilian. For a frame of reference, compare Cheney's eyes to the eyes of someone such as Audre Lorde or Arundhati Roy. Not to just pick on Cheney. This is a great way to make personal assessments of anyone who exerts pathological control over one's environment.

Another fun deconstruction pastime is to bring copies of news articles or other White House Literature, such as Arbusto's 2005 inaugural speech, to the friends 'n' family table. Discuss the way they are written, the slant, the information conveyed (either directly or through allusion), and/or the larger ideological (and corporate) interest permeating every word.

The general rule for analysis of this kind is to take absolutely nothing for granted. Analyze every assertion, word, and comma placement, and respond from your heart and experience, as well as your mind. Examine all repeated nouns and adjectives, for they are rife with clues about what is actually being communicated.

Mainstream reporting almost always follows the exact same formula, so it is illuminating to read articles from the bottom to the top. Introduction paragraphs offer a general overview of all of the information that will follow. All the paragraphs in the middle are designed to support the writer's subjective arguments, though some of these paragraphs invariably present a "dissenting" view or two, usually in the third and fourth paragraphs. The final paragraph—that is, the Last Word—is almost always used to leave the reader with deep suspicions about the "dissenting" paragraphs, a sense that "fair and balanced,"[†] information has been communicated, and rest assured, all government agencies and corporate overseers are the genuine voices of reason.

By reading an article from the end to the beginning, you will see where the author's allegiances lie right from the get-go.

This, too, is a highly beneficial community pastime.

Another kind of article I have noticed a lot in Arbusto's

[†] "Fair and balanced" involves the practice of planting an issue and then focusing on two facets of it. For instance: Drilling for oil in one of the last arctic refuges on earth is an argument between forward-thinking neo-pioneers and whiny environmental groups. There is no room for any other perspective or voice because it's already "fair and balanced" due to the fact that it includes insights from both neo-pioneers and environmentalists, so shut up. The issue has been aired, debated, and decided upon. Go sign a petition if you don't like it.

media is the puff piece meant to convince people that (fill in the blank, but usually Arbusto) is super duper keen and swell. These strange articles are like infomercials for the leader of the free world. It seems oddly insulting that any self-respecting leader would ever *want* such simpering pieces of puffery written about him, but then Arbusto is oddly insulting.

How's this for a mid-2004 campaign headline of an AP exclusive article: "Bush the Mountain-Biker Rides Hard, Shrugs off Crash."[2]

In this specimen of news information, I learn that the AP reporter has been invited to go for a "punishing" mountain bike ride at the Crawford ranch with Arbusto (who "charges" ahead of everyone else), his Secret Service guys (pistols "bulging" under their shirts), and the rest of the entourage. Arbusto leads the way, saying things like, "I'm gonna show you a hill that would choke a mule," right before he eats shit and lands on his back with his $3,100 bike on top of him. Our intrepid reporter must know that Arbusto is a goddamn fool, showing off his ranch like a spoiled kid giving his pals a guided tour of his room of wall-to-wall toys without letting them actually play with or touch anything. To this end, Arbusto, leader of my country on vacation in Crawford, "swats away" any question that does not have to do with the cost of his bike, the material that was used to make his bike, inside jokes about the Tour de France, or the "treacherous" terrain of his beloved "piece of property."

Arbusto's spill is obviously the challenge for the reporter. How to confect a puff piece when the object of puffery executes a slapstick ass plant with his bike landing on top of him, for chrissake? Well, if you are this reporter, you conjure a silent, deadly metaphor. You clue the reader in on how brutal the pathways are, and how our subject charges ahead with courage and speed, and by god, if he eats shit, our subject gets right back on his bike and gloriously announces to the world, "We've got thrills, spills—you name it." You turn the mortal fuckup into a larger-than-life story about how one might go about saving the world. But you never actually come right out and say this. You delve into minutiae, extolling the virility of your subject: "Over an 18-mile ride that lasted an hour and 20 minutes, he burns about 1,200 calories and his heart rate reaches 168 beats per minute. That's nearly four times his resting rate and in the same range as Lance Armstrong's when the six-time Tour de France winner is pedaling hard." You seduce the reader with mundane feats of greatness and a simple moral for everyone who can wrap their mind around an Aesop fable.

In the case of Arbusto's administration and the crimes against humanity it commits, it is not difficult to discern that this silent, deadly metaphor is employed in every facet of the administration's image management—from the attacks on the World Trade Center and Laura's Easter Dinner Menu to carpet bombing innocent human beings and all of their "property" to the aura-like backdrops that often illuminate Arbusto's head during speeches.

The presidency is a show, and there's a slightly different message each time you tune in. And when you can view the spectacle of this, it makes you free.

At the other end of the spectrum, we have the intolerance articles. These tend to be about insurgents, terrorists, terrorist leaders, alleged terrorist leaders, those thought to have somehow abetted terrorists or insurgents, or world leaders who are not, mysteriously, in Arbusto's good graces. These include Chirac, Schroeder, sometimes Martin (depending on whether or not Canada is lubing up its asshole for a good fucking by the U.S. in a timely manner), and always, always, Castro and Chávez.

Fidel Castro is, as everyone with cultural myopia knows, a dictator who does not allow elections and illegally detains innocent people (who plotted to assassinate him). This is a lot different from Arbusto, so let's just move on.

Hugo Chávez, though by no means as well known by the mainstream masses in the U.S., is generally referred to as a "self-styled revolutionary." This mysteriously frequently recurring term always baffles me. What exactly *is* a self-styled revolutionary? One who does not follow the accepted standard of revolution? If Chávez and his administration are democratically elected into office by millions of Venezuelan voters, where does "the revolution of Chávez" begin and the will of the population he represents end?

In a recent spate of articles about President Chávez, I learned he has "annoyed" Arbusto. One particular article, entitled simply "Venezuelan Leader Frustrates U.S.,"[3] really got me racking my memory for a time when anyone who does not do the Arbusto administration's immediate bidding wasn't killed or taken out of power in a coup (tried and failed against Chávez), or hadn't mysteriously committed suicide. I couldn't remember, but it seems that when Chávez announced to the world community that he had evidence that Arbusto was planning an assassination attempt against him, the White House interpreted this as an "attack." Adding further insult, Venezuela nationalized its oil, and quite a bit of the 1.5 million barrels a day it sells to us goes back into the socioeconomic infrastructure of Venezuela instead of Arbusto's oil 'n' energy pals.

That fucker, Chávez.

More on him and his "self-styled revolution" a bit later.

One of Washington's recent "concerns" is Chávez's decision to buy one hundred thousand AK-47s from Russia. My enthusiastic interest in this li'l factoid had little to do with why my government thinks it has any say in what other world leaders do with their money—especially when said world leader happens to know that my government would like said leader's ass served to the world community on a gold-plated platter embossed with his 'n' her cowboy boots. What fascin-fucken-ated me was that Washington's "concern" was printed on March 16, 2005, *a mere nine days* before my government sold F-16 warplanes (heya, Lockheed Martin, don't spend it all in one place) to Pakistan as a "reward" for that government's assistance in the "War on Terror."

Why is it acceptable in my country that headlines state India is "upset"[4] about this transaction? In our narrow view, it makes sense to be "concerned" with Chávez for buying one hundred thousand guns and patronizing toward India for being a sore loser when we plan to supply one of its all-time archrivals with instruments of mass death. This sale to Pakistan forces India (both, um, incredibly poor nations) to buy similar weapons from some other country, but you bet yer ass that the bucks will stop somewhere near some Arbusto somewhere in Texas.

It may take time, energy, and effort to perceive the media in this way, but it also makes you free.

And now, it is time for a poetic interlude, with your effervescent hostess, Inga La Gringa:

> We aren't the world.
> We aren't the children.
> We aren't the ones who make a better day,
> so let's stop thinking
> that we have something to give
> to any other nation,
> when we haven't even paid
> our own reparations.

Ahem.

Let us turn our attention from how our fascinating worldview affects our understanding of global events, to see this learned and chosen cultural affliction functioning domestically.

Initially, I had written this chapter with call-and-response type, paragraph-by-paragraph breakdowns of a speech given at a college in 2004, and a column by Leonard Pitts appearing in the *Miami Herald*. Well, it turns out that the speech-giver was none too pleased with my butchering style of analysis and thus withheld permission. I had picked this particular piece of writing because it quintessentially encapsulated the whole white liberal belief that our country has never committed a single wrong before Arbusto came into office, and, among other things, that the horrifying "abuse scandal"[†] that occurred in Abu Ghraib prison would someday "pass." I could spend a few months counting the millions and millions of Muslims in this world for whom this wholesale abuse, rape, terror, carpet bombing, and war will not pass for many, many generations.

Long story short, I had to cut the speech, which left me with Leonard Pitts's column, and a different dilemma. The speech guy is a white, old-money liberal. Leonard Pitts is an African American liberal. A white woman critiquing an African American man about the function of cultural myopia in a context of racism is not gonna go over well with a number of people. I know this. But with the white guy there, it didn't stand out so bad, 'cause I tore his cracker ass up too.

As it turns out, in my book, as in U.S. history, the white man covered his ass by withholding permission to reprint his speech, and the African American man's newspaper, which retained the rights to give reprint permission, didn't ask to read the context in which I planned to use his article. The first Mr. Pitts will know of this is when it's already a book being sold in stores.

I considered cutting this section as well, but dang, there is just so much myopia going on in this column, I couldn't bring

---

† I gather this has become the "accepted," myopic euphemism for describing the torture, sexual assault, and various other sadistic crimes and humiliations inflicted upon innocent Iraqi people at the hands of the U.S. government. It is not clear to me how (white) soldiers—funded with our tax dollars—riding an old woman like a donkey fits into this euphemism. The term, "scandal" is also problematic. It insinuates a small "blip" featuring "bad apples," rather than the systemic nightmare that it is.

myself to delete it—especially after the, yes, *torture* of deleting
that liberal honky speech. So, as a compromise, Mr. Pitts, if you
would like to kick my ass, email me and I'll fly to Miami, or wherever you live, and just more or less hope you aren't into pointy
shoes or steel-toed boots. For what it's worth (which, I know, is
not much) our culture is *positively rife* with this style of communication. If articles such as this were capable of producing oxygen,
the U.S. could easily save the entire planet from global warming.
And so, without further ado.

In an article originally entitled "Who Cares if Cops Are Watching Rappers?" *Miami Herald* columnist Mr. Pitts asserts that his
views of U.S. culture are some kind of "norm" from which every
"deviating" view emanates.

All unexamined and undefined terms appear in bold for
your redefining convenience.

> Are Miami **police** spying on **rap artists?** And should
> it matter to **you** if they are?[5]

Who is the "you" being referred to here?

When I say "you" in my book, I am talking to a disabled
teenager who was in the wrong place at the wrong time when
bullets were flying. My "you" is her family and friends. My "you"
is a gender-variant person who has considered suicide. My "you"
is all the hookers and strippers and whores who are not respected
for their services to humanity. My "you" is drug dealers and gang
members who are portrayed as two-dimensional thugs instead

of highly complex human beings who are playing the hand they were dealt just like every other person in this world. My "you" is deeply thoughtful, well-meaning white or white-identified people who really want the world to be a better place and can't quite see how their indoctrination manifests in a series of elaborate choices made throughout their daily lives. My "you" is indigenous people or people of color who struggle to see the larger pattern of oppression that is often enacted in an overwhelming series of manifestations in their daily lives. My "you" is the farmers and loggers, fire fighters and ambulance drivers, Teamsters[†] and teachers, librarians and nurses, and everyone else who truly runs this country. My "you" is an aging black nationalist or indian rights activist, an antiwar grandmother, or a Vietnam Brutal Occupation veteran who is maybe feeling despondent about how the imaginations of the youth of this country are under corporate siege. My "you" is rap artists and the cops who don't feel all that comfortable spying on them.

So who is this "you"?

How **you** answer the first question depends on who **you choose** to believe. According to a recent [*Miami Herald*] story . . . **police** in both Miami and Miami Beach have been routinely tailing and surveilling **rap performers** who visit South Florida to work and play.

[†] I mean actual Teamsters, and not the organization that more or less pals around with the U.S. government. Big difference.

This was promptly denied by Miami **Police Chief** John Timoney. However, the piece quotes some of his officers acknowledging their participation in the program. And the assistant **police** chief of Miami Beach unabashedly admits his department's spying. "We have to keep an eye on **these rivalries**," Charles Press said.

"These" rivalries.

The function of the word "these" is to let the reader know we're *really* talking about "those" violent young black men warring with each other again.

Who killed Tupac Shakur? Who killed Biggie Smalls? Has it ever been established that this was really a rivalry? What *exactly* is a "rivalry"? Have these murders ever been fully investigated?

The one fact that I've ascertained about Tupac and Biggie's murders is that they led to an all-knowing mainstream reality that rappers are gat-brandishing "gangsta thugs" who shoot each other up in the course of "these" rivalries.

It would not surprise me in the least if the CIA was behind both of these murders, because any time a fiercely intelligent, passionate, and beautiful black man captivates the imaginations of people, he is generally murdered or framed and incarcerated—and both of these men, to greater or lesser degree, definitely met this criteria. Besides Malcolm X, Dr. King, and Mumia Abu-Jamal, I am still wondering who killed Jam Master Jay. He had nothing to do with gangs, yet every article I read about Jam Master Jay's horrible murder mentions Tupac and Biggie and otherwise alludes to "these" rivalries.

This correlation is completely nonsensical.

Lots of white rock stars are known for committing suicide, overdosing on drugs, and/or beating their wives or girlfriends. Nowhere in the media will you find namesake trends linking all white rock stars to these realities. Rappers and hiphop artists are contextualized by "rivalries" because it serves white supremacist racist power structures and corporations to define rappers and hiphop artists. If they define themselves, they might captivate too many imaginations, and get too many people wondering about the definitions of even more unexamined terms such as "freedom," "liberty," and "democracy."

At the very least, "gang rivalry" is one of those frequently occurring, loaded terms—like "war" and "traditional values"— that inspires many questions about exact contextual definitions.

All of which makes it **difficult** to take **Timoney's denial** at face value. At a minimum, it's clear that **somebody with a badge** is surreptitiously following **rappers** around.

Okay, so here we are at the fourth paragraph of the article, and we arrive at the thoroughly examined, highly qualified point of view that Timoney is lying. If "rappers" were accorded the same amount of discourse and respect as is extended to the police, this article would be completely different. It would, for one thing, *contain perspectives from the people the police are spying on.*

Back in the 1970s, the *New York Times* ran a three-page article on the Puerto Rican American civil rights group the Young Lords.

Autobiography of a Blue-Eyed Devil

The reporter hung out with various members of this group for weeks. The deeply investigative story is beautifully written and pandering to no particular force in any particular power structure. It is not, however, a puff piece. It is a thoughtful story about a complex group of people. Can you imagine such a thing appearing in a large newspaper of today? A fully kickass, three-page investigative report in the *Washington Post* about Black Voices for Peace? Can you imagine the *Los Angeles Times* giving Alejandro Alonso, the creator of Streetgangs.com, a fully autonomous editorship? These ideas are preposterous in the media of today, but they were not preposterous back when the media wasn't owned by a handful of multinational corporations and individual journalists were able to write about things that captivated their imaginations.

This benefit-of-the-doubt shout-out is bestowed upon to Chief Timoney before coming to the conclusion that it is "difficult" to take his denial "at face value."

Why choose the term "difficult"? Why not "patently impossible," "absolutely untenable," or "palpably absurd beyond fiction, nonfiction, and science fiction, combined"?

Two full paragraphs are given over to allow the police the space to deny this allegation because he could lose his job if he pisses off his overseers. This is also why the voices of rappers are completely silenced in this form of journalism.

Which returns **us** to the second question. Should **you** care?

Hmmm.

Should "I" care.

I dunno. It would be a really big stretch of my identity to "care" what happens to (black) rappers. Are we talking just mild spying and not sodomizing with lightbulbs? I mean, a little spying on these violent thugs probably won't hurt anybody, will it? I, for one, would like to know that the police are preempting rappers' violent behavior. You can't be too careful. Why I should reach into the glorious treasure chest of my compassion and potentially squander it on the kind of people who entertain these rivalries.

I'm going to **go out on a limb here** and speculate that **you** are not, **yourself, a rapper. Now if you're reading this in the Jacuzzi in the back of your limousine surrounded by scantily clad women, then I am obviously in error and I apologize.** But I'm going to assume that's not the case.

Oh, hoo-hoo, that is a knee-slapping good one.

Wait, I am still laughing at this little joke about me maybe being a rapper.

Wow. Not only is Mr. Pitts much wiser and more compassionate than violent thugs deserve, but he seems to have quite a grasp on what rappers are all about.

He understands where Immortal Technique is coming from in his devastating eulogy to destruction, "Dance with the Devil."

He has carefully studied Akon's video for his hit single "Ghetto," where he walks around ghettos, barrios, reservations, and rural white communities, singing of the plight of children who have no one to catch them when they fall.

He has a handle on the scathing sociocultural analysis of artists such as Paris, Lyfe, Mos Def, Lauryn Hill, Kam, Eve, M.I.A., Sister Souljah, and indeed, Biggie Smalls and Tupac Shakur.

Seriously, my brain almost cleaved another couple hemispheres when I read this paragraph.

Here are some questions that immediately arose from this cerebral plate shifting:

- Why is someone who entertains stereotypes about rappers enabled to define who rappers are?
- Why does the music industry constantly glorify and stereotype mediocre rappers and hiphop artists who pander to the mainstream's unexamined stereotypes about rap and hiphop music?
- Why is Eminem, as opposed to most black mainstream talents, presented as a deeply complex human being, worthy of adoration and praise, even while one is grappling with the negative aspects of his personality?
- How is it acceptable to assume that anyone who rides around in a limo with a Jacuzzi is a black rapper?
- Who does it serve to perceive "rappers" as people who want nothing more in life than to ride around in limos with objectified women in bikinis?

Indeed, far from being a **rap** star, maybe **you're** one of those folks **of a certain age** for whom **rap is a**

territory only slightly less alien than Pluto. And twice as frightening.

I feel **your pain.** One of the reasons I quit being a **music critic** 10 years ago is that I found it increasingly difficult to appreciate the artistry of **some young man cursing at me over a drum beat sampled from an old James Brown record. Not to mention the violence, always implied and sometimes celebrated in graphic detail in the lyrics of rap songs.**

Here we unveil the mystery of who the "you" describes. This article is for people "of a certain age" who know absolutely nothing about—and indeed, are "frightened" by—the rap and hiphop movements.

As with every musical genre, some rap and hiphop artists speak to me more than others. I am not very taken with a lot of mainstream rappers, but the only thing I find frightening about them is why they are given so much more recognition and money than rappers and hiphop artists who speak their truths from their hearts, lives, consciousness, and history instead of their egos and bank accounts.

If these readers find this immeasurably diverse demographic of musicians, DJs, MCs, dancers, muralists, and artists "frightening," I'm gonna go out on a limb here and guess that he is scared of what conscious people of color, off-white folks, and indigenous folks in the rap and hiphop communities have to say about this environment we all live in together, because I'll tell you what. I look around and straight up, one of the only true, actual bright beacons of hope that I see is in the rap and hiphop communities.

I got me a passel of contemporary white Christian rock CDs at the library the other day and I listened to them closely. The folks were speaking their truths, but it was all completely passive, and steeped in unaccountability. Jesus will love me no matter what I do. I can ax murder an entire rural community and Jesus will still love the fuck out of me, no questions asked. The rapture Christians were even more hard-core, with this consciousness that since Jesus is coming to take all true believers to heaven, then pollution, global warming, and the disappearance of entire species are all just punishments that non-true-believers will have to endure. I mention this because I found these CDs a lot more passively and unaccountably celebratory of violence than any "gangsta" rap song I've ever heard.

Allow me to indulge in addressing one complaint about rap and hiphop that I often hear.

Unconscious white people, especially women, are often quick to point at the misogyny in rap and hiphop.

So like—let me just get this small point out of the way— what, Mick Jagger, Kid Rock, and Axl Rose are a buncha stalwart feminists who would sooner die than treat a woman like a piece of highly expendable shit? *We live in a culture that denigrates women in every facet of existence.* Naturally, then, the rap and hiphop artists who openly denigrate women are more likely to get huge recording deals from the music industry.

Duh.

Aside from that, though, is the much larger point that I don't hear much misogyny in rap and hiphop because I seek out politically and socially conscious artists.

For example, if an unconscious white woman does not see how she perpetuates white supremacist racism by embracing stereotypes about an entire music genre, then where exactly is her ground to stand on, pointing fingers at (some) rapper's unconscious sexism?

If, however, a person chooses to examine the racial and socioeconomic realities that inform any given rapper's misogyny, then that's a different story.

One such examination exists in the words of V.S. Chochezi. She, her mother, Staajabu, and her two daughters, Jessicah and Tisho Pratt, are all poets. This excerpt is from their collaboration, *Scribes Rising*. Ms. Chochezi's piece "Hip Hop Cool"[6] goes, in part, like this:

Hip hop is cool
and whatnot but
Ain't nothin
hip about it
if it's not speakin
consciousness

Talkin about liberatin
workin for and takin
back our freedom

Autobiography of a Blue-Eyed Devil

Rappers are going
To jail as fast as you
Can say, "What's up, man?"

While M.C.s are
squarin off, bitin
cussin carryin on
warrin words on 5.0's
and that might be cool

But callin my sistah's ho's?

Now that ain't cool. . . .

In the ancient griot tradition, history is told through oral stories, to the beat of words or music. Many Africans, Haitians, Dominicans, Jamaicans, and Afro-Caribbean folks, and their descendents in all of the Americas, observed, and continue to observe, this tradition.

Rap and hiphop, along with def poetry and spoken word, are modern incarnations of griot. They poetically speak peoples' various truths—and this is actually the *very reason* that I view the rap and hiphop community as representing so much hope for the future of this country. In no other cultural realm do I see a devout adherence to the power of the past in the present and future, and nowhere else is the practice of holding one's self and community accountable given such high regard.

I came across the writings of Ronald Chatman, a.k.a.

Waving to Stevie

O/G Madd Ronald, from the Rolling 20s Neighborhood Bloods, on Streetgangs.com. Below is an excerpt from his essay "The Peace Process," which is a part of his forthcoming book, *No More Blood Shed,* where he discusses some of his feelings on mainstream rap music:

> I once walked into my own livingroom and saw my kids doing the Cripwalk to a mainstream rapp artist video, where they were doing the Cripwalk in the video.
>
> In this video, they were wearing blue and exploiting the L.A. gang culture.
>
> I felt totally disrespected by the fact that these clown-ass wanna-be gang members are exploiting the mainstream with their bullshit rhetoric about poppin' glocks, smoking kronick, Cripwalkin' and using words that are reserved for the gang community in mainstream rapp videos.
>
> I had to explain, as a parent, not a Blood, that a simple dance or a word like "cuz" can get you killed on Normandie and Adams.
>
> Watch what is it you are wearin' and watch where you are going.
>
> The wrong colors in the wrong place can get you killed.
>
> The wrong words in the wrong place can get you killed.
>
> A wrong turn down the wrong street in L.A. can get you killed.

If you are driving through a hood like the West-side Rollin' 20's and you turn down the wrong block one too many times, don't be surprised if someone fires a round of shots into your car.

It don't sound right, but that's the way things are in Los Angeles.

Rapp music often glorifies my bitch, my glock and my kronick.

How many times have we heard those lyrics and how many different artists are going to use them?

At first it seemed kool, back in the 80's, but now I have two daughters. If my son calls one of his sisters a bitch, it is not his fault. It is my fault for condoning his listening to such dehumanizing lyrics.

If my son picked up a gun and went out and took someone's life, it is not his fault, it is my fault for condoning such dehumanizing lyrics.

It is ridiculous, when I see a rapper with his shirt off, glorifying how many times he has been shot.

I grew up on the streets of L.A., bangin' for real.

As bad as it felt to be shot, there is nothing kool about catching any lead.

When I see you on an album cover, exposing how many times you have been shot, you ain't showing me nothing but how many times you have been victimized.

That is the shit that makes kids think it is kool to get shot.

I have been around people catching lead for years and I don't have one homie who thinks there is anything kool about getting shot at.

We have got to understand the systematic ideology that is portrayed through the media and through music.

Our kids think they can live up to these exploitive messages and images that they get subliminally when they hear these words or see these images.

Another thing is the glorification of using guns in the music or in the movies.

It is actually a double-edged sword when the music is compared to the movies.

We watch Arnold Schwarzenegger terminate the world year after year, but if a young black rapper talks about it in the soundtrack, he gets banned.

I don't support either one.

If we are making music that is shaping the minds of the young to bust shots with their glocks and to maliciously commit genocide, we have a responsibility to speak of the consequences of genocide or else we are hypocrites.

I have spent six years of my life in California's prison industrial complex.

I have been in maximum security prisons with inmates that were doing life for bustin' a few shots with their glocks as if their lives were unfolding to a rapp song.

Ain't no pride in a life sentence.

I have never met a gang member that was doing life for a gang-related murder who was proud of committing such an act of genocide.[7]

Our environment would be drastically different if Pat Robertson and Halliburton held their people to the high standard of accountability to which Ronald Chatman holds his people. Besides right-wing and rapture Christians, war profiteers, and the general U.S. population, Bill Cosby, in particular, would be well served in carefully considering Mr. Chatman's words before ever again opening his trap on the subject of accountability.

There is no place for Mr. Chatman's brilliant perspective in the "mainstream." His voice is never heard in the articles written by all the Leonard Pittses of this environment. Yet, within his perspective lie all the qualities of a true leader. Someone who should have his own media empire, if not a seat in the U.S. Senate.

Many of the people who have inherited or adopted the griot tradition live with memories of slavery and genocide in their DNA. Many grow up in areas where violence and poverty reign supreme. Such topics often arise in rap and hiphop songs because they are lived experiences, and not necessarily because they are always "celebrated."

If an adult was once a child who truly knew hunger, and figures out that by writing songs with dehumanizing lyrics, he or she will quite possibly pass a legacy on to his or her children, so that they will never, ever, ever know hunger, we are dealing with a lot more complexity than mindless "celebration."

If there are "curse" words in songs, it is because these are peerless tools in the service of expressing emotion. Without such words, I, personally, would probably not be able to express myself, verbally or in writing. Sometimes I am upset. Sometimes I am so fucken livid I could shit solid bricks of rage, and that is a fuck of a lot different than being upset.

> Of course, **violence** is more than **a lyric where rap is concerned. The music has been repeatedly stained with the blood of performers and hangers-on, of which the murders of Tupac Shakur and Christopher "Notorious B.I.G." Wallace are but the most infamous examples.**

Now, now.

Here we have it. We CANNOT have an article about rappers without mentioning Tupac and Biggie. This just is not done in the white mainstream media of Amerikkka. Even when these senseless murders have *absolutely nothing to do with the price of fucking tea in China,* the media tosses them into the mix. Always.

Over and over, always. Trottin' out Tupac and Biggie like the imaginations of children depended on it.

> Given all that, should **you and I** be **troubled** that police are spying on **these guys?**

I dunno.

That's an awfully long list of unexamined stereotypes for me to contend with. So far, I've pieced together a narrative that the police might be lying about spying on worthless thugs who entertain these rivalries and kill each other and drive around in limos with half-naked women in Jacuzzis. I am pretty convinced that people of this order are not worthy of my consideration, and maybe Chief Timoney should just be given the ol' winky-winky-wink on this one, but because newspaper and magazine writers are enabled by large mainstream media corporations (or vice versa, I'm not sure which), I am going to follow through on this, and find out what the argument is.

I know there is an argument because the article hasn't ended yet.

Yeah, I think **we** should.

Are you feelin' the benevolence? Are you basking in the warm glow of it? I know I am.

The problem is that police aren't surveilling people whom they suspect of committing **crimes** or even people whom they suspect will commit **crimes.** Rather, they are surveilling an **entire class.** And how **convenient that the vast majority of people in that class are young, male and black.**

In other words, **people whom the mainstream already finds frightening.**

Now this is one of the mainstream media's favorite maneuvers. I call it "dazzle hypocrisy." The writer first creates a reality, and then critiques the very reality he just created. The fear of "young black men" was described and validated from word one and now he is pointing out that it is "convenient" that this is the demographic being spied on *because* "people" are already somehow *organically frightened* of them.

It seems that I am being informed that police are carrying the fear of young black men just a wee bit too far, but the fear itself is perfectly reasonable.

Beyond the **issue** of **racial profiling** of **young black men,** though, is the question of **civil rights** for **all of us** in these **tenuous days post-Sept. 11.** Days in which **Muslim men are rounded up** for no reason other than that they are **Muslim men.** Days in which **the government** refuses to account for the people it detains or even to provide them access to **attorneys.** Days in which the **attorney general** can order the local library to give him a list of the books **you've** been reading.

In other words, days that echo certain other days, **dark days** of **Japanese internment, dirty tricks against Martin Luther King Jr., spying on anti-war protesters, investigating John Lennon.** Taken in context, the surveillance of **rap** stars seems of a piece with the **civil rights erosions we have seen in recent years.** Of a piece with the **bad old days**.

Autobiography of a Blue-Eyed Devil

Here is a nice duck 'n' dodge lip service circumvention of "the issue of racial profiling." This is the first, last, and only time this "issue" is mentioned, though it is, in essence, the crux of the whole matter. By mentioning racial profiling, and then immediately going "beyond" racial profiling, there is no examination of racial profiling at all.

I will be able to look back on the "bad old days" when sixth graders critically analyze newspapers and history textbooks from the past century to learn about how racism, fear, coercion, and ignorance operate on a mass-population scale.

So yeah.

I mean I know it's no longer okay for whites to showcase their weekend festivities in the park with the lynching of a young black man, but still, I am effervescently curious about when the good new days might have started.

> And maybe **this is fine** with **you** because **you're** not a **rapper.** Or because **you're not Japanese or Muslim, not Martin Luther King Jr. or John Lennon.** Maybe **you** just want to **feel safe** and never mind **the cost.**

If I apply logic to the above passage, then as long as "you" are not Japanese American, Muslim, a rapper, Dr. King, or John Lennon, and your sense of security is derived from knowing that there are no terrorists anywhere near you, then you should be able to identify with the writer's inherent viewpoint. None of these realities or appellations describe me, yet I find the entire sentiment of this article repulsive.

> It's a **common view, but a shortsighted one.** And
> what a shame if **civil rights** must **erode from beneath
> you, personally, before you understand that.**
> It's **easy** to **ignore** the **cost** when **someone else** is
> paying. But eventually, **this bill** comes around to **us all.**

This entire article, including the title, calls to mind a similar article I read in a Seattle gay community newspaper a few years back.

The article was about police brutality against black people. It was called "Why Gays Should Care" or something very much like that. The white author went to a protest in a black neighborhood and asked a number of activists and organizers, "Why should gays care about police brutality in black neighborhoods?" For their part, the organizers seemed to understand that this man was at least trying to grope his way out of the abyss of white normative cultural myopia, and expressed sentiments along the lines of "When they came for the Catholics, I didn't say anything because I'm not Catholic, etc. . . . "

The author concluded that "gays" should "care" not because a power structure that sanctions the murder or brutalization of *anyone* can, inherently, serve no one but the elite forces that keep said power structure in place, but because the cops might one day come after gay white men too.

Why did the author feel so comfortable assuming that "gays" are white males? Why was he compelled to go to a community of people who were dealing with an enormous amount of grief and bother them with something that he should have been asking all his white gay male friends? Which, by the way, would have made for more interesting reading.

The article reflected the incredibly limited view of this writer, whose perspective seems not to have extended outside his circle of friends. He was unwilling to look beyond his inner sanctum.

Mr. Pitts's inner sanctum is much larger than this Seattle writer's, but both of them came to the exact same conclusion, using the exact same logic. It's all right if children are starving, if entire communities of color are under economic and judicial siege. It's all right if the CIA and U.S. government insinuate guns and crack into ghettos and barrios, and then, through the mainstream media, explain to "the rest of us" that "these people" are just, well, not quite "civilized." It's all right if entire demographics are disenfranchised. But dag-nab-it all, "we" draw the line when these horrors get too close to "our" world.

This is couched as some kind of benevolent, civil-rights-lovin' courage, and is a frequently occurring symptom of widespread cultural myopia.

Civil and human rights are not available to all citizens at all times, and not all people in this population are accorded a place to present their voices. This is true now, and has been true throughout the history of the United States. So it seems kinda paltry and inefficient to harp about injustice only because you happen to notice it in proximity to yourself.

Family-fun pastimes for examining the media have much in common with a successful trip to the optometrist's shop. Afterward, you see the world more clearly.

Personally engaging with the media in these and other family-fun ways is a very powerful thing to do. Careful examination of the information that is *most readily available* to the widest percentage of the population provides a corrective to cultural myopia and helps one develop a more complex worldview.

To find out, for instance, what is happening with the present criminal case against Warren Anderson, you must hunker down with in-depth, global, often subversive news sources.

Some news sources, however, might not necessarily be considered news sources at all. On the Internet, news bloggers and well as online communities, such as Black Planet, Indianz, Craig's List, Street Gangs, and ButchDykeBoy, provide forums for people to discuss current events at great lengths. There is little or no censorship, and with the added luster of anonymity, people are freer to air their deepest fears, ignorances, epiphanies, theories, and beliefs like I have witnessed in no other medium.

I frequently peruse the Best of Craig's List for this specific reason. While this online resource community is largely perceived to be disgruntled white office workers, the Best of Craig's List defies easy designations.

Autobiography of a Blue-Eyed Devil

On a recent jaunt through the Best of Craigs, I found a Casual Encounters posting that jibed so incredibly well with this chapter, I emailed the anonymous writer and asked for both permission to reprint (having learned my lesson from the speech man) and verification that she did, in fact, work for the mainstream media. She was nice enough to accommodate me on both counts, and so I present to you her posting, "Hate the Media? Fuck Me," in all its glory:

Hate the media? Fuck me! - w4m
Date: Mon Mar 21 21:26:55 2005

Hi. I'm a journalist. Or a reporter. Whatever word pisses you off more, I'm part of the mainstream media, the liberal media, the so-called liberal media. I am the epitome of all that is wrong with contemporary journalism.

That is why I need you to fuck me until I feel as disgraced sexually as I do professionally.

Look, I started my career with a great deal of optimism. I thought I was going to expose some hard truths. I thought I was going to tell stories that mattered to people. I thought I was going to write clever, piquant critiques of popular culture and politics that turned conventional wisdom on its head and opened new avenues of understanding and appreciating the world we live in.

Maybe I did some of that in the years I've been slaving in the salt mines. But mostly, I've capitulated to The Man.

Now, I want to capitulate to an actual man.

There's some sort of odiousness in my professional life that will irritate you no matter what your political stripe.

If you are Republican, I am indeed a liberal. There, I said it. I've left Republican voter quotes out of election stories because they were too infuriating; unless, that is, the quotes made the subject ridiculous and then I played them up. I've ignored your fucking women's clubs and your business "luncheons" (for fuck's sake, "lunch" will suffice!) and I would never deign to profile your pathetic loser hateful whitebread "Pioneers." I have a pitiful, wretched bias against asshole honkies like yourselves that manifests itself in small, ultimately meaningless ways since you never seem to realize the joke is on you.

You are arrogant, deluded and selfish assholes, and if you'd act like a supercilious pig who hates poor people—oh, excuse me, government handouts—and non-WASPs while jamming me with your arrogant cock that'd be great.

If you are a Democrat or progressive, there are reasons aplenty for you to hate me as well. I consistently toe the publisher's line; anytime there's an issue that a certain, moneyed sector of the community helps

the publisher adopt as a cause of the publisher's own,
I make sure all the coverage of said issue is superficial. Hey, I used to fight this, but after I nearly lost my
lousy-paying shitty-benefits job because I told the truth
about a community group with powerful vested interests, I decided the community would lose whether or
not I caved. I don't file FOIA letters, either.

You are right about people like me, and if you
could lord it over me while fucking my brains out,
that might just do the trick.

If you don't hew to any political interests there's
plenty to revile about my professional life which,
sad to say, is the only life I seem to have. I capitalize
Web site and Internet. I never use the passive voice.
This is the longest thing I've written for publication
in ages. I don't use a comma after the terminal "and"
in a series. I rely on the press releases of boring and
often insane community groups to develop stories
around that you don't give a shit about, and I can't
blame you for that!

I'm better-looking than your average reporter—
God knows it's goblins and gnomes all over the news-
rooms of the world—so that isn't saying much. Mostly,
I expect my half-ass way of getting my shit pulled
together to fuel your aggressive, angry libido.

I am everything that is wrong with the media,
incarnated in human form. If you've ever said "Fuck
the media," this is your chance.[8]

⅍

So you see, dear reader, possibly more often than not, even the people who deliver the news are often incredibly unhappy with this situation. Many reporters and journalists would like to seize the opportunity to serve their community, but, under the present model of power, they are unable to do so.

Lordisa bless them.

Pretty much any time you reach into your imagination and somehow or another creatively apply it to the environment we live in, you will experience a deep sense of fulfillment because it always feels real nice to reclaim your heart and mind from bullshit lies. It makes you free.

And here I must give thanks to Robin D. G. Kelley. His book *Freedom Dreams: The Black Radical Imagination* provides a much deeper foray into the power of uncolonized imagination, and demonstrates how change occurs first, foremost, and forever in people's hearts and minds. Before I read his book, I was entertaining the suspicion that imagination is the most empowering force of resistance to oppression, but feared I couldn't communicate this without sounding like some new age life coach or something. So *Freedom Dreams* moshed into my life right around then, and I swear I felt like god was just totally having my back. Investigating all of Dr. Kelley's work is absolutely requisite for anyone who wishes to live a conscious life in the United States of Amerikkka.

✣

If you want to see the power of imagination in full live action, check out the documentary *The Revolution Will Not Be Televised*.

The people of Venezuela figured out that it does not serve them to have some U.S. corporate government Spaniard Muppet ruling their country. It took a period of trial and error, but they figured it out. Not only did they vote Chávez, a man of black and indigenous *(negro y indio)* descent, into the presidency, the people also pitched in to rewrite their constitution, which now includes things like allotting monthly incomes and pension funds to stay-at-home parents. They demanded oil profits be spent on them. And they have organized crucibles of imagination, called Bolivarian Circles, throughout the country. Here's Narco News publisher Al Giordano's description of the Bolivarian Circles:

> To hear the oligarchs and the Commercial Media
> screech about the Bolivarian Circles, you would think
> they are armed paramilitary organizations of vam-
> pires coming to drink their precious children's blood.
> I went and spent time with these Circles. Do you
> know what they're really doing? The old guy in every
> neighborhood who loves the architecture, the history,
> you know him, these guys even exist in San Francisco
> and New York, the one who goes and spends hours at
> the library researching the construction of the local
> church? Well, this guy is now in the Bolivarian Circle.
> And for the first time he has an eager audience of

children and adults and elders all excited to study and learn the history of their barrio. And the lady who understands herbs and natural medicine is holding very popular workshops and training sessions to help everyone understand it. She's the Bolivarian Circle, too. So is the neighborhood baseball team, and kids who do rap or theater. They're the Bolivarian Circles, too. That's what they are "armed" with: library books, herbal remedies, boomboxes and baseball gloves.

And, you know, the upper classes have a point in their fear of this, which is why the Commercial Media preys on this fear: the family using herbal remedies is no longer spending a week's pay on expensive pharmaceuticals. It's healthy without them. There's a self-led reorganization of the economy from the bottom up. Everything is changing.

So the Commercial Media yelps "Beware! Vampire Bolivarian Circles are coming to kill you!" This is why the most popular chant in Caracas today is "Chávez Makes Them Crazy!" Because the people watch these former ruling class members railing all their fears on TV, and they really do have psychological problems with the loss of their illusory power over others.[9]

After watching *The Revolution Will Not Be Televised* for the first of five times, I overheard a man saying, "Well, it will never work. They are always trying to create new governments, and they always fail."

I almost punched him.

Other than back when the "founders" were trampling indians' rights to the sacred lands of their ancestors and securing their own, when have we here in the U.S. ever gathered up the wherewithal to even *consider implementing* a new form of government? When have we had the joy and pride of carrying our constitution that we wrote and voted for from our hearts and minds around in our pockets, as many Venezuelans presently do? I was so fucken jealous watching people *brandish their constitution*[†] in that documentary. When have we ever had the dream of hope and the reality of knowing that our nation's leader truly cares about our entire population?

So now the U.S. government views Venezuela as one of the biggest threats in the world, and U.S. media enablers invalidate this mass political movement by employing "self-styled" word choices. The "opposition," which is always sympathetically portrayed in U.S. newspapers, is filled with some of the most bejeweled, nanny-raised, and chauffeur-driven protesters you will ever lay eyes on.

It is in the interests of the U.S. government to prevent its citizens from seeing what is really going on in Venezuela. After all, we might start using our imaginations to foment our own newly ratified constitutions and home-brewed revolutions.

Here in this country, the people have intimate and boundless knowledge about celebrities, sports stars, music artists, and super-

---

[†] The Venezuelan constitution is bound into a little blue leather book.

models. This is completely rational and makes perfect sense. Meanwhile, our socioeconomic infrastructure is being gutted.

Venezuelan people are not, evidently, seduced by such things and they have the constitution to show for it. So I figure the population squanders its collective imagination on some direct, live-action stuff instead of on vicariously experiencing the lifestyles of the rich and famous.

Freedom and free speech may very well be marketing brands more than they have ever been *actual* lived realities of all Americans. Regardless, these brands influence our imaginations, and so we dream up rose parades, beer bongs, the concept that blue ink on index fingers equals democracy in Iraq, end of discussion, or that a yellow plastic band on our wrists equals supra-human perseverance.

We dream this shit up all the time. I get jittery inside, imagining the possibilities of our collective imagination, were it unfettered by the guiding light of the mainstream media.

Dead Prez says it better than me, but anyway, let's get free.

Full Spectrum Dominance

𝔚hen my Grammy could still walk around just fine, before the arthritis set in too bad, we often strolled around her garden, which wasn't a garden like in the *Better Homes and* sense of the word. She loved all the plants—the ones she stuck in the ground and the ones that grew there on their own recognizance. They were all the same glorious episodes of life to my Grammy. She planted roses, irises, dahlias. They grew happily alongside red clover, yerba buena, dandelions.

Sometimes we'd walk up into the foresty area behind her house and pick wildflowers. Grammy knew the names of pretty much every plant in her world.

Sometimes though, she'd say, "Coo, what are you?"

She would then describe the plant to every person she ran into until she found someone who knew what it was. Also her method for finding out the names of birds, insects, and other fauna, this process could take moments or weeks. She didn't much overconcern herself with actual *people,* but in regard to *the world around her,* Grammy was a nosy parker who had to know all the neighbors' business.

When I was about fourteen, we were walking in the foresty area and I bent down to pick a white flower.

"Hup!" Grammy hollered. "What the HELL do you think you're doing?"

I almost jumped out of my skin. I straightened up and looked into her eyes. They were clouded with dark anger. I shakily told her what I knew she already knew. "I was, uh, gonna pick that flower."

Grammy was sweet as sipping hot apple cider in front of a raging fire with everyone you love. She was also bellicose-prison-matron-esque, and you goddamn well unquestioningly (or questioningly, at great peril) did what she said.

She bellowed, "I never, and I mean NEVER, want to see you picking a flower that you don't know. If you don't know it, then it's none of your business, so leave it the *hellalone.*"

Grammy's verbal caginess entrapped her grandchildren into asking questions that exposed our unthinkingness for all and sundry to hear. By fourteen, I'd learned to consider my position before responding.

She stood, hands on hips, glaring at me, waiting.

A response was most definitely in order.

If I asked, "Why?" I would be indirectly admitting that I had no regard for this plant as a living entity. This unstated admission, I knew from previous experience, would get me into a whole other world of trouble than the one I was already in. But I *did* want to know why. I wanted to know why this was such an important decree, stated with maximum authority.

So I asked her the name of the flower.

"It's a trillium," she snapped and launched into a narrative about how trilliums are among the most amazing flowers in the world and if you pick one, it will not only almost immediately die, but it won't grow back for seven years, and she wonders if there is any connection between picking trilliums and breaking mirrors, she will have to find out.

"BUT. Remember," she wagged her finger in my face, though now there was a smile in her voice and her eyes had gone back to sparkling, "never mess with a plant unless you *know* it."

To this day, I do not pick unknown flowers, and if someone gives me one I'm unfamiliar with, I find out what—or rather, who—it is.

In general, giving me flowers is a touch-and-go kinda thing. While I always appreciate the thought, plantation-slave-produced flowers bring only sadness into my home. They are scentless über-models shaped into existence by servants of a heartless industry.

Most florists deal in these.

The best flowers come from someone's garden, the second best from the local farmer's market, and the third best from a flower stand that buys flowers locally.

Grammy's Flower Decree has some pretty far-reaching implications when taken outside the realm of horticulture and magnified into an elemental tenet of existence:

DO NOT FUCK WITH SHIT THAT YOU DO NOT KNOW.

Severe abrogations of this decree are abundant in our culture.

The land that is called Four Corners in "Arizona," "New Mexico," "Colorado," and "Utah" has been of keen interest to various uranium and coal mining corporations for five or six decades.

This land has been sacred to all Hopi, Dineh, and Navajo people for thousands of years.

Many places in this area have been contaminated by toxic uranium run-off from mining operations that went down in the 1950s and continue to this day.

During the past fifty years, many specific rocks, mountains, rivers, and caverns that held the voices of ancestors were bulldozed.

Strip-mined.

Laid bare.

A gang rape comes to mind.

When uranium is excavated from this holy land, it is manipulated in factories and made into bombs to kill people in Iraq and
Afghanistan. Depleted uranium (DU)—which lingers in the air
long after a bomb's explosion infiltrates the nethersphere—causes
cancer and other debilitating sicknesses in everyone who is
exposed to it. DU does not have patriotic allegiances, so U.S.
soldiers are stricken by exposure as well. It is not difficult to
be exposed. All you have to do is breathe. When DU-exposed
soldiers come home and have children, there are severe birth
defects to deal with.

The Hopi, Dineh, and Navajo people know the indiscrimi-
nate manner in which uranium poisoning makes itself known
in a community, and I often wonder why the reproductive
crimes committed against populations living deep in the shadows of corporate impunity are not part of the discourse of either
mainstream feminists or evangelical pro-lifers.

Traditional indian people do not want this holy ground
desecrated in the name of death to innocents, and they are consequently under siege by any corporation that can afford to hire
a private army—largely by co-opting the local police—and with
(predictably) the full backing of the U.S. government's Bureau of
Indian Affairs, Environmental "Protection" Agency, and Department of "Defense."

One of the only sources of employment in this region—and

one of the only ways for folks in the area to pay their bills and put food on their table—is to work for the mining corporations. This is a morally repugnant proposition, and a percentage of a person's humanity must be sacrificed in order to work in the mine.

Between the choices of dealing with moral repugnancy and watching your grandmother and three children starve to death, however, most folks will go with the repugnancy.

In this situation, as in many latter-day contexts, morality is a luxury.

For those who do not believe that the U.S. has problems similar to those our government has created in so-called developing nations, a conscious and well-informed visit to a place such as Black Mesa, "Arizona," would be rather disillusioning. Just like Palestinian people, the Dineh who live in Black Mesa have been forced from their homes, brutalized, endlessly harassed, and illegally detained—and they too benefit from having outside witnesses living in their community.

The Peabody Coal Company has recently been excavating a sacred place called Big Mountain. The Dineh know that if Big Mountain is killed, a heart chakra of the earth will be killed. Long before satellite photos showed that from outer space Big Mountain looks exactly like a human heart pumping blood, the Dineh were well aware of what it was. They do not need satellite photos to tell them what they have always known. But many other folks aren't as blessed with an upbringing centered around cherishing and respecting the earth.

Evidence is required.

So look it up on the web and see one of the hearts of the

world that a small group of people is fighting for, in the name
of the planet and all the people who live on it, and ask yourself, .
"Why should these folks shoulder the massive responsibility
of defending a heart of the earth? How come me and all my
friends and family are not fighting for life and the planet too?"

Most mountains in the world are sacred to the indigenous
people who live near them and have managed to survive the
slaughter that marks most indigenous people's reality in the
white man's world. Indigenous people do not view mountains as
"challenges" to "conquer," or as a means to prove their mettle to
themselves and their peers.

This may be why one rarely hears of Sherpa guides dying
when they climb Chomolungma—recognized as "Mount Everest" by whites. Chomolungma is a part of the Sherpa people's
backyard. They know it. They respect it. It is alive and they
are on personal terms with Miyo Lungsungama, the goddess of
humans and prosperity who's lived there since THE BEGINNING.

Ad executives from Manhattan who decide it will be a good
bonding experience to climb "Mount Everest" do not know Chomolungma or Miyo Lungsungama.

Neither do movie producers from Beverly Hills.

Even seasoned mountain climbers do not *know* "Mount Everest," or any other mountain other than ones they've lived alongside and respected as sentient beings for many, many years. They
may know the terrain, the weather, the dangers, and the necessary equipment, but they do not know the mountain.

Sherpa folks probably seriously laugh their asses off at the corporate types who think it's some big lifetime accomplishment to climb this mountain that the Sherpas have been on intimate terms with since they were born.

But then again, they probably give thanks to the goddess of prosperity for bringing these people to them, because they pay exorbitant sums for guides. Sherpa people unfortunately need money to survive since the global economics these very corporate types represent are responsible for threatening, damaging, and/or destroying the way of life Sherpa folks have maintained since THE BEGINNING.

People in the United States are famous for demonstrating a lack of respect and humility when dealing with things we do not know, much less understand. Due to the fact that whites make the laws and design the economy, many people in the world— indigenous or not—are coerced into taking part in the profound disrespect of the earth they have otherwise known, cared for, and loved for millennia.

The tourism industry is another place where desecration of Grammy's Flower Decree abounds. The tourism industry caters to fully entitled people from wealthy countries who believe they have the right to venture into any poor, "exotic" nation on the planet and view it as a source of entertainment— a backdrop for their lives.

Many people in poor nations are coerced into pandering to tourists. It is widely believed that tourism boosts a nation's economy, and I suppose it does, if you think that working as a maid or busboy in a U.S.-owned corporate hotel or restaurant is something other than an elaborate form of slavery. Locally owned businesses receive but the merest trickle of the wealth that tourists bring into their countries. The vast majority of tourist money goes right back into the pockets of businesses such as the Hilton, the Hard Rock Cafe, and Hertz car rental agencies. ◆

In Cancún, Mexico, for instance, local people are not allowed to show their faces anywhere near resorts unless they are delivering supplies, employed as servants, or carting tourists to and fro. The tourists probably don't wonder where "they" go when their shift is over, because, like masters throughout history, they do not wonder about the humanity and lived experiences of slaves. And the people do, indeed, report for work, acting out the white-approved role of "festive little Mexicans," because, like I mentioned before, morality is a luxury that people who would otherwise face starvation—or murder, if they were to attempt unionization—cannot afford.

I experienced tourism firsthand when I worked at the Pike Place Market in Seattle, delivering milk and other dairy products to local businesses. This involved hand-trucking cases of milk in plastic jugs and glass bottles through crowds of people to load my delivery van. This action, I soon learned, was deemed "picturesque" by many tourists. A common, ill-fated response was to attempt to film me or take my photo, often with small children being directed to stand near me.

Four cases of milk in glass bottles are heavy and difficult to negotiate through a crowd of people, so I had absolutely no patience for parents who put their children in harm's way by deeming me a potential background for their family photo album. I was infuriated so many times by this. People would tell their six-year-old child to "go stand by that milk girl," without ever considering the possibility that their kid might get in my way and send a cascade of glass, metal, and milk raining down on their child's head. Since—unlike many people in this world who negotiate the ignorance of tourists—I enjoy the luxury of speaking my mind, I would often scream, "Get your kid out of my way, you stupid fuck." People would register a kind of annoyed surprise that not only could I speak, but I had actual thoughts and emotions flurrying around in my head and heart.

I think about this form of total disregard when I see ads about wonderfully "exotic destinations" such as Thailand, Jamaica, and Costa Rica, and I shudder at the thought of how the people in these places are viewed and treated.

I wonder how many tourists pick "exotic" flowers, and I wonder how many women like my Grammy keep their mouths shut about it because in poor countries, everyone knows tourists are allowed to abrogate any decree they so desire.

❧

The term "full spectrum dominance" encapsulates very well
the reality of living as an Amerikkkan at this point in history,
though formally it's just a military strategy engineered by a
team of Arbustos.

Pondering this term not only led me to a chapter title, but
to some other epiphanies. Chief among them was the realization
that the brutal repressions, coups, enslavements, genocides, and
mass rapes resulting from over 250 military occupations orches-
trated by the U.S. government in the past couple of centuries
might be recontextualized as "half-ass dominance."

Full spectrum dominance was coined in "Joint Vision
2020," a government document outlining the vision that the U.S.
Department of Defense will follow in the future. It details "the
ability of U.S. forces, operating alone or with allies, to defeat
any adversary and control any situation across the range of military operations."[1]

In my perception, full spectrum dominance is not just a
sociopathic military doctrine that any serial killer or rapist would
envy, but a name placed upon a fully vested and long-existing ideology. I see full spectrum dominance enacted in every facet of our
existence. Our enemy is not just people in "other" countries, but
the earth itself, as well as anything or anyone we do not know. It
doesn't matter if the "adversary" is the new kid at school, the trees
on your block that are uprooting the street pavement, the entire
prison population, or the rival team's fans—it is perfectly acceptable to view any "adversary" with total vitriol in our hearts.

Autobiography of a Blue-Eyed Devil

Peri Heydari Pakroo called from "New Mexico" the other day, and I've been thinking about our conversation ever since. We were talking about the sadness in the world and the sadness in our environments and the sadness in our lives.

Huge sadnesses, all around.

Peri said, "I remember when I was a kid and went swimming in Lake Michigan all the time. Now the water is too polluted to swim in. I wonder where kids in Milwaukee swim these days."

This was a boding resonation of my own thoughts just a day prior, when I'd been thinking about the deep sadness in my heart.

I'm not sad about any one thing in particular.

Just sad.

And I count the fuckall out of my blessings, too. In my life, there is health, love, deeply meaningful work, nonincarceration, a roof over my head, food, running water, family, friends, and skilled pool players.

All told—and especially in light of the fact that I'm not focused on the ins and outs of famine, mass rape, or people bull-dozing my home, bombing my family, or pulling me over and legally beating me half to death with heavy metal flashlights—not much to complain about.

I see this general sadness in the eyes of everyone I interact with, though.

It is a sadness I have never before seen en masse.

When I was a kid, I saw it in my mother's eyes when she came home from a bad night at the hospital. I have seen it in my family's eyes after Nick died. I have seen it in the eyes of rhesus monkeys in an AP newswire photo, when they were recaptured after escaping from a laboratory where they lived their lives in cages, completely at the mercy of human beings. I have seen it in the eyes of people when war is upon their land, and in the eyes of people in ghettos and barrios and on reservations.

But I have never before seen it in the eyes of just the general population—newscasters and pop star fans and people in the post office.

There is a certain anxiousness around the edges of this huge, general sadness—like that of someone protecting a glass ballerina in the middle of a street hockey game.

In many ways, I do think this is a good thing—that masses of people have sadness in their eyes like lab animals and war orphans. I do not know how humanity, as a whole, can progress in any way until everyone learns to acknowledge and live with the sadness of the present and past.

Most people in my country, however, do not choose to acknowledge the perfectly natural rationale for such huge sadness. Indeed, many people think there is something "wrong" with them, so they go to a doctor who tells them they have a "chemical imbalance" and gives them some antidepressant drug that numbs the pain of living in this environment that is killing the world, thus further removing them from facing the repercussions the human race has created.

Still and all, sad is sad, and strange as it may sound, I do see a great hope in this mass sadness, even if many people in my country and the world are content blaming everything on that entitled fool, Arbusto.

Autobiography of a Blue-Eyed Devil

✄

The Full Spectrum Dominance Amerikkkan Way of Life—the one where corporations provide jobs (as opposed to deeply meaningful work) and suck resources out of the earth like she is a vacant junkie whore in the middle of a Bad Situation—is roughly a century old. I think of this in the context of history—of temples in Peru, Egypt, and Greece. A hundred years is, give or take, a coupla measly human[†] lifetimes. And in just a coupla lifetimes, the Amerikkkan Way of Life has become poised to destroy the entire planet.

Certainly, this lifestyle has evolved from many hundreds of years of imperialism, racism, genocide, destruction, colonization, and enslavement, but if you look at this larger history as a big zit, the U.S. is the whitish green head on the tippy-top.

It is about to pop.

It was really nice talking to Peri because, unlike many people I know and care about, she doesn't choose to pretend that her sadness is just some temporary problem that can be isolated and fixed. She is not afraid to see how she is connected to history. I have noticed this general attitude with many people whose immigrant parents fled oppressive regimes or whose families have experienced mass traumas, such as war, slavery, or genocide. Like many people I know—or don't know, but still

---

† For a great redwood, a century is still prepubescent.

no less care about—Peri is not afraid to see how she is connected to the earth.

And the earth is fucken sad, so it's natural that everything that lives on it is sad as well.

I think about when I am sad, and how every eyelash I have, every meal I eat, every conversation I engage in is informed by my sadness. When my brother died, I was so sad, food felt like sadness in my mouth, so I stopped eating for a while.

At the time, it made sense.

So I imagine the earth's sadness affects every living aspect of it in a very similar manner. Maybe I am projecting, but maybe that doesn't matter because my thoughts are influenced by the fact that I am wholly composed of this earth. Every breath I have ever taken and every mouthful of nutrition and love that sustains my body and life comes from the earth.

I am nothing else.

And dang, it seems like it would hurt like fuckall to be drilled for oil.

It hurts when someone takes a blood sample and, however gently, plunges a hypodermic needle into my arm. So how would I feel if there were regions of my body that were filled with microscopic hypodermic needles, slowly pumping the blood out of me, 24-7.

It would be depressing to experience chronic, inflicted pain like that.

Imagine how coal, uranium, and diamond mining might feel.

And the military testing out its newest weapons deep inside you.

✗

This is why I am sad, and this is why Peri is sad, and this is why everyone is sad. Poverty and brutal military occupations, domestic violence and rape, white supremacist racism and ecocide—all of these things are tortures and diseases humans create and perpetuate, and they are, at the same time, repercussions of the earth's sadness.

It is a cycle of abuse that is mirrored many times over in our relationships with one another and the world around us. The competitive male model of domination and control consumes every aspect of life, whether one is aware of it or not.

When left to our own devices, women† tend to operate under a cooperative model of negotiation. In the U.S., this model is largely found in grandmother-centered, queer, and/ or feminist communities. Matrifocal societies exist, but there is no worldwide model of cooperation counterbalancing the competitive full spectrum domination model. Traditional indigenous people live on the earth by a much more cooperative model, and many of these people continue to exist under physical or economic siege in the name of "progress" and "development."

---

† "Women," in this context, does not refer to women who are completely seduced by the male power structure. "Women" means transgender and biological women who struggle to feed, sustain, and love ourselves and/or others in a heartlessly corrupt environment created and sustained by males. Big distinction.

The opposite of war is probably love,[†] but I cannot think of one worldwide love-based experience that balances out the reality of war. The closest I can come up with is Amma, the woman and goddess incarnation from India who blesses thousands of people with sacred love, in marathon darshans that can last up to thirty-six hours. While there is a middling to pretty good chance that you have never heard of Amma and have no idea how profoundly life-altering it is to be in her arms and feel her Plain Old Love, there is no chance whatsoever that you haven't heard of war.

This is what I mean when I say "male" and "female."

I understand that gender is fluid and the perception of gender is largely based on cultural constructs. One of these constructs, however, is particularly pernicious and happens to rule the world. There is nothing counterbalancing this construct, and it was designed by, for, and about (white and/or ruling) males.

So, maybe I do not mean "women" at all, but I cannot think of any other word or phrase to adequately juxtapose with the unquestionable reality of full spectrum male domination, except maybe Grammy's Flower Decree, which is also, in my imagination, related to the way women see the world. And you know, I think it needs to be stated that my Grammy was an openly sexual and angry woman. She was not averse to patting a man on the ass or telling someone she did not like to get the goddamn helloutta her house. So when I say "women," I am not

---

† Without love, there can never be peace. This truth can be viewed in any family.

thinking of soft and perfect hostesses at the cocktail party, if you know what I mean.

That has never been my experience of women.

Women are people like my mom, who come home from work late at night with blood on their uniforms, and stare into the cup of tea you made for them, wondering if there was some better way to tell two people that three of their five children had died in a car wreck.

Women are people like my aunt Genie, who show you how to get a hook out of a fish's mouth without hurting it too bad in its last moments of life.

Women are people like my Grammy, who tell you that if you want blackberry cobbler after dinner tonight, you better hustle your ass outside and into the blackberry patch with a bucket.

It is crucial to note and consider this overall imbalance because the total absence of women's ways of thinking and problem solving—versus the pathological, highly detailed focus on men's ways—is one of the main reasons why, for milli-instance, it's considered fine and dandy to keep animals trapped in shampoo laboratories for generation after generation. This isn't to say that women wouldn't do this, but *we have no way of knowing one way or the other* because all basis for scientific thought and research comes from an almost ancient history of men figuring things out, then defining and writing about them. Women scientists can "fit in," but they cannot, and have never, defined the overall structure.

This holds true for any branch of what Dr. Frances Cress Welsing refers to as "people activity (economics, education, entertainment, labor, law, politics, religion, sex and war)."[2]

A trial, for instance, is all about which lawyer is best. It is a competition between the prosecution and defense. The clients of winning lawyers get whatever they're after, be it freedom, money, or monopoly rights. Like stud racehorses, the best law competitors command the highest fees. Wealthy people are winning clients and poor people are losing clients. Wealthy people are often white, and poor people are often of color or indian. This is why many black people in the U.S. celebrated when O.J. Simpson walked—even people who felt that he was morally repugnant.

For a lot of folks, it was just, I dunno, *refreshing* to see a black man be a winning client for once. This is also unfortunate because it pitted white women and survivors of domestic violence against the general black population, when in reality, all these demographics are far better served sticking close together, though unity of this kind rarely, if ever, occurs.

Affirmative action, for instance, benefits white women more than any other group, but it has been "branded" a "black" concern by the media. This is why black people marched on the Supreme Court when they were talking about rescinding affirmative action in "Michigan," and white women were nowhere to be found.

꙰

Autobiography of a Blue-Eyed Devil

I got some shit after publishing my last book, for something called "male-bashing." I have little patience for this term. I have lived my entire life with the knowledge of rape dictating many aspects of my existence. I do not walk into any room without assessing the exits, and positioning myself strategically. I never sit with my back to the door or to unfamiliar people in an unfamiliar setting. I do not even think about these actions. I have been stunned many times by police officers, soldiers, and gang members who have told me that some of my specific self-taught survival tactics are included in their formal training. As a veteran woman living in a rape warfare culture, I execute these maneuvers—and many, many more—on autopilot.

If you ever invite me into your home, I will note all potential dangers and visible exits. I'll imagine what can be used as a weapon. I will check out the door lock(s) and, if possible, the window latches. You won't notice me doing any of this because not only will I myself not notice me doing this, I'll be done by the time you close the front door.

Some people consider my choices for survival a form of paranoia. To these folks, I say: You have every reason to invest so deeply in denial. It will probably break your heart to see how intimately male domination has colored your own choices for survival.

My heart has been broken many, many times.

Indeed, I am heartbroken as I write this.

It is heartbreaking to live in an environment that is killing and raping the earth, while surrounded by a population of human beings who, along with myself, survive and abide life in a white supremacist, racist rape warfare culture.

It is heartbreaking to experience and witness the pain and suffering that ensue.

Here is what I was thinking about the day before Peri wondered where kids in Milwaukee swim these days:

Every summer of my entire life, I've had an ocean or river to swim in. The last time I went swimming in my good friend the Pacific Ocean was about four years ago. I dove under a wave and swam around for a while, but the ocean had a message. And the ocean said unto me:

How dare you swim in me and have a good time in
me when I am being killed. Get the fuck out and find
a way to help me before you ever jump into my waters
again. You have the same mouth that my murderers
have. You have the ability to communicate to those
who will not hear me. Use it or lose it, Jack.

I got out of the water, thinking how I have always hated it when the ocean calls me "Jack," and I sat down close to the waves. I watched them crash. Millions and billions of sand flies rose up and swarmed me as my ass, feet, and hands sank into the watery shore. I couldn't remember ever being swarmed by sand flies before, and I realized they were so populous because somewhere along the food chain, the sand flies or their larvae were impacted by the total absence of sand crabs. When I was a kid, I used to scoop up handfuls of wet sand and watch the sand crabs climb out, drop back onto the beach, and burrow into the sand again. It was kind of a gross-out pastime, 'cause the ugly little gray crabs gave me the creeps. But you know, I never questioned their place in the overall scheme of things.

I asked the ocean where the sand crabs went, but all the ocean would say was:

Murder, murder, murder, Jack.

I haven't swum in the ocean since that day, because it is still being murdered, and I know it will call me "Jack" if I go back without some kind of progress report. What the ocean does not perhaps understand is how difficult it is to speak out in its defense without people being dismissive and saying stuff like, "You're such a tree-hugger, Inga." Or maybe, "I thought you were a queer/feminist/anti-white-supremacist-racism-and-imperialism activist. I didn't realize you were an environmentalist too."

In reality, I consider myself none of these things.

I have always been a tad slow on the uptake, which is sometimes embarrassing. But in this context, it means I just have the devil of a time entertaining baseless distinctions.

Last summer, I went swimming in the river not far from my home. Rivers—at least those that aren't formidable like the Mississippi, Nile, or Amazon—aren't generally as matriarchal and draconian as the ocean, but the message was basically the same:

Don't you think it's kind of, umm, rude to have fun splashing around in me, while I am being murdered right in front of you?

So this summer, for the first time in my life, I have not gone swimming.

My grief over this is really quite substantial.

Maybe this makes me an "environmentalist," but probably I am just a selfish fuck who wants to go swimming again.

Wanna walk through the forest without hearing the echoes of everyone in it crying out in sadness, terror, and pain.

Due, in part, to my great sadness about not having a spot in which to go swimming, I went on a road trip by myself last summer. One afternoon, as I was driving along Highway 1, I saw a bunch of cars stopped on the side of the road. A flurry of people were crossing the street, to and from their cars, cameras at the ready. The touring paparazzi had evidently located a "point of interest." I slowed to a crawl and looked out the window to see what the "attraction" was. Standing in a pasture, with a number of horses, were two zebras. They were looking at the people looking at them, with mystification and some other thing I couldn't then name, in their eyes. They watched the people walk up to the barbed wire that kept them out of the pasture. They watched the people take pictures. The zebras looked very bored with the humans.

That's it.

Their eyes were glazed over with profound boredom.

I passed by the people and the zebras and thought about how when the U.S. armed forces captured Geronimo, they "sold" him to the St. Louis Fair. There, Geronimo sat in a cage, and people from miles around came to see the "attraction" of the "savage beast."[3]

I am willing to wager that all of the people gawking at the zebras—and not everyone was whitey—would consider this an unconscionable act. Another one of the famous "dark times" in this country's history.

We would never do something like that again.

I wondered if, in previous incarnations, the people who were staring at the zebras had also purchased tickets to stare at Geronimo.

I felt no need to stare at the zebras.

It was really neat to see them. I felt thankful because I haven't had the opportunity to see many zebras in my life. I also respect that they have a right to live, and nowhere in my definition of "living" is there a part where it's okay for people to gawk at you and take pictures of you and disrupt your day just because you are a "point of interest" from their intensely limited, myopic worldview.

Can you open your heart to the mountain lion who has been attacking hikers? If you were a mountain lion, on a scale from one to ten, how much would you enjoy having contact with the species that is destroying your world?

I mean, ballpark figure here.

How emaciated would you have to get before you attacked someone "enjoying nature" for the day? How many affordable new custom-designed homes would diminish the size of your world to the point where you ventured into areas where people would be found? Mountain lions want *absolutely nothing* to do with people. They're not like Pollyanna dolphins, who make efforts to communicate with us and clue us in on reality.

Mountain lions have no "hope" for humanity.

They straight up think we suck.

Yeah, summer of 2004. An emaciated mountain lion attacked a hiker in "California." One of the hiker's friends stabbed it. The forest officials followed its trail of blood and "destroyed" it, as if it were a condemned building in the new freeway's path.

In Mumbai, they have a similar problem with jaguars, only there it's worse because the jaguars actually prowl around the outskirts of the city, hunting small animals and children. But the forest officials in India have a different approach. They decided to release a bunch of pigs and rabbits in the forest to hopefully repopulate it with meals that the jaguar much prefers. And you know, India is not exactly famous for how wonderfully it treats women and the environment, but the folks who talk shit there talk fucken loudly and articulately, people know how to take to the streets, and there are many goddesses and animals worshipped in the pantheon of Hinduism. The way officials in Mumbai dealt with their jaguar problem, at least from my point of view, reflected a more gender-balanced model of cooperative problem solving. Instead of "Kill them all and let god sort them out," Mumbai officials embraced a "Feed them all and let nature sort things out" approach.

Which reminds me.

You know that saying, "Kill two birds with one stone"? Well, back, back, back in the day, when women had more say, it went, "Feed two birds with one seed."

Natch.

Summer of 2003. Another emaciated mountain lion attacked a person tearing through its world on a mountain bike. It was also "destroyed."

I really ponder the usage of this word in newspaper articles and newscasters' mouths. Wasn't the mountain lion already quite destroyed before it reached the point of desperation, frustration, and rage to attack a human being?

In "California," there have been fewer than twenty attacks by mountain lions in the entire 150-odd years that white people have been encroaching upon their world and destroying them. On average, once every seven and a half years in "California," humans have ventured into a mountain lion's territory and gotten attacked for it. In contrast, humans kill thousands of other humans and millions of animals every single day. By this standard, mountain lions are folks who are willing to put up with a helluva lot of shit before going into attack mode.

Perhaps we could learn a thing or two from them without subjecting them to laboratories and zoological studies.

We do not call them brothers and sisters, who can help us to understand how territory truly operates and how respect for earth and life and Grammy's Flower Decree factors into that. We call them predators, and wild beasts, and other self-projections that are much more aptly ascribed to (white) humans. We mount them in poses of ferocity and call their fur-covered polyurethane corpses "trophies."

We display them as evidence of our total dominion.

Oh, god, we are so gross.

Puke.

One night last winter, a neighbor knocked on the door. She was holding a cat in her arms, and she said, "I think your cat wants inside. He's been crying on the porch all day and night." I found this odd because I hadn't seen him in my comings and goings that day.

However, I responded to the more general reality, and said, "Uh, I don't have a cat."

Be that as it may have been, he stared at me pointedly, jumped out of her arms into my living room, and commenced screaming at me for food.

I bid the neighbor goodnight, and turned my attention to the new situation at hand.

While I had some really nice carrots and tempeh, there was no meat or cheese in my house. I started stressing out with this crazy, demanding cat screaming—really there is no other term to describe the level of volume and insistence he is capable of—at me for food. I tore through my cupboards and remembered I'd bought some tuna for houseguests a while back. I found it behind ten different kinds of canned beans, and fed it to the cat. It gave him diarrhea and he shit all over my bed and in the living room on the very sacred pink velvet blankey that my witchy friend Sybil made for me.

For three weeks, this cat drove me insane. If he wanted something, he would not shut up until he got it.

Boredom and resignation are not a part of his genetic code.

On more than one occasion, while I was deep in thought, writing, he came into the room and screamed at me, and I swear to god my heart just ripped into my throat and I thought I was gonna go into arrest.

I got really freaked out about this cat. He was so neurotic and desperate for love. I wondered what the fuck domestication has done to him and his people. I wondered what happens to you when you are taken away from your mommy when you're little

and so is she,

and so is she,

and so is she,

and so is she.

Ughhhh.

Then people started telling me how I had to get him "fixed," which is another one of those words like "destroyed":

WHAT DOES IT MEAN????

"Fixing" *means* "invasively removing reproductive organs." Choosing to employ some general, decent-sounding term like "fixing" does not change the reality of what is done to the animal.

We have to control the pet population because there are too many strays and unwanted animals in the environment, so it is just assumed to be a kindness to get them spayed and neutered, rather than go to all the trouble of examining our cultural beliefs and attitudes about animals. There are also millions of unwanted children, old people, incarcerated people, and developmentally different folks in this environment. If our population were to view the world from a cooperative perspective, surely our imaginations would alight upon a way to bring all of the "unwanted" animals and people into the thick of things.

This would be a different way of considering the pet population.

If we don't invasively remove their reproductive organs, they'll be "too wild" and "go into heat" or "spray."

Right, so I figure, look, if you have to mangle someone's body in order to be able to hang out with him or her, then maybe y'all shouldn't be friends.

Researchers have *never* spent time finding noninvasive herbal ways to keep animals from getting pregnant. To conceive and implement elaborate schemes for surgically removing animals' reproductive organs, on the other hand, is considered perfectly rational.

If we no longer believed animals existed in our service,

and laws were passed to enforce this, there would also be far fewer neglected, abandoned, and abused animals.

After the movie *101 Dalmatians* came out, doting and unimaginative parents shut up their whining kids by purchasing dalmatian puppies in droves. Within a year after this film's release, the novelty of having a real live movie tie-in product roving around the house wore off, so pet shelters nationwide were inundated with unwanted dalmatians. These puppies were not considered living beings, but live-action toys that inconveniently grew up and had needs and demands.

This would never, never, ever have happened in a culture that respects the life of all living beings.

Those animals who are allowed to have sex lives and reproduce are used in the service of breeding and making money. If you understand animals to be wholly sentient beings, the practice of animal breeding appears truly pathological. Dalmatian-breeding farms exploded after one fucking Disney production. The bitches were put into reproductive overtime in order to meet that economic blowback demand.

I had no intention of getting this cat "fixed."

If he started peeing in my home, I would have a talk with him about it or find some way to make his life as miserable as his piss would make mine. As it turned out, I didn't have to deal with it because Maria took him to the vet and found out the deed had already been done.

He just looks (and acts) like he has balls.

Maria was the big cheerleader for me keeping this cat. I travel a lot, and having a pet just doesn't seem fair. Especially to a needy creep like him, who drove me up the fucken wall. I mean, what kind of asshole bites your arm at three in the morning because he decides that he's done being curled up quietly beside you and now wants to go outside?

I was relieved when Maria found a home for him with a nice dyke family in the country.

The day before he was gonna leave, I looked out the window and saw him crouching under a bush, ass wagging and tail twitching in the way that means a cat's entertaining a truly nefarious plan. I wondered what this plan was, and watched him. Along comes a man with a big, lopey golden retriever. The cat lunged out from under the bush, landed on the dog's shoulders, worked it over with his claws, then sprung off its back, into the street. All of this in, like, eight seconds. The dog was crying and the man looked like he just got his identity stolen in a whirlwind.

I laughed my ass off.

Called Maria and told her to forget it, I'd decided to keep the cat.

Then people wanted to know what his name was. Always asking me what the fucken cat's name was. I called him "Chunklet," which wasn't really his name. It's a generic term I use for anything dear and small, including human children.

This cat is very complex. He isn't just someone you can

call "Patches" and be done with it. I would know what I'd call him over time. Living life with him would inform me. I was really tripping on people's insistence that I immediately name him, as if someone's ability to personify him would be impaired without this crucial information. Why was it so important? Couldn't he just be who he is? Would naming him formalize my ownership over him? Would it announce to the world that this cat was now my possession? One neighbor, especially, thought the name "Chunklet" was some form of mild pet abuse, and asked me if I had "thought of" another name for him every time I saw her.[†]

After a couple months living with him, I realized that he is very wise, cagey, affectionate, playful, and antagonistically demanding. He reminded me of an old patriarch who doesn't suffer fools kindly. "Little grandfather" came to me, and so I call him "Abuelito." I do not know his name for himself, or even if cats think of themselves by name, but I quite enjoy coming home and yelling, "Abuelito, mi querido!" and seeing him run to meet me and start telling me about his day from halfway down the block. He did the same thing back when I called him "Chunklet." I am sure he would greet me just as enthusiastically if I called him "Serial Killer Ax Murderer Piece of Shit from Hell," or, indeed, "Patches."

He hears my voice, and the love and respect I have for

[†] "Her" cats, "Banana" and "Pudding," aren't allowed outside to feel the wind in their fur, chase birds, stare longingly at the chicken next door, or flop down in the blazing sunshine after a hard day's fucking off. She evidently doesn't consider this abusive.

him in my voice. He doesn't need a lot of extra frills dressing up that reality.

So, the whole culture of "pet ownership" encroached upon my life.

People complain to me that he attacked their dog, and I have to say, "Oh, well, I'll put a stop to that immediately. I'm feeling you. That's just too fucked up. I must control that behavior. We're going to the vet right now and I'm gonna get his teeth and claws ripped out. If that doesn't work, I'll take him to a priest and get his spirit completely exorcised." And then the person has to say, "Well, gee, you don't have to be sarcastic. I was just thinking you could keep him inside." And then I have to say, "Oh! Great idea! I'll keep this obviously psycho cat, who is smarter than me, you, and your dog combined, in my home 24-7. He's sure to embrace the concept of a litter box after a few months' imprisonment."

Some of my neighbors told me I needed to make him stop taking naps in the street 'cause he was gonna get hit by a car. I was like, "Look, he's living his life. If that involves getting hit by a car then that will suck, but it's *his fucken life.*"

His life did involve getting hit by a car. He lived through that and doesn't nap in the street anymore.

I don't want to sound callous here.

I unconditionally love this vengeful, megalomaniacal anarchist with all my heart, and part of that love is fully apprehending that he, uh, lives life on the edge. Any cat who attacks dogs for sport is living life on the edge. Any cat who tries to steal a sandwich out of the hands of a construction worker on

445

lunch break, or follows complete strangers down the sidewalk, screaming at them until they stop and pet him,[†] is living life on the edge. This is Abuelito's way. He will never, ever be a mellow cat who lies around the house all day and stays out of trouble.

It's bad enough that *I* have to deal with the culture of "pet ownership"—I have no desire to inflict it on him.

He is not my slave.

Indeed, as time went on and I grew more familiar with the codes and mores of "pet ownership," I was thunderstruck at how many similarities it has with slavery. I started wondering if, perhaps, since people have, collectively, never come to terms with slavery, one of the ways it lives on in our hearts is through pet ownership. And I see quite clearly how white people condoned slavery back in the day—so many aspects of our relationship with animals are based on the idea that this is *Just the Way It Is*.

This phenomenon is on full, decontextualized view in how we regard pets: We exert control over their reproductive systems. We breed those we deem "valuable." We unquestioningly tear babies away from their siblings and parents, and they never see each other again. We call ourselves their "owners" and "masters." We have their claws surgically removed in order to protect our other possessions. We abuse and neglect them. We assume their lack of intelligence, yet

---

† I think the reasoning here goes something like this: "If you're gonna pass my home and territory, you're gonna pay the ferryman, which equals taking a few moments out of your day to give me the love I am pretty much constantly entitled to."

marvel over it whenever they do something we consider "smart." We say they don't have "real feelings," or we project our own onto them. We tie them up, train them to be docile and well mannered, punish them when they are "bad," and give them treats when they are "good." We project our fears onto them. We treat them like stupid sub-children and ourselves as their benevolent overseers.

I would have little insight into any of this if Abuelito hadn't decided that my home would be his home. I don't know where he came from or why he left the place he was living before. He is so very willful, I don't doubt the possibility that someone who wanted a cute little kitty to sit in the window and bat at the flies just tossed him into my neighborhood. But I firmly believe he came to my home because he sensed I would not impose my will upon him. It is difficult being emotionally attached to someone who is positively heedless of the dangers in this world, but I am not going to try to somehow make him "act right" or "keep him safe" just so I won't have to go through the pain of losing him.

I think a lot of people can relate to that one, in many different contexts.

Whenever he uses up the last of his nine lives, he will have lived his life to the fullest, and I will love him and feed him and support him to that end. It was, after all, someone from my species who took him away from his mother in the first place.

And, like his mother probably was, I will be very, very sad when he is gone.

✕

When coyotes in Los Angeles eat people's pets, it's perfectly acceptable to hate coyotes because a pet is a beloved member of the family, and a coyote is a wild and heartless beast who has no respect for human-pet bonds. There is not a lot of talk about what would inspire coyotes to venture into the city because this train of thought would lead folks into discussing our role in the destruction of their habitat, and that might actually lead people to develop more sustainable means of existing in this world, which, everyone who is a real estate magnate can agree, is not profitable.

When salmon runs are destroyed by completely irresponsible farming methods, people show no concern unless the cost of salmon rises. Environmentalists, and tribes along salmon runs who have fishing treaty rights, are pitted against the fishing and farming industries, and sometimes, one another. Under the full spectrum dominance competitive male model of problem solving, this becomes a fight between various human factions, and the salmon die regardless.

Humans care about the world around us and everyone else who lives on it inasmuch as it concerns our specific emotional selves or our economic system.

I find this mystifying.

Since we live in this world, on this earth, shouldn't everything about it concern us, 24-7? If beef cows live a horrifying existence and die brutal deaths and we eat their flesh, then are we not introducing horror and brutality into our bodies?

＊

I heard something once that forever impacted my perception
of food and life and love. I do not remember if I read this, or if
it was a dream, a documentary, or just an anecdote someone
shared with me, but it goes like this:

An old woman in Mexico was given a tortilla-making
machine. It was explained to her how it works, and how much
easier her life would be if she used it, and how much more convenient it is than forming tortillas by hand. She wanted nothing
to do with this machine, and the person who gave it to her tried
to patiently explain that she was being ignorant.

The old woman sighed deeply.

She patiently explained that her life, love, thoughts and
memories all go into each tortilla she makes. It is *this* that
nourishes her family, and the tortilla is merely a vehicle
through which this nourishment is absorbed into the bodies
of those she loves and feeds. A tortilla machine made no
sense to her because it would separate her from the *act*
of making tortillas, which was the whole fucken point of
making tortillas.

So who, exactly, is the ignorant one in this story?

I have thought about this many, many times in my life.

You are what you eat, and when our entire culture eats mass-
produced, machine-made food that is rarely, if ever, touched by

caring human hands, it is no wonder that there is little compassion and respect for our food, our world, and one another.

The difference between my Grammy's blackberry cobbler and a frozen Marie Callender's blackberry cobbler is much more profound than actual ingredients or baking techniques.

I have never eaten a premade frozen cobbler, and gone outside with it still warm in my belly, and lain down on the ground, and watched the sky, high and totally quiet and content as a kite on a gentle breeze, for a whole hour.

Grammy's cobblers hummed inside my body, and now that she is gone and I will never eat one again, the memory of all the cobblers she ever made for us hums inside my body.

Makes my lips tremble and smile and tears flood my eyes.

They tasted so fine.

I stopped eating meat twenty or so years ago. At the time, my intention wasn't to become a "vegetarian"—something I knew almost nothing about. What happened was like a lot of things that happen to me in my life, it seems. I just stumble onto realities that freak me the fuck out an awful lot.

I was at a pot dealer's house. He was a militant vegan. He used absolutely no products made from animals. He wouldn't even burn candles that contained beeswax. Fresh out of Santa Maria into the Big City, I thought this was the weirdest thing I'd ever heard. How the hell could you celebrate a holiday, birthday, new baby, wedding, or NBA championship win by the Lakers without barbecuing a side of beef?

I investigated his bookshelf and saw a book about meat processing. I leafed through it until I came to a photo of a chicken processing plant. It depicted a huge oval conveyor belt up near the ceiling. As big as a football field, right? And every foot or so, there was a clip thing where a living chicken's feet were attached. When the rig was turned on, the conveyor belt spun around at eighty miles an hour, and each individual clip spun at double that speed. The chickens were centrifugal forced to death and defeathered all in one go.

I thought, "Christ, someone *invented* this. Someone is fabulously wealthy because of this machine."

Then I thought, "Oh dear lordisa, I've eaten chickens who were centrifugal forced to death."

It really, like I say, freaked me the fuck out.

When I got home, I pulled a new package of my favorite thinly sliced ham out of the refrigerator and put it in the freezer. I decided I'd stop eating meat for a couple weeks and started looking forward to my ham sandwich. I didn't have the faintest notion of how to feed a vegetarian, so for those weeks, I mostly ate vegetables, pasta, cheese, and bread. When the time was up, I thawed the ham and made myself a beautiful sandwich. Took one bite and gagged.

It tasted like savory and juicy **bad death**.

I never ate meat again and presently border on veganism. That is, I'd prolly be a vegan if I didn't adore cheese.

My family, particularly my Grammy, thought I would die. They carped at me, preached to me, threatened me, and cajoled me.† Grammy would say stuff like, "Pick the goddamn bacon fat out and eat the beans on your plate, Christ Ah Mighty, I don't know how long this vegetarian shit is *gonna go on.*"

Uncle Bruce is always on hand to remind me that "tofu babies" are never the sharpest knives in the drawer, so it might be all right for now, but I better start eating meat again before I have kids.

Other than the general principle surrounding the detrimental effects that the consumption of bad death has on a population, there's not much dogma involved with my borderline vegan-ism. I think some people are meat eaters and some people are not, and just like a brown-eyed family can sometimes pop out a green-eyed kid, a pack of carnivores can sometimes pop out a borderline vegan.

However, I do very much appreciate that my eating prac-tices have led me to investigate what I eat and where it comes from. Inasmuch as I live in the midst of a highly industrialized, corporate environment, I make every effort to procure healthy, locally grown food whenever possible.

A huge war is raging right now between the agribusiness

---

† In the interest of perspective, it is instructive to balance this with their reaction to my being a queer. That was like, "Oh, ho-hum, pass the salt then, you big judy." Even my redneck uncle Allen was unfazed. He has long been obsessed with the fact that all of the Muscios, with the exception of my brother, are girls. Therefore, his thinking goes, the family name is in danger of extinction. His response to my queerness was something like, "Well then, great. Your kids will be Muscios, right?"

industry, particularly Monsanto, and organic farmers. As of this writing, Monsanto has adopted the relatively new tactic of suing and otherwise harassing organic farmers all over the planet for *saving and reusing seeds from the past season's crops*. They seem to have a special obsession with keeping U.S. organic farmers in line, possibly for the sake of the Monsanto global image.

If you can't make your own children mind, then how can you make other people's children mind?

Written into the "constitution" that Arbusto cobbled together for the people of Iraq is a law forbidding farmers from using nonagribusiness seeds. An article called "Iraqi Farmers Aren't Celebrating World Food Day" shed some light on what corporate-sponsored laws look like:

> As part of sweeping "economic restructuring"
> implemented by the Bush Administration in Iraq,
> Iraqi farmers will no longer be permitted to save
> their seeds. Instead, they will be forced to buy
> seeds from US corporations—which can include
> seeds the Iraqis themselves developed over hun-
> dreds of years. That is because in recent years,
> transnational corporations have patented and now
> own many seed varieties originated or developed
> by indigenous peoples. In a short time, Iraq will be
> living under the new American credo: Pay Mon-
> santo, or starve.[4]

⚔

To me, buying food from local producers is not just
a luxurious matter of dietary consideration. It is a choice
between supporting the ~~bad death~~ feeding system that male
domination has created or procuring sustenance by, for, and
from the earth.

In this way of thinking, my local farmer's market is a tiny
battlefield and the four large sunbursting lemon cucumbers
in my bike basket that cost me a dollar—100 percent of which
went into the pocket of the man who grew them—are itsy
golden bullets.

I hear a chainsaw outside today. It is close. It revs and the
steady *brawwwr* coalesces into a keening roar as the chains
cut through, past the end. During this time, the scream of
a tree crashes into my heart, and I am seized with horror.
How many times in my life have I heard this noise? How
many times has it occurred, but I have not heard it? How
many forests, how many trees, how many times a day? How
many times have I chosen to abide by this, thousands or millions? People in the U.S. often express "horror" when they see
images of war-torn countries. Yet, these very same folks can
drive through a clear-cut forest without seeing the exact same
carnage, without thinking of all the surviving fish, birds,
insects, and other animals who live in that clear-cut as war-
torn refugees.

In wealthy countries,[†] the sound of a chainsaw is generally taken to be a temporary inconvenience. In poor nations, where CIA-backed military or drug cartel death-squad juntas rule in all but name, the sound of a chainsaw often carries even more sinister associations.

To me, today, right now, the chainsaw means death and destruction are singing their songs into my home.

It is idling now and I can still hear the tree.

I know very well what will happen if I go out there right now and talk to the chainsawing person. He or she will say pretty much the same thing that any SS soldier said in the aftermath of WWII, and what any U.S. soldier will say during the Iraq brutal occupation crime trials that are almost guaranteed to occur: "Just following orders."

The logger in the rainforest, the captain of the fishing boat, the overseer at the chicken-slaughtering plant, they all say the exact same thing as the crack dealer in South Central Los Angeles, Chicago's South Side, and Jersey City: "Just wanna feed my seed." Crack dealers are part of the economy in their environment no less than pig farmers are part of the economy in theirs, but selling crack is illegal and the mass slaughter of pigs is standard operating procedure.

Does the illegal drug economy cause *more* death and

---

† And how, exactly, do we define "wealth"? Many "poor" nations are quite rich in diamonds, oil, natural gas, coca, or coffee—resources that are legally stolen from them by white imperialists and colonialists.

destruction than legal, corporate animal slaughter and farming practices? Besides the obesity, heart or mad cow disease, E.
coli infections, and hormone ingestion experienced by human
beings who eat animals who died **bad deaths**.

In the Gulf of Mexico, off the coast of "Texas," "Louisiana," and
"Florida," over 5,800 square miles of ocean are *completely devoid of
life*. This area is aptly, but rather generically, called the dead zone.
I just found out about another dead zone, off the coast of "Oregon,"
but I do not know how much space it consumes. In the Gulf of
Mexico, there are no seaweeds, no fish, no lobsters for almost six
thousand square miles. The nitrates from fertilizers and pigshit
and other chemical insecticides and pesticides run into the gulf
from the Mississippi River, completely depleting the oxygen levels.

The pollution is literally taking the ocean's breath away.

I first read about this in 2003.

By 2004, the media enablers of agribusiness corporations
decided to accommodate this atrocity by calling it "the annual
dead zone." Language never fails to amaze me, and I constantly
marvel at the power of just one word. By choosing to qualify the
term "dead zone" with the adjective "annual," a sense of normal-
ization is introduced into this wholesale ecocide.

Here's what a scientist at the Louisiana Universities Marine
Consortium has to say about the dead zone:

Fish and swimming crabs escape (from the dead
zone)," said Nancy Rabalais, the consortium's chief

scientist for hypoxia, or low oxygen, research. "Anything else dies."[5]

Adding insult to injury, one of the main points of the article where this quote appears is that sharks are attacking more people off the coast of "Texas" because there's nothing else for breakfast, lunch, or dinner. The focus is not on the total annihilation of ocean life due to the practices of the agribusiness industry, but on how more people might be in danger of shark attacks because of this "annual summer phenomenon."

As in, "Hey, kids! Stay out of the water today. It's annual dead zone season, and the sharks are on the prowl!"

Drug dealers don't kill on this scale—in fact, in many of the world's ghettos, barrios, and slums, drug dealers provide the only social service net available to their fellow citizens. Unlike huge multinational corporations, it is in drug dealers' best interests to be proactive and supportive members of the community, regardless of the business they are conducting.

I mention this because I have a seemingly endless fount of questions about the concept of "bad guys" when my normal day-to-day life is marked by violence, atrocity, and devastation enacted by entities and individuals who are generally considered to be "good guys."

The jackhammer is another one of those unique full spectrum dominance sounds, akin to the chainsaw. It does not matter if the jackhammering is happening outside my window in the United States, or outside someone's window in Malaysia. It is a universal sound and everyone understands what it means.

Just following orders.

Seriously, jackhammers crack me the fuck up. A jackhammer is an extend-o phallus men use to make it seem as if they were in control of the earth, via, evidently, their dicks.

I always laugh whenever I see a man[†] using a jackhammer—the expression of concentration on his face while he holds a machine, shaped like his dick, at the level of his dick, doing what he is supposed to imagine his dick should do if he is to be considered a "real" man.

He jams the accelerator and jacks the earth.

So hilarious.

I laugh out loud, and do not care who thinks I am a crazy woman.

If I do not laugh, sadness will surely consume me and I will be lost to this world.

This is survival, and I do it every day.

The jackhammering man is subconscious pornography right there on the street, in full view. It's not like there is only One

---

† Jackhammering women don't have the same effect on me, but I only ever recall seeing one in my life thus far.

Way in the Whole Wide World to pull up pavement and con-crete.[†] Just because no one bothers to examine things from non-invasive perspectives doesn't mean there aren't other ways to Get Jobs Done.

I think it has been widely proven that the human imagina-tion kicks ass.

Uh, hello.

Fiber optics? Nuclear war? Saffron ice cream? Nuestra Virgen de Guadalupe? Federal income tax? The annual hajj? Otis Redding? Hello?

Wide shut eyes do not peer into the decontextualized spec-tacle of jackhammering (for instance), which is why it's per-fectly natural for our children to witness such a deeply sexual enactment of male domination on the street outside our homes.

Meanwhile, it makes perfect sense to disdain sex workers and whores for doing the jobs they've quite imaginatively been doing for thousands of years.

Once, I was walking along a busy street in Seattle. Looked up at the sky and saw a hawk carrying something in its talons, blazing through the sky at full speed. A crow clan and all their descen-dents chased after it in a frenzy of speed and velocity. They were on that hawk's ass, hurtling through the air. Hawks are much

---

† Which probably shouldn't be replaced because it probably shouldn't have been laid down in the first place because pavement and lawns greatly assist in sustaining drought conditions.

bigger than crows. In the world of nature, this means hawks don't fear crows. But this hawk was overwhelmingly outnumbered.

I stood on the ground, staring at the sky, my heart pounding.

"What the fuck?" I thought.

As I tried to piece together a reason for this spectacle, the hawk released what it held in its talons. I watched it fall, a little black speck. Two crows shot out of the crowd, straight down, swooping and breaking the fall of the little black speck. It was a baby crow the hawk had stolen. Baby and parents landed with a *whoomp* and a rustle of wings twenty feet away from me. I was riveted as I watched the parents circle round and round their baby, lifting its feathers with their beaks, nuzzling it with their heads. It seemed to be shaken and dazed, but otherwise, just fine.

The hawk did not share a similar fate. I think it was hoping the crows would back off if it dropped the baby. All the crows besides the parents shot off, out of my sight, after the hawk. I imagine it was not a pretty sight when it got caught.

And there is no doubt in my mind that the hawk got caught.

Everyone who knows crows knows that you don't mess with their babies. Baby crows are coveted and adored by their entire family tree. People rarely actually see baby crows because they are so fiercely protected. The youngest crow one generally sees is a teenager. In all my years of appreciating crows, this was the first baby I had ever seen.

Okay, so I was arrested by this high drama, and my heart was racing like a NASCAR driver. My eyes were practically rolling in my head from the adrenaline rush of what I'd just witnessed. I looked around me, to see if there was someone else, someone to whom I could say, "Oh my god, was that the most intense fucken thing, or what?" Almost hyperventilating, I wanted to share this experience with someone.

But there was no one.

That is, there were hundreds of people. Some of them were talking on cell phones. Some of them were talking to each other. No one was looking at the sky. No one's heart was racing but mine and the crow family's.

Suddenly, I felt very, very alone.

So yes, there is a loneliness here, in looking at the world that humans do and do not inhabit. We are coerced into thinking and caring about the intimate lives of celebrities we will never have relationships with, so we don't spend a lot of time thinking and caring about birds right outside our windows.

What if rats, ants, and cockroaches were viewed as a population of sentient beings who had a right to live?

I know this sounds insane, and it is related to the loneliness I am speaking of, but when I live in places with cockroaches, I never have cockroach problems. I talk to them. I say, "Look, mighty cockroach clan, I am a clean person and you will be hard-pressed to find food in my home. If you like, I will leave you cookies in the corner of this cupboard, but I ask you to stay away from the rest of my home, please."

This shit never fails.

I've lived in buildings where all my neighbors have complained about cockroaches, and sometimes the napalmesque-fumigant men come and spray all the apartments except mine, and the cockroaches—who are incredibly psychic—lay low for a while, and come back in a week or two.

This costs me a few cookies a month, but people generally think it is *absurd to try to communicate with lower life forms,* so I've learned not to share my "pest control" techniques.

And there is a loneliness in this.

There was loneliness the time I lived in an apartment overlooking an alley in Olympia, "Washington." The crows all hung out on the wires strung around the street and this alley, and I could see them right outside my kitchen window. So, naturally, I started feeding the crows. Unfortunately, the seagulls figured out that there was food to be had every morning outside my window, and they descended. Seagulls are fucking greedy bastards, and I would not have had any problems with them if they didn't vibe the crows out and gobble up *all* the food. So I started saving all my pennies and keeping them on the windowsill. I'd feed the crows, and when the seagulls descended, I'd lob pennies at them and call them greedy bastards and tell them to fuck off. At first, the crows tripped out on me. Why was I throwing pennies when I had been feeding them so nicely? But within a couple days, they realized that I was *only throwing pennies at the gulls.*

From then on, I'd throw the food down, the crows would hang back and wait for the seagulls to descend, I'd throw pennies at them, the gulls would bitch and moan and squawk off, and the crows would eat their breakfast.

After a while, the gulls figured out that the area outside my window was crow territory, and they stopped dropping in altogether.

And the thing about this was that whenever I was out and about in Olympia, there were always crows near me. They totally watched over me, every moment that I was outside. They would escort me home late at night, and swoop in near if a drunk man got too close. It was really, really fucken cool.

This is a unique situation that someone might want to share with everyone they know and love, but I only told my friends Nomy and Roni because I knew they wouldn't think I was crazy for having this huge and intimate relationship with the crows.

It is interesting, this loneliness.

While my connection to the world around me often alienates me from humans who choose not to apprehend the sentience of all living beings, the feeling of having a place and actually belonging in this world is just a kickass full-infusion self-esteem booster.

My mother always has the poem "Desiderata" hanging in her kitchen. I memorized it when I was a child. There is one particular sentiment that I have chanted to myself all my life, and it goes like this:

> You are a child of the universe,
> no less than the trees and the stars;
> you have a right to be here.

And whether or not it is clear to you,
no doubt the universe is unfolding as it should.

To me, this is another facet of Grammy's Flower Decree.

It means I belong in the world, and no man-made nightmare environment of dominance and control can ever, ever, ever alter that reality.

I don't need detailed and painstakingly researched environmental reports to know that the earth is being killed. It seems that if we just took the time to train ourselves to listen to the world in which we live, and to truly apprehend the reality that we belong here, no one would really need a lot of assistance feeling passionate about this shit.

Somewhere within walking distance of your home, there is stark evidence of the earth's demise.

I bet you fifty bucks you can find it, and I know it takes a lot of courage to speak out in the earth's defense. But, equipped as pretty much everyone is with an infinitely resourceful human imagination, not to mention opposable thumbs, I'll wager you can come up with a clever way to do that too.

Opiate of the Asses

When I was nine, the Kee's Appliance deliveryman knocked at the door. Our mom answered it, and we crowded around her, abuzz with curiosity.

"What's that?" she asks, pointing to a box that clearly stated Zenith State of the Art Color TeeVee on it.

"It's a teevee," said the man.

"Well, why are you delivering it to my house?"

The siblings and I were leery as well. We had been begging our parents for a teevee ever since *Happy Days* came out and kids started dressing like the Fonz at school and we had to pretend that we knew who the Fonz was, and laugh at all the sitcom-inspired jokes we did not understand.

This was no way to live as a child growing up in the United States of Amerikkka.

Like with so many other things, Mom was on our side, but alas, our home ran a lot more along the lines of dictatorship than democracy.

You could work on Dad, wear him down on some things, but when he said "no" it generally meant "Abso-Fucken-Lutely Not," and Dad *hated* teevee.

He hated when we watched it on sleepovers at friends' houses. On Sunday mornings he'd take *time out of his day* to interrogate us about what we'd watched at whomever's house the night before. It made sleepovers a bit of a pain in the ass, but no one wanted to stay the night at our house since we didn't have a teevee and even if we had, there was the unattractive reality of our naked dad to contend with.

We had teevee autonomy at Grammy's, where our father's tyranny held no jurisdiction. She overruled everyone on anything, and her home was an inner-family neutral zone.

I have always, always loved the power of my Grammy.

This teevee on the doorstep was strange and surreal and entirely improbable, much like my father.

"Your husband bought it," the deliveryman said,

"No. You got the wrong house, pal," said Mom: "Get your teevee back in your delivery van and get out of here before my husband comes home and sees that."

"No, Mrs. Muscio. Really, he came into the store yesterday and bought this teevee."

We started shifting our feet and whispering amongst ourselves. Could it be possible? Was this some kind of cruel joke our father and the Kee's Appliance deliveryman were playing? Could it *really happen* that he'd actually hand-truck that sure-to-be-gorgeous simulated wood grain teevee *into our home?*

My mom asked to see the signature on the bill of sale.

She looked at it and showed it to us.

Sure enough, Joseph L. Muscio—familiar to everyone who needed field trip permission slips signed.

Meaning, not Nick. He was only three.

"He bought it, Mrs. Muscio. I saw him in the store myself."

Wordlessly, and kinda staring off, Mom opened the door all the way. As an adult, I now know she was thinking this:

"What the fuck, what the fuck, what the fuck?"

We made a path for the Kee's Appliance deliveryman, and he asked possibly the most beautiful question I had heard in my life up to that point:

"Where do you want me to put your new Zenith State of the Art Color TeeVee?"

When Dad came home, we were all poring over the *Los Angeles Times* teevee guide—a periodical I had been wont to study anyway, in my effort to appear in the know about teevee shows. Reading it with an *actual teevee in the house* was a whole new concept. I felt like a rich person who could buy anything in the J.C. Penney.

We were scheduling our entire childhoods. We had Mondays and Tuesdays agreed upon, and were quarreling about Wednesdays, when our father walked into the room and let us know that it was all, indeed, a cruel joke.

"*Sesame Street*," he intoned. "*Villa Alegre. The Electric Company. Zoom.*"

Having thus communicated with us successfully, he left the room. To anyone who doesn't know our dad, this might not sound like successful communication, but we knew very well what this meant. No *Happy Days*. No *Good Times*. No *Carol Burnett Show*. No nothing except the shows on the public educational channel. Joe B. threw the teevee guide across the room, but I think we were all aware that what this *really* meant was that **when Dad was home,** *Sesame Street, Villa Allegre,* et cetera.

And so it came to pass.

We settled into a furtive and somewhat successful campaign of watching the teevee. Someone was always designated the Watch. This person was in charge of listening for Dad's car and whisperyelling, "Dad!" when necessary.

Someone else—usually Joe B. 'cause he had the longest reach—would zip the channel to PBS quick as lightning, and we would all pretend to be totally absorbed in whatever show was on. This may have been our downfall, because I do not believe our father thought any of his children would actually sit through an entire episode of *Nova*.

That is, besides maybe Liz, who was li'l miss astronomy.

But we got away with this for quite some time. Maybe a year.

Then one day, Dad turned off his headlights before sweeping into the driveway, didn't slam the car door, and probably tiptoed up to the house—the fuck.

He nailed us watching *The Brady Bunch*.

We got lectured and yelled at and told off and bitched out.

Less than a week later, Dad was napping in the back bedroom. He always peed after getting up from a nap, so the Watch merely had to listen for the sound of his loud-ass pee stream hitting the water. Joe B. would then get the word, and lightning-zip the channel knob.

Looking back, I see that it was incredibly nonstrategic of us to be taking a chance like this so soon after getting nailed for *The Brady Bunch*. The lure of the teevee, however, was very difficult to resist, and absent from our family structure was a goody-goody sibling who might have counseled us otherwise—which is probably for the best anyways, as this sibling would have been a wretched and timid soul, accustomed to frequent ass-kickings.[†]

---

† Nick, who was maybe four by this time, was the closest thing we had to a goody-goody. Everyone—even the extended family—was in straight-up consensus that Nick was the nicest kid our parents were evidently capable of producing. He was also a pyromaniac who endangered our home on numerous occasions, so you can imagine what evil bastards the rest of us were.

On this occasion, we were watching the show our father despised above all others: *I Love Lucy.*

Dad *hated* Lucy.

This is the scene.

Four children, semicircling the teevee, completely absorbed in the world of Lucy Ricardo, who was on a vacation in Italy. As I recall, Lucy was enduring the rigors of a severe sunburn while being a runway model in a fancy fashion show where she had to wear an itchy wool suit.

As one indivisible entity, we heard the hall door click.

This was very bad.

Oh so very, very bad.

It meant that our father was not only up from his nap, but had somehow figured out that we listened for him to pee, and so had abandoned this ritual. The teevee was clearly visible from the hallway. If the door had clicked, that meant that it was opening, and there was no chance in hell that Joe B. would have time to do his wonder-zip on the channel knob.

It meant we were completely fucked.

All four of us, again, as one, froze.

The naked father walked past us, into the kitchen. We heard a drawer open and close. We all breathed a dangerous, hopeful sigh of relief. Maybe he was still half asleep and somehow, miraculously, hadn't noticed Lucy in Italy. Gingerly, ever so slow-motionly, Joe B. reached up to change the channel.

Our father walked back into the room with a foot-long, five-pound, shiny red pipe wrench† in his hand.

Our strange, surreal, and entirely improbable father.

He lifted his arm and swung the wrench into the teevee screen.

It shattered thickly and popped.

He walked away.

We heard his pee stream gushing into the toilet.

I bet he had to go pretty bad by then.

He never said a word to any of us about it, then, soon after, or ever.

That was the end of the teevee.

Well, almost.

It made that cool popping noise, which roused our collective interest, and we spent the rest of the evening looking at the teevee insides and ascertaining once and for all that there were not tiny people living in it.

After *that* was the end of the teevee.

When our mom came home from work and saw the imploded teevee in the living room, I bet she said pretty much the exact same thing as when she watched the Kee's delivery-man hand-truck it into the house.

---

† I took this wrench with me when I moved away from home, and somehow or another, I still have it. This pipe wrench, my 1965 *Random House Dictionary,* and a wooden spoon are the only things I have from my childhood home.

Autobiography of a Blue-Eyed Devil

I was two months shy of thirteen when our dad died. Aside from all of the other things that the passing of one's complex, loving, asshole father might mean, his absence led to the almost imme-diate household presence of:

a) sugar-sweetened cereals.
b) lots of friends.
c) a teevee in the living room.

When MTeeVee made its debut, all four of us were present, accounted for, and in complete agreement that video was gonna slaughter the radio star.

Perhaps in a subconscious effort to make up for all the lost years, we watched the teevee morning, noon, and night.

My brothers became adept at monosyllabic, gruntingly pre-occupied conversations. The only way to get their attention was to stand in front of the teevee and duck out of the path of what-ever they invariably threw at you before you could get a chance to tell them whatever it was you had to tell them.

As an added bonus, all four of us knew what the insides of the teevee looked like.

When I left home, I did not have a teevee. I had other things on my mind, I suppose. Like tuning in to the universe via halluci-nogenic mushrooms, but that's another story.

Or maybe it's not.

Taking mushrooms was a time when I began to understand

the power of my imagination, the power of the world's imagination, and the concept of seizing joy, and maybe teevee kinda paled in comparison.

Taking mushrooms involved being in nature. If I took mushrooms in a man-made setting, I had a bad, paranoid trip. Uncle Bruce and Joe B. taught me how to trip. Hallucinogenic mushrooms are an alive, amazing spirit and must be respected. People who do not respect them or who take them to "party" also have bad, paranoid trips. You cannot invite an ancient spirit into your body and expect to have a good time at a keg party.

Ancient spirits do not want to be at keg parties.

On mushrooms, I knew there was a place for me, and I knew the world wanted me. I lay down on the beach, my face three inches from the sand from midmorning until the sun went down. I watched the wind move the grains around while the sunshine sparkled on each little facet of a speck, and the wind riffled my clothing and hair and the sun shone on the crown of my head, and I'll be goddamned if I didn't know I was in the exact right place at the exact right time, and few forces on earth could have moved my ass from that spot. With mushrooms, I sat in trees and felt them deep bass humming with life, felt them breathing, felt them listening to the day's news from the earth.

I bathed in the phosphorescence of the ocean and watched electric-blue lights dancing until my lips were also blue.

I lay in the middle of rural farm roads and watched the sun

rise over my head, with every color the human eye can perceive exploding over my heart, making me cry.

Those were the times that I began to truly wrap my mind around the vast differences between my environment and this world.

I was reared in a place where my environment didn't particularly go out of its way to tell me it wanted me. I wasn't a cheerleader, an Elks Rodeo Queen, or the daughter of a real estate developer. I wasn't the neighborhood cop. I wasn't particularly well liked, though I was well known. I did not get good grades. My teachers looked up at me, shook their heads, and sighed deeply on the rare occasions that I walked into their classrooms.

But on mushrooms, ah.

On mushrooms, I saw that there might not be a place for me in my environment, but the world passionately wanted me.

And you know, I wasn't really in a position to look a gift horse like that in the mouth.

Prior to and during the mushroom period of my life, I probably would not have questioned a teevee's presence in my home. But somehow or other, it just never came up. I vaguely recall my boyfriend buying a little black-and-white teevee at a garage sale, but I have no memory of either of us ever watching it.

When I got older, I had lovers and housemates who owned teevees, but by then, I'd developed an aversion to this presence in my home. The compromise I've generally reached with people I live with is to keep the teevee on a cart in a closet, and wheel it out whenever someone wants to watch it. This way, there's a teevee in the house, but you *really* have to want to watch it if you're gonna go through the rigmarole of retrieving it and plugging it in.

The exception to this was when I lived with Bambi, Sini, Alison, and Shug in San Francisco. We had a gigantic flat, and the teevee was in the teevee room. I could avoid it or not. It was also just vastly entertaining to watch Sini watch teevee. Especially when she was eating barbecue. Sini was *such* an angel about my weird borderline-vegan fetish for watching people tear into messy meats. Not many people in this world (quite rightfully, I might add) will let you invade their sacred eating space as if you were witnessing performance art.

But Sini would just tune me the fuck out and scream into the teevee set, counseling various characters, loudly critiquing their actions and choices, expressing her sexual arousal as inspired by various people, like Scully on *The X Files*.

Sini had the hugest woody for Scully.

Sini's way of watching teevee—especially while she ate barbecue—was, in itself, a vastly entertaining show. In this way, I vicariously enjoyed two things that I, personally, abhor.

It was a beautiful arrangement.

Sini would actually give me the heads-up—bang on my door and holler, "Hey, li'l vegan! I just ordered barbecue!"

When it arrived, I'd go into the teevee room. Sini would ignore me as I sat, completely mesmerized, nay, starstruck, as she ripped into the ribs of painfully deceased pigs 'n' cows, railing at the characters on whatever show she was watching

("Jerry, you need your *ass fucked* by Kramer, and that's all
there is to it, buddy"), and sucking brownish burgundy goop
off her fingers.

Lordisa, how I love that Sini Anderson.

So anyway, as things transpired, I've never owned a teevee.

In the beginning, *it just so happened*.

I'm compelled to qualify this because I know from experience that when avid teevee engagers find out I have never
owned a teevee, there's this guilt-inspired, competition-based
notion that I consider myself some higher life form, aglow in
self-righteousness, when nothing could be further from the
truth. The teevee sucks me in just as successfully as the next
person. Except for *Jeopardy!*, I don't even really seek out *intelligent* programs. I love *Elimidate, Fear Factor,* and *Extreme Make-
over: Home Edition*. I watch bible shows, the mall shopping channel, *Sexos en Guerra,* and *Sabado Gigante*. I used to love watching
the Miss Universe pageant before Donald Trump bought it and
turned it into a right-wing propaganda spectacle, resplendent
with a young Arbusto host.

Some of the fondest memories in my life are of watching *The Price Is Right* with my Grammy. I will absolutely wash
out a mouth with pine tar soap before I hear *a word* against
Bob Barker. When I lived in Los Angeles, Liz, our sister-in-law
Cindy, her friend Lucy, and me all stood in line at five in the
morning to be in the studio audience for *The Price Is Right*.
None of us got called up onstage, but just being in the same

room with Mr. Showcase Showdown was a subtly life-changing experience.

The teevee seduces me no less, and maybe even more, than anyone else. It is human nature to be sucked in by it, which is *precisely why* it is a formidably good idea to maintain absolute control over its presence in your home.

As I've gotten older and seen how much metaphorical, emotional, psychological, economic, and physical *space* a teevee *consumes,* I clearly see the threat to my father's children that got the man so incredibly riled up.

Minus the pipe wrench.

I think the pipe wrench was a bit much.

In New Orleans, I learned about the literally negative power of teevee. I was staying with Miss Pussycat at Pussycat Caverns. She gave me a lovely little loft space to sleep in.

After the first night, I woke up in the morning and felt a vague, but powerful, vacuum of absence.

Couldn't put my finger on it. This happened every morning when I woke up.

It wasn't a bad feeling, but it was noticeable, and I wondered about it. By the fourth morning, I'd spent some time in this city, and come to a small understanding of its spirit. New Orleans thrives on dreams. Lovely dreams, unsettling dreams, nightmares. It is a city built on a swamp, and is always in motion, living out good, bad, and ugly dreams.

New Orleans is the most alive place I have ever been.

So on that fourth morning, I realized that what was missing every day since I'd arrived was my dreams. It wasn't that I simply did not remember them. My dreams were *taken* from me in my sleep by the spirit of the place—hence the vacuum of absence.

I was very cool with this, and formally, consciously offered up my dreams to the spirit of this place each night before falling asleep. The vacuum of absence stopped happening, though my dreams were still very much taken from me. Every time I've since visited New Orleans, I've offered all my sleeping dreams to the place. In return, New Orleans opens itself to me when I am awake.

Another one of those beautiful arrangements life in this world sometimes offers up.

Before going to New Orleans, I was never conscious of the possibility that my dreams could be taken from me while I sleep. After I felt this sensation, however, I was able to easily identify it in other contexts. This is how I happened upon the realization that the teevee is a dream-sucking parasite.

Sometime after that trip, I was staying in a hotel. When I woke up in the morning, I felt that exact same vacuum of absence, but instead of the culprit being the spirit of a beautifully complex and horrifyingly ugly place, this time it was the teevee.

I was so pissed off.

"You asshole," I said, "you stole my dreams."

The maw of its grey-olive-green-black screen stared at me, gloating.

From then on, whenever I sleep in a room with a teevee, the first thing I do is cover it up. I travel with four scarves: two for muting glaring lamps, and two more in case of a big-screen teevee.

Dreams are consciousness.

Jung says so.

If an off teevee sucks dream consciousness, then an on teevee must really do a good job of sucking awake consciousness. This consciousness sucking is a live-action physical negation that we have learned to welcome into our daily lives.

I mean, if you got to read a book all about your life after you died, the hours upon hours of realities that fill your head when you are watching the teevee would provide very little in the way of plot or substance.

There would be huge gaps in the book every time you were watching the teevee in your past life.

That would suck.

But it is also true that the teevee literally drains energy and tires you out much more than staring out the window and day-dreaming or making a mental list of why you love every single person whom you love.

Thoughts, stories, and words have enormous power. They create reality. Therefore, you create your reality when you bring deep and rich stories into your life (such as those found in history, for instance), when you carefully examine the words that surround you.

The teevee has no right to create a person's reality, but in my country 98 percent of the population evidently disagrees.

It is not just that folks could be doing other, more productive things instead of watching the teevee—though that is in itself a valid enough consideration. The teevee *actually, literally takes* from you. It's not like New Orleans, which offers safe passage, heart-stoppingly poignant interactions with other human beings, and endless parades in exchange for a portion of your consciousness.

That's a straightforward business transaction.

You offer up your consciousness to the teevee, and it gives you mean-spiritedness, white supremacist racism, human dominion over animals and the earth, sexism, racial stereotypes, elaborate rationalizations about imperialism and brutal occupations of other countries, white normativity, trite celebrity lifestyle obsessions, mindless violence, and wealthy people and war criminals constantly presented as heroes, icons, and legends of our time.

That's worse than a scam-ass pyramid scheme.

The used-car salesman who uses tigers on leashes to demonstrate his power over others, which will, in turn, somehow seduce people into buying cars on his lot. The white game show host who raises his eyebrows and says, "Ohhh, realllly???" to the young black woman who says she is a genetic physicist. The other game show host who repeatedly uses the word "savage" to describe a young Chicano man's intelligence. The mean-spirited dating show where two white women enact survival of the fittest by racially ganging up on a Korean American woman and then setting upon each other once she has been eliminated. The dating show "prize" who is a lurid misogynist completely obsessed with the reality of breasts.

The fact that people will defend the practice of teevee watching to the bowels of rationality is also quite interesting.

What's to defend?

It is a soul-sucking, ridiculously indoctrinating, absolutely negative use of time. You only watch "intelligent" programs? Well, what other intelligent things can you think of to do that do not involve passively ensconcing yourself in front of the teevee set? Why not take these intelligent viewing practices to another level? What about, instead of watching nature shows, spending three hours an evening tracking the birds in your neighborhood and finding out if there's anything lacking in their diet? Or making nice sandwiches for all the homeless folks within walking distance from your home? Or instead of watching a "news" program about how emotionally unstable and suicidal kids are these days, maybe you could pack up all the kids in the neighborhood and take them fishing. (That is, if there's a relatively unpolluted body of water nearby, and you're not a creepy sexual predator.)

As my friend Ronald frequently points out, "Love is a verb." The teevee sucks away time, imagination, and energy that could easily otherwise be spent enacting love for the world around you.

It repels active engagement with friends, lovers, and family. It robs you of time spent reading books that spark imagination,

learning how to sew, drawing comics, sending love notes to
everyone you know, meditating, writing to your prison pen pals,
doing yoga, making care packages for soldiers whose families are
too poor to send them anything, rebuilding the engine of a clas-
sic car, creating a neighborhood organization to hold the police
accountable for their actions, going for walks, poetically reappro-
priating offensive billboards in your community, putting together
a model 1964 Impala with your kids, and making strawberry-
rhubarb jam for all your friends and neighbors.

I know, I know.

You get home from school or work (or looking for work),
you're tired, and you just want to be left alone. You just want
to turn your mind off for a while and not think. I have nothing
but compassion for this reality. My job is one of those jobs that
never end. For the past six years, I have pretty much *never* not
been thinking about or writing this book. I do watch movies and
documentaries to shut my mind off sometimes, but even then, I
filter everything through the consciousness of my work.

So I have had to learn ways to get some quieter space.
Playing pool is a big one. Reading science fiction is good too.
Learning Wing Chun—the only ancient martial art developed
by a woman—has proven helpful. But really, the biggest thing
is just engaging with the world around me—and this still sometimes involves lying down on the ground and looking at the
world really close up. Watching the industry of ants for even five
minutes can be a seriously rejuvenating activity. Or I stare at a
flower and watch it just be dazzling in the sunshine. There is a
particular golden iridescent sparkling that can only be seen on

the petals of red or bright orange flowers in a certain light, and I spend time looking for that.

Ten minutes of thinking of nothing else but the sky you are staring at relaxes you and clears your mind much more effectively than a numbing hour of watching Donald Trump manipulate corporate-minded protégés into backstabbing, insulting, and cutting each other down.

At the same time that all this is true, maybe you live in the midst of violence and terror, and engaging with the beauty of the world or going outside and looking at the sky is not only a nonexistent possibility, but, in fact, a life-threatening action.

Maybe the teevee drowns the sounds of gunfire outside. In every major city in the U.S., it swallows police sirens and helicopters, car alarms, people fighting on the street, and drunk fools loudly debating the strong and weak points of every "piece of ass" that walks past.

Maybe you are incarcerated or institutionalized, and the teevee provides one of your main connections with the outside world.

The teevee means many different things to many different people. The practice of watching teevee when there are other, more constructive things that one could be engaging in is, in and of itself, a huge luxury.

According to TV-Turnoff Network, the "average American" watches four hours of teevee a day. My home makes up part of the 2 percent of teeveeless homes in the U.S. That's right, a whopping 98 percent of U.S. homes have at least one teevee, which leads me to the realization that one of the only things my people can probably agree upon at this point in our history is our right to be willfully indoctrinated. Forty-one percent of homes in the U.S. feel the dire need for more than three teevee sets. Children between the ages of two and seventeen could hold down a part-time job to fill the space that the teevee takes up in their lives.

If you can't bring yourself to ritualistically assassinate your teevee, then *at least* keep it in a closet. This will, indeed, require you to consciously consider whether or not you truly want to haul the teevee out, rather than just mindlessly hitting the power button.

Changing your teevee-viewing practice is well over half the battle.

Even if you do not watch much teevee, you can do better and watch less.

The opiate of the asses is a major enabler of white supremacist racism and imperialist male domination.

Why defend this?

Why invite this into your home?

How can anyone ever reclaim their imagination with the teevee blaring into, or sucking the life out of, their consciousness?

Enquiring minds want to know.

Like offering dreams to New Orleans, opening yourself up to the world around you garners you a much richer return on investment than allowing the teevee to occupy your imagination.

I suppose this isn't much different from when I was taking mushrooms all the time. Maybe that opened me up to the possibility of being fully enchanted by the beauty of the world I live in, but it is by no means requisite.

It takes time to learn other, positive practices, and if you are not watching the teevee, time is precisely what you will have.

When I was four, my mom took me to the library. I remember looking forward to this event for quite some time. She told me as soon as I could write my name legibly enough to sign the library form, I could have all the books I wanted. I worked hard at learning to write my name because my mother led me to believe that my life would somehow not truly begin until I was able to use the library. She would preface answers to my questions with things like, "Well, when you can go to the library and get a book about [fill in the blank] you will understand better, but I do know that [fill in the blank]."

My mother profoundly gifted me by leading me to believe the library was where it's at. We didn't have much money as a family, but both of my parents were incredibly resourceful at seducing us with activities that happened to be free.

The librarian was very nice to me. She showed me how to find books and gave me a little tour of the children's section.

"I can take *any book in this whole library* home with me?"

"Yes," she said, "as long as you bring it back in two weeks."

I thought the librarian had read every book ever gracing

her shelves, and was deeply in awe of her. This is almost certainly where my adoration of librarians is rooted.

I've run across a few librarians who said, "Shhhhhhh," like they were spewing rattlesnake venom, but by and large, librarians are people who have blessed my life with free knowledge, unflaggingly impressed me with their patience for stupid questions, and inspired me with their devout adherence to free speech.

I could practically write a book all about how wonderful librarians are.

I could write another book about how hungry kids in poor towns, on reservations, and in neighborhoods are often robbed of this self-generating resource, but maybe in a way I already have.

In middle school, I started library surfing. This is a game where you walk around the library, randomly picking books off the shelves, and reading from each one for as long as it holds your attention. If it holds your attention for more than five or ten minutes, you put it in your keep pile and move on to the next arbitrarily selected book.

This practice has led me to imagining the authorized and unauthorized biographical lives of a large and diverse group of people, including Tallulah Bankhead, Billie Holiday, Ludwig of Bavaria, the Dallas Cowboys Cheerleaders, Bugsy Siegel, Imelda Marcos, LaToya Jackson, Maury Povich, and Steve Biko.

I also have a casual knowledge of taxidermy, underwater welding, attachment parenting, marzipan, and ikebana.

I love the library and the library loves me.

✧

My local library employs someone who understands the value of comix and graphic novels. I have tried to find out the name of this person to no avail, so if you happen to be the comix procurer in Portland, "Oregon," I appreciate you very much and wish you job security and good health.

Here is something I have often wondered about in my life: How come science fiction, kids' literature, comix, and graphic novels are generally not taken seriously, yet these genres represent some of the most subversive, deep-thinking writing available in my country?

I do not understand why schools do not use books like Ho Che Anderson's *King* in U.S. history classes. This three-volume comix series delves deeply into the life of Martin Luther King Jr, without idolizing or demonizing this deeply complex individual. Dr. King's right-hand strategist, Bayard Rustin (think of a non-piece-of-shit Karl Rove), is often a bit inconvenient for many homophobic celebrants of the Civil Rights Movement. Mr. Anderson, however, saw no reason to exclude a man who had such a huge impact on our history just because he was gay.

Kids like comix.

A lot of comix writers and artists like history. Seems like a match made in heaven to me, but then, my idea of heaven is a place where there are no unwanted children or old folks' homes.

In my experience, people who do good comix spend an

inordinate amount of time studying human nature in order to make their characters come to life. People who spend a lot of time studying human nature often emerge with an impressive understanding of how fucken insanely complex people, life, and people's life choices are.

Some comix have "good" guys and "bad" guys, but none of the comix I love best have this completely unrealistic worldview. Even the seminal *Elektra: Assassin,* published by Marvel, gives the reader some very good ideas about how our heroes and villains became the people they are.

Gilbert and Jaime Hernandez, or Los Bros Hernandez, have been doing the *Love and Rockets* series for over two decades. Their characters are my friends, and I learn more about them each time I reread a volume.

Gilbert's Luba carries a hammer around with her. It is an incredibly bad idea to cross Luba—which is related to how she became the mayor of Palomar.

I was thinking of Luba the day I bought a heavy hammer at a garage sale. It made me feel like it was an incredibly bad idea to cross me, so I kept this hammer in my bike basket all summer long. *It does not matter whether or not it is, in fact, a bad idea to cross me.* Luba and her hammer forged this reality in my imagination, and inspired me to create my own reality.

This is one of my very favorite things about being human. All we need is an instance that sparks our imaginations and we fucken run with that shit. The more your imagination is sparked, the more stuff you got to propel you along.

Fucken wheeee.

✕

Science fiction is one of the things that help me to consider how environments are constructed and how they evolve over time. Octavia Butler and Ursula K. Le Guin are largely responsible for this teaching.

Ms. Butler is a genius at projecting her imagination onto present-day realities, taking things as they appear to her, and following them along the course of events that might transpire.

Ms. Butler's stories occur mostly on this earth and detail the workings of the human mind and imagination in spectacular, awe-inspiring ways.

Her character Lauren Olamina helped me to understand that it *really is possible* to be hurt in your actual flesh-and-blood body when a tree is cut, a cop kills another young black man, a village is razed, a woman is raped, or a pollutant sickens and kills a population thousands of miles away. Ms. Olamina is an empath, living in a world much like our own but quite a bit more intense, which makes her very vulnerable, indeed.

Being our hero, however, she figures things out.

Ursula Le Guin writes about the multiverse. Her books are set all over time and space.

A common feature in some of her stories is an organization called the Ekumen—a kind of multiplanetary United Nations, but one that hasn't been defanged and manipulated by, say, the United States government.[†]

Envoys from the Ekumen visit various worlds, and the government of each world's ruling country generally tries to hide the bad stuff and put on a happy face. The envoy's job is to sort through the bullshit and figure out the history and present situation of the planet. The story evolves from there.

These are very coarse descriptions of both writers' books, many of which have nothing to do with Lauren Olamina or the Ekumen.

Both of these *thankfully* prolific writers provide me with the opportunity to step back and look at the environment I live in from an empath's or Ekumenical point of view, and I *see* the unimaginative choices people make when they know they are taking part in fucked-up shit but have done so for so long they can't seem to find a way to stop. This exact pattern is holographically repeated not only in our government, but in families, workplaces, schools, and civic organizations. It is our environment, which has—as Ms. Butler and Ms. Le Guin will inform you—been constructed. It is deeply ingrained in every aspect of our existence, from our most intimate relationships to the crimes against humanity that our government commits in our names.

---

† I just recently read an article about some fool right-wing group that wants the UN off of U.S. soil. The reasoning goes: Since the UN was unwilling to back the U.S.'s brutal occupation of Iraq, then the UN harbors and abets terrorists. Big sigh.

꙰

A more jovial but no less scathing appraiser of the state of nature that human beings have forged through racism, imperialism, and warfare is Mr. Terry Pratchett. He writes of a seemingly preposterous place called Discworld, which is a flat world held up by four giant elephants who ride through space on the back of the Great A'Tuin, a humongous turtle. Discworld is populated by trolls, dwarves, elves, gnomes, golems, zombies, vampires, witches, and humans. Oh, and the Wee Free Men, who are criminal-minded drunken bastards with hearts of gold and whiskey.

With sentences that inspire my writer's heart to explode in joy ("Her chest rose and fell like an empire"), Mr. Pratchett uses his characters and their lives to deftly illustrate the ridiculousness of human fears. He is one of my favorite feminists in the whole wide world, and since I have been living in a country run by Arbusto, I have relied on Mr. Pratchett's imagination to see me through with my ability to laugh at my kind intact.

It is a tall order, as I know very well that people are being terrorized in my name as I lay in my warm cushy bed at night. Thanks to Mr. Pratchett's seemingly endless fecundity, I actually do experience sleep without constant anxiety-laced nightmares.

For this service, I owe him a great deal.

Many people have no such luxury.

Children's literature is another genre that suffers from culture-wide underestimation.

I stumbled across *The Golden Compass,* by Philip Pullman, after I had finished reading the latest Harry Potter installment a few years back. After reading *The Subtle Knife* and *The Amber Spyglass*—the other books composing the *His Dark Materials* trilogy—I scoffed at everything Harry Potter, which wasn't such a sad parting after reading J. K. Rowling's subplotted rationalization of slavery in the second Harry Potter book.

In *The Golden Compass,* we meet our heroine, Lyra, and her dæmon familiar, Pantalaimon. The children of Lyra's village are being disappeared by something called the Gobblers, which turns out to be a group of evangelical freaks who are conducting experiments that eviscerate a child from its dæmon familiar. In Lyra's land and time, this is pretty much the same thing as separating people from their very souls. What follows is a peerless, epic saga involving god, satan, polar bear armies, homosexual angels, and the ever-present ridiculousness of human fears.

Philip Pullman is a subversive mutha. One of his earlier trilogies, published in the 1980s and early 1990s and centering around illegal arms deals and drug running, brought keenly to mind many of the U.S. and UK government crimes going on at that time. In that series, our heroine is Sally Lockhart, and the setting is more or less Victorian England, but the Cold War, U.S.-Soviet arms race, and Iran-contra parallels are more than striking.

Likewise, *His Darkest Materials* brings to mind many of the struggles facing humanity today, and I keep thinking about the Gobblers.

In my present world, the Gobblers are also enabled by evangelical freaks, but their objective is to gain access to schoolchildren and seduce them into joining the military. In "Louisiana," for instance, the Gobblers sneakily passed a law so that any child who wants a driver's license is automatically registered with the Selective Service. "Louisiana" officials defend this law by stating that it is *actually* designed to help kids out. Especially, according to the article I read, kids in "the inner city," who might not know that in order to be eligible for certain benefits (these "benefits" were not named in that or any other report I've read on this topic), they must be registered with the Selective Service. The Gobblers are also very busy at high schools across the country, and many parents and caregivers do not know that—unless they fill out some form that no one tells them is in existence—their children's information is freely available to military recruiters. Some of my friends from Los Angeles have told me stories about military recruiters picking kids up from (largely black and Chicano) schools and seducing them with pizza and video games. Parents come home from work and find that their pepperoni-breathed teenager has signed up for the Army and there is nothing to be done about it.

This form of coercion is almost charming when compared to the fate of people who do not have U.S. citizenship. Life-or-death green cards are dangled at Mexican, Jamaican, Haitian, Puerto Rican, and other nationals. If they snap at the bait, they're shipped to the front lines, often without proper training, weaponry, or Kevlar.

They are bodies to wear down "insurgents."

More valuable than goats.

Less valuable than medics.

So yes, Philip Pullman's Gobblers strike a serious chord in my heart right now.

In general, it seems strange and surreal that this environment is filled with people who often pass uninformed and ill-considered judgment on comix, graphic novels, kids' books, and science fiction, when these are some of the best sources of pure, unadulterated imagination readily available at any public library. Meanwhile, folks will watch reality teevee shows, crime scene dramas, or bitch 'n' ho music videos ad nauseam.

I understand that I am a loser in this environment we call a world. I am not the fittest, and the reason I survive is because I have found all manner of ways of taking joy and remaining present and accounted for.

Only losers have chronically broken hearts.

Only losers admit that they are assholes.

When it comes down to it, losers are the only people who spend time looking for pay phones.

I'm such a loser, the one person I would have wholeheartedly voted for in the 2004 presidential elections—Carol Moseley Braun—garnered something like .0 percent of the primary vote.

I'm not even very good at being a loser homo—I recently had sex with a beautiful biological man and can't seem to stop thinking about this interaction.[†]

---

† I said, "Dang, you are like a dyke with a dick," and he said, "Uhm, whutt?" and I said, "Oh, nothing, nothing."

I was telling good ol' Maria about what a loser I am, and she was so sweet, trying to convince me that I am a "winner" in some ways, but I wouldn't concede the point, and she ended up saying that she's a heartbroken loser too, but I already knew that because she and my good pal Ariel recently incorporated Big Mama's Church of Jesus Christ the Girlie-Man, and I figure you gotta be pretty dang present in this world and taking a fuck of a lot of joy if you're gonna start a church called that.

It is a strange thing, a broken heart.

In the generally accepted mainstream of society, a broken heart is something to be avoided *at all costs*, and is almost exclusively associated with the failure of love, sex, or romance. In order to avoid heartbreak of this order, it is acceptable to remain emotionally shut down, to reject those who touch us deeply, to stand guard over the deepest, most human and complex parts of ourselves like K-9 dogs at the gates of hell.

That's not the kind of heartbreak I am talking about, though.

In my experience, that kind of heartbreak heals up as soon as I grow and learn. It's not such a big deal compared to the heartbreak of knowing that somewhere in Mexico, a young child was stolen and all of his organs were removed and drugs were sewn up in his corpse, and his body crossed the border in a car with a man and a woman who seemed like a lovely couple with their sleeping darling angel babyboy in the backseat.

In the environment I live in, this is heartbreak.

'   In the environment I live in, children are sold into sexual slavery by parents who love them with all their genetic makeup, but also must feed their other four kids. Remember *Sophie's Choice?* How people cried and cried to think of that horrible choice? People make Sophie's Choice every day in this free-trade-for-all globalized marketplace, where you may very well shop in a department store owned by someone who fucks little girls who sacrifice their lives so their families can eat.

This is heartbreak.

Gang violence, police murder, torture and brutality, unjust laws, and wrongfully incarcerated human beings are heartbreaking.

Perfectly innocent people sitting on death row is heartbreaking.

Living in an environment where people celebrate the genocide of indigenous people on Thanksgiving and Columbus Day is heartbreaking.

Poverty is heartbreaking.

War is heartbreaking.

It breaks my fucking heart that children in some parts of my country routinely walk past corpses, yellow-taped yards, and coroners' vans on their way to school. Many of the kids who walk past corpses have empty bellies and will eat their first meal of the day when they get to school, after this gruesome impetus to ponder their siblings', their peers', or their own mortality.

This is heartbreak.

At a minimum, 25 percent of all the biological women I see every day have reported being sexually assaulted. This statistic does not reflect everyone who experiences sexual violence yet does not report it—women, children, and men throughout the spectrum of gender and sexual identities—and I don't know how this commonly accepted nationwide statistic can be right, when more like 76 percent of my friends, lovers, and family members have been raped, molested, or otherwise sexually assaulted at least once in their lifetimes.

This is heartbreaking shit.

One of the things I have learned from corresponding with people in prison is the importance of taking joy. To someone in prison, receiving a beautifully packaged letter with a couple of crossword puzzles, some stamps, and maybe a money order for five dollars is a joyous occasion. Likewise, to me, living here on the outside, where heartfelt and meaningful communication is often a rare commodity, receiving a handwritten letter from someone who spent hours expressing his or her deepest thoughts is also a joyous occasion.

I *take* joy.

If there is joy to be had in this world and I see it and do not take it, then, quite frankly, I see no reason why I should take up space on this overpopulated planet. It is another story if I do not *see* the joy because I am stricken with grief, or if, indeed, there is not much joy to be taken.

Like if you are being illegally detained by the U.S.

government, or living in a country where Lockheed Martin bombs are raining down from the sky.

In some situations, joy is a rare commodity; to be hoarded and kept secret because people will try and take it away from you.

I do not know how people being illegally detained in Guantánamo Bay might take joy, but I am sure they must find a way to do so in order to maintain their mental faculties while living through such a terrorizing ordeal. I recently read about a Namibian British detainee who was punished by being removed from the English-speaking population and moved into the Arabic-speaking population. His response was to learn how to speak Arabic. He spent two and a half years of his life in illegal detention becoming proficient in another language.

I am sure he took joy in this.

I have, however, read many reports that people being held in that place are no longer sane, so I do not doubt that joy in Guantánamo Bay is a very, very rare commodity.

And you know, when my friend in federal prison writes me a letter telling me about his relationship with a flower that he can see growing on the other side of a high-security fence, through the slit that passes for a window in his cell, I mean, what kind of a piece of shit would I be if I failed to take joy in all the flowers in my neighborhood?

I mean, for instance.

There are so many people who do not have the luxuries of

freedom, food, shelter, a library, and/or running water, and *they* find ways to take joy.

The Riverbend blogger is a young Iraqi woman, living in Baghdad, who has documented the brutal occupation of her land since that fateful day in March 2003. She often describes ways in which she takes joy, but I was recently interested in her take on terror, which is the opposite of joy:

> Terror isn't just worrying about a plane hitting a skyscraper . . . terrorism is being caught in traffic and hearing the crack of an AK-47 a few meters away because the National Guard want[s] to let an American humvee or Iraqi official through. Terror is watching your house being raided and knowing that the silliest thing might get you dragged away to Abu Ghraib where soldiers can torture, beat and kill. Terror is that first moment after a series of machine-gun shots, when you lift your head frantically to make sure your loved ones are still in one piece. Terror is trying to pick the shards of glass resulting from a nearby explosion out of the living-room couch and trying not to imagine what would have happened if a person had been sitting there.[1]

And here is one of the ways in which the Riverbend blogger takes joy:

E. was the first to hear it. We were sitting in the
living room and he suddenly jumped up, alert, "Do
you hear that?" he asked. I strained my ears for
either the sound of a plane or helicopter or gun
shots. Nothing . . . except, wait . . . something . . .
like a small stream of . . . water? Could it be? Was
it back? We both ran into the bathroom where we
had the faucets turned on for the last eight days in
anticipation of water. Sure enough, there it was—
a little stream of water that kept coming and going
as if undecided. E. and I did a little victory dance
in front of the sink with some celebratory hoots
and clapping.[2]

The Riverbend blogger's reality fills me with outrage and
grief, and I keep her perspective close at hand. When I get
together with my friends and/or family.

Every time I get into my safe and comfy bed at night.

Every time I turn on a faucet.

Every time I look at Abuelito and think, "You, my friend,
have more nutritious food and better healthcare than most
human beings on the planet."

Every time I walk through my neighborhood in the middle
of the night and hear the deep quiet of sleeping beings.

If there is joy to be taken and I do not take it, then fuck
yes, I suck ass.

I do not hug trees because I love them and think they "need a hug" from some jackass. I hug trees because sometimes I need to remember what it feels like to have something to hold on to in this world and I can get a goddamn good grip on a tree.

Ditto large rocks.

And my aunt Genie.

Only through the state of being present can one take joy, and it is impossible to be present in this environment that is called the world without being a heartbroken loser.

So get it the fuck on.

The winners are all busy watching teevee, blaring their contentment with the results of fraudulent elections, and xeno-phobically and pathologically SWAT-teaming themselves against their own humanity.

More fucking power to the winners.

There are old folks to visit and cakes to bake. There are prison sentences to commute and police to videotape. There are brutal occupations to stop and reparations to be made. There are war crimes against humanity to be tried and federal taxes to be reverted into state and city coffers. There are hurtful ads at your bus stop to reconstrue and there are Wal-Marts to be run the fuck outta town.

In almost any given community, there are more kids who need attention, food, shelter, clothing, love, healthcare, and/or books than there are kids who enjoy all these fine trappings.

In most places, the local Humane Society provides a

luxurious life that many children in the foster care system often can't even conceive.

In this way of looking at things, the social fabric of the U.S. has been so completely shredded to bits, there is a gigantic playing field for people to work with.

Especially for those whose imaginations are their own.

And people are all depressed in my country, and the entire world hates our guts and that really hurts our feelings because above and beyond all else, my people love to be loved.

We are a deeply complex and warmhearted people.

We just have our heads up our asses is all.

Gently, gently now.

Haul it on out.

The End

𝕴 am in Manchester, England.

My friends have given me their weekend flat to live in.

It is an old rope factory that is now modern living spaces. You swipe plastic cards instead of using metal keys, and as you step into the hallway the lights turn on.

"Motion sensored," developers call it.

"Creepy," I call it.

⚒

So the rope came from hemp planted and harvested by slaves in England's various colonies, including Amerikkka.

It was brought across oceans and woven into rope by worker-slaves in Manchester.

And now, modern living spaces.

The first three nights, I sleep in the bedroom with the light on.

But then I start feeling like an ass. Jacking up folks' electricity bill just because I can feel the memories of all these slaves.

So I turn off the light.

In the middle of the night, I wake up from a dream where I am being attacked by a bird. I lay in bed for a few moments, heart beating, and realize that even though I am now awake, the feeling of being under seige has not abated in the least.

The entire room is filled with the spirits and the memories of the dead. It is packed like a Madison Avenue rush-hour elevator. I can actually *feel* myself sticking out like a sore thumb in what most people would call "a room with one terrified person lying on the bed."

I am paralyzed with fear, and every fight-or-flight cell in my body is screaming, "Flee! Flee! Flee!" But deep inside, I know if I run away, these spirits will trouble me to no end for the duration of my time in their home.

They know I know they are there.

So I take a deep breath, stay in bed, and be quiet.

Make myself calm down somehow.

Breathe, breathe, breathe.

The second I approach calmness, these dead people start telling me their stories. Not in words or anything, more in the feelings of their memories. A large portion of their collective lament seems to stem from the fact that no one listens to them. They have lived in this place for a very long time—perhaps even before it was a rope factory. A huge population of dead folks contending with these new hallways, digital appliances, and people who completely ignore their existence.

"All the dead ever, ever want," they say, "is for the living to bear witness to the past."

So that is what I do.

I lay quiet, listen.

My heart is still beating and I am still afraid, but I've noted how my calmness changed everything.

And after around twenty minutes, I become overwhelmed with all these memories which are and are not mine.

I unmake the bed and drag the mattress out into the living room where the train-track lights keep the spirits away, because I am just one fucken person and I cannot contain the collective and individual laments of the rope factory dead every night.

I remake the bed and hope that the living will learn to acknowledge the past, until I fall asleep.

A Glossary of Examined Terms

When I travel around the U.S., a proliferation of signs greet me at the entrance to almost every town. They tell me when the place was "founded," and sometimes by whom.

These signs are all, invariably, erected by the victors of history's present telling. They are not unlike those flags mountain climbers stab into the flesh of mountains when they get to the top.

The curiously red cherry on the sundae.

Underneath and/or surrounding the signs are insignias of all the patriarchal groups who represent "the founders" in some capacity or another—the Elks, the Moose, the Lions, ye et cetera Good Olde Boys.

My *Random House Dictionary*, like most English dictionaries, and like Bill Gates's present-day Encarta encyclopedia version of the universe, was written from the perspective of the victors and vanguards of history's present telling. These sources of information offer definitions of terms, but by no means do they provide *the* definitions of terms.

According to my 1965 *Random House Dictionary*, "to found" means "to set up or establish on a firm basis or for enduring existence."

Let's examine this definition from other perspectives.

To set up or establish:

If you're a young girl in the Narranganser tribe living in "colonial times" in a place that a bunch of pilgrimy settler types have recently started referring to as "Massachusetts," when a new town is "set up" or "established" you and your people are no longer allowed to go into that area without arousing, at best, suspicion and disdain and, at worst, certain rape and/or death. Never mind that this area has been a sacred meeting ground for all tribes in the region for the past three thousand years. If you protest, you will die.

You know this from past experience.

On a firm basis or for enduring existence:

If you're a young black man living in "colonial times," when a "firm basis" and "enduring existence" are in place, it means progress is happening and an economy has been successfully created to sustain the lives of all the white founders, so, obviously, you have been forcibly brought here to do all the work. Upon your back, the firm basis will be achieved. Through your sweat, blood, tears, and heartbreak, the enduring existence of this new town will be assured. You will be beaten, tortured, mutilated, humiliated, and offed if you protest.

You know this from past experience.

It is only grudgingly that dictionaries and encyclopedias take into consideration the stories of the people who are not the victors. Dictionary writers don't get to *be* dictionary writers unless they know how to represent the stories of the victors.

For instance, I would like *nothing more* than to be a dictionary writer, but I am not "qualified." In order to be "qualified," I have to go to schools where I won't pass unless I get the victors' stories straight in my head.

It wasn't until the year 2001—or 136 years after the abolition of the legal Amerikkkan version of slavery—that the *Merriam-Webster's Dictionary* caved in to the reality of existing mainstream designations and made the landmark decision to designate the term "nigger" a racial slur, and no longer synonymous with "African American."

Many viewed this as an improvement. A positive sign.

It's disgusting that we live in a society that would ever think to "rejoice" about a dictionary recanting the definition of "nigger" in 2001. I think the correct emotional response is outrage that it wasn't until the beginning of the twenty-first century that the people at Merriam-Webster finally felt enough pressure to change the definition of "nigger."

"Improvement," my white cracker ass.

Words such as "found" and "nigger" have been incorporated, without examination, into our means of communication. Many words and terms are candidates for more imaginatively conceived definitions. Below, I have provided a glossary of terms that are used, or consciously *not* used, throughout this book.

African American: I employ this term when it is used by people who identify as African American.

American Indian: I employ this term when it is used by people who identify as American Indian.

Arbusto: "Bush" or "shrub" in *español*. Arbusto was also the name of George W.'s oil company plaything. I believe that words give off resonations of power, and I think some people already have too much—partially because their names are invoked so often in our everyday lives. "Arbusto" is therefore employed throughout this book to connote not only the man and his administration, but also the four-generation family dynasty that has been fucking shit up since well before World War II, and is presently ruling the world.

Asian/Asian American: This term, or worse, "Oriental," is used by people in the U.S. to describe an achingly diverse population of human beings. "Asian" can mean any of the following demographics, in any combination: Hawai'ian, Indonesian, Chinese, North or South Korean, North, Central, or South Vietnamese, Japanese, Burmese, Malaysian, Mongolian, Filipino, Thai, Timorese, Tibetan, and many other folks. I tend to shy away from this term because it just seems so much more respectful to find out *which* Asian ancestry/ancestries someone is from.

autogenocide: Referred to as "gang violence" or "gang warfare" in the U.S. media, autogenocide is a self-sustaining form of genocide the U.S. government has created in ghettos, barrios, poor communities, and entire nations, where people are divided and conquered to the degree that they are unable to see who their actual adversary is. Poverty and illegal economies are crucial in maintaining a state of autogenocide.

black: I use this term to describe the collective population of U.S. and global citizens of, for instance, African, Haitian, Jamaican, Dominican, Afro-Cuban, Afro–Puerto Rican, Belizean, Brazilian, Ethiopian Jewish, and/or Afro-Caribbean descent. I know that "African American" is considered the most polite and respectful term by many people, especially in the southern states. I intend no disrespect by using the term "black." It was only after much thinking and many conversations that I decided upon this term.

    For one thing, many well-intentioned (and not so well-intentioned) (white) people have grown accustomed to using "African American" as a blanket term to unthinkingly describe all black people. It doesn't quite make sense when the person in question is French Canadian.

    I once saw some show where Maury Povich was interviewing two people from Nairobi, and kept referring to them as "African American." They had no idea what he was talking about, and I marveled at Mr. Povich's obliviousness to the straight-up confusion on his guests' faces.

    Another consideration was pointed out by a friend of mine. He said, "I'm not an immigrant. 'African American' sounds like I'm an immigrant. This is my fucken country and I still want to know where my forty acres and goddamn mule are."

    I do not have the experience to make such assertions, but I'd like to note that this basic sentiment thrives in the imaginations of many of my friends.

Chicano/Chicana: A person of indigenous, mestizo, and/or Mexicano ancestry, whose family has been in the U.S., often since long before it stopped being Mexico.

coincidence theorist: I discovered this wonderful term on Paris's website, Guerrilla Funk. Coincidence theorists are people who believe that things just kinda end up happening so that white men in power always end up on top. They are unable to rebut allegations about U.S. government crimes against humanity without heavy reliance on the following adjectives: "absurd," "ludicrous," "ridiculous," "insane," and "far-fetched." They are also fond of the adverb "patently." When coincidence theorist politicians start saying that the prospect of the U.S. bombing a certain country is "sheer paranoia," it is the perfect time for folks in that country to start digging bomb shelters.

conspiracy theorist: A person who looks at the end result of crimes against humanity and figures out who, exactly, benefited.

cracker: See "ofay."

democracy: As of this writing, I know of only one country in the world that embraces democracy: Venezuela. If you wish to know what democracy looks like, I recommend a subscription to Narco News (www.narconews.com). If this is not possible, get your local video store to carry *The Revolution Will Not Be Televised,* or go in on a copy with a bunch of friends. There is also democracy in certain regions of the world, such as Chiapas, Mexico. In a democracy, old people and children dance. Women are unquestioningly part of the process, and so are homos and trannies, old people and children. Plants, animals, the earth. Everyone has a say in a democracy.

discover: What happens when white supremacist racists and imperialists are able to perceive, define, and infiltrate something.

dyke: This word should almost only be used by people who are queer, or are in love with everything queerbaity. I say "almost" because I have heard this term used disparagingly by gay men, which sucks, but there you have it. My straight sister can happily call me a big faggot dyke, but there're a lot of people I would also happily sucker punch for doing so. "Dyke" is one of the many disparaging words in our language that have been reclaimed by those they were once used to denigrate. As such, these words should only be used by those who have historically been victimized by them. See also "fag/faggot" and "nigger/nigga."

fag/faggot: Generally pertains to men, but I call myself and my dyke friends "fag" and "faggot" a lot because I like the sound of both words. Otherwise, see above, including the part about disparaging use. Also used in similar respects as the loathsome marketing creation "metrosexual"; a queer might refer to him- or herself as a "big fag" in reference to his or her penchant for home decor, hair care, and/or fashion ensembles.

First Nations people: This is a term widely used in Canada. It would be nice to see it adopted in the U.S. because it acknowledges that there were nations of people here before the white man came.

freedom: In the chapter "Full Spectrum Dominance," I copped the definition for the same-named military doctrine off the Department of Defense's website. After reading Arbusto's 2005 inaugural address, where he mentioned the word "freedom" at least 38,214 times, I realized that the definition for full spectrum dominance is, in fact, also Arbusto's definition of freedom. To wit: "the ability of U.S. forces, operating alone or with allies, to defeat any adversary and control any situation across the range of military operations." This should clear things up for folks who are sometimes confused by the widespread usage of "freedom" in Arbusto's Amerikkka.

My definition of freedom, almost needless to say, differs quite significantly, and generally involves imagining life.

For many inmates in the U.S., freedom is what happens when unjust laws are not arbitrarily enforced and years of your life are not stolen from you and your family.

For many indigenous people on the planet, freedom is the ability to live how your people have traditionally lived, in a self-sustaining manner, with the blessings of your ancestors upon you.

For lions and tigers and bears, freedom means forests instead of housing developments.

For many women, freedom is living without the intimate terrorism of male domination sundering your life and the lives of your children, if you have children.

For a gang member, freedom might mean a library that you can access without risking death by having to go through someone else's territory.

Freedom is many things to many folks.

That is the most important thing I know about freedom.

freedom fighter: See "terrorist."

gay: 1) Happy. I often remind people to "be gay!" when I am bidding them adieu. 2) A homo who thinks that he or she can somehow "fit in" to mainstream society and gain "acceptance" through increasing "tolerance" and the hallowed heterosexual halls of legislation. Gays think people will somehow "evolve" on this subject of "the gay lifestyle" without ever recognizing the *massive continuum of oppression* that espouses "intolerance." Gays don't seem to notice that most self-identified gays are white and male. Like their heterosexual counterparts, gays also tend to have a lot more money, power, property, and cultural entitlement than dykes, homos, queers, and fags.

Hispanic: A person of Spanish ancestry. Hispanic people generally represent the previous colonial powers in Mexico, the Caribbean, and the central and southern Americas. This term is frequently used in the mainstream media to describe people who have some, very little, or absolutely no Spanish ancestry—and who were, in fact, subjugated by the Spaniards. An overwhelming population of people from the Americas does not identify as "Hispanic."

homo: I like the word "homo." It is a happy-sounding word to my ear. It means you love/fuck whomever you want and usually, but not always, you want to love/fuck people who identify as the same sex/gender as you.

indian: The original inhabitants of the Americas. When speaking about many specific tribes, or entire populations of indigenous peoples, I frequently use the word "indian." This, too, is a reflection of the people I am close to. To many of my friends, using the term "Native American" to describe their ancestry does not make any sense because their people were here long, long before this place was called "America." Wherever possible, I use the name of a specific tribe a person comes from, but when describing the collective population of people who lived here before the white man came, I use "indigenous" (which I don't really like 'cause it sounds so laboratory) or "indian." As with my use of most racial terms used in the mainstream lexicon, I intend no disrespect and have put a lot of thought into my choices. Meanwhile, I remain mindful of the fact that the road to hell is paved with good intentions.

Indian: This word is capitalized when describing people from India. Again, it is best to find out which area of India a person's family comes from. It is also important to note that people from Nepal, Pakistan, and Kashmir are often called "Indian" in the U.S., and that is straight-up wrong. Moreover, there are Hindus, Muslims, Christians, and Sikhs in these regions, not to mention many other religious groups, and India is a complex-ass place. The term "Indian" is no more descriptive than "African," "European," "Asian," "Hispanic," or "American."

indigenous: This describes all of the people on the planet who lived in their respective lands long before whitey showed up, and can, at times, pertain to "whites," such as indigenous Irish folks like my crazy-ass, beautiful mother.

Latino/Latina: A term I more or less shun because there is no such place as "Latin America." There is a Central America, a South America, a Caribbean, and a Mexico. These massive areas are filled with diverse countries, states, cities, and villages, which are, in turn, populated by an incalculable variety of people. I have never been able to discern a homogeneous "Latin" culture, religion, flavor, or ideology.

lesbian: See "gay."

lifestyle: Something gays, the rich, and the famous evidently have.

Lucky Sperm Club: I was turned on to this term by a woman who dated a wealthy Texan. She told me that this was how he and his coterie referred to themselves. I find this term just incredibly amusing, and double over in unseemly fits of haglike cackling when I imagine the dicks this "lucky sperm" hails from.

manifest destiny: See "survival of the fittest."

manufacturing consent: A favorite pastime, if not the sole function, of the U.S. mainstream media, largely involving bizarre rationalizations of white supremacist racism, imperialism, and male domination. The manufacture of consent is employed with great effect in coercing entire populations to avert their gaze from atrocities occurring in their midst.

minority: A relativity-based value judgment. "Minorities" exist through the inculcation of racist/ethnic/gender/sexual/religious supremacy—generally revolving around whiteness, maleness, heterosexuality, and/or Christianity, in my country. It is just as credible to call the perceived "majority" "indoctrinated racists" as it is to call any demographic a "minority." If a Cuban American male is a fully assimilated, white-identified, racist, heterosexual, fundamentalist Christian, only in one constructed identity—race—would he qualify as a "minority." This term also does not take into account the myriad, deeply intimate complexities of mixed races, skin tone, hair, and facial features. Also, whites are a "minority" in

"California," though white Californians are, to my knowledge, never referred to as such.

Dr. Frances Cress Welsing's definition of white supremacy (racism) helped me to gain a deeper understanding of why I dislike the term "minority" so much. The rationale for usage of this term has been patiently explained to me by many people. White people compose the majority here in the United States, and therefore it is perfectly acceptable to describe everyone who is not "white" as a minority. I understand that there are borders and counties and laws and census counts that are very real in legislative, economic, and judicial senses, and according to these designations, whites are the majority.

I guess I tend to look at things from a global and historic perspective. In this light, whites are the minority. One out of five people on the planet is Chinese. Throw in Africa, India, the Middle East, the Americas, and all Asian nations, and you too will have a difficult time with this term. The demographic that is fast overtaking whites in the rest of the country is people of mixed races and ethnicities. This is the exact point at which the federalist, fundamentalist, right-wing Christian, Mormon, and Aryan Nation terror of genetic annihilation comes in.

Native American: I employ this word when it is used by people who identify as Native American.

nigga/nigger: These words belong to black people. No one else should use them. However, I have employed "nigger" a few times in this book when making a point about white people's ignorance, and am speaking from the voice or perspective of a bigoted white person. I probably shouldn't do this, but I am presently not evolved enough to refrain from mocking white racists.

ofay: A disparaging term for a white person. At this point in history, I like the terms "ofay" and "cracker" because they point out whiteness. The more white people recognize whiteness, the better our chances of facing the past.

off-whites: Conscious white people who have spent years examining history and unflinchingly recognizing their present involvement with white supremacist racism. In general, off-whites in the Americas do not believe the past will be faced until reparations are paid and the sacred land of people's ancestors is given the fuck back.

queer: Another good general term for everything and everyone homo, but I still like "homo" better. The thing with "queer," though, is that lots of "straight" people identify as queer because they revere the never-ending complexities of sexuality and gender. Saying you are queer doesn't necessarily mean you are also a homo. Try and keep up here.

settle: This term, like many found in the vernacular of white imperialism, is highly problematic for me. "Settle" is used to describe what the French, Dutch, and British did in the northeast. The Spaniards similarly "settled" in much of the southwestern territory. All of this land, however, was already quite settled by intricately structured and governed indian nations who had lived here for thousands and thousands of years. Every tribe within every nation had its own ways, means, beliefs.

The millions and millions of people who lived in the

"Americas" had been settled for quite some time. Europeans were, if anything, unsettlers, and our descendents have spent the past five hundred years unsettling cultures, traditions, and land.

survival of the fittest: A bullshit story that corroborates white supremacist racism, male domination, and imperialism.

terrorist: I am not sure what a terrorist is, as I have never met someone who identifies as a "terrorist." For many people who work at women's health clinics, white fundamentalist Christian men who firebomb their places of employment are terrorists. For family farmers, agribusiness corporations—which work through the U.S. government and banks to take people's land and livelihood away—are terrorists. Polar bears and salmon live under the auspices of terrorism pretty much constantly. I am certainly terrorized by U.S. advertisers and the corporate media, but I do not think any of the people involved in these industries think of themselves as "terrorists." The definition of "terrorist" also raises some deeply philosophical questions in my mind. Such as: To a tree, are the terrorists the developer and surveyor who walk around and tie plastic neon pink ribbons around you, or are the terrorists the actual people who come and chainsaw everyone who has a pink neon ribbon? I know I am supposed to think of "Middle Easterners" as terrorists, but all of the people I have ever known who are from this massive, complex, and highly diverse region seem to be the type of people who invite me over for dinner, or answer my questions about Islam and history, or ask me questions about women, dykes, and homos in the United States. I suspect I will figure out exactly what a terrorist is in the same moment that I figure out exactly what a freedom fighter is.

transgender/gender-variant: These terms describe people who do not, in whole or part, identify with the one-dimensional cultural gender assigned to them at birth. Many folks have a difficult time imagining the wide range of genders that make up humanity because we are taught that one is either a man or a woman. Looking at gender as *a range* has improved my own personal outlook. I am very happy with my biological gender, but my attempts to be a "woman" as defined by my society were frustrating and self-defeating. When I realized the possibility of a range of genders, I came to a deeper understanding of my nature.

Like everyone else on the planet, transgender/gender-variant folks represent wildly diverse demographics.

tolerance: Supposedly, the world will be a happy place when everyone can "tolerate" everyone else. I, personally, do not want to be tolerated. If you "tolerate" me because I am a homo/white/Irish Italian/non-Christian/non-Muslim/non-Jewish/a woman/Amerikkkan, there's a 99.9 percent chance that I cannot stand being in the same room as you, and do not, by any stretch of the imagination, "tolerate" you. Who the fuck is anyone to "tolerate" anyone else? Either you are a compassionate, open-minded person with love in your heart and the passion to live a glorious, sacred life, or you're not. In general, "tolerance" is a courageous and commendable response when your four-year-old is pitching a fit in the grocery store.

unconscious white/white-identified person: Someone who has not taken the time to reeducate him- or herself about the history of the United States and apply that history to his or her own, and everyone else's, present lived reality. There are many forms of unconsciousness, ranging from blatant racism to "progressive" liberal celebration of multicultural diversity.

war: When the U.S. is involved, a war is almost always, in fact, a brutal occupation. When the U.S. is not involved, wars can almost always be traced to the autogenocidal version of divide and conquer set up and established by huge multinational corporations representing the governments of the U.S., France, Britain, Germany, Saudi Arabia, Israel, Canada, Japan, China, Russia, or Australia.

white/white-identified: In this book, "white" generally means the dominant culture and those who unconsciously and/or silently abide by and/or identify with it. "Whiteness" as a race—as opposed to an ideology—is identified in a variety of fractalized contexts. Dr. Flusty makes many valuable points about the perception of race and whiteness in the foreword, so go back and read that if you are a foreword skipper.

white supremacist racism: The unquestioned ideology—rooted in the terror of genetic annihilation—that permeates every facet of existence in the United States of Amerikkka. See Dr. Frances Cress Welsing's definition of white supremacy (racism) in the preface.

Foreword

1. Sven Lindqvist, "Guernica in the Global History of Warfare," *La Vanguardia* (Madrid), 2003. Also see Lindqvist, *Exterminate All the Brutes: One Man's Odyssey into the Heart of Darkness and the Origins of European Genocide*, trans. Joan Tate (New Press, 1997). To force, however, I would add the King's English, bearing in mind that a lingua franca ain't nothing but a dialect equipped with an imperial expeditionary force.
2. For a thorough exploration of this, see Luigi Cavalli-Sforza. Anything by Luigi Cavalli-Sforza.
3. Stole this one from Pauliina Raento, in conversation.
4. Schlomit Keren Stein, also in conversation.

Preface

1. Dr. Frances Cress Welsing, *The Isis Papers: The Keys to the Colors* (Chicago: Lushena Books, 1991), ii.

Part 1: Roots

Introduction

1. James W. Loewen, *Lies My Teacher Told Me: Everything Your American History Textbook Got Wrong* (New York: The New Press, 1996), 42.
2. Ibid., 42.

Columbus and the New World Order

1. Howard Zinn, *A People's History of the United States: 1492–Present*, rev. ed. (New York: HarperPerennial, 1995), 1.
2. Eduardo Galeano, *Memory of Fire: I. Genesis* (New York: Pantheon, 1985), 49–50.
3. Loewen, 79–80.
4. United States Army School of the Americas website, http://carlisle-www. army.mil/usamhi/usarsa.
5. Ginger Thompson, "Behind Roses' Beauty, Poor and Ill Workers," *New York Times*, February 13, 2003.
6. Noam Chomsky, "The Manufacture of Consent," in *The Chomsky Reader*,

ed. James Peck (New York: Pantheon, 1987), 121–22. Quoted in Arundhati Roy, *War Talk* (Cambridge: South End Press, 2003), 86–87.

7. Zinn, 11.

God Told Me to Kill You

1. John O'Sullivan, "Annexation," *The United States Magazine and Democratic Review* 17 (July 1845), 5–10. Quoted in "John O'Sullivan Coins the Phrase 'Manifest Destiny,'" History Tools.org: Resources for the Study of American History, www.historytools.org/sources/manifest_destiny.pdf.
2. *Random House Dictionary* (New York: Random House, 1965), 872.
3. Associated Press, "Robertson: God Says It's Bush in a 'Blowout' in November," *USA Today,* January 2, 2004, www.usatoday.com/news/politicselections/nation/2004-01-02-god-bush_x.htm.
4. Eduardo Galeano, *Memory of Fire: II. Faces and Masks* (New York: Pantheon, 1987), 179.
5. Laura Ingalls Wilder, *Little House on the Prairie* (New York: Harper Trophy, 1953), 47.
6. Ibid., 55.
7. Ibid., 211–212.
8. Ibid., 237.

Five Hundred Years of Servitude

1. George Lipsitz, *The Possessive Investment in Whiteness: How White People Profit from Identity Politics* (Philadelphia: Temple University Press, 1998), 3.
2. Loewen, 259. Emphasis is Loewen's.
3. Galeano, *Faces and Masks,* 248.
4. Lipsitz, vii.

Manifest Destiny Variety Show

1. Eduardo Galeano, *Memory of Fire: III. Century of the Wind* (New York: Pantheon, 1988), 121.
2. Carrie McLaren, "The Great White Way: Daniel Kevles on the History of Eugenics in the US," *Stay Free!,* no. 22 (Spring 2004), 12–13.
3. Galeano, *Century of the Wind,* 126.
4. Ryszard Kapuscinski, *Shah of Shahs* (San Diego: Harcourt Brace Jovanovich, 1985), 23–24.
5. Ibid., 28.
6. Russell Mokhiber and Robert Weissman, "We Had a Democracy Once, But You Crushed It," originally published in the *Guardian,* published

by Common Dreams, August 10, 2003, http://commondreams.org/ views03/0810-06.htm.

7. Galeano, *Century of the Wind,* 149. Emphasis is Galeano's.

8. "CIA and Assassinations: The Guatemala 1954 Documents," http://hartford-hwp.com/archives/47/156.html.

9. Galeano, *Century of the Wind,* 151.

10. Langston Hughes, "Merry Christmas," in *The Collected Poems of Langston Hughes,* ed. Arnold Rampersad and David Roessel (New York: Alfred A. Knopf, 1994), 132.

11. Galeano, *Century of the Wind,* 152. Italics are Galeano's.

Postage Stamp Redemptions

1. Malcolm X, *Malcolm X Speaks* (Atlanta: Pathfinder Press, 1965). Quoted in Zinn, 449.

2. Sarah Ruth van Gelder, "Freedom Sings: An Interview with Harry Belafonte," *Yes! Magazine* (Spring 2002), www.yesmagazine.com/article.asp?ID=487.

3. Arthur Schlesinger Jr., quoted in Taylor Branch, *Parting the Waters,* 918–19. Quoted in Loewen, 235.

4. Arthur Schlesinger Jr., "When Ethnic Studies Are Un-American," *Social Studies Review,* no. 5 (Summer 1990), 11–13. Quoted in Loewen, 302.

5. June Jordan, *Some of Us Did NOT Die: New and Selected Essays of June Jordan* (New York: Basic/Civitas Books, 2002), 30–31.

6. Alejandro A. Alonso, "Black Street Gangs in Los Angeles: A History," Streetgangs.com, www.streetgangs.com/history/hist01.html.

7. Cress Welsing, iv. Emphasis is Welsing's.

8. Paris, "Black on Black Violence—Real Talk," *Guerrilla Funk,* December 6, 2003, www/guerrillafunk.com/thoughts/doc4651.html.

9. Gary Webb, *Dark Alliance: The CIA, the Contras, and the Crack Cocaine Explosion* (New York: Seven Stories Press, 1998), 27–29.

10. Ibid., 20.

11. "McKinney Raises US Government's 'COINTELPRO' Program with UN Human Rights Commissioner," *Truthout,* September 2, 2001, www.truthout.org/docs_01/0563.McKinney.CON.UN.htm.

12. Black Commentator, "Mass Incarceration and Rape: The Savaging of Black America," *Black Commentator,* no. 95, June 17, 2004, www.blackcommentator.com/95/95_cover_prisons.html.

13. Ibid.

14. Paul Street, "Those People in That Prison Can't Vote Me Out: The Political Consequences of Racist Felony Disenfranchisement," *Black Commentator,*

no. 68, December 11, 2003, www.blackcommentator.com/68/68_street_prisons.html.

15. Dan Pens, "Oregon's Prison Slaveocracy," *Prison Legal News*, May 1, 1998.
16. Ibid.
17. Ibid.

Reckoning
1. Immortal Technique, *Revolutionary 1* (New York: Viper Records, 2001), liner notes.
2. Roy, *War Talk*, 78.
3. Sarah Ruth van Gelder, "Freedom Sings: An Interview with Harry Belafonte," *Yes! Magazine* (Spring 2002), www.yesmagazine.com/article.asp?ID=487.

Part 2: Branches of Oppression

Introduction
1. "The Wolves Within," a Native American tale told many times around the Sacred Fire. *Manataka*, www.manataka.org/page104.html.

Tiptoeing around Noah's Big Drunk Ass
1. Derrick Jensen, *The Culture of Make Believe* (New York: Chelsea Green, 2002), 57.
2. Ibid., 62. Emphasis mine.
3. Scott Glover and Matt Lait, "Ex-Officer Calls Corruption a Chronic 'Cancer,'" *Los Angeles Times*, September 21, 1999, appearing on Streetgangs.com, www.streetgangs.com/topics/1999/092199excopcancer.html.
4. Anne-Marie O'Connor, "FBI Pressured INS to Aid L.A. Police Anti-Gang Effort," *Los Angeles Times*, February 29, 2000, appearing on Streetgangs.com, www.streetgangs.com/topics/2000/022900fgi.html.
5. Luis J. Rodriguez, *Always Running, La Vida Loca, Gang Days in L.A.* (Willimantic, CT: Curbstone Press, 1996), 72.
6. Madd Ronald, "Blood Is Love, Blood Is for Life!!" *Streetgangs Magazine*, September 2, 2003, wwwstreetgangs.com/newsletter/090203bloodin.php?vo=15.
7. "LAPD Blues," program #1915, original airdate May 15, 2001, *Frontline*. Transcript at www.pbs.org/wgbh/pages/frontline/shows/lapd/etc/script.html.

8. "The Streets of Rampart Today," www.pbs.org/wgbh/pages/frontline/shows/lapd/later/streets.html.

9. Ibid.

10. Ibid.

11. Cara Mia DiMassa, "Community Rallies Behind Beleaguered Videographer," *Los Angeles Times,* July 14, 2002, B1.

12. Ibid.

13. Ibid.

14. Jacqueline Carpenter, "Anti-Police Rally at African-American Community Church," Los Angeles Independent Media Center, July 13, 2002, www.la.indymedia.org/news/2002/07/17777.php.

15. Jeffrey Gettleman, "Prosecutors' Morbid Neckties Add to Criticism," *New York Times,* January 5, 2003, www.nytimes.com/2003/01/05/national/05NOOS.html.

16. Ibid.

17. Sharon Churcher, "Violent Past of U.S. Army's Torturer-in-Chief," *Daily Mail,* May 9, 2004, www.dailymail.co.uk/pages/live/articles/news/worldnews.html?in_article_id = 301191&in_page_id = 1811&in_a_source = .

18. Silja J.A. Talvi, "The New Plantation," AlterNet, July 9, 2004, www.alternet.org/rights/19182. Emphasis in original.

19. Transcript of phone call available at the Memory Hole, www.thememoryhole.org/drugs/noelle-call.htm.

20. E., "Voices of Women in Protest," Portland Independent Media Center, August 23, 2002, http://portland.indymedia.org/en/2002/08/104730.shtml.

Eenie, Meenie, Miney, Mo, Catch a Cracker by the Toe

1. Sharon Basco, "Bamboozled by Ads: Politics, Propaganda and Advertising," interview with Jean Kilbourne, TomPaine.com, April 7, 2003, www.tompaine.com/feature.cfm/ID/7489.

Cards on the Table

1. Javier Moro and Dominique Lapierre, *Five Past Midnight in Bhopal: The Epic Story of the World's Deadliest Industrial Disaster* (New York: Warner Books, 2002), xvii.

2. Luis Rodriguez in an interview with Joseph Rodriguez, *East Side Stories: Gang Life in East L.A.* (New York: powerHouse Books, 1998), 180–81.

3. James Diego Vigil, *A Rainbow of Gangs: Street Cultures in the Mega-City* (Austin: University of Texas Press, 2002).

4. Eldridge Cleaver, *Soul on Ice* (New York: McGraw Hill Company, 1968), 14–15.
5. Tom Roeder, "Army Set to Injure Goats for Training," originally published in the *Colorado Springs Gazette*, September 8, 2004, reprinted on Common Dreams, www.commondreams.org/headlines04/0908-04.htm.

Waving to Stevie

1. *Random House Dictionary*, 946.
2. Scott Lindlaw, "Bush the Mountain-Biker Rides Hard, Shrugs Off Crash," Associated Press, July 26, 2004, www.boston.com/news/politics/president/bush/articles/2004/07/26/ap_exclusive_bush_the_mountain_biker_rides_hard_shrugs_off_crash?pg=full.
3. "Venezuelan Leader Frustrates U.S.," March 16, 2005, http://story.news.yahoo.com/news?tmpl=story&cid=1512&ncid=1512&e=9&u=/afp/20050316/wl_afp/usvenezuela_050316184307.
4. Anne Gearan, "U.S. to Sell Jets to Pakistan; India Upset," Associated Press, March 25, 2005, http://news.yahoo.com/news?tmpl=story&u=/ap/20050326/ap_on_go_pr_wh/us_india_pakistan_18.
5. This and all subsequent excerpts are taken from Leonard Pitts Jr., "Surveillance of Rappers Is a Threat to All," *Miami Herald*, March 22, 2004, www.realcities.com/mld/miamiherald/living/columnists/leonard_pitts/8244442.htm. Originally published under the title "Who Cares if Cops Are Watching Rappers?"
6. V.S. Chochezi and Staajabu, *Scribes Rising* (Sacramento: Straight Out Scribes, 2002), 130.
7. Ronald Chatman, *No More Blood Shed*, forthcoming from Senegal Press.
8. Anonymous, www.craigslist.org/about/best/sea/64876377.html.
9. Nessie, "SF IMC Interviews Al Giordano on Venezuela, the Media and Anarchism," San Francisco Independent Media Center, December 20, 2002, www.sf.indymedia.org/news/2002/12/1552703.php.

Full Spectrum Dominance

1. Jim Garamone, "Joint Vision 2020 Emphasizes Full-spectrum Dominance," DefenseLINK, www.defenselink.mil/news/Jun2000/n06022000_20006025.html.
2. Cress Welsing, ii.
3. Galeano, *Faces and Masks*, 252–53.
4. Nelson, Jeff, "Iraqi Farmers Aren't Celebrating World Food Day," appearing on VegSource, November 11, 2004, www.vegsource.com/articles2/iraq_seeds.htm.

5. Jeff Franks, "Annual 'Dead Zone' Spreads Across Gulf of Mexico," Reuters, August 4, 2004, published on the Forest Conservation Portal, http://forests. org/articles/reader.asp?linkid=34024.

Opiate of the Asses
1. Baghdad Burning, January 15, 2005, http://riverbendblog.blogspot. com/2005_01_01_riverbendblog_archive.html.
2. Ibid., January 27, 2005.

Acknowledgments

This book could not have been written without two specific writers:

James Loewen, who bolsters me.

Arundhati Roy, who gives me courage and wherewithal.

Thank you.

I am starting to feel like I can't write a book without Jenny Goode editing it. I got all the credit for *Cunt,* but in reality, it would not have been the great book it is without her tempering my anger and general vitriol, and patiently culling the deeper love in my heart. Thank you, Jenny. You bring out the best in me.

Thanks to everyone at Seal/Avalon for being behind this book. Ingrid, I miss you, and thank you for all of your love and insights. Brooke, Krista L-G, and Krista R., thank you for jumping in with such verve. Thank you for listening, and offering trust and respect.

Thanks to Faye Bender and Michele Karlsberg, my agent and publicist, respectively. I don't know if I am batting on your team, or you are batting on mine, but either way, I am thankful to you both.

Thanks to Miss Pussycat and Mr. Quintron for *always* finding ways to be beautiful and shining, no matter what is happening in the world.

Eli Halpin. Thank you for the book cover. I am deeply honored to live in a world that contains your divine gifts.

Jon and Patrick, thank you for giving me a home and leaving your delightful cookies and scones on my doorstep.

Thanks to Garcia for talking to me sometimes and for leaving me alone sometimes. You got that balance down, my friend.

Danica Anderson, my witch therapist. I love you for going to places where crimes against humanity have been committed, and for doing your deeply sacred and divine work. I love you for digging into humanity's consciousness. I thank you—and Bogie, Phil, Dayo, and Marko—for giving me the time of day.

Thanks to Riz. Whether you are on this earth or somewhere else you will always be love, and you're not some lame-ass, blissed-out herbal tea love. You are love like god means when god talks about love, and I fucken love you.

Stan Goff, Bryan Proffitt, Derrick Jensen, and Dr. Steve Flusty. The four of you give me profound assurance about humanity, and I thank you for this blessing. Stan, you've shifted your military skills into your life and writing, rendering a great and generous gift to humanity. Bryan, your openess, courage, and love stuns me. Derrick, your words heal my heart, no matter how painful they are. Steve, my ballerina. You have helped my to apply terms and concepts to my experiences and feelings many, many times. You are all dearly, dearly loved by me, Inga La Gringa.

Elizabeth Sadler. Your insights, appreciation and respect for the (spirit) world have given me a deep sense of validation on many occasions. I thank you, and love you.

Acknowledgments

Peggy Seltzer, my platonic soulmate. I thank you for inviting me into your heart, for giving me books and music and laughter when I didn't feel like there were any words or songs or happiness. You have single-handedly healed my heart in places where I did not know I was hurt. Thank you.

Rya Joy Frances Hickey. Thank you for showing me the correct manner in which to hold a grudge.

Cedric, my kindest and most gentle friend. There will come a time in our lives when you no longer resoundedly beat my ass in chess. It will most likely be a while, but your godlike patience can easily contain that.

Ariel, Maia, and Maria. Thank you for loving me. Thank you for accepting me as I am. Ariel, thank you for that beautiful smile, but at the same time, always being a tad cranky. Maia, thank you for your straightforward grace, which I rely on. Maria, thank you for prodding me along by asking, "Is it finished yet? When's it gonna be finished? How much longer do you think until it's finished so I can read it? I wanna read it."

Ronald Chatman. You take the time to listen to me, and I completely trust you to respond from your heart. I thank you for teaching me about courage, loyalty, honor, and, of course, the art of war.

Robin D.G. Kelley, Margaret Cho, Luis Rodriguez. Mostly I thank you all just for being in the world, doing the work you do. But also, you've been kind to me, and I am indebted to you for the added bonus of that.

Sadiki, Romeo, and Ase. I only know you from corresponding through the mail, but you have all profoundly enriched my life. You inspire me to deeply appreciate many things. I imagine your freedom every day.

All my pool buddies at the Goodfoot. Special thanks to Angie, Andrew, Chris, and Burroughs. Also, thanks and love to the employees at the Goodfoot: Sandy, Jonathan, Q, Sabrina, Jesse, and everyone else.

There are a number of people that I have not seen in a while, who have had a significant impact on my worldview. This includes: Reuben Roqueñi, Shannon Funchess, Chris Omowale, Fiona Brigstocke-Ngo, Hannah Class, Mamie Williams, Deanna Baldivez, Andrew Vasquez, Eddie Andrade, Junior Zepeda, Steve Arredando, Eddie Vela, Gerod and Cedric Sloan, Juanita Uribe, Lisa Tiger, Bob Jordan, Mariko Marrs, Michael Garcia, Sheri Ozeki, Leta Gild, Beaver Chief (R.I.P.), Nemo, Rob Williamson, and Guy Davis.

I have a rather large posse of friends who offer up a tremendous amount of support and love. Among these are Roni, Lynnee, Miss Tea, Alex, Sini, Nomy, Jude, Krystee, LaniJo, Roger, Jason, Lia, Peri, Turtle, Parisha, Cristien, Vasant, Bao, Dawn Kiss, Dawn Adell, Gabrielle, Mel, Leigh-Anne, Cath, Karin, Emira, Lauren, the Lunapads Familia, and raisedeyebrow.com. Special shout-outs to Emira for reading parts of my book when I was feeling defeated and vulnerable, and for being beautiful and gentle with me.

Mom, thank you for putting me on the planet. Thank you for working your fingers to the bone so your children can afford luxuries and entitlements. I love you with all my heart.

Dad and Nick. There have been times when I wished I had a chance to talk with you. So it has been nice that you've both been present throughout this book, and I thank you.

JoeB, Cindy, Nicholas and Joseph, Liz, Josh, Evan and Avery. Thank you for being patient and loving with me when I have been so neglectful to you in the past couple years. I can always count on you people to challenge me and talk general shit. Special thanks to Josh and Cindy for being good to me and for loving my family so dearly.

Grammy (R.I.P.), Aunt Genie, Uncle Bruce, Uncle Allen, and all the cousins, thank you for teaching me cool stuff about the world and engaging with me in a real way throughout my life.

Thanks to Cousin Jimmy, Carole, and the family for being so loving to me when I visited England and Ireland. Carole, I pine for your Tea N' Bam Cakes almost every day.

I am also deeply grateful to the earth.

Special shout-outs to the Pacific Ocean, Oaks, Cedars, Passion Flowers, Jasmine, Horsetails, Hyacinth, Roses, Wisteria, Butterflies, Bamboo, Dandelions, Swallows, Crows, Ospreys, Dolphins, Whales, Mountain Lions, Grunion, Salmon, Horses, Monkeys, Gorillas, and the mighty-ass Rabbit Clan. You teach me more than I deserve to be taught. Thank you.

Special thanks to Abuelito and Diabla Blanca. You bring warmth, joy, and the blood-spattered semi-corpses of rodents into my life, all of which inspires me to keep things real. Thanks.

In general, my day-by-day support network came from the

spirit world. There are a lot of beings who have resisted white (male) domination, and they will not rest until their deaths are no longer in vain.

I thank all of the spirits who have come to me and helped me with this book. Some of you, history remembers. Some of you have been relegated to the children's section in public libraries. Some of you are never mentioned.

I thank you all the same.

Most importantly, Nuestra Virgin, Mata Kali, Erzuli Danto, Kwan Yin, and Holy Durga; Slayer of Ignorance. You have given me protection, love, and a deep understanding of divine vengeance.

In my heart and prayers, I thank you every day.

Inga Muscio is a public speaker and author of *Cunt: A Declaration of Independence.* She lives in Portland, Oregon.

Steven E. Flusty, PhD, is Assistant Professor of Geography at York University. His primary obsession is the everyday practices of global formation, a topic he has interrogated most ruthlessly in *De-Coca-Colonization: Making the Globe from the Inside Out.* His work has also appeared in assorted electronic media and a selection of academic, professional, and popular journals of varying degrees of repute.

Credits

Selected Titles from Seal Press

For more than twenty-five years, Seal Press has published groundbreaking books. By women. For women. Visit our website at www.sealpress.com.

Cunt: A Declaration of Independence by Inga Muscio. $14.95, 1-58005-075-1. An ancient title of respect for women, "cunt" long ago veered off the path of honor and now careens toward the heart of every woman as an expletive. Muscio traces this winding road, giving women both the motivation and the tools to claim "cunt" as a positive and powerful force in the lives of all women.

The F-Word: Feminism in Jeopardy by Kristin Rowe-Finkbeiner. $14.95, 1-58005-114-6. An astonishing look at the tenuous state of women's rights and issues in America, this pivotal book also incites women with voting power to change their situations.

The Truth behind the Mommy Wars: Who Decides What Makes a Good Mother? by Miriam Peskowitz. $15.95, 1-58005-129-4. This moving and convincing treatise explores the new-century collision between work and mothering.

The Pirate Queen: In Search of Grace O'Malley and Other Legendary Women of the Sea by Barbara Sjoholm. $15.95, 1-58005-109-X. A fascinating account of an intriguing Irish clan chieftan is joined by tales of cross-dressing sailors, medieval explorers, storm witches, and sea goddesses.

I Wanna Be Sedated edited by Faith Conlon and Gail Hudson. $15.95, 1-58005-127-8. With hilarious and heartfelt essays from writers such as Dave Barry and Barbara Kingsolver, this anthology will reassure any parent of a teenager that they are not alone.